NATIONAL IDENTITY AND ETHNICITY IN RUSSIA AND THE NEW STATES OF EURASIA

THE INTERNATIONAL POLITICS OF EURASIA

Editors:
Karen Dawisha and Bruce Parrott

This ambitious ten-volume series develops a comprehensive analysis of the evolving world role of the post-Soviet successor states. Each volume considers a different factor influencing the relationship between internal politics and international relations in Russia and in the western and southern tiers of newly independent states. The contributors were chosen not only for their recognized expertise but also to ensure a stimulating diversity of perspectives and a dynamic mix of approaches.

Volume 1
The Legacy of History in Russia and the New States of Eurasia
Edited by S. Frederick Starr

Volume 2
National Identity and Ethnicity in Russia and the New States of Eurasia
Edited by Roman Szporluk

Volume 3
The Politics of Religion in Russia and the New States of Eurasia
Edited by Michael Bourdeaux

THE INTERNATIONAL POLITICS OF EURASIA
Volume 2

NATIONAL IDENTITY AND ETHNICITY IN RUSSIA AND THE NEW STATES OF EURASIA

Editor:
Roman Szporluk

M.E. Sharpe
Armonk, New York
London, England

Copyright © 1994 by M. E. Sharpe, Inc.

All rights reserved. No part of this book may be reproduced in any form
without written permission from the publisher, M. E. Sharpe, Inc.,
80 Business Park Drive, Armonk, New York 10504.

Library of Congress Cataloging-in-Publication Data

National identity and ethnicity in Russia and the new states
of Eurasia / Roman Szporluk, editor
p. cm. — (The International politics of Eurasia: v. 2)
Includes bibliographical references and index.
ISBN 1-56324-354-7.   ISBN 1-56324-355-5 (pbk.)
1. Nationalism—Former Soviet republics.
2. Former Soviet republics—Ethnic relations.
3. Former Soviet Republics—Politics and government.
I. Szporluk, Roman. II. Series.
DK293.N38 1994
947.086—dc20   94-11527
CIP

Printed in the United States of America

The paper used in this publication meets the minimum requirements of
American National Standard for Information Sciences—
Permanence of Paper for Printed Library Materials,
ANSI Z 39.48-1984.

BM   10   9   8   7   6   5   4   3   2   1
BM (p) 10 9   8   7   6   5   4   3

Contents

About the Editors and Contributors — vii

Preface
   Karen Dawisha and Bruce Parrott — xi

1. Introduction: Statehood and Nation Building in Post-Soviet Space
   Roman Szporluk — 3

I. Russia — 19

Map — 20

2. Center–Periphery Relations in the Russian Federation
   Elizabeth Teague — 21

3. Russian Minorities in the Newly Independent States: An International Problem in the Domestic Context of Russia Today
   Nikolai Rudensky — 58

4. The Paradox of Russian National Identity
   Gregory Guroff and Alexander Guroff — 78

II. The Western Newly Independent States — 101

Map — 102

5. The Influence of Ethnicity on Foreign Policy: The Case of Ukraine
   Ilya Prizel — 103

6. Development of Belarusian National Identity and Its Influence on Belarus's Foreign Policy Orientation
   Jan Zaprudnik — 129

7. The Influence of Ethnicity on the Foreign Policies of the Western Littoral States
   Algimantas Prazauskas — 150

8. Baltic Identities in the 1990s:
   Renewed Fitness
   Walter C. Clemens, Jr. — 185

III. The Southern Newly Independent States — 207

   Map — 208

9. Nation Building and Ethnicity in the Foreign Policies
   of the New Central Asian States
   Martha Brill Olcott — 209

10. Ethnic Demography and Interstate Relations in Central Asia
    Robert J. Kaiser — 230

11. The Ethnic Factor in Central Asian Foreign Policy
    James Critchlow — 266

12. War in Abkhazia:
    The Regional Significance of the Georgian-Abkhazian Conflict
    Gueorgui Otyrba — 281

   Appendix: Project Participants — 311

   Index — 315

About the Editors and Contributors

Roman Szporluk is professor in the Department of History, Harvard University, where he holds the M.S. Hrushevsky Chair in Ukrainian History. He was educated at Lublin, Oxford, and Stanford universities. From 1986 to 1991 he served as director of the Center for Russian and East European Studies at the University of Michigan, where he was professor of East European History. Professor Szporluk's many publications include *Communism and Nationalism: Karl Marx versus Friedrich List*, *The Political Thought of Thomas G. Masaryk*, and a forthcoming history of Ukraine in the nineteenth and twentieth centuries, *From Little Russia to Independent Ukraine: The Emergence of a Nation*.

Karen Dawisha has been professor in the Department of Government and Politics at the University of Maryland at College Park since 1985. She received her Ph.D. from the London School of Economics in 1975. Her publications include *Russia and the New States of Eurasia: The Politics of Upheaval* (coauthored with Bruce Parrott, 1994), *Eastern Europe, Gorbachev, and Reform: The Great Challenge* (2nd ed. 1990), *The Kremlin and the Prague Spring* (1984), and *Soviet Policy Toward Egypt* (1979).

Bruce Parrott is professor and director of Russian Area and East European Studies at the Johns Hopkins University School of Advanced International Studies where he has taught for twenty years. He received his B.A. in Religious Studies from Pomona College in 1966, and his Ph.D. in Political Science in 1976 from Columbia University where he was assistant director of the Russian Institute. His publications include *Russia and the New States of Eurasia: The Politics of Upheaval* (coauthored with Karen Dawisha, 1994), *The Dynamics of Soviet Defense Policy* (1990), *The Soviet Union and Ballistic Missile Defense* (1987), *Trade Technology and Soviet-American Relations* (1985), and *Politics and Technology in the Soviet Union* (1983).

Walter Clemens, Jr., is an associate at the Harvard Russian Research Center and an adjunct research fellow at the Harvard Center for Science and International Affairs. He has taught at Boston University since 1966. Dr. Clemens is the author of a number of books, including *Baltic Independence and Russian Empire* (1991), *Can Russia Change?* (1990), *National Security and U.S.-Soviet Relations* (1982), and many articles.

James Critchlow has been a fellow at the Russian Research Center at Harvard University since 1987. Before coming to Harvard, he was visiting professor in the Department of Political Science at the University of Illinois (Urbana-Champaign). He has worked for the Board of International Broadcasting, Radio Liberty, and the U.S. Information Agency. His published work on Central Asia includes a book on Uzbekistan, contributions to several other books, and numerous articles.

Alexander Guroff received his A.B. from Princeton in 1990 and is currently a research assistant at the Center for Strategic and International Studies. He is a graduate student at the School of Advanced International Studies, Johns Hopkins University.

Gregory Guroff is a senior associate at the Center for Post Soviet Studies. He was previously the coordinator of the President's U.S.-Soviet Exchange Initiative at the U.S. Information Agency, where he has held numerous positions since 1977. Before joining the Agency, Dr. Guroff taught in the Department of History at Grinnell College. He is the editor and author of several books and articles.

Robert Kaiser is assistant professor of geography at the University of Missouri (Columbia). He has had a number of fellowships, including those from Duke University's East–West Center and from the Social Science Research Council. Dr. Kaiser's publications include *The Geography of Nationalism in Russia and the USSR* (1994).

Martha Brill Olcott is professor of political science at Colgate University, where she has been a member of the faculty since 1975. Dr. Olcott is the author of *The Kazakhs* (1987) and editor of *The Soviet Multinational State* (1990). Over the years, she has published numerous articles in academic journals and books, including "Central Asia's Catapult to Independence" (1992), "Central Asia's Post-Empire Politics" (1992), and "The Slide Into Disunion" (1991).

Gueorgui Otyrba is professor in the Department of Modern History at Abkhazia State University. Trained as a scholar of Italian history, Dr. Otyrba is currently researching the history of Abkhazia and is compiling reference collections of documents and materials on Abkhaz-Georgian relations, 1989–1993. He has written several articles on Abkhaz-Georgian relations, most recently "Clashes of Interests: Tbilisi-Suhum" (1992).

Algimantas Prazauskas is a senior researcher at the Institute of Oriental Studies of the Russian Academy of Sciences. He has written extensively on ethnicity and politics in India and the former Soviet Union. His books and articles include *Ethnic Conflicts in the Countries of the East* (1991), *Ethnicity, Politics and State in Modern India* (1990), "Authoritarianism and Democracy in Multinational Societies" (1991), "Ethnic Conflicts in the Context of Democratizing Political Systems" (1991), and "The Baltic Problem" (1990).

Ilya Prizel is associate professor of Russian Area and East European Studies and coordinator of East European Studies at the School of Advanced International Studies, Johns Hopkins University. Dr. Prizel is the editor of *Post-Communist Eastern Europe: Crisis and Reorientation* (1992), and author of *Latin America through Soviet Eyes* (1990). He is currently writing a book titled *Russia, Poland, Ukraine: National Identity and Foreign Policy Formation.*

Nikolai Rudensky is a researcher at the Institute for the Economy in Transition in Moscow (since 1993). Previously he was a researcher at the Institute for USA and Canada Studies of the Russian Academy of Sciences. In 1994 Dr. Rudensky was awarded a two-year fellowship from the Social Science Research Council. He is the author of many books and articles, including "War as a Factor of Ethnic Stability and Conflict in the USSR" (1992), "The Nationality Problem and the Rights of Peoples in the USSR" (1991), *Ethnic Processes in the Modern World* (1987), and *Peoples of the World: A Historical-Ethnographic Encyclopedia* (1988).

Elizabeth Teague is a senior research analyst at the RFE/RF Research Institute in Munich, where she has specialized in Soviet and Russian political developments since 1981. She is the author of *Solidarity and the Soviet Worker* (1988), and a regular contributor to the *RFE/RL Research Report*. Her articles have also appeared in *The New York Times*, *The Wall Street Journal*, *Problems of Communism*, *Government and Opposition*, and others.

Jan Zaprudnik is adjunct professor at the Harriman Institute of Columbia University and the director of the Belarusian Institute of Science and Arts in New York. Dr. Zaprudnik worked at Radio Liberty from 1954 to his retirement in 1991. He has written a number of articles on Belarus and its literary tradition. He is the author of *Belarus: At a Crossroads in History* (1993) and is currently working on a *Historical Dictionary of Belarus*.

Preface

This book is the second in a projected series of ten volumes produced by the Russian Littoral Project, sponsored jointly by the University of Maryland at College Park and the Paul H. Nitze School of Advanced International Studies of the Johns Hopkins University. As directors of the project, we share the conviction that the transformation of the former Soviet republics into independent states demands systematic analysis of the determinants of the domestic and foreign policies of the new countries. The series of volumes is intended to provide a basis for comprehensive scholarly study of these issues.

The present volume analyzes the impact of the quest for national identity on the foreign relations and internal structure of the new states. The collapse of the Soviet Union and the discrediting of Marxism–Leninism as a source of political legitimacy have prompted a search for fresh principles of political organization in all the post-Soviet countries. In this search, one of the strongest potential sources of guidance is an intensified sense of national identity. The quest for national identity, however, can have various political consequences, depending on the specific form of identity that becomes prevalent. This book examines which patterns of national identity have begun to emerge within the new states, along with the role of these national sentiments in relations with the outside world. The book also explores in some detail the political impact of the heightened sense of ethnicity and of the mixed ethnic composition of most of the post-Soviet countries, particularly the presence of sizable numbers of ethnic Russians in several of the new states.

We would like to thank the contributors to this volume for their help in making the first phase of the Russian Littoral Project a success and for revising their papers in a timely fashion. We are especially grateful to Roman Szporluk for supporting the Russian Littoral Project since its inception, for contributing insights that were pivotal in structuring the project's treatment of national and ethnic issues, and for editing this book.

In addition, we are grateful to Janine Ludlam and Florence Rotz for their skillful handling of the complex logistics of the workshops on which the book is based and for their unstinting labor in preparing the final manuscript.

Russian Littoral Project

The objective of the Russian Littoral Project is to foster an exchange of research and information in fields of study pertaining to the international politics of Eurasia. The interaction between the internal affairs and foreign policies of the new states is being studied in a series of workshops taking place in Washington, D.C., London, Central Asia, and other locations between 1993 and 1995. Scholars from the new states, North America, and Europe are invited to present papers at the workshops.

Focusing on the interaction between the internal affairs and the foreign relations of the new states, the project workshops examine the impact of the following factors: history, national identity and ethnicity, religion, political culture and civil society, economics, foreign policy priorities and decision making, military issues, and the nuclear question. Each of these topics is examined in a set of three workshops focusing in turn on Russia, the western belt of new states extending from Estonia to Ukraine, and the southern tier of new states extending from Georgia to Kyrgyzstan.

The Russian Littoral Project could not have been launched without the generous and timely contributions of the project's Coordinating Committee. We wish to thank the committee members for providing invaluable advice and expertise concerning the organization and intellectual substance of the project. The members of the Coordinating Committee are: Dr. Adeed Dawisha (George Mason University); Dr. Bartek Kaminski (University of Maryland and The World Bank); Dr. Catherine Kelleher (The Brookings Institution); Ms. Judith Kipper (The Brookings Institution); Dr. Nancy Lubin (Carnegie Mellon University); Dr. Michael Mandelbaum (The School of Advanced International Studies); Dr. James Millar (The George Washington University); Dr. Peter Murrell (University of Maryland); Dr. Martha Brill Olcott (Colgate University); Dr. Ilya Prizel (The School of Advanced International Studies); Dr. George Quester (University of Maryland); Dr. Alvin Z. Rubinstein (University of Pennsylvania); Dr. Blair Ruble (The Kennan Institute); Dr. S. Frederick Starr (Oberlin College); Dr. Roman Szporluk (Harvard University); and Dr. Vladimir Tismaneanu (University of Maryland).

We are grateful to the John D. and Catherine T. MacArthur Foundation for funding the workshops from which this book is derived; we are especially grateful to Kennette Benedict for her firm support of the whole project from the beginning. The Friedrich Ebert Stiftung (Dieter Dettke) also contributed valuable funding for these workshops. For funding the workshops on which several future volumes will be based, we express our thanks to the MacArthur Foundation, the Pew Charitable Trusts (particularly Kevin Quigley and Peter Benda), the National Endowment for the Humanities, and the Ford Foundation (in particular Geoffrey Wiseman).

We also wish to thank President William Kirwan of the University of Maryland at College Park and President William C. Richardson of the Johns Hopkins University, who have given indispensable support to the project. Thanks are also due to Dean Irwin Goldstein, Associate Dean Stewart Edelstein, Director of the Office of International Affairs Marcus Franda, and Department of Government and Politics Chair Jonathan Wilkenfeld at the University of Maryland at College Park; to Provost Joseph Cooper and Vice-Provost for Academic Planning and Budget Stephen M. McClain at the Johns Hopkins University; to Professor George Packard, who helped launch the project during his final year as dean of the School of Advanced International Studies, to SAIS Dean Paul D. Wolfowitz and to SAIS Associate Dean Stephen Szabo.

Finally, we are grateful for the guidance and encouragement given by Patricia Kolb at M.E. Sharpe, Inc. Her confidence in the success of the project and the volumes is deeply appreciated.

Karen Dawisha
University of Maryland
at College Park

Bruce Parrott
The Johns Hopkins University
School of Advanced International Studies

NATIONAL IDENTITY AND ETHNICITY IN RUSSIA AND THE NEW STATES OF EURASIA

1

Introduction

Statehood and Nation Building in Post-Soviet Space

Roman Szporluk

The fall of the USSR did not bring about the "end of history" in its former space. If anything, history is being made there anew. The collapse of the Soviet Union has opened the historical stage to a whole host of new actors, new participants, who are determined to shape their own destinies—and the destinies of others. This in turn has forced traditional players to face problems never dreamt of, and has given us an unprecedented opportunity to observe phenomena well known from other historical situations but now taking place in a setting never seen before—a postcommunist world.

There exists a vast literature on ethnicity, nation formation, and nationalism in "capitalist" societies. The world has less empirical knowledge, and even less theory, about the same kinds of phenomena in communist and especially postcommunist societies. How do nations constitute themselves after the collapse of a polity that defined itself in terms of the universal, internationalist ideology of Marxism-Leninism? How will the new international politics, the new system of international relations, affect the formation of national identities within new states? How will internal processes express themselves in turn in the international sphere? What will be the place and the role of ethnicity as compared with the role of political and social institutions and values in shaping the new identities of the new states? Will they take language and the ethnos as the defining, decisive marker of nationhood, or will they seek to substitute for ethnicity some other criteria of nationhood? Will they be able to transform their present political systems, which at best are "proto-democracies," into working and stable democracies?[1]

The contributions to this volume address some of these questions, and pose other issues, as they seek to diagnose the present condition of the former republics of the USSR and to discover the tendencies of their future evolution as well as their import for the world community. These are not simply academic questions. The emergence of fifteen new states in the space vacated by the USSR has created a new international environment that also includes, and has a profound impact on, the states that used to be neighbors of the USSR. Interstate and interethnic wars are raging in much of the formerly Soviet space. Those wars are sufficiently dangerous to merit the attention of the world. The very fact that a new interstate constellation has emerged poses a host of practical questions for the diplomats and generals of the old and new states. Even heavier challenges await the leaders of the new states, and their political and intellectual elites, as they face their internal problems.

Commentators in recent years have been pointing out three tremendously difficult changes the former USSR faces: the transition from empire to independent states, the transition from a Communist Party–run centralized economy to a market economy, and the transition from a totalitarian system to a pluralist and democratic one. Now, several years after 1991, the difficulties involved in all these transitions have become only too evident. Indeed, in several cases there has been a retreat from reforms in some or all of these areas. The contributions to this volume give us a sobering indication of how all three kinds of transitions are in reality combined or fused in the chaotic and extremely difficult process of formation and transformation of states and nations.

Key questions of national identity and international relations in the new geopolitical space that has emerged outside Russia are addressed here in chapters by Prazauskas, Zaprudnik, Otyrba, Rudensky, Critchlow, Prizel, Clemens, Olcott, and Kaiser. Three papers—Guroff and Guroff, Teague, and Rudensky—address the Russian question directly, but the role of Russia in the area is so major that all the chapters in varying degrees discuss Russia as they investigate its legacy and its relations with the new states or the crucial problem of Russian minorities in what Russians call the "near abroad."

The many legacies of the Soviet Union include the Soviet theory and practice of "the nationality question." Not only did the late Soviet regime create its own economic, ideological, and political system, but over the years to a large extent it defined ethnicity itself within its territory. It virtually created nations and nationalities following criteria and purposes that were its own, and in conformity with these it charted out "national" or "republic" borders. The Soviets thus created a host of ethnic problems that they proved incapable of dealing with in the final years of the USSR, and left as their legacy to their successors. One of the fundamental aspects of the entire Soviet experience with ethnicity was to connect nationality and the rights of nationalities to territory. The Soviets did not invent the concept of ethnic homeland, of course, but they did much to make it even more central to the idea of nationality than it had been earlier. Virtually all the ex-Soviet peoples, large and small, have some places in ex-Soviet space marked as their "ethnic homelands," even if the nominal or titular nationality forms a minority in the overall population of "its" land, and even if most of that nationality's members live elsewhere, in the "diaspora." Those homelands are said to be connected with some special bonds to the titular nation. Equally, if not more importantly, all those ethnic homelands enjoyed under the Soviets the status of political entities, and even the smallest, and thus ranking lowest in the hierarchy of autonomous regions and republics, formally enjoyed at least rudiments of "statehood." (See especially Teague, Olcott, Kaiser, Rudensky, and Critchlow.) Those nationalities that lived in the USSR at the time of its dissolution had been traditionally defined—by themselves and by others—with ethnic criteria, primarily by language. To what extent has the experience of communism resulted in a change of those markers that define a nation?

The Soviets did not intend to create nations and "their" corresponding states as entities capable of independent or autonomous existence. As became evident immediately after Gorbachev's rise to power, if not earlier, some creations of Moscow, most notably Nagorno-Karabakh, lacked both national legitimacy and a capacity to function as administrative, let alone political, entities. Moscow's purpose in creating "nations" and "republics" was to promote the creation of Soviet man and Soviet woman, members of one *Soviet* people, living in one *Soviet* state. This policy of "internationalization" to a large extent became synonymous with, and was perceived by other nations as, Russification. The modern Soviet person was to adopt the most important mark of ethnic Russian nationality—the language—because the Russian language enjoyed a special position as the language of the emerging communist civilization. But the full definition of Russianness was the privilege of the party, and the Communists chose only those other elements of Russian traditional identity that suited them—for example, an authoritarian political system—and even the Russian language and Russian culture were promoted in a Sovietized form.

This selective and manipulated resort to Russian identity contained within itself a potentially explosive contradiction between the Soviet identity, defined ideologically and politically, and a Russian identity rooted in culture and history. One of the most important developments of the post-

Stalin era was the gradual emancipation of Russia from "Sovietism," in other words, the emergence of an anti-Soviet Russian national movement and national identity.[2] In 1990–91, this new Russia found itself in a state of revolt against Moscow and "the center." Some people abroad mistakenly saw the conflict between Russia and the union in a personalized and thus trivialized form, as a struggle for power between Yeltsin and Gorbachev. Of course, it was that too, and this aspect did matter as well, but if these two men had not been identified with what at that historical juncture were two opposing political entities—Russia contra the Soviet Union—there would have been no breakup of the USSR as occurred in 1991.[3]

In 1991, Russia returned—or so it seemed—to where its "normal" course had been interrupted by Lenin and the Bolsheviks in 1917. When the Bolsheviks came to power, modern, European-style nation building in Russia itself had not yet been completed. After the revolution and civil war, a "Russian Soviet Federated Socialist Republic" did exist within the larger structure of the Soviet Union, but it was not taken seriously, by Russians or non-Russians, as the Russian nation-state or the national homeland of the Russian people. In the prevailing view of the Russians, the whole of the USSR was the real Russia. The architects of the USSR did not treat the republics as real or potential nation-states. Moscow delineated their borders deliberately so as to make the republics incapable of independent existence. By putting together different peoples within one political entity, the party created the conditions under which its "leading role" would be necessary for the operation of that complex system of "autonomous" districts and regions and "republics" within "republics." This ethnic mixing within ethnically designated territorial units could work only if the Communist Party remained in control.

Precisely because Russia itself had not yet resolved the key issues of its modern identity when the Bolsheviks won—the relations between state and society, between nation and empire—the same issues reemerged as Soviet power was disintegrating. In a real sense, among the post-Soviet nations facing the problem of nation and state building, the Russians are in a particularly difficult situation. They were used to being "the leading nation" in the USSR, but they were also an object of manipulation and a victim of political manipulation—their identity made and remade by the party.

Moscow had never intended that it should be so, but its purely opportunistic policy has left an ineradicable legacy. The nationalities have come to see themselves as existing properly only through and within their own "national" states. Thus, virtually all post-Soviet national identities are now political; they are defined by the state. What used to be fiction under the Soviets is now, or is desired to be, a reality. This is a point of departure for any future solution of post-Soviet conflicts. The question is not whether the USSR, or Yugoslavia, can be reconstituted—they cannot—but whether their successors, which have chosen to declare themselves nation-states (rather than multi- or supranational entities), will develop a civic or an ethnic definition of nationality.

Thus, at this important point in their history, as they try to move from totalitarianism to political pluralism, and from a command economy to free markets, the post-Soviet nations are also constructing their states, and in so doing are also reshaping their national identities. In this process, the outlook and psychology of peoples in the new states is changing. They are creating their own armies, forming their diplomatic corps, entering the world community under their own flags. Whether or not all those newcomers to the world of nations survive as independent states, the promises and hopes of the post-1991 era will remain a key component of their collective memories and thus of their recast identities. Those politicians and analysts who imagine that a multinational state run from Moscow can be restored along the lines of the pre-1991 USSR ignore at their peril the psychological impact of the moment of national liberation. For many, especially the young people who are the first generation formed by the experience of 1991, the post-Soviet world is normal, the world as it should be. They do not "miss" the USSR.

New kinds of international relations are especially important in forming and re-forming post-Soviet national identities and states. External relations among the new states are making them increasingly different from each other as ex-Soviets, and this is especially true of the younger generation. Their Russian is getting worse as they increasingly speak English—even when communicating with their immediate neighbors in what used to be the "Soviet bloc," or indeed, even their fellow "Soviets." New international neighborhoods are emerging, and in them identities are being transformed. Old commonalities derived from a shared Soviet experience are receding into the past and new ones are being forged. A young Lithuanian discovers more to talk about with a Pole or a Swede, and correspondingly less with a Tajik or a Georgian.

By relying on the current political aspirations of the peoples concerned, as well as on their geography and history, as a guide, it is possible to identify at least four major post-Soviet "neighborhoods":

1. The Baltic zone, consisting of Estonia, Latvia, and Lithuania, together with the Scandinavian countries, and Poland and Germany.
2. The "East-Central European," with Ukraine and Belarus, but also Lithuania, in a neighborhood where Poland is the focal point, but

which also includes Hungary, Slovakia, and Romania. Moldova, together with Ukraine, may form a subgroup tying a part of the ex-Soviet space to the Balkans.
3. The "Caucasus neighborhood," which consists of the three former Soviet republics in Transcaucasia, but also extends to the Russian Federation in the north and to Turkey and Iran in the south.
4. The whole area of Central Asia, with its new external connections.

Obviously, other combinations can be sketched out: for example, there is some basis for speaking of an actual or potential community of nations of the Black Sea region, including the Caucasus, Turkey, Russia, Ukraine, Romania, and Bulgaria as well as Greece.

What matters most about these "neighborhoods" is that they facilitate political de-Sovietization and economic marketization in all ex-communist countries that would become their members. The formation among the latter of new national and political identities would thus tend to go hand in hand with economic and political departures from the imperial legacy and Soviet way of life and thought.

The converse point can be made even more strongly. The stronger the ties between the ex-Soviet republics and Moscow become, the more likely it is that the old political and economic structures within those republics, and in Russia itself, will be revived. The entry of Belarus into closer economic ties with Russia, announced early in 1994, appears to be producing this effect in both Minsk and Moscow.

Many people in the new states would probably agree with the comment made by the president of Kazakhstan, Nursultan Nazarbaev, at the December 1993 CIS summit: "We realized we have little in common." The people in Moscow who propose to rebuild the USSR would be wise to bear in mind the broader validity of this observation and to reflect on what the effect of "reintegration" would be on Russia itself.

The Russian case calls for a special discussion, because geopolitically Russia is in a class by itself. As the state that claims to be the heir and legal successor of the USSR, Russia needs to address problems of postimperial space and sovereignty as they relate to the "near abroad," but it is also required to define itself as a nation-state where within its sovereign limits it is presented with numerous national challenges. Do Russians in Estonia have a stronger right to national self-determination than the Tatars of Tatarstan within Russia, for example? The very concept of a near abroad implies some central location, an empire of the middle; in the meantime there are people clamoring inside.

The age-old question, What is Russia? is still being asked. Russia has rejected its previous communist form, but it needs to construct itself in positive terms rather than just by rejecting the Soviet model. The discussion of Russian identity includes geography, ethnicity, language, history, culture, and religion.

Current discussions invoke traditional visions of what Russia is, and involve the centuries-old question of whether Russia should look to the West or East.

To understand these different visions one must look at Russia's history, at how the empire was formed. Since the times of Peter I, Russian intellectual and political history has been preoccupied with the "Russia and Europe" problem. Historians of Russia are well used to discussing its past and its present in terms of grand dichotomies, such as state and society, nation and empire, and viewing Russia itself in terms of its being alike or unlike "the West," with a corollary question of the compatibility or lack of compatibility between Russia and democracy and liberalism. The answer to the question about Russia's relation to the West is more than a question of geography—it is an answer to the question about Russia's internal political and social organization.

All these considerations help us understand what being in a Russia without Ukraine and Belarus may now mean to the Russian public. Unlike all the other formerly Soviet nations, whose distinct identity the Russians recognize, Ukrainians and Belarusians are commonly perceived in Russia as being Russian, not only by imperial or statist but also by historical and cultural/ethnic criteria. Their "leaving" is felt very strongly because it is costly not only economically but also emotionally. Many Russians have believed that the western East Slavs, because of their centuries-long association with the West politically (Poland) and religiously (Catholicism), are more European than the core "Muscovite" lands. Their union with Great Russia in the seventeenth–eighteenth centuries, therefore, contributed to the Westernization of Russia from within, as it were, since they became internal elements of the Russian body national. Conversely, the departure of Ukraine and Belarus makes the post-1991 Russia feel less "European" than it was before.[4]

The Baltic states also provide us with an insight into the relation of Russia to Europe. Is Russia willing to treat the Baltic nations as the east of the West or the west of the East? The new Russia, as many Russians see it, is one that has been deprived of its Baltic region—which had been a part of the empire from 1721 to 1991, with an interlude of 1918–40, in the case of Latvia and Estonia, and from 1795 to 1991 (with the same interlude) in the case of Lithuania.

To appreciate the place of the Baltic region and Ukraine and Belarus in the present Russian thinking, it is helpful to turn to earlier reflections made by Ken Jowitt (in 1986) on the meaning of Eastern Europe to the Soviet leadership in Gorbachev's time:

> Eastern Europe isn't simply territorial "booty"; it is an integral and concrete expression of a political generation's revolutionary credentials and achievements, its revolutionary "patrimony." That explains Brezhnev's blunt assertion to the Czechoslovak leadership in the late 1960s that the Soviet Union would never give up Eastern Europe.[5]

Thus, while Peter and his successors saw joining Europe as remaking Russia in the image of a Europe that was "the Other," their Soviet successors made Russia European by creating a Europe in the image and likeness of Soviet Russia. This construction worked for several decades, from 1945 to 1989. Then there was the brief moment when, after giving up its socialist alternative Europe, the Soviet Union hoped to be included in a much larger "common European home."

But the Soviet Union ceased to exist shortly after the collapse of the socialist Europe of which it had been the central, constituting part. The old, pre-Soviet theme—the question of *"Russia* and Europe"—returned. Now it was a noncommunist Russia's challenge to define itself with reference to Europe on new terms—and, because of the collapse of the "union," in addition to the collapse of communism, in a new geographical form.

It was in connection with this that, in Moscow's view, as accounted by Jowitt, the attempts by West European Communists to develop an alternative socialist model to that created in the USSR threatened to condemn the Soviet regime to "ideological marginality."[6] Jowitt speculated that as Soviet ties to the non-European world became stronger—he was writing when Moscow was deeply engaged in Afghanistan, Ethiopia, and Vietnam—the Soviets would intensify their attention to the "eastern part of Europe." As Jowitt understood well, Eastern Europe was "a vital component of the Soviet leadership's conception of itself as a European political and ideological, not simply military and economic, force." Because of this, he expected that Gorbachev's "commitment to Eastern Europe" would be "exceptionally strong."[7]

At the same time Russia always was, and wanted to be, an Asian power too. Already in the eighteenth century, Russian schoolchildren read in their geography textbook:

> Q. What is Russia?
> A. A vast empire, located in Europe and Asia.
> Q. And how is Russia generally divided?
> A. Into two main parts: European and Asian.[8]

In the twentieth century the view that Russia is also a part of Asia is even stronger. In his book on Russia's Asian connection, the title of which repeats a question asked by Dostoyevsky, *What Is Asia to Us?*, Milan Hauner cites those Western commentators who have ironically remarked on how many "common homes"—European, Asian, Eurasian, Arctic, Pacific—Russians have claimed to be living in at the same time.[9] But irony aside, it is enough to take a look at St. Basil's Cathedral in Moscow to become aware that, while indeed Russia is situated both in Europe and in Asia, "the East" happens to function also as an authentic "Constituting Other" of Russia: It commemorates and honors the conquest of Kazan. (How well this memory plays in the capital of Tatarstan today is another matter.) Acknowledging the enormity of this Eastern connection, one of the most interesting ideological currents in twentieth-century Russian thought, the Eurasian School, proposed to redefine Russia as a power that was both European and Asian, both Christian and Islamic, as one that accepted as its own historical legacy the period of the so-called Mongol yoke over Slavic and Christian Russia.

Eurasianism represents an interesting chapter in Russian intellectual history, and it does have some followers today, but it runs against the much stronger pro-European tendencies in Russia. Many see dangers in Russia's becoming too "Asian." A Russia that stresses its Asian credentials too much, they feel, will be less convincing as a European nation and state. For those who wish to retain close ties with their fellow East Slavs, a Russia looking to the Pacific would become more alienated from Ukraine and Belarus, both of which are seeking to establish themselves in an East European neighborhood, and have no claims to common homes beyond Europe. The Belárusians do not want to fight in Tajikistan or the Caucasus. The same can be said almost certainly about the Ukrainians. It is doubtful that the border of Tajikistan with Afghanistan is also Ukraine's border, although Russians (at least according to Moscow editorial writers) view it as Russia's border.

Another very famous and very central theme of modern Russian history is again on the table: the relation between the Russian people or nation, *russkii narod,* on the one hand, and the Russian state, *rossiiskoe gosudarstvo,* on the other. What form of government, of political organization, is the most appropriate for Russia, for the Russian people?

Today, this question is being formulated with reference to geography as well. Many hold the view that for the Russian nation, a Russia understood and constituted as a nation-state is not an adequate political form: for its well-being, they hold, the Russian nation requires an empire, preferably within the limits of the former USSR, as its proper living space.

While it is mainly the Communists and radical nationalists who are for the union/empire, some Russian democrats, too, speak the language of empire, even when their vocabulary is less brutal or less candid than that of Vladimir Zhirinovsky. For them, too, the present-day Russian Federation is not Russia, and they do not limit their territorial claims to Ukraine and Belarus. Rather, leading figures in the pro-Western camp are calling for the creation, or restoration, of a *Russian* state within the 1991 boundaries of the USSR. They obviously expect that the "near abroad" will become less "abroad" and more "near." The first issue of *Izvestiia* in 1994 carries an article titled "The Russian [*russkii*] Question in Russian [*rossiiskoi*] Politics of 1994." Its opening sentence reads, "The Russian question—that is the most important problem of Moscow diplomacy in the new year." The article goes on to say that "the opposition" has been using the question against President Yeltsin with unfailing success. The opposition defines "the Russian question" as the issue of Russians living in the former republics outside Russia. For those people, the only acceptable solution to the Russian problem is to include all those territories back under Russia.[10]

To say that the plight of the 25 million Russians outside the Russian Federation is the top priority on the current Russian agenda is another way of saying that the condition of some 125 million Russians *inside* Russia, together with the 25 million or so other citizens of Russia, is not the top priority. Empire takes precedence over reform.

The prominent Russian political commentator Aleksei Pushkov articulates this point of view for the Western public. He declares that "Economically, the Soviet Union was a single body. After the country [*sic*] fell apart, it is not surprising that, after a short period of local elites' assertiveness, trends toward economic union and a common ruble zone are winning out."[11]

Thus, as we see, in Pushkov's view the USSR was, and implicitly is, one country, although it is divided up now. He does not specify exactly what economic union is possible under the aegis of Moscow in the post-1991 conditions—other than one based on plan and central command.

In his view, "none of the former Soviet republics can gain access to markets outside the former USSR and all of them depend on the same economic area. They can be neither included in any economic bloc that would drag them to modernity, nor assisted sufficiently to reconstruct their economies and reorient their exports and imports." From this it follows naturally "that in this setting Russia acts as the economic nucleus of an emerging community."[12]

Pushkov recommends that Russia's leading role in the CIS should be accepted by the United States, since "In any case, nothing seems to be able to prevent Russia from playing that role. . . . it is not by chance [*ne sluchaino*] that . . . Kozyrev has started to drift in that direction."[13]

This call for the West's acceptance of the restoration of the USSR is combined with a warning against "the second mistake," which "would be to attempt to marginalize Russia—for instance, by accepting the East European countries into NATO while leaving Russia outside."[14]

How does one "marginalize" a Russia that is a global power even in its present borders, and one that would include, by the author's preference, also the lost republics, as its sphere of influence if not directly its provinces?

We are back to the question Ken Jowitt raised about the USSR in Gorbachev's time. The "marginalization" some Russians fear now is a psychological, not a political or economic, threat; it is about identity, not security. In a recent article, Iver B. Neumann speaks of "Russia as Central Europe's Constituting Other." In developing his argument regarding the identity of Central Europe, Neumann offers his own, "a radically different perspective." Identity, he says, should be seen "not as something to be had, but as something to be done." Neumann calls for treating identity "as a *relation, always forming and reforming in discourse, rather than as a possession.*"[15] Thus, it is evident that for some Russians today, closer relations between East-Central Europe and the West threaten to "marginalize" or "Asianize" Russia. The same fear is reflected in the view that emigration of Jews and Germans from Russia has already contributed, and continues to contribute, to what a Polish author, Ryszard Kapuscinski, calls the "Asianization" of Russia —that is, its "marginalization" or "de-Europeanization."[16]

The opposition of Moscow to the Visegrad Group's joining NATO can be better understood by taking into account Russian problems with national self-definition, such as those raised by Jowitt, rather than by any real military considerations. Entry of the Czech Republic, and even more so Poland, into NATO would further marginalize Russia—not in reality of course (a good argument can be made that such a move would bring all of Eastern Europe, including Russia, to "Europe"), but because of the Russians' uncertainty about their identity.

While Russia as a real continental power is defining its identity in relation to both "Europe" and "Asia," Ukraine and Belarus are seeking to define themselves within a much narrower geographical—and cultural— horizon. The elites of Ukraine and Belarus, as well as Lithuania, and especially the younger generation of those nations, are looking to their immediate Western neighbors, especially Poland.[17] One may speculate that the Russian election of December 1993 has increased the number of people in Warsaw who will be sympathetic to the concerns of the Eastern nations with whom so much of Polish history had been tied. In the new constellation of states created by the breakup of the USSR, Czechoslovakia, and Yugoslavia, it may well prove to be the case that Poland, with its forty million people and its good relations with all its neighbors, will play a significant and positive role in the development of its "neighborhood." While before 1939 Poland's claims to the role of a "regional great power" were disputable, the situation now may actually warrant such a status.[18] This new neighborhood, consisting of several former Soviet republics and several East-Central European nations, is only emerging. For the Ukrainians or the Balts, however, it provides a mental map that is quite different from that of the "near abroad" with a center in Moscow. One of the potentially most significant new linkages emerging is that between Kiev and Warsaw.[19]

Such developments, which are only beginning, need not be perceived as a threat to a Russia that concentrates its attention on its real—that is, its internal—problems, rather than on restoration of the empire. Preoccupation with the latter, it would seem, impedes rather than promotes the rise of a new Russian national and state identity.

A major "internal" problem that the Russian Federation faces today is the relations between its ethnic Russian majority and its non-Russian nations. These questions are examined in this volume. One should not be deceived by numbers: Indeed, the percentage of Russians in Russia is higher than that of Ukrainians in Ukraine, not to mention the percent share of the Kazakhs in the population of Kazakhstan. What matters is that such "Russian" nationalities as the Tatars, Bashkirs, Yakuts, Chechens, and many others have their homelands in the Russian Federation. The national aspirations of the Tatars cannot be satisfied by "repatriation"—they have nowhere to go—or by border adjustments. The nationalities problem of the Russian Federation is qualitatively different from the problem of Russians in the non-Russian republics. Its resolution will depend on the creation of a political identity of Russia that satisfies both the ethnic Russians and the other nations whose homelands are in Russia.

Even within its present borders, Russia is a great power. As such—as Russia, that is, in its nonimperial identity—it needs to develop relations not only with the "near abroad" but with Europe, Asia, and the world community.

There are people in Moscow who advocate precisely this kind of approach. Thus, for example, in a lecture delivered at the Kennan Institute for Advanced Russian Studies, Andrei Tsygankov argued against the current tendency in Moscow to promote the restoration of the USSR. (He referred to Andrei Kozyrev's pledge before his voters to work for restoring the USSR "by peaceful means" as an example of the emerging trend in Moscow.) He predicted that if a nonimperial Russian identity, a new liberal national identity, is not formed, "the alternative will not be a new totalitarian regime, nor a democratic government, but disintegration and civil war."[20]

Even if this scenario is pessimistic in the extreme, the case of Yugoslavia, where war and massacres were preceded by "historical" and "philosophical" debates among poets and professors, should be a warning. Current Ukrainian-Russian disputes involve fundamental issues. They are at the same time about Ukraine's identity, its very legitimacy, and about Russia's national and political identity.

Let us restate in this connection an underlying theme of this introductory chapter: The relations between the ex-Soviet republics have become interstate relations. This means that the parties have at their disposal military power. In a recent study, Barry R. Posen has examined what he calls the problem of "emerging anarchy" that arises after the collapse of empires:

> The longest standing and most useful school of international relations theory—realism—explicitly addresses the consequences of anarchy—the absence of a sovereign—for political relations among states. In areas such as the former Soviet Union and Yugoslavia, "sovereigns" have disappeared. They leave in their wake a host of groups—ethnic, religious, cultural—of greater or lesser cohesion. These groups must pay attention to the first thing that states have historically addressed—the problem of security—even though many of these groups still lack many of the attributes of statehood.[21]

The collapse of the Soviet Union did not create a "sovereignty vacuum" in Russia or Ukraine, or in most other republics. New "sovereigns" in the republics appeared on the stage before the demise of the "sovereign" in Moscow, and by their very rise they directly contributed to the latter's demise. Moreover, the successor republics, or at least Russia, Ukraine, and Kazakhstan, from the very beginning defined themselves as political, not ethnic, entities; they were not created by, and for, an ethnic group. The concept of a "people of Ukraine" was civic and territorial, not linguistic or ethnic. The post-Soviet Ukraine was not an entirely new entity, but a state that claimed to be the legal continuation of the Ukrainian Soviet Republic. Ukraine's withdrawal from the USSR was carried out by constitutional bodies of the Ukrainian Soviet Republic. This secured acceptance of the new state's independence by until-then loyal Soviet citizens, and at the same time prevented the rise of rival claimants to power from among opponents of communism. The actions of political actors of all persuasions thus made it possible to avoid a civil war between "Sovietists" and nationalists, between ethnic groups, between regions. And equally importantly, it was possible to avoid a war with Russia or "the center." All of these points can be applied, *mutatis mutandis,* to the other successor states of the USSR (except those of the Transcaucasus).

The mode of dissolution of the USSR would seem to provide the successor states with a precedent on which to build their future relations. The question is whether the most important of the successor states will accept this outcome as final. It is too early to tell whether neoimperialism will prevail over the nonimperial nation-building model in Russia. Many Russians know very well that an attempt to restore the USSR would be extremely costly to Russia. They understand that a reabsorption of the ex-republics by Moscow, were that to prove feasible, would not restore the status quo ante 1991. All the post-Soviet nations have moved far ahead in the definition and redefinition of their own distinct identities. It is possible to envisage arrangements under which they can cooperate, bilaterally or in multilateral structures, in economic, security, and other matters. But the time when Moscow could play the role of a recognized elder brother has passed. Lenin understood that only communism, not Russian superiority, could legitimize Moscow's rule over Kiev and Minsk and Tashkent. What universal principle or idea could legitimize the inclusion of Ukraine in an avowedly Russian state? And what kind of Russia would Russia have to be if it wanted to keep the Ukrainians and Tajiks, the Belarusians and Georgians together, in some future "common home?" An imperial Russia would have to be a dictatorship. Even if some ex-republics were to be brought under Moscow's control economically, without giving up formal attributes of political independence, this would have to be done by means of command-economy methods. The surest way to shift the balance of Russian politics away from democracy would be to bring the ex-republics back into Moscow politics as an enlarged Russia's problems. Democracy and empire are incompatible.[22]

Notes

1. See Timothy J. Colton, "Politics," in *After the Soviet Union: From Empire to Nations,* ed. Timothy J. Colton and Robert Legvold (New York: W.W. Norton, 1992).

2. See Roman Szporluk, "Dilemmas of Russian Nationalism," *Problems of Communism,* vol. 38, no. 4 (1989). Reprinted in *The Soviet Nationality Reader: The Disintegration in Context,* ed. Rachel Denber (Boulder: Westview Press, 1992).

3. See John B. Dunlop, *The Rise of Russia and the Fall of the Soviet Empire* (Princeton: Princeton University Press, 1993).

4. See John Morrison, "Pereyaslav and After: The Russian-Ukrainian Relationship," *International Affairs,* vol. 69, no. 4 (1993); and Roman Solchanyk, "Ukraine, The (Former) Center, Russia, and 'Russia,' " *Studies in Comparative Communism,* vol. 25, no. 1 (March 1992).

5. Ken Jowitt, *New World Disorder: The Leninist Extinction* (Berkeley: University of California Press, 1992), p. 217.

6. Ibid., p. 218.
7. Ibid.
8. Bassin, Mark, "Russia Between Europe and Asia: The Ideological Construction of Geographical Space," *Slavic Review,* vol. 50, no. 1 (spring 1991), p. 8.
9. See Milan Hauner, *What Is Asia to Us? Russia's Asian Heartland Yesterday and Today* (Boston: Unwin Hyman, 1990).
10. Leonid Mlechen, "Russkii vopros v rossiiskoi politike 1994 goda," *Izvestiia,* 4 January 1994.
11. Alexei K. Pushkov, "Letter from Eurasia: Russia and America: The Honeymoon's Over," *Foreign Policy,* no. 93 (winter 1993–94), pp. 88–89.
12. Ibid., p. 89.
13. Ibid., p. 90.
14. Ibid.
15. Iver B. Neumann, "Russia as Central Europe's Constituting Other," *East European Politics and Societies,* vol. 7, no. 2 (1993), p. 349.
16. Ryszard Kapuscinski, *Imperium* (Warsaw: Czytelnik, 1993), p. 327.
17. See Stephen R. Burant, "International Relations in a Regional Context: Poland and Its Eastern Neighbours—Lithuania, Belarus, Ukraine," *Europe-Asia Studies,* vol. 45, no. 3 (1993); and Stephen R. Burant and Voytek Zubek, "Eastern Europe's Old Memories and New Realities: Resurrecting the Polish-Lithuanian Union," *East European Politics and Societies,* vol. 7, no. 2 (1993).
18. See Iver B. Neumann, "Poland as a Regional Great Power: The Inter-war Heritage," in *Regional Great Powers in International Politics,* ed. Iver B. Neumann (New York: St. Martin's Press, 1992), pp. 121–50.
19. Ian J. Brzezinski, "Polish-Ukrainian Relations: Europe's Neglected Strategic Axis," *Survival,* no. 3, 1993, pp. 26–37.
20. "Russia in Need of Moderate Nationalism," Kennan Institute for Advanced Russian Studies, *Meeting Report,* vol. 11, no. 7 (1994).
21. Barry R. Posen, "The Security Dilemma and Ethnic Conflict," *Survival,* no. 1, 1993, pp. 27–28.
22. This point has been recently argued by Zbigniew Brzezinski, "The Premature Partnership," *Foreign Affairs,* vol. 73, no. 2 (March–April 1994).

I

Russia

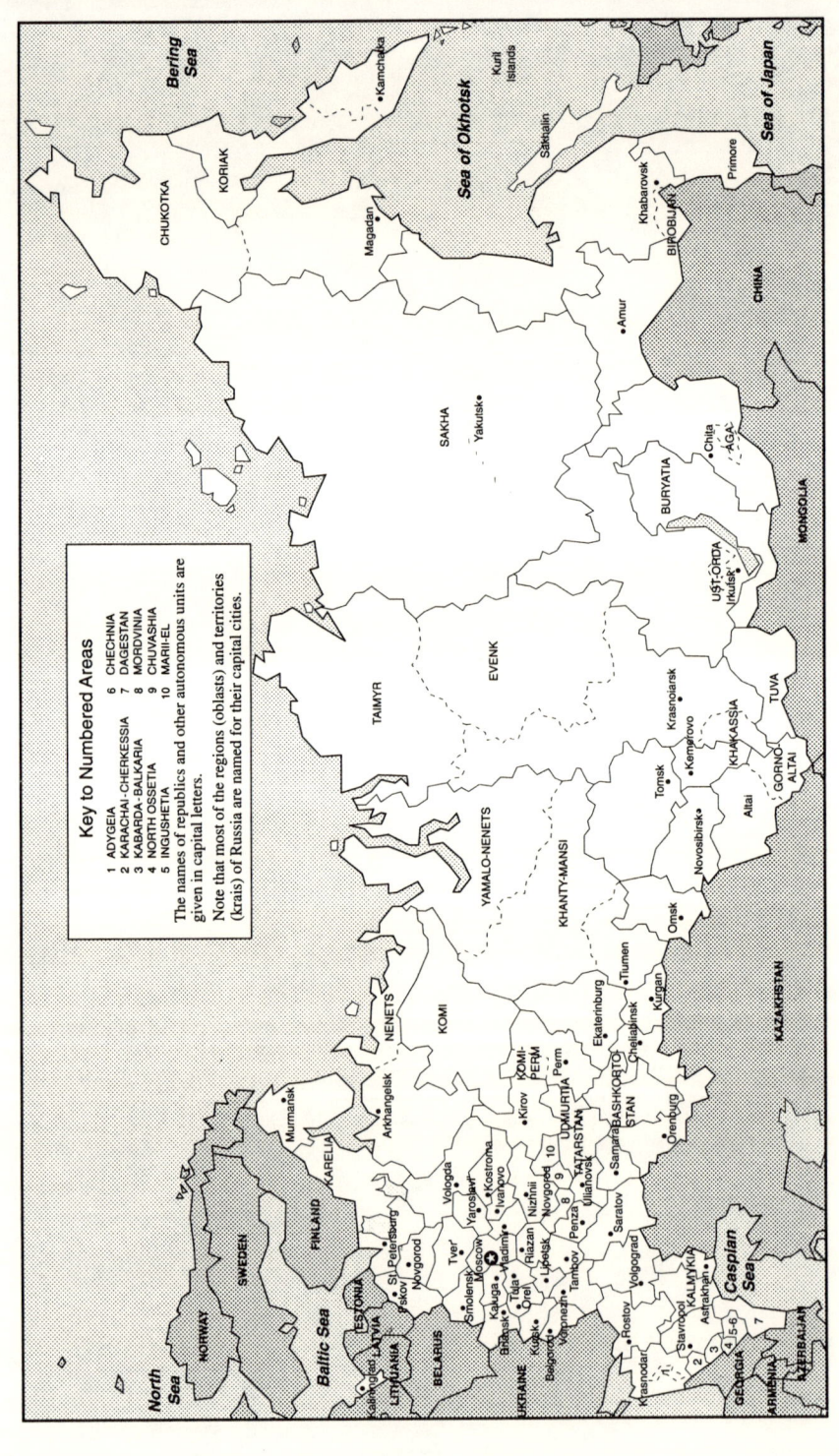

2
Center–Periphery Relations in the Russian Federation

Elizabeth Teague

A redistribution of power between the center and the periphery is essential if the Russian Federation is to become a stable democracy and a reliable member of the world community, able to live at peace with itself and its neighbors. It is no longer possible (if indeed it ever was) to govern the world's largest country from a single center. Regionalization—used here to describe the devolution of economic and political power from Moscow to the provinces—is already well advanced in Russia. As this chapter seeks to show, there was between 1991 and 1993 a major shift of power from the federal center to the country's constituent units.

Regionalization alone, however, will not ensure that the Russian Federation evolves into a stable democracy. Also necessary will be the successful conclusion of what is generally described as the federalization of Russia.[1] Federalization requires the adoption of constitutional provisions that would put relations between Moscow and the regions on a firm legal basis and allow for a division of powers and resources between the two that would be generally viewed as fair and just. The present system, which divides Russia up into a patchwork of ethnically based republics and territorially based regions, is unstable because it is not seen as equitable by a majority of Russia's regions.

Numerous efforts have been made to reform Russia's administrative system but, while regionalization is already a reality, federalization was stalled throughout much of 1993. In the best of circumstances the redistribution of powers between the center and the provinces would be a sensitive issue. In Russia the process was complicated by the ruthless struggle for power between President Boris Yeltsin and the Russian parliament, which came to a head in the confrontation of September–October 1993. Center–periphery relations became a political football as president and parliament competed for allies in Russia's regions and cities. In the process, both sides lost prestige in the public eye and there has been a dramatic decline in the authority of the state.

The result of the paralysis of central power is that devolution has occurred in a chaotic and unplanned way. Regional autonomy in the Russian context in 1993 meant region after region declaring that its laws took precedence over those of the center, threatening to withhold federal taxes, and getting away with such behavior unpunished. At the same time, the struggle between executive and legislature that has crippled the center has been mirrored in many of the regions. According to Charles Neff of the University of Alaska, the present situation is best described "neither as Moscow running things from the center nor as complete local control" but as a mixture of the two that creates "a gridlock of competing legal requirements." The frequent result, Neff concludes, is that in the provinces "no one is really in charge."[2]

The erosion of central authority has implications for Russia and for the rest of the world. It is generally agreed that Russia's peaceful evolution into a decentralized federation is a desirable goal. This might at some future date lead to the further splitting-up of the federation into a number of independent states but, for the time being, the breakup of the country is not generally seen as desirable. Since no one inside Russia at present wants to see the breakup of the Russian Federation, the country would be unlikely to split up without disruption or even violence.

To start with Russia itself, it goes without saying that federal leaders in Moscow want to maintain the country's integrity. The overwhelming majority of Russia's provincial leaders want that too. Regional officials are pushing hard to get local control over natural resources and avidly exploiting the opportunities for personal enrichment offered by the privatization of state property but, rightly or wrongly, few of them appear to believe that their regions have sufficient resources to flourish as independent states. Nor are many of them willing at present to shoulder the responsibilities involved in statehood. Indeed, in places where regional executives are in conflict with the corresponding legislatures, the former are keen to canvass the support of Russia's president against their own parliaments.

Since neither the center nor the periphery wants to see the breakup of the Russian Federation there is a danger that, if Russia did disintegrate, it might do so in a spontaneous manner accompanied by violence. A particularly dangerous situation would arise were the loyalties of the Russian army to be split: Civil war would then result. This has implications both for Russia's immediate neighbors and for the rest of the world.

The prospect of Russian disintegration presents the countries on Russia's immediate borders with a particularly complex dilemma. These are the states Russians tend to call the "near abroad." The last thing any of them wants is the reemergence of a militarily self-assertive and expansionist Russian Empire. At the same time, a Russia so weakened that it collapses inward is likely to be only slightly less dangerous for the countries on Russia's borders because of the risk that civil war might ensue and spill across frontiers because of the large concentrations of ethnic Russians living in the countries on Russia's periphery.[3] None of Russia's neighbors, with the possible exception of Ukraine, is yet in possession of the kind of army that could protect it from such spillover (to which Ukraine's high population of ethnic Russians makes it especially vulnerable). Nor is any of Russia's neighbors well equipped to cope with a sudden influx of Russian refugees.

The rest of the outside world—what Russians call the "far abroad"—is also alarmed by the prospect of the violent breakup of the Russian Federation. This is both because of the danger that the conflict might spill over into adjacent countries and because Russia remains a nuclear power. Turbulence within Russia's borders would create the danger of the further proliferation of nuclear states on the territory of the former Soviet Union.[4] For these reasons, to quote the *Christian Science Monitor,* "An unstable Russia means an unstable world."[5]

Russia's Imperial Legacy

The Russian Federation has never been a true federation in the sense in which that word is used in the Western literature.[6] Instead, it was an artificial creation established by the Bolsheviks in November 1917 in an attempt to legitimize the continuation of the Russian Empire.[7] Russia today is still governed by the constitution adopted in 1978, when the Russian Federation was part of the Soviet Union.[8]

While federalism takes a variety of forms, a federation has been defined as a voluntary association of sovereign states coming together for a common purpose within an overarching political system and delegating a limited number of powers to a central authority.[9] The powers of the federal center are constitutionally enumerated, and all remaining powers are reserved to the constituent states of the federation. This may come about in one of two ways. The first, as observed in the Constitution of the United States, applies when all powers that have not been specifically retained by individual states are automatically transferred to the federal center. The second, or Swiss, model stipulates that all powers that have not been specifically granted to the center remain with the individual states.[10] This definition of federalism is broad enough to embrace the political systems of the United States or Canada, Germany or Switzerland, but is not an accurate depiction of the relations that pertained until the collapse of the Soviet Union between the Russian Federation and the USSR or those currently pertaining between Russia and its constituent parts.[11] The Russian Federation is still governed by a constitution that was not designed for a sovereign state. The Soviet Union was run as a unitary state by the Communist Party (CPSU) but the party was not constructed along federal lines. The CPSU has been described by Mark Frankland as the "nervous system through which the leadership imposed its rule on a country the size of a continent."[12] Local leaders (even those supposedly elected) were appointed by the central party apparatus, on which they relied for career advancement; as a result, officials looked for their instructions upward rather than downward. Just as Estonia or Ukraine under Soviet rule could not put up a statue to a national hero without Moscow's permission, so today the Irkutsk region complains that Moscow is still trying to determine matters as trivial as fishing and hunting regulations for Irkutsk's lakes and forests.[13] Many Western cities—to say nothing of larger units such as the states of the United States, the cantons of Switzerland, or Germany's *Länder*—have more autonomy than Russia's republics and regions.

The collapse of the CPSU in 1991 turned Russia, to quote Frankland again, into "something disturbingly like a giant animal that has lost control over its limbs."[14] But it is not the absence of the Communist Party that is rendering Russia's constitution unworkable so much as the rejection by the drafters of successive Soviet-era constitutions of one of the fundamental principles of liberal democracy: the separation of powers. Russia's 1978 constitution provided for no separation of powers, no system of checks and balances to ensure that no branch of government was able to dominate the others.[15] Parliament was supreme, and whoever controlled parliament controlled the country. Until Yeltsin's rise to power that meant the CPSU, since the party controlled the elections to parliament. Then, onto a constitution that declared (Article 104) that "The Congress of People's Deputies is the highest body of state power of the Russian Federation," Yeltsin grafted an amendment (Article 121.1) that read "The president is the highest official of the Russian Federation."[16] The result was a head-on clash between executive and legislature, a feud between parliament and a popularly elected president that left Yeltsin's repeated attempts at economic and political reform dead in the water. While the Supreme Soviet's own draft constitution was scuttled by opposition from Russia's ethnically based republics, parliament blocked all Yeltsin's attempts to adopt a new constitution that would give the chief executive enough power to govern effectively.

On 21 September 1993, after six months of seeking accommodation with the Supreme Soviet, Yeltsin tried to cut the Gordian knot. Appearing live on evening television, the Russian president announced that he was dissolving parliament with immediate effect and calling new parliamentary elections for December. Yeltsin had no constitutional right to do either of these things. In a decree entitled Step-by-Step Constitutional Reform, he ordered that in the period before elections to a new parliament the country would be ruled by presidential and government decree.[17] Yeltsin's action set off a new phase in the power struggle. In contrast to August 1991, when events in the provinces were of minor significance and the defeat of the putsch was wrought by the few thousand people who came to Yeltsin's support at the Russian White House, in September 1993 the reaction of Russia's regional leaders was of great importance. Provincial leaders did not, perhaps, play the most crucial role in 1993: That part was assigned to the security forces, who remained united and obedient to Yeltsin. But, once it was clear that the military was loyal to the president, then the reaction of Russia's republics and regions took on major significance. These events showed clearly that, in just two years, the balance of power had shifted decisively from Moscow to the provinces. The rest of this chapter seeks to explain how that came about.

Russia's Territorial-Administrative Structure

Today's Russian Federation has inherited, with some modifications, the structure created by Lenin and Stalin in the early days of Soviet power. This consists of a hierarchy of both ethnic and territorial subdivisions (for a list, see the Appendix to this chapter).

On the top rung of the ladder are twenty republics formed according to the national principle (twenty-one if the Chechen Republic, whose 1991 declaration of independence has not been recognized by Moscow, is included). During the Soviet period, these were known as "autonomous republics" to distinguish them from the fifteen union republics that made up the Soviet Union. Artificial creations designed to give Russia's minorities a semblance of statehood, Russia's republics act as "national homelands" for some of the largest ethnic groups—Tatars, Chuvash, Mordvins, and so on—that have for centuries inhabited the territory over which the Russian Federation now extends.[18] The republics account for 28.6 percent of Russia's land mass and 15.2 percent of its population.[19]

The second rung of the ladder is occupied by six territories (krais) and forty-nine regions (oblasts). These entities are territorial in character and bear no ethnic connotations. In addition, two "federal cities," Moscow and St. Petersburg, have the same rights as Russia's regions, as do Russia's ten autonomous districts (okrugs) and sole remaining autonomous oblast (the Jewish Autonomous Oblast).[20] Like the republics, the autonomous districts and the autonomous region are ethnoterritorial in nature, that is, they are located on the traditional territories of the indigenous groups after whom they are named (for details, see the Appendix).

Russia's 1978 constitution endowed the republics with privileges that the regions did not enjoy. Unlike the regions, the republics are endowed with the trappings of statehood (flag, national anthem, and so on); they have constitutions, not charters as the regions do; they are led by presidents, not so-called heads of administration; they elect Supreme Soviets, not Soviets of People's Deputies; and they adopt laws rather than decisions. "In other words," writes one observer, "the republics claim to be states that have united in a federation (even though nobody knows when this is supposed to have happened) while all the other 'subjects of the federation' are merely administrative components in a unitary state."[21]

Given the centralized character of the Soviet system and the intrusive power of the Communist Party and secret police, the republics' autonomy was illusory as long as the USSR was still in existence. That situation changed once the Soviet Union collapsed. The regions now began to bitterly resent the republics' higher status because, being on average far more populous[22] and industrialized than the republics, the regions were paying far more into the state budget than the republics did. Indeed, many of the republics were net recipients of state funding whereas the regions were paying considerably more in taxes than they got back in state subventions.[23] According to Vice President Aleksandr Rutskoi, the contributions made to the federal budget by the krais and oblasts amounted to "as much as 85 percent" of the total; the tax burden of the republics was "80 percent lower" than that of the regions; and some republics contributed nothing to the federal budget at all.[24] Accordingly, the regions felt that the republics were being subsidized by their tax rubles. This is a source of much bitterness on the part of the regions.

A combination of territorial and ethnic divisions within a single state does not automatically create problems. The example of Canada and Switzerland —both of which are federations that make territorial provision for ethnic minorities—shows that, while such systems require delicate handling, they can work successfully.[25] The real problem with Russia's setup, as Paul Goble of the Carnegie Endowment has argued, is not that it combines ethnically and territorially based divisions, but that it includes an anomalous class of territories that purport to be founded on the ethnic principle but where the indigenous nationality is heavily outnumbered by ethnic Russians. Extreme examples are furnished by entities such as the Khanty-Mansi Autonomous Okrug, an area the size of France that produces more oil each year than Kuwait[26] and where the indigenous Khants and Mansi made up 1.3 percent of the population at the time of the 1989 census, or the Jewish Autonomous Oblast, created by Stalin in 1928 and where Jews were only 4.1 percent of the population in 1989. Indeed, the titular nationality represents an absolute majority of the population in only five of the twenty-one republics of the Russian Federation—in Chechnia, Chuvashia, Dagestan, Tuva, and North Ossetia (for details, see Table 2.1). Goble identifies this anomaly as the main source of interethnic resentment in Russia today.[27] The Khants and the Mansi number fewer than thirty thousand but, were they to claim ownership of the natural resources in the region that bears their name, they could cripple Russia's oil production.

The Khants and the Mansi are an extreme example and unlikely to hold Russia's oil industry for ransom. Nonetheless, the Soviet system gave certain privileges to the members of some of the smaller national minorities (a guaranteed proportion of official posts, for example) that bore little relation to the actual weight of these ethnic groups in the population. A number of the ethnic conflicts on the territory of the former Soviet Union today have been exacerbated (though not apparently caused) by the unwillingness of members of a given ethnic minority to relinquish privileges enjoyed during the Soviet period. (This is a factor, for example, in Abkhazia's struggle to secede from Georgia; Moldova's battle of wills with the Russian-speakers in Trans-Dniestria; and Ukraine's uneasy relationship with the Russian population of the Crimea. Its influence can also be seen in the Russian Federation in, for example, Tatarstan.) Moreover, the inequality built into the Soviet system by Stalin gives entities at every level an incentive to try to hoist themselves up to the next rung of the ladder; this also fosters political instability.

Table 2.1
Population of Russia's Autonomous Formations (1989 census)

	Total population	Titular nationality (%)	Russians (%)
Republics			
Adygeia	432,046	22	**68**
Altai Republic	190,831	31	**60**
Bashkortostan	3,943,113	22	**39**
Buriatia	1,038,252	24	**70**
Checheno-Ingushetia	1,270,429		
Chechens		**58**	23
Ingush		13	■
Chuvashia	1,338,023	**68**	27
Dagestan	1,802,188	**80**	9
Kabardino-Balkaria	753,531		
Kabardians		**48**	32
Balkars		9	
Kalmykia	322,579	**45**	38
Karachaevo-Cherkessia	415,970		
Karachais		31	**42**
Cherkess		10	
Karelia	790,150	10	**74**
Khakassia	566,861	11	**79**
Komi Republic	1,250,847	23	**58**
Marii-El	749,332	43	**47**
Mordovia	963,504	32	**61**
North Ossetia	632,428	**53**	30
Sakha (Yakutia)	1,094,065	33	**50**
Tatarstan	3,641,742	**49**	43
Tuva	308,557	**64**	32
Udmurtia	1,605,663	31	**59**
Autonomous Oblast			
Jewish	214,085	4	**83**
Autonomous Okrugs			
Aga Buriat	77,188	**55**	41
Chukchi	163,934	7	**66**
Evenki	24,769	14	**67**
Khanty-Mansi	1,282,396		
Khants		0.9	**66**
Mansi		0.4	
Komi-Permiak	158,526	**60**	36
Koriak	39,940	16	**62**
Nenets	53,912	12	**66**
Taimyr	55,803		
Dolgans		9	**67**
Nenets		4	
Ust' Orda Buriat	135,870	36	**56**
Iamal Nenets	494,844	4	**59**

Sources: 1989 census as reported in USSR State Committee on Statistics, *Natsional'nyi sostav naseleniia SSSR* (Moscow: Finansy i statistika, 1991).

Note: Bold type indicates that a given ethnic group represents either a majority or a plurality of the population of a given republic or region.

"As Much Autonomy as You Can Swallow"

In the late 1980s the three Baltic states launched their drive for full independence from the Soviet Union, and the USSR began, gradually at first, then with increasing speed, to unravel. Independence campaigns were mounted in Armenia, Georgia, and Moldova. Encouraged by these examples, Russia's autonomous republics began to demand more freedom to run their own affairs. Mainly they did this not because they desired full independence but because they hoped to obtain greater benefit from the exploitation of their considerable natural resources. Several of the union republics had smaller territories or populations and fewer natural resources than the larger Russian republics. Oil-rich Tatarstan, for example, with its population of 3,641,000, complained about having fewer rights than Estonia, which in 1989 (when the last USSR census was taken) had a population of 1,464,000.

The independence drive accelerated in April 1990 when, at the behest of Soviet leader Mikhail Gorbachev, the Soviet parliament passed the All-Union Law on the Delimitation of Powers Between the USSR and the Subjects of the Federation.[28] This law declared that the USSR's fifteen union republics (Ukraine or Russia, for example) and Russia's autonomous republics (such as Tatarstan or Tuva) were all "subjects of the federation." Whereas the autonomous territories had had this status all along, the union republics had until then been described as founders of the Soviet Union; the implication was that the union republics and they alone had entered the USSR voluntarily and therefore retained some kind of right to leave.

The apparent intention of the April 1990 legislation was to downgrade the union republics and hamper the efforts of the independence-minded among them to free themselves from the USSR. However, the law had other, unintended effects. First it provoked the more reticent union republics to emulate those in the forefront of the independence drive. One after another they declared themselves sovereign and that their laws took precedence over those of the USSR. On 10 June 1990, the Russian Federation proclaimed itself a sovereign state.

By implying that the autonomous republics enjoyed equal status with the union republics, the law had the second unintended effect of provoking a string of declarations of sovereignty by Russia's autonomous republics. These were initially resisted by the Russian leadership, since they were seen as threatening the dismemberment of the Russian Federation.[29] It was not long, however, before Yeltsin himself, looking for allies in his fight against Gorbachev and the central Soviet leadership, took a leaf out of Gorbachev's book and began to woo Russia's autonomous republics. In August 1990 Yeltsin told the leaders of Tatarstan (and, by implication, those of Russia's other autonomous republics) to "take as much autonomy as you can swallow."[30] By the end of 1990 almost all Russia's autonomous republics and autonomous oblasts had heeded this advice. Adopting declarations of sovereignty, they proclaimed themselves full republics and declared that their laws took precedence over those of the Russian Federation.[31] Like the union republics, Russia's republics declared that all the land, industrial assets, and mineral resources on their territory belonged to them. Many of them went on to claim the right to enter into treaties and economic agreements with other governments as well as the right to secession and self-determination.[32]

Yeltsin used the assertiveness of Russia's republics as a weapon in his struggle with Gorbachev and the Soviet center. Therefore, his leadership did not react publicly to their sovereignty declarations. According to RFE/RL's Ann Sheehy, Yeltsin's attitude was "to let the autonomous republics adopt them if they wanted on the grounds that Gorbachev's attempts to prevent the union republics taking such steps had only aggravated interethnic relations."[33]

Republics and Regions as Rivals

Yeltsin's encouragement of Russia's autonomous republics was to prove a two-edged sword. When the Soviet Union collapsed at the end of 1991, Russia's republics began to demand the economic and political autonomy they had been promised. Fearful that their leaders might stir up ethnic tensions and separatist sentiment, Yeltsin tried to appease the republics with tax breaks and other concessions. This served, however, only to alienate the leaders of Russia's regions. Meanwhile, the leaders of the republics, not satisfied with what they received, clamored for more. All of a sudden, Yeltsin found himself facing the threat that the Russian Federation, like the USSR before it, might fall apart.

The Russian leadership had been hoping that the adoption of a new constitution would ward off centrifugal tendencies by establishing a more equitable division of power between Moscow and the republics and regions. Work on a new constitution had begun in 1990, but drafting a constitution that was acceptable to all concerned was to prove a gargantuan task. Initially, responsibility for drafting the new constitution was assigned to the Constitutional Commission of the Supreme Soviet, whose executive secretary, Oleg Rumiantsev, unveiled the first draft in November 1990.

Rumiantsev's original idea was to phase out the Soviet-era hierarchy of ethnoterritorial units (autonomous republics; krais and oblasts; autonomous oblasts and autonomous okrugs) and replace it with a federation of territories, each of which would have equal rights.[34] As a step toward this end, Rumiantsev's first draft reduced the hierarchy to two levels: (1) "national and territorial state formations, having the status of equal republics" (that is, the former autonomous republics), and (2) "federal territories" (the krais and oblasts). However, this distinction was not intended to be permanent. The aim was to turn Russia into a true federation organized into some fifty new territorial divisions modeled on the *Länder* that make up the Federal Republic of Germany. The status of the regions would gradually be raised until they eventually enjoyed the same status as the republics.[35] In this way, divisions based on ethnic distinctions would be phased out; all Russia's provinces would become equal in status; and ethnicity would be disentangled from the state to become no more than "the private affair of the citizen."[36]

The word "land" (*zemlia*) was included in the first draft of the constitution drafted by Rumiantsev's commission, and was still there when the second draft constitution was published in early October 1991. At that stage, however, the autonomous republics put up such strong opposition to the scheme, which would have deprived them of their privileged place in the pecking order, that the whole idea of switching Russia to a system modeled on Germany's had to be abandoned.[37] Alarmed by threats from the republics that they would leave the Russian Federation if such a constitution were adopted, the Congress of People's Deputies refused to discuss the constitution when it convened at the end of October 1991, and the draft was sent back to the Constitutional Commission for further work.[38] Rumiantsev described the word "land" as "a red rag to the autonomies,"[39] with the fiercest opposition coming from Sakha, Checheno-Ingushetia, and Tatarstan.[40] All the autonomous republics had by this time declared themselves full republics, and many of them had proclaimed that their laws took precedence over those of Russia; they were alarmed that they would lose their identity and their privileges and that their national statehood would be diluted if they were included in the *Land*-type formations Rumiantsev's commission had in mind.[41]

On 20 January 1992, the Presidium of the Supreme Soviet of the Russian Federation adopted an interim decision on the division of authority between the center and the constituent parts of the Russian Federation. A distinction was made between two kinds of subjects. The first category was composed of Russia's twenty republics (comprising all the former autonomous republics plus four of the five former autonomous regions, all of them founded on a nominally ethnic basis); these won the right to have their own constitutions and laws, form their own governments, have automatic representation in federal bodies, and nominate judges to the supreme court.[42] The second category comprised Russia's regions, the "federal cities" of Moscow and St. Petersburg, and the territories that had previously comprised the third rung of the hierarchy—the sole surviving autonomous region (the Jewish Autonomous Oblast) and ten autonomous districts. None of these won the right to its own constitution, though they could have their own charters and form their own legislatures. Olga Glezer of the Moscow-based Institute of Geography declared in evident disgust that this meant that "23 million Russian subjects will live in a federation, and another 124 million will live in a unitary state."[43]

So, after months of heated discussions, Russia found itself still saddled with territories based on the ethnic principle and with its old multitiered structure.[44] This structure is patently inequitable. A large number of populous ethnic groups—Russia's 842,000-strong German population, for example—do not have autonomy, though the Germans, whose Volga German Republic was abolished by Stalin in 1941, have a clear moral right to such status. Another ethnic group that lacks its own territory, as the historian Mikhail Gefter has pointed out, is the Russian nation itself.[45] Less provocatively, representatives of many of Russia's krais and oblasts drew attention to the fact that they had populations far larger than those of the republics.

The republics had already declared themselves sovereign. Now it was the turn of Russia's regions, who objected to the idea of being relegated to secondary status, to begin to declare themselves republics. Thus, there was talk in Russia's vast, mineral-rich Krasnoiarsk Krai of creating a Enisei Republic, while the leaders of Primorskii Krai threatened to re-create the Far Eastern Republic that had existed between 1920 and 1922.[46] Activists in Tiumen' Oblast spoke of joining with the Sverdlovsk and Kurgan oblasts to set up a "Urals Republic."[47] There was talk of a "United States of Northern Asia" stretching from the Urals to the Pacific and cut off from Central Russia by the two Volga republics—Tatarstan and Bashkortostan.[48] Meanwhile, Tatarstan and Bashkortostan set off alarm bells in Moscow when, in January 1992, they dispatched representatives to a "Pan-Turkic assembly" in Almaty, the capital of Kazakhstan.[49] This reawakened old Russian fears that Turkish influence over the Turkic-speaking republics on Russia's southern rim might lead to Turkish domination not only of Central Asia but of Bashkortostan and Tatarstan; these republics, which are Turkic-speaking and have a strong desire for autonomy, occupy Russia's heartland, straddling its main railway and pipeline communications systems. Meanwhile, the Confederation of Mountain Peoples of the Caucasus brought together representatives of fourteen North Caucasian peoples in the Chechen capital, Groznyi, in February 1992 and announced that, if the Russian constitution was adopted in its then form, they would set up an independent confederation stretching "from the Caspian to the Black Sea."[50]

The Federal Treaty

Alarmed by parliament's failure to move forward on a new constitution even as parts of the country seemed to be escaping from central control, the Yeltsin leadership concluded that, if the Russian Federation was not to fall apart, another solution would have to be found. To escape from the constitutional dead end in which Russia found itself, the government switched its priorities. Putting the constitution on the back burner, the Yeltsin government resolved to tackle the vexing question of the powers of the federal authorities vis-à-vis the constituent parts of the Russian Federation. Power sharing between the center and the periphery would be codified in a Federal Treaty that would later form the cornerstone of the new constitution. To sweeten the pill, the government promised that the new agreement would devolve more powers to Russia's republics and regions than they had previously enjoyed. Many of the republics were nonetheless unhappy with Yeltsin's proposals and complained that Moscow was not offering them enough autonomy. The strongest objections were put up by Sakha, Bashkortostan, and Karelia. Tatarstan refused even to consider signing the Federal Treaty, insisting that the only kind of agreement it would enter into with the Russian Federation was one that recognized Tatarstan not as a subordinate but as an equal partner.[51] (Tatarstan is maintaining this position to this day.)

Meanwhile Oleg Rumiantsev and the Constitutional Commission continued work on the draft constitution. Rumiantsev told a press conference in early March 1992 that the chapter dealing with the respective powers of the federation, republics, and regions was proving the most sensitive of all. Rumiantsev called fruitlessly on deputies to adopt his draft; if they did not, he warned, republics such as Tatarstan and Sakha would try to split away "and the Russian Federation will be destroyed from within." Rumiantsev spoke as parliamentary deputies from Siberia were preparing to meet in Krasnoiarsk to discuss the "decolonization" of Siberia. Though the deputies denied that secession from the Russian Federation was on the agenda, the meeting was said to have provoked "something akin to panic" in Moscow.[52]

Moscow's alarm was misplaced—at least at that time. The Krasnoiarsk meeting showed that Siberia's regions were not ready to assume the responsibilities that would accompany political independence and were not, accordingly, seeking to secede from the Russian Federation. A few separatist calls were heard in Krasnoiarsk, but they did not win the support of the majority. What did, however, annoy the deputies attending the congress was Moscow's management (or mismanagement) of the economy. They were tired of being ordered about by the center and felt that they could hardly fail to do a better job of running their own economies than Moscow had. The center, they complained, took no account of local conditions, and the reforms being carried out under the leadership of Yegor Gaidar treated all Russia's regions as if they were identical. This put Siberia in a particularly disadvantageous position. The region produces raw materials and has little agriculture. Therefore, the high food prices that followed Gaidar's liberalization of consumer goods prices in January 1992 hit the population of Siberia at a time when a sharp fall in production all over the rest of the former USSR was reducing demand for the raw materials that are Siberia's staple product. According to one of the documents adopted at the end of the Krasnoiarsk congress, Siberia was being "forced to beg for social and humanitarian aid, although it is the country's main source of fuel and raw materials."[53] The deputies demanded changes in the reform program to take account of regional differences.[54] They wanted Siberia's regions to have the right to issue their own export licenses and to sell most of their raw materials themselves at world prices, instead of having to sell them at fixed prices to Moscow, which could then resell them and keep the profit. They also demanded that their territories be recognized under the constitution as "equal subjects of the Russian Federation," that is, be granted equal status with the republics and the right to pass local laws and levy their own taxes. The opinions heard in Krasnoiarsk indicated that, as Michael Bradshaw of Birmingham University has stressed, Russia's resource-rich regions would not contribute to the country's recovery unless there was further devolution of power from the center and they were allowed to manage their own economic interests.[55]

Even as Russia's regions were toughening their demands, the Yeltsin leadership was bargaining hard to persuade the republics to sign the Federal Treaty. The dispute over who should qualify for the designation "subject of the federation" proved so bitter that it was resolved only by drafting not one but three separate treaties—one for the republics, another for the regions, and a third for the autonomous districts and sole surviving autonomous region.[56] In the end, the three treaties were signed in the second half of March 1992 and the only republics that refused were Tatarstan and Chechnia.[57] Other republics, such as Kalmykia, appended amendments intended to enable them to cut deals with Moscow later and gain greater control over their mineral wealth or the right to levy local taxes. Bashkortostan agreed to sign only at the very last moment. Its amendments included statements that Bashkortostan was the owner of its land and natural resources and that it had the right to trade with other countries and to run its own legal system. The republic had earlier persuaded Yeltsin to let it keep 75 percent of the foreign currency earned by its enterprises (as opposed to 70 percent, which was the norm both for the other republics and for the regions).[58]

The Federal Treaty outlined the division of authority between Moscow and the republics and regions, specifying which functions should be exercised by the federal center alone, which fell into a catchall category of functions exercised jointly by the federal government and the regions, and which residual functions would be devolved to the republics and regions.

To the center ("the federal organs of state power of the Russian Federation") went exclusive jurisdiction over:

- establishment of bodies of executive, legislative, and judicial power at the federal level;
- adoption and amendment of the Russian constitution and other federal laws;
- enforcement of federal law;
- approval of changes in internal borders and regional subdivisions;
- protection of Russia's external land borders, territorial waters, and airspace;
- protection of the human and civil rights of citizens of the Russian Federation and of ethnic minorities;
- citizenship issues;
- control over the federal procuracy, the codes of criminal law, criminal procedure, and legislation regarding amnesties and pardons;
- federal financial policy, including elaboration of the federal budget, issue of money, levying of federal taxes and customs, control of the central bank, and allocation of federal funds for regional development;
- energy policy;
- transport and communications;
- space exploration;

- weapons production;
- foreign policy (including making war and peace, and signing international treaties);
- defense and security policy;
- foreign economic relations of the Russian Federation;
- administration of federal property.

While the center's responsibilities were clearly delineated, the category stipulating which functions should be shared between the center and the republics or regions was vague. Included under this heading were the administration of border areas; maintenance of law and order and protection of public safety; protection of the rights of ethnic minorities; environmental protection; health care; culture; and education. Responsibility for the collection of taxes and duties was to be shared by the federal center and the republics, but not by the regions. How these joint functions were to be carried out was not specified, however, and there was therefore plenty of scope for subsequent disagreement over who had the right to do what.

The provision of a mechanism to mediate disputes between the center and the periphery is one of the hallmarks of the federal system as described in the Western literature.[59] Russia's Federal Treaty states that disputes over issues of jurisdiction between the federal government and the constituent republics and regions are to be settled by the Constitutional Court. This does not, however, seem to have been enough to ensure the smooth functioning of the treaty, and in the period since its signing, the republics and regions have complained constantly about the center's failure to implement the treaty's provisions. In the absence of a mechanism for the exercise of joint powers, it seems, the center has gone its way while the republics and regions have gone theirs, and the result has been more or less total confusion. "Moscow tends to handle 'joint' issues by itself, while the regions do the same," was the verdict of one Russian journalist who reported high dissatisfaction with the Federal Treaty even in Yeltsin-loyalist Ekaterinburg (the former Sverdlovsk).[60]

The section of the Federal Treaty that dealt with the residual rights belonging to the republics and regions stated that "all spheres of state power" not explicitly assigned to the federal center or to the joint jurisdiction of the center and the republics or regions were to be exercised by the republics and regions independently. The rights of the republics and regions were, however, circumscribed by the stipulation that they must be exercised in accordance with federal law. A reasonable enough requirement on the face of it, this implies that the center retains the right to determine how the republics and regions exercise their rights. For example, the Federal Treaty gave both the regions and the republics the right to act as "autonomous parties to international and foreign economic relations and agreements with other republics, krais and oblasts . . . of the Russian Federation." At the same time, the treaty reserved the final say not only in foreign, defense, and security policy, but also in foreign economic relations for the central government. It is therefore questionable how much autonomy Russia's republics and regions really won when they signed the Federal Treaty.

Yeltsin's proposal that the Federal Treaty should be incorporated into Russia's new constitution was opposed by Rumiantsev on the grounds that the treaty gave the republics too much autonomy. There were two main areas in which the Federal Treaty favored the republics. The first had to do with property rights. While the Federal Treaty stated that "the land, minerals, water, flora, and fauna" on the territory of a given republic were to belong to the people living in that republic, no such right of ownership was given by the Federal Treaty to the populations of Russia's regions. On the face of it, this placed the populations of the republics at a marked advantage over the populations of the regions.

But how much real power did the Federal Treaty give the republics over the natural resources on their territories? The answer seems to be not a lot. The Federal Treaty went on to state that, where republic property rights were concerned, "Questions connected with the possession, use, and disposal of land, minerals, water and other natural resources will be regulated by the fundamental legislation of the Russian Federation and of the republics of the Russian Federation." In other words, the republics must exercise their property rights in line with federal legislation. Not, again, an unreasonable requirement; nonetheless it implies that, in the final analysis, the center reserved the right to decide what use should be made of the natural resources of the republics.

The second area in which the Federal Treaty granted the republics greater rights than the regions had to do with the center's power to declare a state of emergency anywhere in the Russian Federation. In the case of a republic, the treaty stated, federal authorities must obtain the preliminary consent of the organs of state power of the respective republic before introducing a state of emergency. In the case of a krai or oblast no such prior consent was required. Apart from the republics' slightly dubious property rights, this is the only place in which the Federal Treaty seems to have discriminated between Russia's republics and its regions. All other powers of any significance were either the exclusive domain of the center or to be shared between the center and the republics; in the latter case, the wording was hazy and the question of who had real responsibility was fudged.

The chairman of the Russian Constitutional Court, Valerii Zorkin, expressed dismay that no fewer than nine of the republics attached conditions to their signatures when they signed the Federal Treaty. This, he asserted, created first- and second-class members of the Russian Federation, to say nothing of the special class into which Tatarstan fell, since it was allowed to get away without signing the treaty at all.[61] Zorkin predicted (correctly, as it turned out) that it would be only a matter of time before the "second-class" regions started to demand the same privileges given to the "first-class" signatories. As for those republics that refused to sign the treaty, Moscow expressed itself willing to conduct bilateral talks with them. After Tatarstan refused to sign, Rumiantsev was quoted as advancing the idea of giving some republics the status of "freely associated states."[62] This concept has since been written into Tatarstan's constitution, even though it has no official basis in Russian law, and negotiations are continuing between Moscow and Kazan over Tatarstan's status. At the time of writing only Chechnia continues to insist that it does not consider itself part of the Russian Federation, but even its leaders have expressed willingness to open negotiations over a treaty normalizing relations between Chechnia and Russia on the basis of some kind of confederation.[63] Chechnia may eventually, therefore, fall into the same position vis-à-vis the center as Tatarstan.

"Regional Economic Autonomy by Default"

Although legislation to determine how the respective powers of the center, the republics, and the regions should be exercised had not yet been adopted, local leaders were not idle. Far from being hindered by the vagueness of the Federal Treaty they turned it to their own advantage and, following Yeltsin's advice of 1990, grabbed as much autonomy as they could. The result was a radical shift of power away from Moscow and toward the provinces.[64]

Devolution was not entirely spontaneous. In the first half of 1992—Russia's first year of independence—the reformist wing of the Russian government led by Gaidar pursued policies consciously designed to encourage economic decentralization. Gaidar's aim was to promote Russia's transition to a market economy by fostering the emergence of large, economically strong "mini-common markets." In particular, Gaidar hoped that economic associations would emerge that drowned out nationalist sentiment by uniting both republics and regions under one roof.[65] By the second half of 1992, however, interests hostile to market reform had regained the initiative and forced the Gaidar team to make compromises that undermined its reform program. Meanwhile Yeltsin, too, became locked in struggle with parliament and was driven onto the defensive. As the government became paralyzed and the authority of the center eroded, devolution assumed an unplanned and chaotic course. Federal laws were almost universally ignored in the provinces as regional leaders seized the opportunity to run things their own way. Where their actions did not meet with Moscow's approval, the center was largely powerless to intervene. This prompted alarm that the country was becoming ungovernable by the center.

Meanwhile, the government's attempt to move to market prices and to effect the crash privatization of state property combined to offer regional leaders, many of whom had been members of the Communist Party nomenklatura, an unprecedented opportunity to parlay their former political clout into economic power. Many seized it with avidity. Even those provincial leaders who did not particularly want more autonomy were obliged, as Moscow launched its program of market reforms, to assume responsibility for events at the local level. The disruptions caused by the dismantling of central planning required local leaders to take matters into their own hands to protect their populations from shortages and ensure that production continued in enterprises on their territory. As a result, the year 1992 saw what Robert Osborn of Temple University has termed "regional economic autonomy by default."[66]

The first thing regional officials took charge of was supplies. At the end of 1991, local leaders began to hoard food stocks in anticipation of the liberalization of most consumer prices set for 2 January 1992. The head of administration in Krasnodar Krai in southern Russia, for example, set up what amounted to a customs service to restrict the outflow of farm produce from his territory and to collect duties on the export of both industrial and agricultural goods from it.[67] He must have reaped a tidy profit when food prices leaped in response to liberalization, but he was not alone. The Postfactum News Agency reported that, by the end of January 1992, local governments had taken control of almost all regional branches of banks as well as of law enforcement agencies.[68]

Some local leaders were slower to react, and restricted their activities to selling licenses and leasing premises (at a profit, to be sure) to aspiring new entrepreneurs. But even those officials who initially tried to resist the reforms of the Yeltsin government took action once it became clear that, if they did not, they might find themselves facing demonstrations, strikes, or food riots. Plant directors struck barter agreements with neighboring farms and factories and did their best to ensure that supplies were not interrupted, production continued, workers remained employed, and families were fed. Activity of this sort goes a fair way to explain why 1992 witnessed so few protests against the government's reforms. Indeed, strike activity not only did not rise in 1992 but actually fell by comparison with 1991. Despite the upheaval caused by the Gaidar reforms, Russia's unemployment rate remained throughout 1992 and well into 1993 one of the lowest in the world.

As the value of the ruble fell in spring and summer 1992, inflation created widespread shortages of cash. Unpaid workers threatened to strike and, in response, regions started to issue their own surrogate money. Although such actions were strictly forbidden by Moscow, the center was powerless to intervene. Reformist leaders in Nizhnii Novgorod Oblast were among the first to introduce their own money, while in Sverdlovsk Oblast, local officials reached a private agreement with the state printing works in neighboring Perm' Oblast: In return for locally produced goods, Sverdlovsk received freshly minted bank notes straight from the printing press.[69] Many regions began to build their own foreign trade networks: Irkutsk Oblast signed a bilateral agreement on economic cooperation with Kyrgyzstan; Iaroslavl' Oblast entered into an agreement with Ukraine; other regions began to court Western investors and to develop what amounted to their own foreign trade policies, and so on.[70]

Even during the Soviet period, the vagaries of central planning had obliged enterprises that wanted to keep their workers to maintain their own supplies, farms, retail outlets, kindergartens, and so on. So, far from weakening once central planning was demolished, the trend toward enterprise autarky increased in Yeltsin's Russia because inflation deprived money of much of its value. Autarky also prompted the decentralization of Russia's formerly Communist-dominated trade unions. Soviet trade unionists had always acted more like personnel managers than Western-style shop stewards. Now, as Russian enterprises became more self-reliant, trade union officials began to transfer their loyalty from the Moscow-based confederation to the management of their particular enterprise. In 1993, local unions were reported to be refusing to transfer dues to the Moscow federation on the grounds that they needed the money on the spot to care for their members. In 1992, it had still been possible to describe Russia's official union federation as the only organization to have survived the collapse of communism with its property and membership more or less intact; by 1993, the unions were beginning to fragment.

The pace of large- and small-scale privatization varied widely from region to region. To combat widespread initial resistance, the Yeltsin government changed its tactics in the fall of 1992. Abandoning its earlier "top-down" approach, it designated fourteen specially selected regions to act as models. Each of the regions, which included Nizhnii Novgorod and Volgograd oblasts, had a reform-minded local leadership.[71] As a result, the pace of privatization speeded up substantially in regions outside Moscow.[72] So-called nomenklatura privatization was extensive. The case was reported in 1993, for example, of two enterprising women who made a fortune by buying a goldmine in Magadan in Russia's Far East. Both had worked for the mine when it was state-owned, one as an economist and the other as chief bookkeeper. They were able to buy the mine by (1) fixing the accounts in the period prior to privatization to make it look as if the mine was making a loss, and (2) buying up large numbers of privatization vouchers at a time when the price of vouchers had dropped to about 4,000 rubles for 10,000 rubles face-value. However, alarm was also expressed because some of the new patterns of ownership emerging in Russia (often involving enterprises supposedly passing into the hands of the work force) appeared to be highly protectionist and ultimately hostile to the emergence of an effective and competitive market economy.

According to Gaidar, one of the chief factors undermining the central government's leverage over the regions was Russia's high rate of inflation. "Regionalism is the most serious problem created by inflation," the architect of Russia's reforms said in spring 1993. "The center has lost its chance to influence the regions because money doesn't work any more."[73] However, the government's attempt to reduce inflation by balancing the federal budget deficit produced unwelcome side effects. Early in 1992 the government shifted responsibility for financing social protection and price subsidies from central to local government, but made no attempt to adjust the share of revenue going to the republics and regions to ensure that their incomes would be sufficient to cover their higher spending responsibilities.[74] This provoked much resentment on the part of local leaders who, while responsible for collecting taxes, have little power to levy their own taxes or to determine what should be taxed and at what rate. In retaliation, several regions, including some Siberian oblasts, withheld taxes from the center. Others concentrated on trying to cut special deals with Moscow, which included demands to be allowed to levy their own taxes and launch their own currencies. Chechnia opted out entirely and refused to transfer any taxes to the center. Chechnia might have been dismissed as a special case had not oil-rich Bashkortostan and Tatarstan both declared fiscal sovereignty; that is, they claimed complete control over all tax revenues collected on their territories and asserted that they would in future make only voluntary payments to the center. Sakha, which produces 90 percent of Russia's diamonds and 60 percent of its gold, went its own way, negotiating a lower tax share with the center than the rest of Russia. In addition, Sakha nationalized its territory and natural resources and declared that in future Russia would have to pay rent for mining rights.

As 1993 progressed, the tax war heated up. It was reported in September 1993 that, by then, thirty-one of Russia's eighty-nine republics and regions were withholding taxes from the center and that the number was increasing daily. Local leaders said that they had been driven to this step by Moscow's failure to send them enough money to pay police and teachers or to purchase grain.[75] Commentators recalled that a decision by Yeltsin's Russia to withhold federal taxes from Gorbachev's Moscow had been one of the factors contributing to the collapse of the USSR. In an effort to restore order, Russia's Finance Ministry announced plans to introduce a uniform tax system in January 1994 that would be applicable to all of Russia's eighty-nine republics and regions without exception.[76] The plan seemed certain to run into strong resistance from many regions.

The Constitutional Battle Resumes

The signing of the Federal Treaty in March 1992 brought only a temporary respite in the struggle between Moscow and the republics and regions over their respective powers. In fact, the Federal Treaty created fresh problems because the republics began to demand that the rights they claimed to have gained under it should be enshrined in the new Russian constitution. Rumiantsev was strongly opposed to this, arguing that the Federal Treaty had given the republics too much power. In this he was supported by parliamentary speaker Ruslan Khasbulatov, who accused Yeltsin of risking, through his concessions to the non-Russian republics, the disintegration of the Russian Federation. Khasbulatov began to court the leaders of Russia's regions, while Yeltsin continued the policy he had adopted earlier of favoring the republics. While this angered the regions and drove them into Khasbulatov's camp, it did not win Yeltsin the unconditional support of the leaders of the republics either. Unlike Yeltsin, the republic leaders really had no interest in the adoption of a new constitution. From their point of view, the longer relations between Moscow and the periphery remained fluid, the more power they could amass in their own bailiwicks. Therefore, while Khasbulatov matched any promise that Yeltsin made, and both men tried by every means at their disposal to win the support of one or another branch of the provincial leadership, local bosses pursued a highly effective policy of playing president off against parliament. As of September 1993, for example, ten republics had with impunity defied Russia's 1978 constitution and declared that their laws took precedence over those of the Russian Federation.[77]

There is no need to detail here all Yeltsin's attempts to get a new constitution adopted or all the roadblocks he encountered.[78] It should, however, be stressed that Yeltsin appealed to the republics time and again, offering them all manner of concessions to win their support against parliament. He was becoming increasingly anxious to secure the adoption of a constitution that would create a strong Russian presidency and give him the powers he felt he needed to implement his policies; in the meantime, he was having to govern by means of emergency powers, which parliament constantly threatened to withdraw. When the Constitutional Commission of the Russian parliament was first set up in 1990, Yeltsin had chaired it. In spring 1992, finding himself opposed by Rumiantsev, Yeltsin washed his hands of the parliamentary commission and instructed his aide Sergei Shakhrai to come up with an alternative draft. This Shakhrai accordingly did.[79] However, both "presidential" and "parliamentary" drafts ran into such fierce resistance from the republics that both were rejected by the Congress of People's Deputies at its April 1992 session.

Yeltsin made fresh efforts to beguile the republics in October 1992, when he set up a Council of Heads of Republics. The council was to meet under his chairmanship, and, although it was to be only consultative in nature, Yeltsin promised it a say in the elaboration of all important decisions. In fact, it turned out to be largely symbolic, offering republic leaders little more than the chance to appear to be negotiating with Yeltsin on equal terms; it nonetheless infuriated the heads of the regions, who were not given such treatment.[80] When Yeltsin tried to break the logjam with parliament in November 1992 and announced his intention of calling a referendum over the constitution, the leaders of the republics scuttled his attempts by declaring that they would not hold it. When the referendum was eventually held on 25 April 1993, it contained no reference to the constitution.

This did not prevent Yeltsin from acting as if his victory in the April 1993 referendum gave him a moral right to try again to create a strong presidency. At the end of April he unveiled a new draft constitution at a meeting of the Council of Heads of Republics.[81] Yet again, Yeltsin offered the republics an extravagant concession. Proposing the creation of a new bicameral parliament—the Federal Assembly—the draft stated that Russia's thirty-three "autonomous formations" would be guaranteed at least 50 percent of the seats in the upper house. This was patently inequitable, since the "autonomies" have only 18.5 percent of the population of the Russian Federation.

Under the 1978 constitution only parliament may make changes to the constitution. Knowing that parliament would never adopt the kind of constitution he wanted, Yeltsin resolved to circumvent it. On 5 July 1993 he convened a Constitutional Assembly and tasked it with examining both his draft and that of parliament's Constitutional Commission. Many of the delegates to the assembly had been hand picked by the presidential staff, but even so Yeltsin did not get everything his own way. Although the "presidential" draft was heavily weighted in their favor, the representatives of the republics objected that it failed to acknowledge their declarations that they were sovereign states and that their entry into the Russian Federation had been voluntary (the implication being that they had the right to secede).[82] The republics also complained that while the presidential draft incorporated the three versions of the Federal Treaty (which the parliamentary version omitted) it did nothing to create the long-awaited mechanism for translating the Federal Treaty into life. (The parliamentary draft, which sought to equalize the rights of the republics and regions, was for obvious reasons a nonstarter as far as the republics were concerned.)

For their part, the representatives of the regions protested so loudly at the attempt to stack the upper chamber in favor of the republics that the proposal was removed from the draft constitution that the Constitutional Assembly approved on 12 July.[83] In its final form, the draft (which had no legal force) gave every subject of the federation, regardless of whether it was a republic or a region, two seats in the upper chamber. A concession to the republics, about which several of the regions protested, was the fact that the draft (Article 5) called the republics "sovereign states within the Russian Federation" whereas the regions were described merely as "state-territorial formations." Noting that the draft did not specify what the two terms actually meant, the Russian journalist Kronid Liubarskii commented that it was nonetheless clear that the choice of phrasing was not accidental: "It is understandably better to be a 'state' than some sort of 'formation' and more pleasing to be 'sovereign' than not, as 'sovereign' definitely signifies more opportunities, well, perhaps not now, but with the passage of time."[84] In addition, the draft made allowance (Article 66) for "individual components of the federation" to negotiate separate bilateral treaties with Moscow; this clause had been inserted at the insistence of Tatarstan.[85] However, there was one major concession that Yeltsin refused to make: the draft stated that the territory of the Russian Federation was indivisible; that is, the republics did not win the right to secede.

After its approval by the Constitutional Assembly the document was sent for review to the legislatures of the regions and republics. This was a recipe for further delay and revision, especially since only eight of the twenty republics[86] represented at the Constitutional Assembly and two-thirds of the regions had initialed the draft text at the close of the Constitutional Assembly.[87] Even those that signed made it clear that their legislatures reserved the right to demand further revisions.[88]

To sum up, the draft constitution approved in July 1993 retained the inequality of status between republics and regions that dates back to the early years of the Soviet system. Lamenting that Russia had still not succeeded in shedding the legacy of the Leninist nationalities policy, Liubarskii called this inequality "a minefield" that would have to be defused sooner or later.[89] The chairman of the Krasnoiarsk Oblast Soviet warned that designating the autonomies sovereign states was "a time-bomb" that would transform Russia "from a federation into a confederation."[90] Most cogent of all was the comment of the head of administration of Tula Oblast. He said his region had no use for the trappings of sovereignty and could get along very well without its own anthem and flag. What Tula did want was economic equality for all the subjects of the federation so that it would no longer be paying taxes to subsidize the republics.[91] Clearly, the issue of taxation remained very much on the agenda.

A wave of "republicanization" followed in the summer and fall, as region after region unilaterally declared itself a republic and claimed the privileges associated with that status.[92] To mention only a few, Sverdlovsk Oblast declared itself the Urals Republic; Primorskii Krai called itself the Maritime Republic; Krasnoiarsk and Irkutsk oblasts combined as the East Siberian Republic; Cheliabinsk Oblast proclaimed itself the South Urals Republic; Orel joined other oblasts in the Central Russian Republic; and representatives of fourteen Siberian regions (and, significantly, republics) met in Novosibirsk at the end of September to discuss the formation of a Siberian Republic.

In mid-August 1993 Yeltsin held a summit meeting with the leaders of the republics and regions in Petrozavodsk, capital of Karelia. He proposed the creation of a new consultative body to be called the Federation Council, composed of the regional heads of administration (the executive branch) and the heads of the provincial soviets (the legislative branch). All these officials would hold their seats on the Federation Council *ex officio*. Yeltsin's proposal was vague (one journalist alleged that he made it up on the spur of the moment),[93] but many observers suspected that his aim was to create an unelected body to act as a substitute for the Russian parliament. At a follow-up meeting of provincial leaders in Moscow on 18 September, the idea of the Federation Council was rejected not only by the leaders of the republics, who were unwilling to allow regional leaders to enjoy the same status as themselves, but also by regional leaders furious at the idea that Yeltsin might be trying to use them as a pawn against Khasbulatov.[94] Yet another of Yeltsin's initiatives had run aground. Meanwhile, at the end of September, the Russian parliament was planning to adopt legislation stripping the president of most of his powers. That is how matters stood when, on 21 September, Yeltsin appeared on television to announce that he was dissolving parliament and calling fresh parliamentary elections. Until those elections had been held and a new constitution adopted he was, in effect, suspending the constitution.

In the crisis that followed, a key role was played by the republics and regions. Both parliament and president appealed to provincial leaders. This was in marked contrast to the situation during the attempted coup of August 1991, when the struggle was resolved by a small group of people in Moscow largely regardless of what happened in the provinces, and it underscored the extent to which power had in the intervening two years passed from the center to the periphery. This is not to say that everything was decided in the provinces: In the first few days of the 1993 crisis, a crucial role was played by the fact that the army and police remained loyal to Yeltsin. But once it became clear that Yeltsin had the support of the security services, all eyes turned to the local bureaucracies in Russia's republics and regions. Clearly, it was there that power now lay.

The picture that emerged was not clear-cut. Generally, regional parliaments expressed opposition to Yeltsin, while the administrators, most of whom he had appointed, expressed solidarity. Thus, Khasbulatov was supported by about two-thirds of the soviets—the local government councils which Yeltsin had told the Constituent Assembly in June must be abolished—in both the republics and the regions.[95] Yeltsin had the backing of the mayors of Moscow and St. Petersburg and of almost all the eighty-eight regional heads of administration. Moscow and St. Petersburg were typical of much of the rest of the country: In both cities the mayors spoke out in support of the president while the soviets voted in favor of parliament. This was not true everywhere, however. In Kemerovo and Briansk oblasts, for example, the heads of administration supported parliament rather than the president. And Boris Nemtsov, head of administration in Nizhnii Novgorod, refused to take sides: The leader of Russia's most market-oriented region said the continuation of his own reforms was more important than loyalty to any particular politician in Moscow.[96]

On 30 September 1993, leaders of the soviets of fifteen Siberian regions met in Novosibirsk and threatened that, if Yeltsin did not withdraw his decree on the dissolution of parliament, they would create a Siberian Republic, withhold all taxes from Moscow, and block the Trans-Siberian railway.[97] Meeting in Moscow that day, the leaders of sixty-two Russian regions (dominated by leaders of regional soviets but also including eighteen heads of administration) voted to set up an entirely new federal body. To be called the Council of the Subjects of the Federation, this was apparently intended as a rival to the Federation Council Yeltsin had been trying to create.[98] Shakhrai dismissed the decision as "blackmail" but was forced to admit that regional leaders could impose effective financial sanctions against Moscow if they carried out their threat to withhold federal taxes and natural resources.[99]

Conclusions

Since Russia's emergence as an independent state, relations between the center and the periphery have been caught up in the struggle for power that has been raging in Moscow between the Russian parliament and the president. Each of the central players has tried to win the provinces over to his side while, in some republics and regions, the power struggle at the center has been mirrored at the local level. The Yeltsin leadership has pursued a fairly consistent policy toward Russia's provinces. Time and again the Russian president has favored the republics, which act as "national homelands" for some of the largest ethnic groups inhabiting the territory of the Russian Federation, over the territorially based regions. This has caused Yeltsin to lose the support of many of the leaders of the regions, which are more populous and which pay higher taxes than the republics. Since this is a costly policy, it is necessary to ask why Yeltsin chose it.

It seems safe to assume that the immediate concern of the Yeltsin leadership is to ensure that the Russian Federation does not follow the example of the Soviet Union by disintegrating. The Russian columnist Vitalii Ganiushin could have been speaking for the whole Russian government when he wrote in 1993, "We could survive the breakup of the USSR but not the breakup of Russia."[100] The center must therefore be on the lookout for any signs of separatism or nationalism. Does Yeltsin's policy mean that he views the republics as being more likely than the regions to fall prey to the kind of ethnic unrest that might spark secession? If so, that might explain why Yeltsin has taken special precautions to keep the republics contented.

The idea that militant nationalism is likely to gain the upper hand in Russia's republics does not stand up to examination. Ethnic Russians are widely scattered throughout the territory of the Russian Federation, where they make up 81.5 percent of the population, and they are well represented even in the "non-Russian" republics (for details, see Table 2.1). Ethnic Russians are a majority in nine of the republics and a plurality in three more, and they occupy leading posts in almost all the republics. Members of the titular nationality, on the other hand, make up a majority of the population in only five of the twenty-one republics that bear their names. That this is in many cases the result of Stalin's policy of deporting entire nationalities and resettling others in their lands does not alter the fact that Russia's "ethnic" republics are artificial creations where the proportion of ethnic Russians in the population is often only slightly lower than it is in some of the "Russian" regions.

Geographer Lee Schwartz has argued that it is regionalism or localism, not nationalism, that is the main centrifugal force at work in the Russian Federation today.[101] There are separatist movements in several of Russia's republics, as there are in some of the regions, but these do not, at least at present, seem to represent the majority view. In many cases, Russia's provinces appear to be using the threat of secession or separatism merely as a bargaining chip to gain greater autonomy from Moscow. Local leaders are not keen to shoulder the fiscal and other responsibilities that secession from the Russian Federation would entail, and most threats to leave the Russian Federation seem to be motivated by dissatisfaction with Moscow's management of the economy and the conviction that Russia's provinces possess valuable reserves of raw materials—timber, oil, natural gas, gold, and diamonds—from which they are not reaping their rightful due.

For these reasons Ramazan Abdulatipov, chairman of the Council of Nationalities of the Supreme Soviet, has argued that the national factor will never be the cause of the collapse of the Russian Federation. However, Abdulatipov has conceded, the ethnic factor might well serve as the *pretext* for such a collapse.[102] This suggests another possible explanation of why Yeltsin backed the republics even when this meant losing the support of the regions. Yeltsin may have feared that ethnic unrest could be whipped up in the republics by members of the former nomenklatura. As mentioned above, the Soviet system offered members of some of the smaller national minorities privileges bearing little relation to the weight of these ethnic groups in the population; ethnic Russians also achieved positions of power and privilege in the "non-Russian" republics in which ethnic Russians make up a majority. Many such people remain in power today and would stand to lose status and privileges if Russia's administrative boundaries were to be redrawn to eliminate the anomalies, or if the relative ranking of the republics and regions was altered to redress the balance in favor of the latter. In resisting change forced on them by Moscow, such people would surely be unable to resist playing the ethnic card.

Some members of the nomenklatura may already be trying to turn the ethnic factor to their advantage. According to the Postfactum Agency, Russian entrepreneurs have "gone native" in that part of Krasnodar Krai that is historically identified with the Shapsug people and that contains the Black Sea coastal resort, Sochi.[103] The agency identified Russian managers of a Krasnodar enterprise as being behind a campaign for the reestablishment of the Shapsug National Okrug. The businessmen were hoping to use the aspirations of the Shapsugs as a front to obtain real estate concessions in the popular holiday resort area, the agency alleged, and concluded that "emerging groups of entrepreneurs have an interest in the ethnic sovereignization of [Russia's] regions as a means of preserving and heightening their own influence."[104]

It has been argued here that devolution of political and economic power ("regionalization") is already a reality in Russia, and that the key role played by the provinces in the constitutional crisis of September 1993 bears out that assertion. Russia's republics and regions have acquired enormous autonomy during the past two years. It has also, however, been argued that Russia's present administrative structure is perceived by many of the country's regions as inequitable, and that a sweeping restructuring of the system ("federalization") is necessary to eliminate interregional rivalry and resentment. These problems might have been alleviated had the original constitutional scheme of federalizing Russia by dividing it up into fifty or so nonethnically based German-style *Länder* been accepted when it was first proposed. But schemes to create a truly federal system ran into strong opposition and, as a result, the country remains divided into territorially based regions and nationally constituted republics and districts.

In light of the fact that a federal solution now seems politically unacceptable to Russia's republics and regions, the emergence of strong trading blocs and economic associations formed on the basis of economic interest and financial advantage may hold the best hope for overcoming the legacy of the past. Most highly developed of these is the "Siberian Agreement" economic organization. Set up in October 1990 to coordinate economic activity between the eastern and western Siberian economic regions, "Siberian Agreement" is now said to be acting as a virtual parallel or alternative government in western Siberia.

The Yeltsin government has not interfered with such developments, which it regards as essentially healthy. Yeltsin appears to have learned his lesson from the ignominious defeat Russia suffered when, in the fall of 1991, it sent troops to Chechnia to bring the independence-minded republic to heel. Instead, Russian troops were sent packing by the Chechens, and Chechnia immediately declared its intention of leaving the Russian Federation altogether. Since then Yeltsin has eschewed the use of force. His leadership reacted calmly (too calmly, in the eyes of its parliamentary and Russian nationalist critics) to assertions of regional autonomy and declined to take punitive action against Tatarstan for its 1992 refusal to sign the Federal Treaty or, in 1993, the unilateral declarations by many regions that they are raising themselves to the status of republics. The policy of the Yeltsin government amounts, in other words, to a Russian version of "don't ask, don't tell." It is based on the premise that, as long as the center does not try to curb the provinces' accumulation of economic and political power, the republics and regions will have little incentive to try to leave the Russian Federation. Judging from the lessons of the Soviet breakup and given the weakness of Yeltsin's strife-torn central leadership, this may be the best of a range of not very attractive options. Moscow might have been heeding Donald Horowitz's warning in his study of South Africa: "The fact of the matter is that early, generous devolution is far more likely to avert than to abet ethnic separatism.... Unfortunately, a good many governments have proceeded on the opposite assumption—that devolution feeds centrifugal forces. The unhappy results are visible in large parts of Asia and Africa."[105] So far, it is worth noting, no other territory has tried to follow Chechnia out of the Russian Federation.

Nonetheless, it is not difficult to imagine scenarios in which the Russian Federation might unravel. As Paul Goble has argued, the Yeltsin leadership could provoke such disintegration if it attempted to clamp down on the republics and regions and to claw back the autonomy the provinces have gained since the Soviet Union broke up.[106] A similar result might be expected, Peter Reddaway of Georgetown University has argued, were an extreme right-wing Communist or nationalist government to be elected and set about bringing the provinces to heel.[107] Faced with such action by the center, rebellious provinces would feel they had no choice but to leave the Russian Federation altogether. Their departure could provoke a general stampede and the collapse of the Russian Federation. In the words of Afanasii Illarionov, legal aide to Sakha's president Mikhail Nikolaev, "Trying to impose decisions on us would actually lead to the collapse of Russia."[108]

The collapse of the Russian Federation would have significant consequences for the rest of the world. Russia may no longer be a superpower, but it is still the world's biggest country and the second largest nuclear power. It retains a permanent seat on the United Nations Security Council, and its troops are still deployed throughout most of the other Soviet successor states. It remains a major regional power in Eastern Europe, the Baltic region, the Transcaucasus, Central Asia, and the Far East. Western policy makers should be aware that there is no consensus as yet in Russia about the form the country should take or the values it should pursue. Russia's foreign policy over the coming period cannot fail to reflect the present state of muddle and confusion in the country itself.

Appendix

Signatories of the Russian Federal Treaty

Republics: Adygeia; Altai;* Bashkortostan; Buriatia; Chuvashia; Dagestan; Kabardino-Balkaria; Kalmykia; Karachaevo-Cherkessia; Karelia; Khakassia; Komi; Marii-El; Mordovia; North Ossetia; Sakha (Yakutia); Tuva; Udmurtia.†

Krais (territories): Altai; Khabarovsk; Krasnodar; Krasnoiarsk; Primorskii; Stavropol.

Oblasts (regions): Amur; Arkhangel'sk; Astrakhan'; Belgorod; Bryansk; Cheliabinsk; Chita; Iaroslavl'; Irkutsk; Ivanovo; Kaliningrad; Kaluga; Kamchatka; Kemerovo; Kirov; Kostroma; Kurgan; Kursk; Leningrad; Lipetsk; Magadan; Moscow; Murmansk; Nizhnii Novgorod; Novgorod;

---

*Altai Republic is the name adopted by the former Gorno-Altai Autonomous Oblast; the region, which was formerly subordinated to Altai Krai, declared itself sovereign in 1990.

†Not signing the Federal Treaty were the republics of Chechnia and Ingushetia (formerly Checheno-Ingushetia) and Tatarstan.

Novosibirsk; Omsk; Orel; Orenburg; Penza; Perm'; Pskov; Rostov; Ryazan'; Sakhalin; Samara; Saratov; Smolensk; Sverdlovsk; Tambov; Tomsk; Tula; Tver'; Tiumen'; Ul'ianovsk; Vladimir; Volgograd; Vologda; Voronezh.

Federal cities: Moscow; St. Petersburg.

Autonomous oblast (region): Jewish.

Autonomous okrugs (districts): Aga Buriat; Chukchi; Evenki; Iamal Nenets; Khanty-Mansi; Komi-Permiak; Koriak; Nenets; Taimyr; Ust' Orda Buriat.

Notes

This chapter was written while the author was a 1992–93 Jennings Randolph Peace Fellow at the United States Institute of Peace, whose generous support is gratefully acknowledged. The views expressed here are her own and are not necessarily endorsed by the U.S. Institute of Peace. The author is grateful for comments on the first draft of this chapter to participants in the workshop held on 28 May 1993 under the auspices of the Russian Littoral Project, especially to Karen Dawisha, Bruce Parrott, Peter Reddaway, Blair Ruble, Lee Schwartz, Roman Szporluk, and Vladimir Tismaneanu. Philip Hanson also made valuable comments on an early draft, while superb research assistance was provided by Michael Conway and Natalie Melnyczuk.

    1. This process is referred to by some authors as "refederalization" but, because the Russian Federation never has been a true federation, the word "federalization" is used here.
    2. Charles B. Neff, "Russia's Booming Far-East Frontier," *Washington Post*, 27 August 1993.
    3. For discussion, see Elizabeth Teague, "Russians Outside Russia and Russian Security Policy" (paper presented at a conference of the United States Institute of Peace on "The Emerging National Security Doctrine of a New Russia," Washington, DC, 17–19 March 1993).
    4. For discussion of this issue, see David Beachley, "The Status of FSU Nuclear Weapons and the Weapons Industry" (paper prepared for the Fifth Bedford Colloquium on Military, Political and Economic Affairs of the Former Soviet Union, Bedford, Nova Scotia, 26–30 July 1993).
    5. Editorial, *Christian Science Monitor*, 22 March 1993.
    6. Daniel Elazar, "Federalism," in *International Encyclopedia of the Social Sciences*, ed. David L. Sills (New York: Macmillan and Free Press, 1972), vol. 5, pp. 353–67; *New Encyclopaedia Britannica*, 15th ed.; Stephan Kux, *Soviet Federalism: A Comparative Perspective* (New York: Institute for East-West Security Studies, 1990).
    7. Scholars have disagreed over whether or not the USSR or its largest component, the Russian Federation (RSFSR), should be described as the heirs of the Russian Em-

pire. Arguing that the concept of "empire" requires an element of foreign domination that was absent in the USSR and the Russian Federation, where Russians counted themselves among the oppressed, some have stated that neither entity should be so described. An authoritative source defines an empire as a political system in which a single political community or nation extends its rule over other political units "without fully incorporating them into a framework of common political symbols and identity" (Shmuel N. Eisenstadt, "Empires," in Sills, ed., *International Encyclopedia of the Social Sciences,* vol. 5, pp. 41–49). This definition fits the Russian Empire but not the USSR and RSFSR, where power was exercised by a monolithic Communist Party that did all it could to force a single set of symbols and a common identity onto a multiethnic population. A looser definition is offered by *Webster's New Collegiate Dictionary,* which calls an empire "a major political unit having a territory of great extent or a number of territories or peoples under a single sovereign authority." Unlike Eisenstadt's, this definition is broad enough to fit the USSR and RSFSR as well as the Russian Empire.

8. Parliament has amended the constitution more than three hundred times since its adoption in 1978. The majority of these changes have been made in the past couple of years.

9. Elazar, "Federalism."

10. The second model implies a more radical devolution of power than the first. The two models were outlined by Gordon Paul Hediger in a letter to *Financial Times,* 9 November 1992.

11. When the USSR collapsed, 25.3 million ethnic Russians found themselves living "abroad," that is, on the territory of the former Soviet Union but outside the borders of the Russian Federation in one of the fourteen other Soviet successor states. At the same time, 27 million non-Russians lived inside the Russian Federation. In all, non-Russians represented just under 20 percent of Russia's population (although, taken individually, only four of the country's more than one hundred ethnic groups composed more than 1 percent of the population). To be precise, ethnic Russians at the time of the 1989 census made up 81.5 percent of the Russian Federation's total population of 147,022,000. Tatars accounted for 3.8 percent; Ukrainians 2.7 percent; and Chuvash 1.2 percent. Census data for 1989 as reported in Goskomstat SSSR (USSR State Committee on Statistics), *Natsional'nyi sostav naseleniia SSSR* (Moscow: Finansy i statistika, 1991).

12. Mark Frankland, "Beware the Bear on the Loose," *Observer,* 1 August 1993.

13. Leyla Boulton, "Reform Still Selling Down on Karl Marx Street," *Financial Times,* 22 September 1993.

14. Frankland, "Beware the Bear."

15. S.E. Finer, *Five Constitutions* (Harmondsworth: Penguin Books, 1979), p. 29; Elizabeth Teague and Dawn Mann, "Gorbachev's Dual Role," *Problems of Communism,* January–February 1990, pp. 1–27 at p. 4.

16. *Konstitutsiia (Osnovnoi Zakon) Rossiiskoi Federatsii—Rossii* (Moscow: Izvestiia, 1992).

17. ITAR-TASS, 21 September 1993; *Izvestiia,* 22 September 1993; see also *RFE/RL Daily Report,* 22–24 September 1993.

18. Lee Schwartz, "Regional Population Redistribution and National Homelands in the USSR," in *Soviet Nationalities Policies,* ed. Henry Huttenbach (London: Mansell Publishing, 1990), pp. 121–62. Ann Sheehy, "Russia's Republics: A Threat to Its Territorial Integrity?" *RFE/RL Research Report,* 1993, no. 20, pp. 34–40 at p. 34.

19. Sheehy, "Russia's Republics," p. 34.

20. On 2 June 1993, the Council of Nationalities of the Russian parliament passed a resolution giving the autonomous okrugs, which until then had occupied the lowest rung

of the ladder, the same rights as the krais and oblasts (*RFE/RL Daily Report*, 8 June 1993).

21. Vladimir Portnikov, "Union of Russian Emirates?" *New Times*, 1993, no. 37, p. 12.

22. The regions have an average population of 2.5 million people each, while the republics have an average of 1.2 million.

23. In 1992 Sverdlovsk Oblast paid 95 billion rubles in taxes and received in return state subventions amounting to 30 billion. The Republic of Tatarstan, by contrast, paid 93 *million* rubles in taxes in 1992 and got back 38 billion rubles (*Knight-Ridder Newspapers*, 23 August 1993).

24. *Sovetskaia Rossiia*, 13 July 1993.

25. Ronald Watts, "The Soviet Federal System and the Nationality Question in Comparative Perpective," in *Soviet Federalism, Nationalism and Economic Decentralisation*, ed. Alastair McAuley (Leicester: Leicester University Press, 1991), pp. 196–207.

26. *Baltimore Sun*, 17 November 1991.

27. Goble, "The Ethnic Factor."

28. *Izvestiia*, 3 May 1990.

29. Sheehy, "Russia's Republics."

30. TASS, 7 August 1990.

31. Ann Sheehy, "Fact Sheet on Sovereignty Declarations," RFE/RL Research Institute, Munich, 31 October 1990.

32. Robert J. Osborn, "Russia: Federalism, Regionalism, and Nationality Claims," in *Russia and America: From Rivalry to Reconciliation*, ed. George Ginsburgs, Alvin Z. Rubinstein, and Oles M. Smolansky (Armonk, NY: M.E. Sharpe, 1993).

33. Sheehy, "Fact Sheet."

34. Sergei Parkhomenko, "Rumiantsev's Draft Suffers Its First Defeats," *Nezavisimaia gazeta*, 18 March 1992, p. 2.

35. Germany's *Länder* are Western Europe's most politically powerful regions. They have large budgets allocated by the central government, out of which they pay teachers, police, and other public servants. Income taxes are collected by the federal authorities, but the *Länder* may levy their own taxes on wine and beer (*Sunday Telegraph*, 8 March 1992).

36. Galina Kovalskaya, "The Caucasus: A Mechanism for Settling and Averting Conflicts Has Yet to be Found," *New Times*, 1993, no. 5, pp. 6–9.

37. Olga Glezer, "Russian Republic: No Longer Soviet Socialist Federative," *Moscow News*, 1992, no. 7, p. 7.

38. Parkhomenko, "Rumiantsev's Draft."

39. *Moscow News*, 1992, no. 10.

40. TASS, 2 November 1991.

41. *Guardian*, 18 September 1991; ITAR-TASS, 8 March 1992, reported in *RFE/RL Daily Report*, 9 March 1992; Glezer, "Russian Republic," p. 7.

42. With parliamentary recognition of the division of Checheno-Ingushetiia into separate Chechen and Ingush republics in June 1992, the number of Russia's republics increased to twenty-one. But, because of Chechnia's insistence that it has left the federation, many commentators describe Russia as consisting of twenty republics.

43. Glezer, "Russian Republic."

44. The Brezhnev leadership ran into similar difficulties when drafting the 1977 Soviet constitution. Then the sticking point was the role to be assigned to the union republics. See John N. Hazard, "Codification of Soviet Nationality Policies," in *Soviet*

Nationality Policies: Ruling Ethnic Groups in the USSR, ed. Henry R. Huttenbach (London: Mansell, 1990), pp. 47–61 at p. 57.

45. Russian Television, 29 March 1992.

46. Set up in 1920 to act as a buffer between the USSR and Japan, the Far Eastern Republic was replaced two years later by a Far Eastern region, reorganized as the Far Eastern area in 1926, and finally dissolved in 1938.

47. *Moscow News*, 1992, no. 7.

48. The Novosibirsk newspaper *Ekonomika i resursy* was cited by TASS on 19 January 1992 and by AFP on 20 January 1992 as proposing the creation of a "United States of North Asia."

49. The assembly was attended by representatives of Kazakhstan, Turkmenistan, Kyrgyzstan, and Uzbekistan (*Libération,* 21 January 1992; Reuters, 22 January 1992).

50. Radio Rossii, 28 February 1992; reported in *RFE/RL Daily Report,* 2 March 1992.

51. *Moscow News,* 1992, no. 10.

52. Mary Dejevsky, "Russian Unity Comes Under Fresh Threat," *Times* (London), 27 March 1992.

53. *Financial Times,* 30 March 1992.

54. ITAR-TASS, 26 March 1922.

55. See Michael J. Bradshaw, *Siberia at a Time of Change: New Vistas for Western Investment* (London: The Economist Intelligence Unit, 1992); Idem, "Siberia Poses a Challenge to Russian Federalism," *RFE/RL Research Report,* 1992, no. 41, pp. 6–14.

56. For the text of the Federal Treaties as signed by representatives of the three levels of territorial-administrative region, see *Etnopolis,* 1992, no. 1, pp. 17–32.

57. Ingushetia, which did not officially split away from Chechnia and become the Ingush Republic until June 1992, did not sign either, but its leaders expressed general willingness to do so. In 1993, angered by the failure of the Yeltsin leadership to take their side in a territorial dispute with neighboring North Ossetia, the leaders of Ingushetia threatened not to sign the Federal Treaty after all.

58. *Nezavisimaia gazeta,* 7 March 1992.

59. Elazar, "Federalism."

60. Galina Kovalskaya, "Yeltsinburg," *New Times,* 1993, no. 18, pp. 10–13.

61. *Nezavisimaia gazeta,* 2 April 1992.

62. Central Television, 24 March 1992, as reported in *RFE/RL Daily Report,* 25 March 1992.

63. Ann Sheehy, *RFE/RL Daily Report,* 2 June 1993.

64. This section draws on the author's contribution to a Heritage Foundation symposium on "Regionalism, Federalism, and Constitutional Reform in the Russian Federation," Washington, DC, 26 May 1993.

65. Institute for the Economy in Transition, *Rossiiskaia ekonomika v 1992 godu: Tendentsii i perspektivy* (Moscow, 1993), pp. 25–28.

66. Osborn, "Russia: Federalism, Regionalism."

67. *Rossiiskaia gazeta,* 4 December 1991, cited by James H. Noren in *Soviet Economy,* January–March 1992, p. 28.

68. Postfactum, "Regionalization and Prospects of Breaking Up of Russian Federation into Several States," mimeo, 1992.

69. Postfactum, 25 March 1992.

70. *Moscow News,* 1992, no. 7.

71. Philip Hanson, "Russia: Economic Reform and Local Politics," *The World Today,* April 1993.

72. *Financial Times*, 6 May 1993.
73. *Newsweek*, 5 April 1993.
74. Christine I. Wallich, *Fiscal Decentralization: Intergovernmental Relations in Rusia* (Washington, DC: World Bank, 1992), p. 5.
75. *Nezavisimaia gazeta*, 1 September 1993.
76. *Financial Times*, 15 September 1993.
77. *Novoe vremia* (1993, no. 37) listed Bashkortostan, Buriatia, Chechnia, Kalmykia, Karelia, Komi, Sakha, Tatarstan, and Tuva; these were later joined by Udmurtia (ITAR-TASS, 23 September 1993).
78. These details may be found in Vera Tolz, "Drafting the New Russian Constitution," *RFE/RL Research Report*, 1993, no. 29, pp. 1–12.
79. *Nezavisimaia gazeta*, 28 March 1992.
80. *Economist*, 27 March 1993.
81. *Izvestiia*, 30 April 1993.
82. *Nezavisimaia gazeta*, 15 May 1993.
83. *Izvestiia*, 16 July 1993.
84. Kronid Lyubarsky, "New Wine in Old Wineskins," *New Times*, 1993, no. 30, pp. 6–7.
85. *Financial Times*, 13 July 1993.
86. Chechnia sent no representative.
87. *New York Times*, 13 July 1993.
88. *Financial Times*, 13 July 1993.
89. Kronid Lyubarsky, "All Forms of Authority but Soviet Power Are Good," *New Times*, 1993, no. 25, pp. 6–7.
90. Quoted in *New Times*, 1993, no. 29.
91. ITAR-TASS, 14 September 1993.
92. Vsevolod Rybakov, "'Parade of Sovereignties' Again, Now Within Russia," *New Times*, 1993, no. 22, p. 3.
93. Sergei Parkhomenko, *Nezavsimaia gazeta*, 11 September 1993.
94. Vladimir Orlov, "Political Crisis in Russia Reaches its Peak," *Moscow News*, 24 September 1993.
95. The regional soviets were elected in March 1990, at the same time as the Russian parliament. Many of their members are former Communist Party officials.
96. *Economist*, 2 October 1993.
97. Reuters, 30 September 1993.
98. AFP, 30 September 1993.
99. AFP, Reuters, 30 September 1993.
100. *New Times*, 1993, no. 30.
101. This point was stressed by Lee Schwartz in a talk delivered at the Woodrow Wilson Center, Washington, DC, 19 October 1992.
102. *Trud*, 27 February 1993.
103. Until the 1860s the Shapsugs were numerically the largest of the western Circassian tribes of the North Caucasus, inhabiting the strip of Black Sea coastline that includes Sochi and extends to the slopes of the Caucasus Mountains. In the mid-1860s, following Russia's victory in the Caucasian War, most of them fled to Turkey. In the late 1920s and 1930s the Shapsugs were classified as a distinct ethnic group and had their own Shapsug National Okrug. Their autonomous district was disbanded in the late 1930s when they and other tribes were officially reclassified as Adyges. They have recently begun to agitate for the return of their territorial and cultural autonomy. See Ronald Wixman, *The Peoples of the USSR* (Armonk, NY: M.E. Sharpe, 1984).

104. Postfactum, "Regionalization."
105. Donald L. Horowitz, *A Democratic South Africa? Constitutional Engineering in a Divided Society* (Berkeley: University of California Press, 1991), p. 224. The author is grateful to Pierre du Toit for drawing her attention to this study.
106. Goble, "The Ethnic Factor."
107. Peter Reddaway, "Russia on the Brink?" *New York Review of Books,* 28 January 1993, pp. 30–35.
108. Quoted in *Christian Science Monitor,* 12 February 1993.

3

Russian Minorities in the Newly Independent States

An International Problem in the Domestic Context of Russia Today

Nikolai Rudensky

Among the many consequences of the collapse of the Union of Soviet Socialist Republics, one of the most important is the formation of a new Russian diaspora—ethnic Russian and Russian-speaking minorities in the newly independent states (NIS) of the former Soviet Union. The largest European nation, with a long record of imperial domination, suddenly became a divided people with vulnerable peripheral groups. It is only natural that such a historical development would be extremely painful for Russian national identity. The sentiment of national deprivation and humiliation, aggravated by the current socioeconomic and political crises in the Russian Federation, may have disastrous implications not only for Russian society, but also for international stability in the post-Soviet geopolitical space and beyond. Suffice it to remember how a similar feeling was exploited by the Nazis in Germany in the aftermath of World War I. A more recent and also tragic analogy may be drawn from the rise of aggressive national-communism in Serbia after the disintegration of Yugoslavia.

The problem of Russian minorities, admittedly a top priority in emerging international relations between Russia and the other ex-Soviet states, is also a highly important and divisive one on Russia's domestic political scene. Across the entire political spectrum there is little if any doubt that the government and society should be concerned with the destinies of kinfolk in the NIS, trying to protect their legitimate rights and interests, and helping them to promote their culture and identity. There is, however, a striking divergence of opinion when it comes to ways and means of intervention on behalf of Russian and Russian-speaking minorities. The attitude at issue has become a litmus test of political orientation—the national-patriotic "war party," with its claims to restoring the Soviet (or, for that matter, Russian) empire, versus liberal-minded politicians, committed to the principles of international law, and aiming to integrate Russia into the world community of civilized nations.

Russian Minorities in the NIS: Demography and Socioeconomic Status

According to the data of the last Soviet population census of 1989, the number of ethnic Russians in Soviet republics outside Russia was 25.3 million,[1] or about 17 percent of the total Russian population of the USSR and about the same share (18 percent) of the total population of the fourteen non-Russian republics. Other nationalities of Russia that have their autonomies in the Russian Federation were also well represented in the Soviet republics: for example, 1.1 million Tatars (mostly in Uzbekistan and Kazakhstan), 842,000 Jews (mostly in Ukraine and Belarus), and 209,000 Lezgins (predominantly in Azerbaijan). The total number of people of Russian-based nationalities outside Russia was 28.2 million, with ethnic Russians constituting nearly 90 percent of this total.

The term "Russian-speaking population," often used to describe the Russian diaspora in the NIS, is not precise enough. If this category is meant to include everyone who has (or claims) good knowledge of the Russian language, it would cover about two-thirds of the total population of the NIS (and, of course, nearly all inhabitants of Russia proper). It is hardly possible to consider this heterogeneous mass as having common problems and well-defined interests.

On the other hand, in the ex-Soviet republics there are many people of ethnic stock other than Russian who regard the Russian language as their mother tongue. The 1989 census gave the total number of these "linguistic Russians" (as distinct from Russians in ethnic terms) outside the Russian Federation as 11.2 million. Most of them live in Ukraine, Kazakhstan, and Belarus (see Table 3.1). It would seem advisable to apply the term "Russian-speaking population" or "Russian-speakers" to these particular linguistic minorities in order to distinguish them from ethnic Russians.

This distinction is, however, somewhat incorrect logically, since virtually all ethnic Russians are naturally speakers of Russian. Moreover, one might doubt whether Russian-speakers in this sense should be regarded as

Table 3.1

Ethnic Russians and Russian-Speakers* in Soviet Republics Outside Russia, 1989

Republics	Ethnic Russians	Russian-Speakers
Armenia	52,000	16,000
Azerbaijan	392,000	137,000
Belarus	1,300,000	1,900,000
Estonia	475,000	78,000
Georgia	341,000	142,000
Kazakhstan	6,200,000	1,600,000
Kyrgyzstan	917,000	174,000
Latvia	906,000	228,000
Lithuania	344,000	100,000
Moldova	562,000	446,000
Tajikistan	388,000	107,000
Turkmenistan	344,000	87,000
Uzbekistan	1,700,000	500,000
Ukraine	11,400,000	5,700,000

*Persons of non-Russian ethnic origin regarding Russian as native language.

an integral element of the Russian diaspora: Most of them, being of Ukrainian or Belarusian ancestry, are ethnically affiliated not with Russia but with Ukraine or Belarus, and would accordingly seek political and cultural protection from these countries. Nevertheless, it seems reasonable to suggest that the Russian government and society should offer cultural assistance to all minorities identifying with the Russian language and culture, irrespective of ethnic origins. To be sure, such initiatives should by no means infringe on the sovereignty of the states in question.

The total size of the new Russian diaspora, in the broadest sense of the word (people affiliated with Russia ethnically and/or linguistically), may thus be estimated at over forty million people.

According to the 1989 census,[2] the proportion of Russians in the total population is particularly high in Kazakhstan (41 percent in 1979, and 38 percent in 1989), Latvia (33 percent and 34 percent respectively), Estonia (28 percent and 30 percent), Ukraine (21 percent and 22 percent), Kyrgyzstan (26 percent and 21 percent), Belarus (12 percent and 13 percent), and Moldova (12.8 percent and 13 percent). Their percentage is relatively minimal in Armenia (2.3 percent in 1979, and 1.6 percent in 1989), Azerbaijan (7.9 percent and 5.6 percent), and Georgia (7.5 percent and 6.3 percent).

Most Russians in the NIS are urban dwellers: from 95 to 97 percent in Turkmenistan, Azerbaijan, and Uzbekistan and from 85 to 86 percent in Georgia, Moldova, and Latvia. In Kazakhstan the Russians constitute 51 percent of the total urban population, in Latvia 41 percent, Kyrgyzstan 40 percent, Estonia 39 percent, Ukraine 29 percent, Moldova 24 percent.

Between 1979 and 1989 the number of Russians outside Russia increased by 1.4 million, or 5.9 percent, while the total population of the Soviet republics except Russia grew by 11 percent. The natural increase among Russian populations tends to be significantly lower than among native ethnic groups. The growth of the Russian populations was relatively more rapid in Belarus (by 18 percent, against the total population increase of 6.5 percent), Estonia (16 percent versus 6.9 percent), Lithuania (14 percent versus 8.4 percent), Moldova (11 percent versus 9.8 percent), Latvia (10 percent versus 6.5 percent), and Ukraine (8.4 percent versus 3.7 percent). A decrease in the number of Russians during the same period, mostly due to out-migration, was noted in Armenia (27 percent); Azerbaijan (17 percent), Georgia (8.2 percent), Turkmenistan (4.4 percent), Tajikistan (1.7 percent), and Uzbekistan (0.7 percent).

It is important to note that many Russians who permanently settled in non-Russian republics can be rightly regarded as native inhabitants, since they were born in those republics. The highest percentage is in Kazakhstan, where 67 percent of all Russians were born on the territory of the republic. In Azerbaijan the share of "natives" among the local Russians is 66 percent; in Kyrgyzstan, Ukraine, Uzbekistan, Latvia, Moldova, and Turkmenistan more than 50 percent; in Lithuania 49.7 percent; and in Tajikistan, Georgia, Estonia, and Belarus between 42 and 48 percent. It is only in Armenia where this proportion is relatively low, at 26 percent.

In most republics more than one-third of the total Russian population has lived in the respective republics for more than twenty-five years; the percentage is somewhat lower (26 to 32 percent) in Belarus, Moldova, Kazakhstan, Kyrgyzstan, and Tajikistan, but higher in Ukraine (36 percent), Latvia (37 percent), Georgia (43 percent), and Azerbaijan (50 percent).

On the other hand, relatively few Russians have so far been disposed to master local languages. In Kazakhstan, for example, less than 1 percent of the Russian population has a good command of the Kazakh language. The percentage is not much better in Kyrgyzstan (1.2 percent), Turkmenistan (2.5 percent), Tajikistan (3.5 percent), and Uzbekistan (4.6 percent). Bilingualism is somewhat more widespread among the Russians in Moldova (12 percent), Azerbaijan (14 percent), Estonia (15 percent), Latvia (22 percent), Georgia (24 percent), and Belarus (27 percent). It is only in Lithuania, Armenia, and Ukraine that more than one-third of the local Russians are fluent in the national languages of the republics (37 percent, 34 percent, and 34 percent respectively).

The level of education in the Russian diaspora is higher than among most core nations. In all former Soviet republics the percentage of Russians among highly skilled workers and professionals (holding college or university degrees) by far exceeds their share in the total population. Russians in Tajikistan, for example, account for a mere 7.6 percent of the population, but make up 21 percent of specialists with higher education; in Turkmenistan the figures are 9.5 percent and 22 percent respectively; in Uzbekistan 8.3 percent and 17 percent.

It should be noted, however, that the relative predominance of Russians in the intelligentsia of non-Russian republics has largely been offset by the growth of native ethnic elements in this social group. Since the early 1960s Russians in most Soviet republics were already losing in the bitter if latent ethnic competition for professional jobs.[3] Naturally enough, the trend could only gain momentum once these republics became independent states.

For all the regional differences in their socioeconomic status, Russian groups in the former Soviet republics tend to hold similar positions in the so-called ethnic division of labor. Relatively most Russians are employed in industry, typically holding blue-collar or middle management jobs. The proportion of industrial workers among Russians in Estonia, for example, is 44 percent versus 25 percent among ethnic Estonians. The corresponding figures for Ukraine are 39 percent and 31 percent, Latvia 37 percent and 25 percent, Lithuania 36 percent and 28 percent, Moldova 35 percent and 17 percent, Azerbaijan 34 percent and 18 percent.

In some republics many Russians have jobs in construction: in Tajikistan and Turkmenistan 16 percent, Uzbekistan 15 percent, Kazakhstan 13 percent, Kyrgyzstan 12 percent, and Lithuania 10 percent.

Transportation and communications account for 13 percent of Russian employment in Turkmenistan; 12 percent in Kazakhstan; 11 percent in Azerbaijan, Lithuania, and Georgia; 10 percent in Estonia, Latvia, and Uzbekistan.

The economic importance of farming is comparatively low: In most republics the proportion of the agriculturally employed among Russians ranges between 2.3 percent (in Turkmenistan) and 5.3 percent (in Georgia). There are relatively more farmers among the Russians in Kazakhstan (10 percent), Kyrgyzstan (8.5 percent), Ukraine (8.1 percent), Moldova (7.8 percent), Belarus (7.2 percent), and Latvia (6.8 percent).

This general pattern of employment goes back to the period of the 1930s to the 1950s, when Soviet authorities promoted the large-scale migration of workers, predominantly Russians, to areas of prospective industrial development, including Kazakhstan, parts of Central Asia, and (after 1945) the Baltic republics.[4] Incidentally, one might reasonably suggest that, apart from economic considerations, this centralized effort was motivated by a political goal: "internationalization," that is, Russification of the ethnic periphery. This planned migration was a major factor in the process of industrialization in many non-Russian areas of the Soviet Union, leaving its lasting imprint on the ethnic composition of the working class. Even now many former Soviet republics rely heavily on Russian workers for their industrial potential. In Turkmenistan, for example, ethnic Russians make up nearly 100 percent of all workers in the engineering industry and about 50 percent of all workers in the textile industry; in Ukraine about 50 percent of all miners; and in Estonia more than 50 percent of all shipbuilders. According to some estimates, the Russian labor force in Latvia creates about 70 percent of the country's gross national product.[5]

It is, however, precisely the importance of Russians in the industrial sector of the NIS that makes their socioeconomic status extremely vulnerable in the present-day economic situation. Many industrial enterprises in the ex-Soviet republics, particularly those related to the disintegrating military-industrial complex, are hardly able to survive under the numerous pressures of market transition. Their bleak situation is further aggravated by the almost total disruption of interrepublican economic links after the collapse of the USSR. As a result, industrial jobs have become increasingly scarce, and many Russian workers are bound to be affected by the mounting unemployment.

Russians in the Disintegrating Union: The Painful Transition to a New Status

The deteriorating socioeconomic condition of Russian minorities in the NIS is closely related to the radical change in their political status. To have a better understanding of this change, it is necessary to look at its historical antecedents.

During the last decades of the Communist regime in the Soviet Union, the situation in the non-Russian republics was characterized by growing alienation and tensions between the so-called titular nations and local Russian populations. On the one hand, many Russians outside Russia never perceived themselves as minority groups: just the opposite, they considered themselves representatives of the dominant nation in the multinational state. Accordingly, they displayed national loyalty neither to the republics of their permanent residence nor to Russia (the Russian Federation), but to the Soviet state as a whole. Sociological polls conducted in the early 1980s indicated that while most representatives of non-Russian nationalities strongly identified with their republics, most Russians outside Russia (70 to 80 percent) gave their supreme allegiance to the multinational entity, regarding the whole USSR as their motherland.[6] Because of this basic attitude, most Russians felt no need whatsoever to master local languages and traditions. Many of them, in fact, showed contempt for the cultural patterns of their ethnic environment, which could hardly have improved their relations with native ethnic groups.

On the other hand, many titular nations were biased against the Russians in their republics, identifying them with the Communist regime and blaming them for the past and present crimes of that regime against their peoples. This attitude was particularly widespread in those regions that had been relatively recently incorporated into the USSR: the Baltics, Moldova, and western Ukraine.

These hidden ethnic tensions became visible in the late 1980s, as many Soviet republics (Estonia, Georgia, Latvia, Lithuania, Moldova, Ukraine) saw the rapid development of mass national movements aimed ultimately at gaining (or restoring) national sovereignty. The newly elected republican parliaments started taking legal measures against what was perceived as the forced assimilation (Russification) of their nations. At this early stage particular emphasis was placed on the effort to strengthen the status of the national languages and to limit the social function of the Russian language, resulting in the abandonment of the time-honored slogan of bilingualism, which had indeed become a synonym for Russification. Naturally enough, the issue was extremely sensitive for the Russians in the republics, but their political response was far from uniform.

From 1988 to 1991 there emerged three major political currents in the Russian diaspora. Some ethnic Russians and Russian-speakers (in fact, rather few of them), favoring adaptation to the new conditions in their republics and advocating the general idea of democratic change, supported the so-called popular fronts—mass democratic movements dominated by native leaders. Others, politicized to a lesser extent, but also inclined to adaptation, formed nonpolitical associations to promote Russian language and culture. Active opponents of the popular fronts organized the so-called international fronts (interfronts), which made desperate attempts to prevent the secession of their republics from the Soviet Union and to restore the influence of communist ideology.

The interfronts received both open and covert support from the central authorities in Moscow, seeking to use the internal struggles in the republics for their own purposes. Tensions were running particularly high in the Baltics, culminating in bloodshed in Vilnius and Riga in January 1991, when the center tried to crush the Baltic drive for independence by force, using the pretext of alleged mistreatment of the local Russians and relying on support from the interfront-type organizations. Of course, the tragic events could only aggravate the lack of understanding between local Russians and the native ethnic communities.

Acute political confrontation between the titular nation and the Russian and Russian-speaking population also evolved in Moldova. Already in 1990 the ethnopolitical conflict led to the proclamation of the so-called Dniester Moldovan Republic on the left bank of the Dniester River, populated mostly by Russian-speakers (ethnically more Ukrainian than Russian).

Another region of ethnopolitical tension was Crimea, which now has the status of a republic within the state of Ukraine. It is the only region of Ukraine with a clear-cut majority (67 percent) of ethnic Russians in the population. Local claims for more autonomy and even secession from Ukraine were reinforced by the position of some influential political forces in Russia who regarded Crimea as historically Russian territory.

In the republics of Central Asia and Transcaucasia there was no political confrontation between the titular nations and the Russian populations. Still, sociological polls of 1990–91 indicated that Russians and Russian-speakers in these regions (particularly in Central Asia) showed maximum (compared to other Soviet republics) levels of anxiety and uncertainty about their future because of general political instability.[7]

Facing New Realities

The overall condition of Russians and Russian-speakers outside Russia has changed radically since the collapse of the USSR in December 1991. All of them now have to rethink their social status and assimilate new patterns of social behavior characteristic of minority groups. Of course, the process can only be long and difficult, its local patterns being determined by various external factors. Some sociopolitical attitudes prevalent among Russian minorities in the NIS have been revealed by representative opinion polls of 1991–92, conducted by the All-Russian Center for Public Opinion Research (VTsIOM) and the Institute for Employment Studies of the Russian Academy of Sciences. (The results of these polls still remain largely unpublished.)

Interestingly enough, in late 1991 Russians in the Baltic states indicated a higher level of identification with their republics than did Russians in other regions. In 1992, however, Russians in Latvia displayed more concern about the consequences of the collapse of the USSR than they had a year before (26 percent of those polled in 1992, versus 19 percent in 1991). The same trend was noted in Kyrgyzstan (38 percent versus 30 percent). In Moldova, however, the problem was now perceived as less important than before (23 percent versus 46 percent), which may indicate some degree of stabilization in the republic.

In 1991 Russians in non-Russian republics were much more disapproving of the dissolution of the USSR than Russians living in Russia. And yet, the fait accompli impelled many to adapt to the situation by applying for new citizenship (in 1991–92 the number of those willing to do so nearly doubled).

More than 50 percent of those polled thought that Russians should be actively involved in the political life of the NIS. Many of them—57 percent in Moldova (69 percent on the left bank of the Dniester), 50 percent in Kyrgyzstan and Tajikistan, 43 percent in Latvia, and 34 percent in Uzbekistan—believed that responsibility for protecting the rights and interests of Russian minorities should lie with the government of the Russian Federation. Nearly all of those polled claimed that the current policies of the Russian leadership did not help to resolve ethnic issues and even aggravated them. Assessing their prospects for the future, about two-thirds of those polled (average for different republics) expressed the view that Russians in the NIS would exist as second-class citizens, while one-third believed that Russian groups would be dissolved in the majority populations.

About 28 percent of the Russians polled in Moldova said they were firmly resolved to leave the republic, while 38 percent said they were determined to stay. The corresponding figures for those polled in Uzbekistan were 31 percent and 33 percent, Kyrgyzstan 36 percent and 25 percent, and Tajikistan 52 percent and 17 percent. Many of them said they would be willing to move to central Russia, even if the resettlement involved a change in occupation. On the other hand, most of those polled failed to indicate the time of their planned departure or describe the necessary steps they had already taken (preliminary arrangements about transportation, housing, and jobs). Many of the potential migrants were not certain whether their living conditions would change for the better once they moved to a new place.

About one-third of those polled, however, said they would be willing to stay in their republics on the condition that the republican parliament adopted laws guaranteeing the rights of the Russians and other national minorities; there were no threats of dismissal from a job for nonproficiency in the national language; and freedom to receive education at all levels in Russian was ensured.

Many of those polled believed that their situation would be more stable if Russia concluded an agreement with their republic on the status of the Russian population. Some of them also thought that Russia should be prepared to use military force in case the security of the local Russians was threatened.

The issue of possible involvement in political action to protect the interests of Russian minorities has proved highly divisive. Many of the polled (46 percent in Latvia, 27 percent in Moldova, 26 percent in Uzbekistan, 45 percent in Kyrgyzstan, and 34 percent in Tajikistan) said they were ready to take part in mass rallies, demonstrations, and strikes and even to enlist in self-defense groups. But many (26 percent in Latvia, 34 percent in Moldova, 45 percent in Uzbekistan, 34 percent in Kyrgyzstan, and 44 percent in Tajikistan) spoke against such actions, viewing them as harmful to the Russian population of the republic.

These were the views of Russians and Russian-speakers as polled in October 1992. Of course, the prevailing attitudes within the Russian diaspora groups strongly depend on changes in their situation. There are reasons to suggest, for example, that many more Russians in Tajikistan wished to leave the republic after the recent outbreak of civil war there. The basic trends revealed by the poll, however, seem more or less steady.

Minority Rights Violations: Real or Alleged?

Although in all former Soviet republics Russians face socioeconomic hardships and suffer from traumatic psychological experiences, their overall situation is not so bleak in terms of legal status and human rights. Despite the association with discrimination invoked by the very notion of the term "minority," it would be wrong to assume (as some, in fact, do) that all Russian and Russian-speaking minorities in the NIS are discriminated against. In Ukraine, Belarus, and Kazakhstan, where the bulk of the new Russian diaspora is concentrated, ethnic Russians and Russian-speakers have so far enjoyed, for all practical purposes, full equality with the rest of the population. In Central Asia (particularly Tajikistan) and Transcaucasia Russian minorities are vulnerable because of general instability and political conflicts, which have caused many to become refugees; however, there has been no formal discrimination against Russians in these regions, either. The only region of the former USSR where the legal status of Russians and Russian-speakers raises real concern is the Baltics, more specifically, Latvia and Estonia.

The three Baltic states—Estonia, Latvia, and Lithuania—were the first ex-Soviet republics to receive recognition from the world community as sovereign nations, even before the dissolution of the USSR (indeed, most Western governments had never recognized the forcible incorporation of these states into the Soviet Union, which took place in the early period of World War II). Now the Baltic governments, supported by the overwhelming majority of the native populations, rightfully assert that their countries had never joined the USSR and regard the five decades between 1940 and 1991 as the period of unlawful Soviet occupation. After restoration of independence the basic political goal is formulated as liquidating the consequences of the occupation period (so-called de-occupation).

By de-occupying, the Baltic governments seek to reverse the radical change in the ethnic structure of the population that occurred during that period owing to a massive influx of migrants—mostly ethnic Russians and Russian-speakers. This ethnodemographic change was particularly sharp in Latvia, where the share of ethnic Latvians in the population fell from 76 percent in 1935 to 52 percent in 1989, and in Estonia, where the proportion of ethnic Estonians decreased from 92 percent to 63 percent between 1934 and 1989. In Lithuania ethnodemographic proportions were altered to a much lesser extent: in 1989 Lithuanians still made up more than 80 percent of the population of their republic. Obviously, with such a large native population, Lithuania is less tense, allowing the government to be more tolerant of nonnative groups. Indeed, in Lithuania the legal situation of minorities, including Russians and Russian-speakers, is much more favorable than in Latvia or Estonia.

Probably the same logic may be used to explain the fact that in Latvia, where the ethnic Latvians are just a marginal majority in the population, the Russians and Russian-speakers have the most serious reasons to be concerned for their future status and civil, political, and economic rights. The most painful issue is that of citizenship. In late 1991 the Latvian parliament adopted a provisional resolution under which citizenship is recognized only to those who were citizens on 17 June 1940 (the moment of Soviet occupation), and their descendants. Other residents could acquire citizenship by naturalization following the adoption of a citizenship law, the draft of which is still under consideration by the parliament.

According to the draft law, certain categories of inhabitants closely linked to the former Soviet army, police, and security service would be permanently excluded from acquiring Latvian citizenship through naturalization. Other permanent residents of Latvia may acquire citizenship through naturalization, according to yearly quotas to be established by the parliament (many nonnative Latvians fear that the quotas would be too low, and naturalization of all residents might take several decades). The basic conditions of naturalization are sixteen years of permanent residence; mastery of the Latvian language at a conversational level, to be established through examinations; a loyalty oath; knowledge of the basic principles of the constitution; and renunciation of (expatriation from) previous citizenship.

Although the requirements for naturalization may hardly be seen as discriminatory in nature, much would depend on how these requirements are understood in their practical application. There is fear among the non-Latvian population that, for example, many permanent residents may in fact be disqualified because of temporary sojourns abroad, including for purposes of study. There are also reported cases of denying naturalization to persons only marginally linked to the former Soviet army, even to long-divorced wives of Soviet officers. A big problem is also posed by the procedure of language examination (required, incidentally, not only in connection with naturalization, but also in relation to access to public employment and education, according to the Language Law of 1989). Many Russian-speakers perceive the examinations as a form of harassment.

The issue of citizenship is vital indeed for the minorities (Russian and Russian-speakers) not only for political reasons. Besides being excluded from political life through denial of suffrage, noncitizens expect to receive unequal treatment economically—they might be discriminated against in the privatization process (distribution of privatization certificates). Many non-Latvians fear that they might not even be able to acquire the apartments where they currently reside.

There may also be discrimination against minorities with regard to freedom of movement, since the relevant Latvian law grants the right "to freely leave Latvia and to freely return to Latvia" only to its citizens, which may imply that noncitizens do not enjoy the right to return to Latvia.

In Estonia the legal status of Russians and Russian-speakers is basically the same as in Latvia. After February 1992, when the Estonian parliament reenacted the citizenship law of 1938, most of them became noncitizens; besides being disenfranchised, they are now subject to a degree of discrimination with regard to public employment and some other types of jobs, landownership, freedom of expression, and political activities (these and other legal limitations for noncitizens have been inserted into the constitution). On the positive side, however, there is some hope for eventual facilitation of the naturalization procedure. A draft law that is now under consideration by the Estonian parliament would grant Estonian nationality to some categories of present noncitizens: spouses and children of Estonian citizens, and natives of Estonia applying for citizenship a year before they come of age, among others.

Abiding by International Human Rights Standards: The Case of Latvia

It is highly debatable whether Latvian and Estonian minority policies[8] are in violation of international law and generally accepted human rights standards.

Naturally enough, both Baltic governments deny allegations of such violations, whereas the government of Russia, and Russian national-patriots, insist that violations exist. In this context particular importance should be attached to the views of the international community and its authoritative organizations concerned with human and minority rights protection. It would seem that, at least until recently, the United Nations, the Conference on Security and Cooperation in Europe (CSCE), the Council of Europe, and other influential international organizations were just not responsive enough to the issue, despite the persistent diplomatic efforts of the Russian Foreign Ministry.

The first practical action taken within the UN framework was sending a fact-finding mission to Latvia on 27–30 October 1992 to "investigate alleged discriminatory practices against minorities in that country." The mission met with the highest Latvian officials as well as with representatives of different minority groups and associations. It considered and analyzed a number of relevant legislative acts and government instructions, and received several hundred petitions from groups and individuals.

The mission made the following general assessment of the situation in Latvia:

> Latvia is going through a transitional period following the reestablishment of independence. During this period the Latvian government is endeavoring to redress certain historical inequities and injustices perpetrated during Soviet rule from 1940 to 1991.
>
> This has given rise to anxiety among the non-ethnic Latvians about their future status and role in the country. It is this sense of insecurity rather than any gross violation of human rights that is most characteristic of the situation prevailing in Latvia today.[9]

The principal conclusion was that

> The information received and examined by the Mission does not reveal gross and systematic violations of human rights in Latvia. Individual violations which have been reported are limited and not related to discriminatory policy as such and they should and can be remedied at the appropriate level. On the positive side, it should be emphasized that no instances of violence, no mass dismissals from employment, exclusion from educational establishments, eviction from apartments, or expulsions were reported.[10]

The report of the mission admitted, however, that

> A large percentage of the residents of the country do not yet have Latvian citizenship and they fear marginalization. The fear of marginalization by denial of citizenship and of fundamental rights related to it is real and in some cases well-founded. This creates a situation which is not conducive to harmonious inter-ethnic relations and as such poses a potentially destabilizing factor.[11]

The mission offered the Latvian government several concrete recommendations, advising it, for example, to amend the draft law on citizenship so as to lower the residence requirement from sixteen years to five years; to grant noncitizens more rights, including that of participation in the privatization process; and to ease the language requirements to obtain citizenship.

It is particularly noteworthy that the mission, though recommending that Latvia, for humanitarian reasons, should extend nationality to the majority of its permanent residents, found that "Latvia is not in breach of international law by the way it determines the criteria for granting its citizenship." Of course, many would disagree with this conclusion; indeed, a situation in which nearly 50 percent of the population of a state are regarded as stateless or foreigners, despite the fact that most of them were born in that country or have lived there for many years, hardly seems compatible with basic human rights standards. It would seem that the Latvian (and Estonian) situation reveals some fundamental shortcomings in international legal provisions concerning the granting of citizenship. In any case, the very precedent of invoking international law and assistance from international organizations in the field of minority protection in the NIS should be perceived as encouraging.

The Impact of the Minorities Issue on Russian Domestic and Foreign Policies

As noted, the problems of the Russian diaspora in the NIS are highly important in the context of domestic political and ideological struggles in Russia. The issue is actively played upon by the conservative opposition to the president and the government, which is now a coalition between Communists and Russian nationalists or, as they prefer to call themselves, patriots. For all the original ideological differences between "proletarian internationalists" and "great-power chauvinists," both groups have found a fundamental common value: the ideal of a strong centralized multinational state modeled either on the tsarist Russian Empire or the Communist Soviet Union.

The "communo-patriots," often dubbed the "Red-and-Brown," perceive the very existence of numerous Russian populations in the ex-Soviet states, let alone real or alleged mistreatment of the Russian groups, as powerful substantiation of their favorite idea of restoring the unity of the empire, be it Russian or Soviet. Before this goal is attained, they demand that Russia ensure the rights and interests of its "compatriots" in the neighboring states by forcible methods, completely ignoring the sovereignty of those states. They vehemently attack the government, and Foreign Minister Andrei

Kozyrev personally, for what they call betrayal of Russians outside Russia to "local nationalists" and "world imperialism."

The so-called Russian National Council, headed by former KGB general Aleksandr Sterligov, states in its program documents:

> Many thousand Russians, making up nearly 80 percent of the working population in the republics, became hostages in the intrigues of political leaders, and found themselves, despite the historical rights of the Russian people, on the territories allocated to other states. The Russian National Council warns all existing governments on the territory of the CIS as well as all public organizations and parties that they are responsible for ensuring the rights and interests of Russian people.[12]

Rhetoric on the problem of the Russian diaspora has been used not only by the hard-boiled Red-and-Brown, but also by so-called enlightened patriots —politicians trying to combine commitment to democracy and reform with emphasis on patriotism and traditional national values. Sergei Stankevich, for example, a prominent, if young, politician who until recently served as personal advisor to President Yeltsin on political issues, has written,

> In the newly emerged sovereign states outside Russia there are over twenty-five million people affiliated with us historically and culturally. Russia is responsible for their destinies. And it will not allow anyone to humiliate them, to slight them, to discriminate against them. Let alone to kill them.
>
> From now on in dealing with Russia you will be facing not a ruined empire, but a power [*derzhava*]. The Russian power has a millennium-long history, legitimate vital interests, and longstanding serious traditions in defending these interests.[13]

With full understanding of the risk involved in historical analogies, one might compare Stankevich's statement with an excerpt from Hitler's speech in the German Reichstag on 20 February 1938:

> Over ten million Germans live in two of the states adjoining our frontiers. There must be no doubt about one thing. Political separation from the Reich may not lead to deprivation of rights—that is, the general rights of self-determination. It is unbearable for a world power to know there are racial comrades at its side who are constantly being afflicted with the severest suffering for their sympathy or unity with the whole nation, its destiny and its *Weltanschauung*. To the interest of the German Reich belongs the protection of those German peoples who are not in a position to secure along our frontiers their political and spiritual freedom by their own efforts.[14]

Even without invoking such ominous associations, it is quite obvious that if Russia really chooses to intervene on behalf of Russian minorities in, say, Latvia or Estonia, by force or threat of force, the result would be disastrous not only for Russia (such a development would certainly disrupt friendly relations between Russia and the West, with many adverse political and economic implications), but also for the minorities thus "protected." In the words of Andrei Kozyrev:

> None of the conflicts can be resolved by force! There are only two possible ways of action. Either to be consistent, acting in the spirit of "The Father of Peoples" [Stalin], in the spirit of the GKChP [the leaders of the August Coup of 1991]—that is, to occupy the territories of the republics with troops, to exile and shoot millions of people, to establish a reign of terror. Or to resolve everything peacefully, on the basis of international law, in a civilized way. There is no other method to protect Russian-speakers among other peoples. You cannot send a "blue helicopter" to guard every Russian-speaking child on his way to school. What are we going to bomb—perhaps cities with mixed populations? And if our blunders provoke Russophobia there—that would be a real national betrayal perpetrated by national-patriots.
>
> Russians in the republics may become hostages of national-patriots if they are perceived not as loyal citizens, highly skilled workers and bearers of European culture, but as a sort of "fifth column" of an imperialistic power. They would have either to emigrate, or to take up arms. The decent way of behavior is to accept the sovereignty of the country and its laws, asserting one's rights by legal means.[15]

Russian policy on the issue of Russian minorities in the NIS should be based on the internationally recognized priority of human and minority rights over the prohibition of intervention in the internal affairs of the state. Russia may and should be concerned not only for its ethnic kinsfolk in the NIS, but for the general condition of human rights in these countries. To be sure, this concern does not exclude special assistance to Russian and Russian-speaking minorities, to help them preserve and promote their culture and identity. In case of gross violations of human and minority rights in some of the NIS states, Russia should use all possibilities of control and mediation provided by international organizations involved in human rights protection, such as the UN, the CSCE, and the Council of Europe.[16]

It seems natural to suggest that minority rights protection in the NIS could also be facilitated through an international organization uniting most of the independent states (except for the Baltics, Georgia, and Azerbaijan) —the Commonwealth of Independent States (CIS). Such hope was recently expressed by President Boris Yeltsin in his address to the leaders of the CIS countries:

> We in Russia deem it important that our cooperation should involve joint protection of internationally recognized human rights from manifestations of

aggressive nationalism. The Russian Federation guarantees all its citizens, irrespective of ethnic or other differences, equal rights and freedoms, promotes necessary conditions to preserve and enhance the linguistic, cultural, and religious identities of all peoples inhabiting Russia. Of course, we expect that ethnic Russians and Russian-speakers in other states would be granted the same rights. I believe that the world community would meet positively a clear and firm position taken by the CIS countries on this problem, largely determining the prospects for our cooperation in other fields, including economic interaction.[17]

Many analysts (including this author) think, however, that the general potential of the CIS is, and will remain, essentially limited. The member countries of the commonwealth are too diverse in terms of economic development, political systems, cultural characteristics, and international orientations. Moreover, political discords between some of them (most notably, between Russia and Ukraine) are now deeper than between them and third parties. The rudimentary supranational bodies of the CIS are bound to remain weak, and this weakness will preclude effective integration. So it seems reasonable to suggest that Russia develop its relations with the NIS mainly through bilateral contacts as well as within broader international frameworks provided by the UN and the CSCE. Of course, this conclusion also applies to diplomatic interaction concerning the problems of the Russian diaspora.

Among the many specific issues in bilateral relations between Russia and the NIS, and closely associated with the situation of Russian minorities, there is one that deserves special mention. This is the problem of the withdrawal of Russian (former Soviet) military forces from the Baltic states, particularly Estonia and Latvia. It seems that this issue is one of the few points on which Russian foreign policy has been heavily influenced by pressure from the nationalistic opposition.

The approach of the Russian leadership to the problem has been anything but consistent. Since fall 1991 leading Russian bodies and officials, including the Supreme Soviet, the president, and the defense minister, have repeatedly come out in favor of the idea of linkage between the timetable for troop withdrawal from the Baltics and the condition of minorities (Russians and Russian-speakers) in these states. Many of these statements were eventually retracted, only to be reiterated afterward. The latest linkage-favoring statement was made by Yeltsin at a press conference in Vancouver on 4 April 1993.[18]

The idea of this linkage clearly contradicts international legal provisions prohibiting a foreign military presence in peacetime on the territory of a state without its explicit consent. Moreover, any protraction in Russian troop withdrawal from Latvia and Estonia can only aggravate internal tensions, leading to further deterioration in the condition of Russian minorities. A relevant observation has been made by Tatiana Zhdanok, a member of the Latvian parliament and a prominent champion of minority rights:

> I cannot understand the linkage between human rights issues and troop withdrawal from the Baltics. The Latvian parliament has just passed a resolution saying that granting citizenship through naturalization is impossible in the presence of Russian troops. One of the deputies remarked, "As long as the army is here, not a single noncitizen will be granted nationality. Don't you even dream of it."[19]

It is no coincidence that the linkage idea is resolutely opposed by Western governments: Stern statements on the issue were recently made by the defense ministers of the United States, Great Britain, the Netherlands, Iceland, and Canada.[20] The Russian government should not risk opportunities of cooperation with the world community in the field of human and minority rights protection in the NIS. It should be noted that these opportunities have become better, thanks to the renewed emphasis on human rights by the new U.S. administration. The issue of Russian minorities in the former USSR was recently mentioned in the Vancouver declaration by Presidents Yeltsin and Clinton on 4 April:

> Admitting that violation of rights of minorities and ethnic communities has been an increasingly important source of international instability, both parties have emphasized the importance of full protection of human rights, including the rights of ethnic Russians and other minorities on the territory of the former USSR. The presidents reaffirmed their commitment to peaceful settlement of conflicts in that region on the basis of respect for independence, territorial integrity, and security interests of all states—members of the UN and the CSCE.[21]

Of course, statements like this should not make one overoptimistic with regard to immediate prospects for international (for that matter, U.S.) involvement in the field of minorities protection in the post-Soviet space. As far as Russian foreign policy is concerned, however, the most promising, if not the only sound, approach to the issue implies invoking the relevant international legal provisions and seeking mediation and cooperation from the international community.

There is reason to believe that the massive "patriotic" propaganda effort that intended to use the plight of Russian minorities to trigger violent nationalistic outbursts in Russia has so far evoked only limited response among the population at large. In February and March 1992 the Vox Populi public opinion service, headed by sociologist Boris Grushin, undertook a representative poll asking two thousand subjects in all major regions of Russia about their attitudes toward the Russian minorities issue.[22] As might have been expected, most of those polled proved to be somewhat biased in their judgments: 35 percent of them attributed the minority-related tensions to the "negative attitude toward Russians among the indigenous populations," 22 percent to the "discrimination against Russians by the local governments," and 25 percent to "lack of protection of Russians from the government of Russia." Yet only 14 percent admitted that the unhappy situation resulted from the Russians themselves being "reluctant to adapt to other national cultures." Moreover, the poll has indicated that no more than a quarter of the Russian electorate advocate toughening Russian policies on the minorities issue. Obviously, even fewer people in Russia would now support actual use of force to resolve the problem of the minorities. And yet, a new wave of aggressive Russian nationalism is by no means inconceivable. Any tangible improvement in the condition of the Russian minorities in the NIS would certainly help prevent it.

Notes

1. Here and below statistical data are drawn from unpublished sources of the Russian State Committee on Statistics (Goskomstat).
2. The data below refer only to ethnic Russians, since the category of Russian-speakers has not been covered by the statistics. There are, however, reasons to believe that there is no great difference between ethnic Russians and Russian-speakers in terms of demographic characteristics or socioeconomic status.
3. See Iu.V. Arutiunian and L.M. Drobizheva, "Russkie raspodaiushego soiuza," *Otechestvennaia istoriia,* 1992, no. 3, pp. 4–6.
4. Some of this migration took place in the course of evacuation of industrial personnel to the east of the country in the initial phase of the Soviet-German war (1941–45). See N. Rudensky, "War as a Factor of Ethnic Conflict and Stability in the USSR," in *Effects of War on Society,* ed. G. Ausenda (San Marino, 1992), p. 189.
5. See "Government Policy to Support Russians in Former Soviet Republics: Social and Economic Aspects" (unpublished report prepared by the State Committee for Cooperation with the CIS Countries [Goskomsotrudnichestvo], Moscow, 1993), p. 5.
6. L.M. Drobizheva, "Russkiie v novykh gosudarstv: Izmenenie sotsial'nykh rolikh," in *Rossiia segodnia: Trudnye poiski svobody,* ed. L. Shevtsova (Moscow, 1993), p. 213.
7. See A. Vishnevskii and Zh. Zaionchkovskaia, *Migratsiia iz SSSR: Chetvertaia volna* (Moscow, 1991), vol. 3, p. 12.
8. It should be noted in passing that the term "minority" is, technically speaking, hardly applicable to nonnative populations of Latvia and Estonia, since in international law the concept of national or ethnic minority is usually confined to citizens of the state in question.
9. From preliminary draft report provided by the commission to the Committee on Human Rights of the Russian parliament.

10. Ibid.
11. Ibid.
12. "Materialy Uchreditel'nogo s''ezda Russkogo natsional'nogo sobora," Nizhnii Novgorod, 1992.
13. S. Stankevich, "Iavlenie derzhava," *Rossiiskaia gazeta*, 23 June 1992. By the way, in the fall of 1992 President Yeltsin put Stankevich in charge of compiling a comprehensive report on the problem of Russian and Russian-speaking minorities in the NIS. Unfortunately, the report, completed in early 1993, has not been made public.
14. Quoted by W. Shirer, *The Rise and Fall of the Third Reich: A History of Nazi Germany* (Greenwich, CT: Simon & Schuster, 1960), pp. 453–54.
15. A. Kozyrev, "Partiia voiny nastupaet," in *God posle Avgusta: Gorechi' i vybor*, ed. Iu. Afanas'ev and Iu. Burtin (Moscow, 1992), p. 163.
16. In this context Russia's ill-fated attempt to obstruct Latvian and Estonian membership in the Council of Europe was clearly counterproductive.
17. *Nezavisimaia gazeta*, 18 March 1993.
18. A complete rejection of the linkage was voiced some days later by Sergei Stepashin, chairman of the parliament's Committee on Defense and Security. See *Nezavisimaia gazeta*, 13 April 1993.
19. T. Zhdanok, "Russkii vopros v Latvii: Narushenie prav chelovek," *Izvestiia*, 28 September 1992.
20. See N. Pachegina, "Moskva priostanavliavaet vyvod voisk iz Pribaltiki," *Nezavisimaia gazeta*, 31 March 1993.
21. *Izvestiia*, 6 April 1993.
22. See B. Grushin, "Russkie men'shinstvo v vospriiatii russkogo bol'shinstva," *Problemy Vostochnoi Evropy*, 1993, no. 37–38, pp. 226–34.

4
The Paradox of Russian National Identity

Gregory Guroff and Alexander Guroff

Russia is a puzzling, unknown country. It has turned out that we know nothing about it. Therefore it is probably why we have lived with such difficulty and so stupidly. Where is the path to the renaissance? A people without its own clan, without tribes, without parents, without history, without historical experience, will never be able to get onto that path. Thus, we have to remember who we are, who are our parents, who is the mother of our land . . . Russia.

Stanislav Govorukhin, *The Russia We Lost*

The paradox of Russia's current search for a national identity is readily apparent on the streets of Moscow. Just a few years ago, Boris Yeltsin stood on a tank in front of the Russian "White House" and stared down the leaders of the August putsch. Today, members of the "State Committee for the State of Emergency" (GKChP) rally their supporters in front of this same building under banners demanding a return to a bygone era. Meanwhile, Yeltsin and his advisors have taken up residence in the Kremlin buildings that had been the headquarters of the GKChP in August 1991 and, until December 1991, had been the focal point of Communist Party power in the former Soviet Union. This turn of events is illustrative not only of the two main forces currently fighting to define Russia's future; it is also illustrative of the evolving paradoxes and fluctuating currents of the debate itself.

In studying the collapse of the Soviet Union, Western observers have paid little attention to Russian ethnic identity. As Russians struggle to assert a new identity in the post-Soviet world, the West has paid little attention to this process. The West has rallied to support all forms of nationalist movements within the former republics of the Soviet Union with the explicit exception of Russia. These movements for local control coincided with the West's desire to break up the Soviet Union. Little attention was actually paid to the substance of these movements, as the primary goal was destruction of the empire. More often than not, however, the Russian search for ethnic identity was defined by its radical fringe. Ignoring the need for national renewal and a strengthened Russian national identity, the West has opposed growing Russian nationalism for fear that it represents a return to a Moscow-centered empire. The presence of such elements in the current wave of Russian nationalism is undeniable, but it is the degree of influence of such elements that must be weighed. In the end, this analysis is often the victim of its own hysteria, for it fails to examine the healthy development of a new Russian identity and focuses only on its most diseased aspects.

When Aleksandr Solzhenitsyn's article "How Are We to Structure Russia?—A Modest Contribution" appeared in *Komsomol'skaia pravda* and *Literaturnaia gazeta* in September 1990, it marked not only the first time his work had appeared in the Soviet press since *Ivan Denisovich,* but also the beginning of a debate in the mainstream media on Russia's new identity in the post-Soviet world. Certainly, a reevaluation of the Soviet Union's global role had begun several years before in the early stages of glasnost, but this article focused on Russia and the Russians.

In 1988 Russian nationalists began to form organizations and parties that advocated a return to Russian roots. For these movements, this meant a return to autocracy, anti-Semitism, and xenophobia. Although well publicized and well organized at the time, these ultranationalist parties were largely marginal. In 1989 and 1990 candidates running on electoral slates endorsed by Pamyat and other nationalist organizations failed to gain popular election to either the USSR or RSFSR Congresses of People's Deputies.[1] The publication of the Solzhenitsyn article brought the issue to the mainstream press. In his article, Solzhenitsyn formulated the question as follows:

> This notion of "Russia" is already tattered and torn; everyone uses this notion, whether appropriately or not. When the monstrous USSR went to grab slices of Asia or Africa, the entire world repeated: "Russia, the Russians ... "
> *What* exactly is Russia? Today, and tomorrow (even more importantly). *Who* sees himself as part of the future Russia? *Where* do the Russians themselves envisage the borders of Russia?[2]

It is this question that was echoed by Stanislav Govorukhin nearly two years later when he released his documentary film, *The Russia We Lost.* While the question today is well formed, the answer remains difficult and vague. In fact, it is this ambiguity that defines the current level of debate about national identity in Russia. After a thousand years of history, Russia finds itself a country without a national identity, whose future is uncertain and whose past full of suffering and tragedy. Russia is a country struggling to emerge from the remnants of a collapsed empire, an empire built, in large part, on Russian tradition, an empire that since 1917 had been the cornerstone of Russian national identity. Russian identity today is in many ways the product of great achievements as much as it is the victim of those achievements. Russian identity today is the paradox of power and the powerlessness engendered by the dissolution of this power.

To understand the present situation and future course of Russian national identity, it is necessary to look first at the constant determinants, geographic and others. It is important to begin with the basic elements of Russian identity and the concrete aspects of its national interests. From there, the historical components of Russian identity will be analyzed. Finally, the impact on Russian foreign policy of this evolving Russian identity will be examined.

Russian Identity: A Product of Geography

Russia's geographical position itself defines many of the country's strengths and weaknesses. The Russian physical landscape reflects many of the strengths and weaknesses of the Russian experience. It is a country at once geographically imposing and geographically weak, a country of lengthy borders that provide no natural barrier to invasion, a country of great expanses of land that are largely uninhabitable and infertile.

Russia is a country whose land stretches across both Europe and Asia. The sheer spread of the land provides Russia with natural strategic interests throughout Europe, the Middle East, the Indian subcontinent, and the Far East. Without any expansionary interests, Russia as a country must carefully monitor events in these regions, as any one region's problems could potentially spill into Russia. Russia is a country whose geography has provided scores of invaders from the Mongols to Napoleon to the Nazis with easy access to its heartland. At the same time, it is a country whose brutal weather has repelled these same foes with equal power.

Russia's geographical position is a fundamental factor in the Russians' sense that they are different—not part of the European family or the West, but surely not part of Asia either. The Westernizer-Slavophile battles, often based in geographical or geopolitical terminology, of the nineteenth century were but one episode in a struggle for the Russian consciousness that has gone on for centuries. Held deeply is the sense that there is (or at least there ought to be) a Russian path that belongs uniquely to Russia. It is a feeling of being part of a long, tortured history.

Many Western experts have written that the primary goal of the current reform movement in Russia is to transform the country into a Western-style democracy and market-based economy. While Yeltsin in many ways seeks the approval, advice, and assistance of the West, it is his goal to reform and redefine Russia within a unique Russian framework. Successful reform in Russia will have more to do with its Russian past and traditions than its Western advisors. This is not to say that Russia must be governed autocratically because it has in the past. It is to say that Yeltsin and his allies do not see the current reform process as an attempt to re-create the United States or any other country on Russian soil. Reform in Russia is to rebuild Russia while maintaining the fundamental belief in Russia's unique place in the world.

No less important than the size and location of the country, the Russian land itself has symbolized the essence of Russia and Russian identity in the country's intellectual debates. Writers from Aleksandr Radishchev and Fyodor Dostoevsky to Valentin Rasputin and Aleksandr Solzhenitsyn have elevated the Russian land to the status of a religion in and of itself. The Russian steppe, the Siberian taiga, and the peasant villages of the Black Earth region are all aspects of Russia's traditional identity. Even today, urban Russians regularly flee the city to return to their dachas in the countryside, or, for a decreasing number, the villages of their ancestors, preserving at least symbolically the attachment to the land. As Yevgeny Yevtushenko put it, the rapid increase in the construction of dachas around Moscow is representative of Muscovites' desires to "touch one's land with one's own hands."[3]

It is the paradox and tragedy of contemporary Russia that the land that is so vital to its own identity has been one of the primary victims of its most recent history. The Soviet period and the triumphs of industrialization exacted a heavy toll. Once fertile lands now lie barren from overfertilization. Great expanses in Siberia have been ravaged for the natural resources they contain. Many of the rivers of Russia are now impassable as a result of the debris on the riverbeds. Lake Baikal, one of the great treasures of the world, has been irreversibly contaminated by a pulp plant operating on its shores. In Moscow, the population halted the traditional mushroom harvest in September 1992 for fear that the mushrooms had been irradiated.[4]

The place of the Russian land in the national identity of Russians was clearly evidenced in the mid-1980s. It should not be forgotten that the sources of early Russian national movements under glasnost lay in popular environmental movements. Russian popular movements to oppose the diversion of Siberian rivers, the pollution of Lake Baikal, and the expansion of the nuclear power industry were some of the most successful early features of democratization during the mid-1980s. These movements grew into focal points for the rebirth of Russian nationalism. It should be noted that this process was not unique to Russia, but also was witnessed in Belarus, Ukraine, and Kazakhstan. It was revelations about environmental degradation throughout the regions of the Soviet Union that propelled the early grassroots movements for local control.

Russian Identity: A Product of History

In the fifteenth century, two monks, Iosif Sanin and Nil Sorskii, battled for the soul of Russia. It was an obscure battle, but one that had a profound impact not simply on the Russian church but also on the development of Russian culture and society. It was the first in a series of such battles that would lead to the emergence of the Old Believers in the seventeenth century. The battle took place in a society where national identity was defined not by ethnicity but by religion. To be Russian was to be *pravoslavnaia* (Orthodox). Sanin held that proper belief came from the repetition of ritual, from the visual splendor of the churches and their iconography. To produce this overpowering church culture, the church required land and wealth. Nil Sorskii believed that religious truth came from inner struggle. Sorskii's church required neither wealth nor power. The clergy through their own example of simple living and religious searching would lead the people.[5]

Ivan III (the Great), the ruling monarch, was attracted by Sorskii's vision because he could enrich the state by seizing church lands. Sanin's view, however, which saw the head of state as the head of the church, provided a much stronger bedrock for the creation of a glorious and wealthy monarchy. Ivan III, therefore, opted for the Sanin approach. The Orthodox Church slowly became an instrument of the state, but the state was also created in the image of the church. Both in religious and civil affairs, creativity and individuality were shunned in favor of ritual response, for ritual response would eventually be internalized and turned into positive belief. It was important to learn not only the right answer, but the proper method to the answer as well. Within Russian culture, the method itself became a correct answer.

The infinite flexibility of the Russian people to live in two worlds, however, allowed the Sorskii approach to live in harmony with the established church. The Russian religion had itself been created on the basis of a dual belief (*dvoeveriia*). From the outset, Russian Orthodoxy was distinguished from Western Catholicism. Conversion in the "Greek" or Eastern Orthodox Church utilized the vernacular language, even when written languages had to be created by the missionaries themselves. Local priests depended on oral communications, for they often could not read the original Greek scriptures and scholarly texts. In such circumstances it was easy to incorporate local customs into the religion, and one could remain true to both the new and the old beliefs. Both church and parishioners were pleased. The church won its converts, and the parishioners, while participating in the new church, were able to maintain their old beliefs and traditions. Given these circumstances, local variations were quick to develop, and regular convocations of church elders were necessary to bring a sense of order and coherence to church rituals and doctrine.

Two hundred years after the Sanin-Sorskii confrontation, the Great Church Council of 1666 met to resolve a similar confrontation between churchmen. In this debate, however, the state played an even more commanding role. Patriarch Nikon had attempted to elevate his position of patriarch to that of coequal with the young Tsar Aleksei Mikhailovich. Nikon had utilized the "regathering" of the Russian lands and the reestablished connections with Byzantine scholarship through the Kievan clergy to assert the authority of the church in matters of faith and ritual. But because this modification of the rituals was accomplished by reference to the Byzantine books, the reaction among the parish priests was fierce. Led by Father Avvakum, they argued that these changes in ritual had to be confirmed by the church elders and not simply by reference to recently discovered scriptures.

The Church Council of 1666 was to include all the Eastern Church Patriarchs (Constantinople, Alexandria, etc.) partially in an attempt to give the council greater legitimacy by invoking the wisdom of the church elders to support the decisions. The council, while approving the Nikonian reforms, removed him from office and exiled him for exceeding his authority. At the same time, the council rejected Avvakum's opposition and condemned him to death. The state was the big winner, gaining prestige from the Church Council and removing rivals on all sides. Like Sanin and Sorskii before them, Nikon and Avvakum fought heroically against each other, only to witness the further advance of the secular state that they both had opposed.[6]

The important point for our purposes is that for the population the acceptable authority came from the accumulated wisdom passed down through the generations. Scholarship based on analysis of written documents was treated with skepticism that verged on total rejection. And, in good Russian tradition, some of the Old Believers left the society, condemning it as anti-Christian, but the great majority of people who accepted the tenets of the Old Belief stayed, at least formally, with the church. It was estimated that nearly half of the Orthodox believers at the beginning of the twentieth century continued to adhere to many of the tenets of the Old Belief, but regularly attended the established church.

It may be too great a leap to suggest that this medieval tradition is the basis of Russian identity today. The development of the Russian Orthodox

Church, however, provides both a background and a framework for understanding many of the issues in the present search for a new Russian identity. Russian Orthodoxy has evolved through centuries of crisis and conflict, but remains today a unified entity. It is, nonetheless, an entity whose future is clouded and uncertain. Russian Orthodoxy must renew itself to push on into the next century. The history of Russian Orthodoxy is not the history of Russia or the Russians, but they have all traveled the same path and today stand at similar crossroads.

From the above discussion, many aspects of Russian culture can be understood. It is, for example, easy to see the source of the contemporary belief that what people read in the press is much less believable than what is passed on to them by close friends. Even today, Russians still feel that they must read between the lines to figure out what is really happening. Equally clear is the persistence of folk remedies and faith healers, which naturally calls scientific practices into question. These phenomena can be explained by the clearly unbelievable information conveyed, for generations in the Soviet press and the truly abysmal state of Soviet medical care. Nonetheless, the tradition of oral wisdom has prepared the soil for the acceptance of this pattern. And, because it is so deeply laid in this society, it will survive despite accurate information from official sources.

The history of Russian Orthodoxy provides insight into the Russians' ability to preserve within themselves an acceptance of the Russian church, often including belief, while appearing at the same time to adhere to Soviet-imposed atheism. It is this tradition perhaps more than anything else that helps us understand how the trappings of Soviet society have so quickly disappeared. While many Russians followed Soviet dictates, this practice concealed an underlying connection with more distant Russian roots.

In the case of other peoples of the former Soviet Union, similar phenomena are observable. Much of the Islamic culture of Central Asia was preserved among the peoples of the region. The Baltic peoples also maintained strong ethnic identities. The preservation of the native culture in these areas was fueled by local attempts to resist Moscow-imposed control and assimilation. Cultural identity became a fundamental weapon in the battle against the Soviet state. For Russians, however, the Soviet state had adopted many Russian traditions. The maintenance of these traditions in many ways contributed to the authority of the Soviet system.

The evolution of the Russian Orthodox Church as an instrument of the state also provides a clear parallel for the development of Russia within the Soviet state. The church has always been an organ of the Russian state, both under the tsar and under the Soviet Union. Likewise, the tsar employed the power of the church to validate his rule. Only in 1905 was the magical religious power of the tsar over the people of Russia truly broken. After the October Revolution, the Orthodox Church sought to preserve itself through subjugation to the atheist policies of the Soviet state. The church's commitment to the state as an institution was, it would appear, stronger than its commitment to worship and to the celebration of God. Neither in tsarist Russia nor in the Soviet Union has the Orthodox Church played an active role in the protection of human rights or religious tolerance. After the collapse of the Romanov dynasty, the church was forced to assert its own identity. Simultaneously, the Bolshevik leaders were faced with the need to establish their own legitimacy. Under Stalin, the Soviet state moved to adopt many of the traditions of the Russian Orthodox Church as a means of supporting the Soviet state. Some members of the hierarchy of the Russian Orthodox Church responded to Stalin's overtures.[7] During this period, the established church became a pillar of support for the Soviet state. However, by the curious logic of the Soviet system, the church was also a locus of potential opposition that had to be contained. Church property was confiscated, monasteries and church schools were closed, and the clergy was systematically annihilated. The church hierarchy that emerged was totally subservient to its new Soviet masters.

As with the rest of Russian society, the Russian Orthodox Church is once again facing an identity crisis. The established church has been rocked by revelations about direct involvement of many church leaders with the KGB. While millions of Russians search for traditions to cling to, they have not all necessarily returned to Orthodoxy. Even many of those who have attended church services do not always share any religious fervor, but rather come out of curiosity. In search of spiritual fulfillment, Russians today have in increasing numbers turned to Mormonism, Baptism, and Buddhism. Possibly as a result of its past subservience to the Soviet state, Orthodoxy can no longer lay claim to the same allegiance of the Russian people. This fate may not be unique to Orthodoxy, as other traditional Russian values and icons once manipulated by the Soviet state may find themselves discarded by postcommunist Russia.

Today, Russians must define a new identity separate from the one that previously rested squarely on the international power of the Soviet Union. The Russian people must define themselves as independent of that which had been their most visible symbol. They must separate themselves from what they were and establish what they will be.

For years, we have asked friends, family, colleagues, and acquaintances what it means to be Russian. One would expect that the answers would come easily and naturally, but quite the reverse is true. Answers come haltingly, often with great reluctance. In an era of heightened national consciousness throughout Eastern Europe and the former Soviet Union, ethnic origin has once again become the basis for the creation of states. Conflict based solely on ethnic origin has scourged the land. In such an environment, one would think that Russians, over 150 million strong, would not hesitate to voice their own ethnic pride. However, today more than ever before, the concept of "Russianness" is complicated even for Russians to express.

In part, as we argue above, the national consciousness of many nationalities within the former Soviet Union was honed in opposition to the Soviet center. The Soviet center, however, was undeniably Russian in many of its core components and symbols. While the peoples of the Baltics and Central Asia could attack the Soviet state as a foreign occupier, this argument was more difficult for the Russians to pursue. Russians may view themselves as the victims of the Soviet system, but it was in so many ways their system. Expressions of Russian consciousness have long been discouraged and Soviet traditions have been mixed with Russian. As a result, Russians find themselves implicitly at war with themselves and their past in their current search for a national identity.

The difference between "Russian" and "Soviet" is certainly one that has been blurred by time and place. Russian traditions did not stop in 1917. The experiences of seventy-four years under Soviet rule have become inextricably intertwined with and part of the Russian identity. The blending of "Russian" and "Soviet" was not only present in terms of the Communist Party ideology, but was even more pronounced in the daily practices created in the society and fostered by the isolation from the outside world imposed by the Soviet regime. This distinction is further blurred today as Russia maintains many of the political borders of the old Soviet Union. Many right-wing politicians in Russia demand the return of "Russian" lands lost in the collapse of the Soviet Union, one of the more recent examples being the Russian parliament's declaration that Sevastopol in the Crimea is Russian. For Russians themselves, the redefinition of Russia and what it is to be Russian is an even more important and complex question than it is for Western observers.

This distinction is frequently lost in the West, which has carelessly used the terms "Soviet" and "Russian" interchangeably. In 1962, Harrison Salisbury published a book titled *A New Russia?* Certainly, he was writing about the Soviet Union, but the distinction at that point may have seemed insignificant. At the same time, Adam Ulam noted that to understand Soviet foreign policy, it was necessary to examine objectively the dynamics of "Russian politics."[8] Once again, while the focus was the Kremlin and the political circles of the Soviet Union, the term "Russian" was carelessly and mistakenly applied. Soviet leaders themselves were often guilty of the same indiscretions. Gorbachev, on one visit to Kiev, twice referred to the local inhabitants as Russians. Today, we continue to hold Russia responsible for these semantic inconsistencies of the past.

Russians have long argued that one of their principal attributes and chief strengths is their willingness to sacrifice and suffer for their society— indeed, to suffer more than other peoples, especially potential adversaries. This view may be fatalistic, but it also flows from a Russian Orthodox tradition that identifies suffering as the way to salvation. Solzhenitsyn has argued that, today, it is the suffering of the Russian people that is the essence of their identity. It is through this suffering that the Russian people have advanced to a higher level of humanity.

World War II and the continuing memory of the war in the minds of Russians is largely explicable against the background of these beliefs. It is true that the suffering and losses of all the peoples of the Soviet Union are colossal by any measure and would naturally imprint themselves in the memory of anyone. With the Russians, however, there is something more: Ask a Russian about the war and the discussion will begin with the suffering and the losses. There are many messages here, but the most intriguing is the relationship between the feelings of enormous loss and suffering, and the consequent righteousness of the people who suffered and thus the inevitability of victory.

As the war developed, it became increasingly a war for Russian survival, for the *rodina*. The utilization of Russian cultural and historical symbols as synonymous with Soviet traditions had been developing throughout the thirties, nowhere more obviously than in the cinema, with the spate of historical films culminating in the release of *Aleksandr Nevskii,* pitting the Russian peasants against the Teutonic Knights to the strident themes of Sergei Prokofiev. As the western and southern republics were severed from Soviet control, the use of Russian symbols became even more obvious, especially with the partial return to favor of the Russian Orthodox Church. Stalin consciously exploited the remaining vestiges of Russian nationalism that had not been destroyed in the first twenty-five years of Bolshevism to propel the people to heroic deeds in the victory over fascism.

Until recently even the questions of how and why people died during the war were simply not raised.[9] No one asked, for example, if the Soviet leadership and Stalin, in particular, were responsible for the deaths of millions during the war through inadequate prewar preparations and wartime errors. Moreover, the scale of the victims of repression throughout the 1930s was little discussed in public. The fact of the suffering and loss was what was most important.

Finally, World War II was the defining event for the Soviet Union. It can be argued that the Soviet Union was born in the crucible of that war.

Throughout the history of the Soviet Union, successive policies served in large measure to split society. The Red Terror, attacks on specialists, collectivization, industrialization, and the purges all resulted in deep schisms within Soviet society. World War II was the singular event in Soviet history that brought the population, particularly the Russian population, together in opposition, albeit in opposition to an even more horrible alternative.

The powerful hold of World War II on Russian national identity is yet another example of the paradox in which Russians find themselves. Victory over Nazi Germany is their greatest achievement, while the losses incurred are their greatest tragedy. World War II was the high point of Russian unity, but in many ways it was a war that had been fought for a false god. Surely, Stalin had manipulated Russian patriotism to aid the war effort, but just as surely many Russians had fought for Stalin and for the Soviet Union. Stalin, who had cut such deep scars in society through his terror, became the primary unifying symbol of the war as well.

With the demise of the Soviet Union, and with the inexorable march of time, the memory of the war for Russians will inevitably change as Stalin and Soviet history are further debunked. The generation that personally experienced the war is gradually leaving the stage of history. Once every school had veterans visiting the children on holidays; every family could cite from personal experience those relatives who had died. The personal link was critical in keeping the memory alive. How it will change is less certain than the fact that it will change.

Russian Identity: Russian Pride

In his September 1990 article, Solzhenitsyn wrote, "Nothing will convince us that our famine, poverty, premature deaths, the degeneration of children—that any of these troubles are of greater importance than our national pride!"[10] This sentiment is well known to anyone who went shopping with wide-eyed visitors from the Soviet Union, who despite their zeal to purchase Western goods would never admit it. They would discuss it sheepishly and in the end would insist, "*U nas to zhe samoe!*" (We have the same thing) or "*U nas luchshe!*" (We have it better).

Russian pride has developed over the thousand-year history of the people. It is the product of the great military victories won over the centuries. Russian pride is cultivated by its cultural heroes, its composers, its writers, its painters. Russian national pride was augmented by the achievements of the Soviet era in space exploration, athletics, and science. The Russians were proud of the fact that the Soviet Union played an influential role in world events. The Soviet Union had but one equal—the United States.

Few things happened in world affairs without the involvement of the Soviet Union.

December 1991 brought many aspects of Russian national pride to a thunderous halt. The collapse of the Soviet Union, while limiting Russian influence in neighboring republics and countries, marked the end of its influence in Latin America, Africa, and the Far East. The collapse of the Soviet economy has crippled the vaunted military and space program. In fact, the space program in which the Russians had taken such great pride is now headquartered in Kazakhstan as a result of the dissolution of the Soviet Union. After three hundred years as a great power, or as part of a great power, Russia is now looking for financial handouts and humanitarian assistance. Russian athletes competed at the Barcelona Olympics, but had no national anthem to hear on the victory stand. Furthermore, the mythology of the Soviet state has crumbled as material has flowed from the archives illustrating the atrocities and tragedies of the era.

This wave of revelations about the Soviet past has had the most devastating impact on Russian national identity. Not only had the framework of Russian national identity been destroyed, but the responsibility for the creation of this framework was undeniable. It was no longer possible to avoid the complicity of the Russian population in the great Soviet experiment. Russia as a country was forced to deal with the grisly facts about the gulag, the abuse of human rights, the environmental destruction of the land, and the foreign policy legacy of the Soviet Union. To many outside the Soviet Union it was not Ukraine or Belarus that had invaded Hungary in 1956, Czechoslovakia in 1968, or Afghanistan in 1979. It was the Soviet Union that was responsible, and Russia now carried the mantle of the Soviet Union in the popular perception. As James Billington has noted, "There was [in January 1992] a sense that almost everyone had been implicated in the moral degradation of Communism and was now involved in his or her own process of self-cleansing."[11]

In many ways this period of Russian history and Russian national consciousness can be compared to the post-Vietnam/post-Watergate period in the United States, but on a much darker and more grotesque scale. Glasnost opened a Pandora's box of facts and revelations about just how far society had fallen during the Soviet period. The mood at the time seemed to encourage a veritable explosion of muckraking journalism on the horrors of Soviet history as well as on the problems of contemporary society. Russians were treated not only to unceasing exposés of the Stalin period, but also new sensationalism in revealing the devastation of the environment, the rise in crime, and the decay of traditional social values. Public self-flageilation led by the media and the intelligentsia was bound to be of short duration, before the reaction of a proud people began to set in. With a sometimes forced pride, often tinged with some arrogance, Russians are putting an end to their self-deprecation and beginning to search for their new identity in the post-Soviet world.

Much of today's Russian nationalist movement is a direct response to the loss of this pride and national self-assuredness. One of the primary goals of Russia's more assertive foreign policy has been the demand that Russia be treated with respect. This new facet of Russian foreign policy is clearly evident in today's international arena. It is not that they will not support UN action in Bosnia; in many ways it is that they just want to be asked first. As Yeltsin said, he felt the United States had begun to dictate policy to Russia, and he wanted to make clear that Russian foreign policy was formulated in Moscow.[12] The underlying sentiment in current Russian foreign policy pronouncements is that though they may not be a great power at present, they will be again shortly. Russian policy is based on the principle that policy toward Russia should be formulated today on the basis of what Russia will be in the future. This is a tone apparent from Russian talks with Ukraine, Estonia, the United States, and other countries throughout the world.

The Future of Russia: Russian Radical Nationalists

A discussion of the impact of Russian nationalism would be both incomplete and unbalanced without a discussion of the radical elements of Russian nationalism. As noted at the outset, these parties had little electoral impact in 1989 and 1990. By 1991, however, Vladimir Zhirinovsky, running on an openly Russian chauvinist platform, garnered more than six million votes in the Russian presidential election.[13] In 1992, they successfully forced the Yeltsin government to modify its foreign policy and have caused great alarm in the West. In the last several years, the ultranationalist movement has grown in number and sophistication. Many members of the Russian legislature have begun to voice ultranationalist positions. The National Salvation Front has gained much attention for its denunciation of the Yeltsin government and its reform program. The Don Cossacks have undergone a dramatic rebirth in the last two years and now lobby for full-fledged Russian assistance to Serbia. Pamyat has grown in size and has resorted to physical intimidation and virulent anti-Semitism. At a recent trial in Moscow, members of Pamyat packed the courtroom and began to chant, "Save Russia! Kill the Jews!" At the same time, nearly every sober analysis of the real political strength of these groups characterizes them as potentially serious competitors for power in the future, but quite marginal players for now.[14]

Even more alarming is the fact that these extremists have begun to conduct their own foreign policy. Many Don Cossacks have gone to assist Serbs in their war against Bosnian Muslims. Zhirinovsky is training mercenaries to aid the Serbs in the Balkan conflict. Even more alarming is Zhirinovsky's assertion that these people fighting for the Serbs are simply preparing for the larger battle to take place in the future in Russia.

Radical Russian nationalists are xenophobic, racist, and reactionary.[15] Increasingly so, these parties also stand among the most organized groups in current Russian politics. While these forces present a horrible future Russia for the West, questions remain as to their mainstream support and political impact. Until now, Russian ultranationalists have been able to focus attention on themselves and their rhetoric. They have focused Western interest groups on the threat they pose both within Russia and without. It will be up to the more liberal nationalist movement in Russia to confront the ultranationalists. The failure of the more moderate forces in Russia to do so will significantly increase the likelihood of an ultranationalist victory.

Clearly, these groups have forced shifts in government policies and raised issues that have become part of the mainstream debate. They have successfully provoked confrontation with the established government. The future success of ultranationalism in Russia will be determined at the ballot box. The movement currently thrives on the disillusionment and uncertainty of the Russian population. Therefore, it would appear that the creation of a moderate, positive Russian identity would greatly hinder the development of the radical nationalists.

The Future of Russia: Russia and the "Near Abroad"

By far the most complex foreign policy issue for the new Russian state has been relations with the countries of the former Soviet Union. These states were categorized by Sergei Stankevich as the "near abroad." This concept provided a clear expression of the Russian view of these new countries. For Moscow, the former Soviet republics were now independent states, but not entirely foreign countries. Within the "near abroad," there is a broad range of Russian interests and Russian policy.

One of the most pertinent issues in the "near abroad" is the issue of the Russian minorities in this region. It is a ready-made issue for Russian politicians. Though foreign policy is of little concern to the majority of Russians, there is a high level of agreement that Russia must look out for the interests of the Russian minorities. In a December 1992 opinion poll,[16] over 85 percent of the respondents felt that at least under certain conditions Russia was obligated to look out for these minorities.[17]

• Misha is a thirty-year-old metallurgical engineer, who lives with his family in the city of Donetsk. As far as he knows, his forebears left the villages to work in the steel plants and mines emerging along the Don River in the 1880s. His father worked in the same steel factory that Misha now works in.

- Tania is the daughter of well-known musicians who trained generations of musicians in Tashkent. Her father adapted local folk music to symphonic form and has been praised by the local party leadership. She never has known exactly how the family found its way to Tashkent, but it had been talked about in hushed tones and seemed tied to the Great Terror of the 1930s. Her parents always felt themselves among the lucky survivors.
- Boris is a retired naval captain who served in Riga and in the Baltic fleet for nearly his entire adult life. He retired to a small flat in Jurmala, Latvia, by the sea. He and his cronies in this "retirement" colony all considered the sea, the *Pribaltika,* and Jurmala to be their home.
- Slava sits in a crowded flat in Moscow with several friends. They are all refugees from Baku, driven out during the past two years by a rising tide of nationalism, mostly aimed at Armenians, but almost equally affecting Russians. Slava's ancestors came to Baku in the mid-nineteenth century, first as traders, then as managers in the vast oil fields. He continues to speak of Baku as home, although one senses that he knows he will never return.

What all these people have in common is that they are Russians who, until very recently, lived in the Soviet Union. They were Azerbaijani, Latvian, and Uzbek residents, but first and foremost they were Russians who lived in the Soviet Union. Many had roots in the area going back generations. They held prestigious jobs and were part of the privileged class. Suddenly, they found themselves uncomfortable and unwelcome, but with no place to go. First from the Caucasus, especially Baku, the Russians began to move, forced out, migrating north toward Moscow and an uncertain fate. Then from Central Asia, the migration continued. A 1993 study by Moscow's Center for Public Opinion Research estimated that in the former Soviet republics between 10 percent and 37 percent of the Russian population planned to migrate in 1992 alone—37.4 percent in Central Asia and Kazakhstan; 17.9 percent in the Baltic states, Moldova, Georgia, and Armenia; and 10.5 percent in Belarus and Ukraine. This alone would represent a migration of nearly three million people. Tatiana Regent, head of the new Federal Migration Service, has suggested that there may be as many as six million migrants coming to Russia.[18]

Most Russian politicians understand the public mood and have given voice to these concerns. One need not look far for reasons that even the most "liberal" of Russian politicians have expressed concerns about Russian-speaking compatriots. Forced migration caused by ethnic conflict, particularly in Azerbaijan and Tajikistan, keeps the issue alive. Restrictive citizenship laws in Estonia and Latvia[19] have also served to foment Russian anger on this subject. In an election campaign, it would stand to reason that some of the candidates will try to exploit this issue. With the prospects of early elections on the horizon, Yeltsin should take note that more respondents in the December 1992 poll felt that Vice President Aleksandr Rutskoi could best deal with the issue of Russians in the "near abroad."[20]

To Russians, it appeared that the West, in its zeal to put pressure on the Soviet Union, supported almost any national movement that was perceived to be in opposition to the center. The United States embraced movements and individuals as disparate as Rukh and Viacheslav Chornovil in Ukraine, Sajudis and Vytautas Landsbergis in Lithuania, Zviad Gamsakhurdia in Georgia, and Birlik and Mohammed Salykh in Uzbekistan. Simultaneously, Russians observed that while there were more than 150 million Russians searching for their identity, Russian nationalism was usually caricatured, represented by only the most extreme elements.

Relations with the Baltic states are in many ways the most vexing for the current Yeltsin government. Yeltsin and his advisors have felt betrayed by the leaders of the Baltic independence movements, who they feel have forgotten the support they received from the Russian government in their secession movements. This is a sentiment voiced not only by the political elite of Russia, but throughout society. It was Yeltsin who journeyed to Lithuania six weeks after being elected president of Russia to recognize the independence of Lithuania. Nonetheless, it would appear that Russia and Russians have become the chief targets of the assertive foreign policies pursued by the governments of the Baltic countries.

While many Russian leaders express concern for the fate of Russians living in the former Soviet republics, there is a particular edge regarding Russians in Latvia and Estonia. Gennadii Burbulis said in an interview in September 1992 that the Russian democrats felt betrayed by the Baltic leaders. "We marched arm in arm with them to ensure that their independence would be peacefully attained, and then as soon as they were independent they became nationalists and began discriminating against the Russian-speaking population. They betrayed their friends." Similar sentiments were expressed by Sergei Stankevich, Evgenii Ambartsumov, and a range of other political leaders interviewed at the same time.[21]

The independence of Ukraine from Russia is by far the most difficult issue relating to Russian nationalism. Ukraine and Russia have been united for at least three hundred years. The historical ties between the now independent countries date back a thousand years. *Nestor's Chronicle,* the eleventh-century chronicle of Russian history, notes that Kiev is "from whence the Russian land came to be." Ukraine is the land that brought Orthodoxy to Russia, that brought Russian to Russia. As Metropolitan Kirill of Smolensk stated in January 1992, the separation of Russia from Ukraine shattered "the commonalities of a thousand years."[22] What is important is less the historical accuracy of these views than the perceptions of the population. Russians believe that there is a direct transference from Kiev to Moscow.[23]

The issue of Crimea has become a focal point of the tense relations between Moscow and Kiev. Ukraine claims the land as its own because it was transferred to Ukraine by Khrushchev in 1954. It had at no prior time been Ukrainian territory. From the Russian perspective, Crimea became part of the Russian empire after an eighteenth-century war with Turkey. In fact, much of Crimea remains Russian (well over 65 percent, by most accounts). In the beginning of 1993, not one of Crimea's 529 schools used Ukrainian as the primary language of instruction, and the predominant language of the region is Russian. Ukraine continues to assert its control over the area, but has adopted a policy of considerable compromise. Yet recent surveys indicate a hardening of Russian attitudes, where nearly 75 percent of the Russians surveyed do not even consider themselves citizens of Ukraine.[24] Many feel that Crimea is the next flash point in the former Soviet Union. Were the dispute between Russia and Ukraine over Crimea to come to military confrontation, it would have a devastating impact on the stability of the entire region. The latest agreement between Kravchuk and Yeltsin on the fate of the Black Sea fleet still needs to be implemented. The issues are critical, particularly given the military significance of the area as well as the scale of weapons available in the immediate vicinity.

Another problem posed by the newly independent countries that surround Russia is the growing spread of ethnic violence. Civil war has erupted all along Russia's southern flank. In Moldova, Georgia, Armenia, and Tajikistan, Russian troops have become involved in the fighting. It is unclear to what extent these troops are pursuing policies directed from Moscow or whether they are operating independently. Either way, the more involved Russian troops become in these battles, the more likely Russia will be drawn into military confrontation in the region.

The "near abroad" for Russia poses additional problems for the Russian government on a conceptual level. In many ways the countries of the former Soviet Union need one another to guarantee reform domestically. They need one another for the markets they provide. They need one another for the economic ties established during the Soviet period. They must work together because they all face the same problem of moving from the Soviet period to a new period of independence. With the exception of the Baltic republics, none of the other former Soviet republics has experienced real independence for several centuries.

Aside from Russia, the dissolution of the Soviet Union meant independence for all the other republics. For Latvia, Ukraine, Georgia, and the other republics, independence movements sought to break ties with Moscow. For the Russians, they too sought independence from the center, only to realize that to their neighbors they still represented the center. While economic integration and military cooperation seem reasonable approaches to overcoming the legacy of the Soviet empire, Russian politicians are frequently bewildered by their neighbors' refusal to participate in joint efforts to resolve the problems that face the region. Institutions like the CIS, though poorly functioning in practice, can play vital roles in the development of reform throughout the area. Even the CIS has been attacked by Western observers as simply a tool of maintaining and expanding Russian influence throughout the former Soviet Union. Any proposal from Moscow for increased cooperation in the region is generally dismissed out of hand for fear of increased Russian involvement in the region.

The Future of Russia: A New Role for Russia?

In many ways, the foreign policy of Yeltsin's Russia has followed the advice of Talleyrand, who wrote at the time he abandoned Napoleon's dream of world domination, "To be great again, France must cease to be colossal."[25] From the outset it has been clear that the new Russian state has cast off many of the old Soviet concepts of national interest. Boris Yeltsin's first foreign visit as president of Russia was to the Baltics. As the leader of the largest Soviet republic, he sought to unite the independence movements of all the Soviet republics to destroy the center that Mikhail Gorbachev presided over. To be sure, Russia maintains wide-ranging security interests; however, only in the words of people such as Zhirinovksy do we still find calls for Russian support of Cuba and other far-flung outposts of Soviet influence.

Yeltsin's foreign policy has represented a fundamental break even from Gorbachev's policy of "new thinking." At the United Nations, in early May 1993, Russia exercised its veto power for the first time since 1984. It was not that Russia necessarily opposed the policy issue in question. It was most likely that Russia could simply not afford to pay the $2 million that would have been required by the resolution to provide mandatory funding for UN peacekeeping forces in Cyprus. Yet it is worth constantly keeping in mind that Russia is consciously searching for its own policy, and Yeltsin himself keeps reminding us that Russia will not always simply say "Yes!"

The global pretensions are gone. The ideological rhetoric disappeared overnight. With the demise of the Soviet Union, Russia has increasingly articulated its lack of interest in Latin America and Africa and other parts of the developing world, except those that border Russia or the former Soviet Union. Russia, it seems, has begun to adopt goals more in conformity with its realistic possibilities as well as the desires of its population. In international relations, most Russians would prefer to see themselves as part of the First World, rather than as the habitual spokesperson and apologist for the Third World.

Russian policy toward Bosnia and Serbia belies an even more fundamental commitment to a positive role for Russia in the international arena. The ethnic and cultural ties between Russians and Serbs are quite close. It was in defense of Serbia that the Russian Empire entered World War I. It was in many ways a war that led to the downfall of the Romanov dynasty, consumed the Provisional Government of 1917, and led to the October Revolution. Yet, despite a widespread pro-Serbian lobby in Russia and a general anti-Muslim bias among Russians, the Yeltsin government has been one of the most steadfast in seeking to resolve the Balkan conflict. While the world has focused on Russian opposition to further pressure on Belgrade, the Russian government has yet to become an obstacle to such a policy. In fact, it would appear that it is the West European countries that have been the most reluctant to take decisive action in the region.

While Russian policy toward the Balkans is indicative of the new policy pursued by the Yeltsin government, Russian-Japanese relations provide an interesting counterexample. Prior to being elected president, Yeltsin had repeatedly pledged to return the Kuril Islands to Japan. However, in the last two years, Yeltsin has canceled or postponed two trips to Japan and repeatedly refused to discuss the islands as preconditions for further talks with the Japanese. Five years ago, it was likely that 75 percent of all Russians could not have located the Kuril Islands on a map, let alone understood the Soviet-Japanese dispute. Today, however, Russians across the country have voiced strong opposition to the return of the islands to Japan. This issue alone is indicative of both the power and ambiguity of Russia's nascent national identity.

Since February 1993, President Yeltsin and Foreign Minister Kozyrev have pushed an idea that would demand a fundamental change in Western concepts of Russia's role in the world. Both men have advocated a "special status" for Russia as guarantor and protector for the region of the former Soviet Union.[26] This is an idea worth pursuing. Europe has failed to respond to the crisis in what used to be Yugoslavia, and has failed to end the bloodshed in Tajikistan or Armenia and Azerbaijan. How will Europe respond to future conflicts in the region? Most likely, it will not.

Russian peacekeeping forces can play a vital role for UN policy. The Russians want to take an active role in preventing the spread of conflict in the region of the former Soviet Union. As the West continues to grapple with the Bosnia debacle, it should seriously consider the events in Tajikistan and Armenia, where CNN does not provide daily pictures of the suffering, but thousands continue to die. Russian troops could establish control over these regions and the UN could mediate the disputes.

Russia's role of peacekeeper in the former Soviet Union must be based on the immediate withdrawal of Russian troops from the Baltic states and other republics that have demanded this. Russian peacekeeping must be encouraged only on an as-needed basis as defined by either an existing multilateral group or some newly created regional authority. Many of the countries of the former Soviet Union have been highly skeptical of Russia's desire to exercise a "Monroe Doctrine" in the region. Ukraine is particularly opposed to any hint of Russian expansionism.[27] To counter Ukrainian skepticism, the Ukrainians and the other former Soviet republics should be encouraged to become involved with Russia in this peacekeeping force.

Conclusion

As one friend said recently, the tragedy of the Russian people was not only in its poverty and its repression, but that the society raised a people in such a way that they have no idea that life can indeed be better. Or as another friend remarked in describing the consequences of the Stalinist repressions, the tragedy is not that we are now allowed to say things that we were forbidden to say in the past, but that we believed, sincerely believed, what we were told. Moreover, we continued to believe even after we had begun to understand. At present, Russia is freeing itself and its past from the tragedy of the Soviet era.

We ought to temper forecasts of the directions of Russian foreign policy with an appreciation of Boris Yeltsin's political and policy flexibility. For example, Yeltsin has been able to avoid constraining his action by strong commitments to specific policy options or to specific advisors. He has twice canceled trips to Japan in response to strong opposition to negotiation on the Kuril Islands dispute. Each time he has appeared to act on his own rather than look like he was conceding. Nonetheless, Yeltsin ventured to Tokyo for the G–7 meeting and hinted at another attempt at a Russo-Japanese summit meeting. Similar ambiguity has been voiced in government pronouncements regarding the Baltic republics. The tone of Russian statements has frequently verged on military threat, reminding their Baltic neighbors that Russia is still a powerful country with the ability to impose its will.[28] However, it seems highly unlikely that, at present, the Russian government is willing to sacrifice relations with the West through the use of military force in the former Soviet Union. In short, Yeltsin has demonstrated considerable flexibility in foreign policy.

Today, Russians continue to face the questions posed by Solzhenitsyn a few years ago. They are questions that are not yet answered. Neither should the answers be expected, for they are questions that have been politically relevant for only a few years. Russia, however, is moving toward a definition of what Russia is and what its interests are. This is a process that the West must recognize and encourage. The development of a positive national identity and a constructive foreign policy is as vital to the future stability of Russia as is the creation of a market economy and a democratic political system. The failure to develop such a concept in Russia will leave a major void, which the ultranationalists will seek to fill.

Simultaneously, the West too must grapple both with the answers to these questions and their implication for Russia's foreign policy. However, the questions must be answered by the Russians themselves. The more the West seeks to impose a definition of what it is to be Russian and what Russia's role in the world is, the less likely it is to be effective in securing a stable and peaceful Russian foreign policy.

An aggressive nationalist government in Russia may pursue an aggressive militaristic policy toward the countries of the "near abroad." Unfortunately, there is little the West can do or will do to prevent such a policy were it to be implemented, nor will the West be in a position to provide much resistance.[29] The West must, therefore, take advantage of the situation that currently exists and encourage Russia to become involved in the protection of peace in the region of the former Soviet Union. Such an approach by the West will diffuse some of the ultranationalist rhetoric in Russia and provide the reform movement with much-needed support that cannot be gained through additional IMF loans.

In seeking to evaluate the impact of Russian national identity on the foreign policy of Russia, it is essential to remember that while Russia is at once a very old country rich in tradition, it is today a country seeking to redefine its past as well as searching for an identity in the future. The West must realize that while it can respond to this developing national identity, there is little it can do to guide the process. The West must ask itself if it is prepared to deal with a resurgent Russia that has clearly defined national interests. The West must ask itself if it is prepared to deal with a Russia whose national interests change with time. The West must ask itself if it is prepared for a Russia that pursues an assertive foreign policy without being expansionary. If the answers to these questions are "no," the West must begin to reevaluate its foreign policy framework. If the West wishes Russia to join the ranks of "normal" countries, it must understand that Russia will do so only as a country that perceives itself as a "great power," with consequent special international standing and regional responsibilities. It will do so only as a country that is able to define and articulate its national security concerns in its own terms, not simply as a repetition of Western policies and judgments. It will do so only as a country whose national interests are determined domestically.

Notes

1. This is not to say that there are, or were, no ultranationalist leaders in these bodies. No one, however, was specifically elected in popular elections of these slates. Sergei Baburin, for example, was elected to the Russian Congress of People's Deputies in 1990 as a member of the DemRossiia electoral slate. Another such example is Valentin Rasputin, who was elected to the Soviet CPD in 1989 by the Union of Writers.
2. "Solzhenitsyn Publishes Essay in Moscow Weekly," Foreign Broadcast Information Service, *Daily Report: Soviet Union,* (FBIS-SOV–90–187) 26 September 1990, p. 37 (*Literaturnaia gazeta,* 1990, no. 38 [18 September], pp. 3–6).
3. Interviewed on NBC News, 5 July 1993.
4. For a catalogue of the environmental destruction of the Soviet Union, see Murray Feshbach and Alfred Friendly, Jr., *Ecocide in the USSR: Health and Nature Under Siege* (New York: Basic Books, 1992).
5. For further discussion of this debate, see James H. Billington, *The Icon and the Axe* (New York: Knopf, 1966); and Georgii Fedotov, *The Russian Religious Mind* (Belmont, MA: Norland, 1975).
6. For further discussion of this conflict, refer to Billington, *The Icon and the Axe;* and Father Georges Florovky, *Ways of Russian Theology* (Belmont, MA: Norland, 1979).
7. To be sure, not all members of the church hierarchy approved of this. Those who resisted ties to the Soviet state found themselves exiled abroad, imprisoned, or murdered.
8. Adam Ulam, *The New Face of Soviet Totalitarianism* (Cambridge: Harvard University Press, 1963), p. 8.
9. A few intrepid historians, led by Aleksandr Nekrich, did dare to ask. Even though the discussions were carried on in scholarly terms and accessible to very few, the scholars found themselves shut down quickly, and Nekrich himself found himself in exile in the West.
10. "Solzhenitsyn Publishes Essay," p. 38.
11. James H. Billington, *Russia Transformed: Breakthrough to Hope* (New York: Free Press, 1992), pp. 168–69.
12. Boris Yeltsin made particular note of this fact in Moscow on 25 January 1993 shortly after a U.S. attack on Iraq. Yeltsin noted, "The United States has a certain tendency to dictate its own terms." *RFE/RL Daily Report,* 26 January 1993.
13. According to official voting returns, Boris Yeltsin received 45,552,041 votes (57.3 percent), Nikolai Ryzhkov received 13,395,335 votes (16.85 percent), and Vladimir Zhirinovksy received 6,211,007 votes (7.81 percent). Vadim Bakatin, Aman-Geldy Tuleev, and Al'bert Makashov also received votes in the election.
14. For a good recent article on the ultranationalists in Russia, see Celestine Bohlen, "Cradle of Russian Revolution is Hotbed of Disgust," *New York Times,* 22 June 1993.
15. For a lengthy treatment of the current state of the ultranationalists in Russia, see Walter Lacquer, *The Black Hundreds: The Rise of the Extreme Right in Russia* (New York: HarperCollins, 1993).

16. The poll was conducted by Vox Populi under the direction of Boris Grushin. For the poll, 1,988 people were questioned between 21 November and 8 December 1992. The poll was conducted throughout Russia.

17. In the poll, 52.6 percent responded "Yes, under any conditions," and 33.2 percent responded "Yes, under certain conditions." This is in spite of the fact that "Relations with Russians in the 'near abroad'" were listed as the eleventh most serious problem facing Russia, 0.5 percent, out of a list of twelve.

18. "Does Russia Need New Russians? An Interview with the Head of the Federal Migration Service," *Komsomol'skaia pravda,* 4 June 1993 [provided by Federal News Service in English].

19. As Paul Goble has frequently noted, Latvia presently has no current citizenship law. However, the draft laws that have been circulated have caused great alarm among Russians.

20. In the Vox Populi poll, 20.5 percent of the respondents favored Rutskoi, while 15.7 percent favored Yeltsin on the issue.

21. Interviews conducted by Gregory Guroff in Moscow in September 1992.

22. Billington, *Russia Transformed,* pp. 164–65.

23. This view contrasts markedly with the historical analysis presented in Edward Keenan's chapter, "On Certain Mythical Beliefs and Russian Behaviors," in vol. 1 (S. Frederick Starr, ed., *The Legacy of History in Russia and the New States of Eurasia*) of this series. However, in this case it is the popular perception of history that heavily outweighs the accuracy of historical scholarship.

24. For a good analysis of the current situation in Crimea, see Ian Bremmer, "Ethnic Issues in Crimea," *RFE/RL Research Report,* 22 April 1993.

25. Adam Ulam, *Expansion and Coexistence: Soviet Foreign Policy, 1917–73* (New York: Holt, Rinehart and Winston, 1968), p. 752.

26. Yeltsin initially broached the subject when he stated at a Civic Union conference in late February 1993, "the time has come for respective international organizations, including the United Nations, to grant Russia special powers as a guarantor of peace and stability on the territory of the former Soviet Union" (quoted in "Reaction to Russian President's Speech to the Civic Union Congress in Kiev and Tbilisi," *Izvestiia,* 2 March 1993 [provided by Federal News Service in English]).

27. As recently as 13 July 1993, Ukrainian Foreign Minister Anatolii Zlenko renewed Ukrainian opposition to any special role for Russia in the region of the former Soviet Union (*RFE/RL Daily Report,* 13 July 1993).

28. In Russia's official response to the recent Estonian law On Foreigners, the government noted, "it seems that the Estonian government has misjudged Russia's goodwill and, giving way to the pressure of nationalism, has 'forgotten' about certain geopolitical and demographic realities. The Russian side has means at its disposal to remind Estonia about these" ("'Text' of Yeltsin Statement," FBIS-SOV–93–122, 28 June 1993, p. 8).

29. For thoughts on this possibility, see Stephen Sestanovich, "U.S. Power Less than Super," *New York Times,* 23 March 1993.

II

The Western Newly Independent States

5
The Influence of Ethnicity on Foreign Policy
The Case of Ukraine

Ilya Prizel

Few topics are more problematic and difficult to present to an American readership than the issue of ethnicity and its influence on the formation of a country's foreign policy. The prevalent political theories of Western, and particularly American, scholarship are deeply rooted in the "realist" school of foreign policy, built around the assumption that countries have an objective definition of "national interest" that is a product of rational forces such as "balance of power," economic interests, and so forth.[1] It is symptomatic of this state of mind that America's two most controversial and widely read articles in international relations theory did not even allude to the power of ethnic identification and nationalism. Francis Fukuyama, in his "End of History,"[2] assumed that with the defeat of communism, the entire international system would move to a homogenized bourgeois market economy, paying scant attention to the powers of nationalism, religion, and ethnic identification as potent political forces. Similarly, John Mearsheimer, in his article "Back to the Future,"[3] analyzes Europe's emerging political configuration entirely in terms of the concept of "balance of power," ignoring the vexing and irrational power of ethnonationalism.

Yet ethnic identity does matter. America and some other English-speaking countries are unique in terms of their political orientation—a product of eighteenth-century rationalism developing until the twentieth century in a climate of virtually absolute security. On the Continent, however, since the early nineteenth century, nationalism has become the most persistent force. Indeed, the potency of ethnonationalism seems to run parallel to the relative "youth" of national awareness. Thus, while the impact of nationalism in the old and well-established countries of Western Europe may, in fact, have peaked before World War II, in Eastern and Central Europe ethnonationalism, with all its historical baggage, continued to be an ascending political force. Although the power of ethnonationalism may appear "irrational" to an American observer who often tends to confuse America's successful export of its popular culture with a political homogenization of the world, it is this kind of ethnonationalism that forms the *Weltanschauung* of much of the world and impels most countries to make decisions of momentous importance.

Ukraine's Ethnonationalism in Modern Context

The discussion of Ukraine's ethnonationalism presents unique problems. Ukraine is among the oldest nations in Europe, with a rich cultural heritage and a distinct language and style of architecture as well as a literary genre (*dumki*). Nevertheless, Ukrainian nationalism is particularly hard to identify and classify, given the country's interrupted and tortured history. Because of the vast size of the country and its central position at the intersection of the Catholic, Byzantine, and Muslim worlds, Ukraine only partially meets the definition of nation. The unfortunate history of the country has continued to place serious obstacles in the way of its formation of an easily defined national entity. Ukraine easily meets Rousseau's definition of a nation as a "spiritual community." However, the divisions between east and west as well as the center and the south, a result of historical linguistic and religious differences, continue to pose serious difficulties in shaping a clear national identity and, hence, a well-formulated national agenda. Similarly, if one were to apply Edmund Burke's definition of a nation as an "authentic community" with its own unique customs and institutions, again Ukraine, with its distinct tradition of the Sich and Hetmanite state, clearly possesses the attributes of a nation. However, once again, the traditions of the Cossacks hardly affect the fortune of millions of Ukrainians living in Right Bank Ukraine and, even less so, those in Galicia.[4] Problems such as these, however, while they may be somewhat more extreme in the Ukrainian case, are not unique for a country of its size.

What makes Ukrainian national rebirth and development of a sense of identity particularly complex is the fact that successive generations of conquest, be it Polish, Russian, or Soviet, have managed either, at worst, to destroy Ukraine's political elite or, at best, to thoroughly "denationalize" it. As a result, although an old nation, Ukraine is currently engaged in the process of nation building, a process that entails not only an assertive remaking of internal institutions but also a new sense of history and new symbols. The development of foreign policy, especially toward powers that previously dominated a country, is a key ingredient of nation building. As the Ukrainian émigré historian Ivan L. Rudnytsky observed,

> History means a constant *confrontation*, interaction and interpretation of communities and cultures. The uniqueness of a nation actualizes itself through this very process. (emphasis added)[5]

This process of "confrontation" as a means of "actualization" is vital for Ukraine in its relationship with Poland and Russia, given the centuries of domination by these powers and the profound cultural imprint they left on Ukraine.

Since the Polish domination of Ukraine (1339–1939) was longer than the Russian (1654–1991),[6] and there is a greater historical distance, which allows for a more detached examination, it is logical to start with a discussion of the impact of ethnonationalism on Ukrainian-Polish relations and then proceed to analyze the parallel situation with Russia.

Ukraine and Poland: Ethnonationalism and the Burden of History

Ivan Rudnytsky, in his thoughtful article "Polish-Ukrainian Relations: The Burden of History,"[7] observed that it was the centuries-old struggle between Poland and Ukraine that ultimately resulted in both countries' loss of independence and their disappearance from the map of Europe. While Rudnytsky is probably correct, a secondary fallout of this struggle was that it engendered and sharpened the national consciousness of both peoples.

For the Poles, the notion of being a Latin Catholic Western bastion locked in a struggle with the "primitive" Byzantine East was born primarily as a result of their struggle first with the Ukrainian Cossacks and later with the Russian tsar. It was this struggle that gave Poland a strong sense of nationhood and national purpose. Ukrainian national consciousness was also greatly shaped by this protracted struggle against Poland. The Polish-Ukrainian struggle provided both nations with powerful myths and symbols in their efforts to establish their national identities. Taras Shevchenko (1814–1861), Ukraine's national poet and the person most responsible for Ukraine's national awakening, in his epic poem *Haidamaki,* glorified the Cossack myth and exhorted the Ukrainians to "Strike, strike the Poles all down!" (*Byite Lakhiv! Byite!*).[8] Similarly, Nikolai Gogol's (Mykola Hohol') depiction of the Poles in his novel *Taras Bulba*[9] extolled the courage of the freedom-loving Cossacks when confronting the perfidious and repressed Poles. Conversely, in the first volume (*Ogniem i mieczem* [With Fire and Sword, 1884]) of a historical trilogy, Poland's Henryk Sienkiewicz

(1846–1916)—one of the leaders of Poland's literary renaissance in the late nineteenth and early twentieth century (during what Norman Davis called the "positivist" period of Polish history) and one of the first winners of the Nobel Prize for literature (1905)—depicts the Poles as a civilizing people locked in a battle of life and death against the cutthroat Ukrainians. In fact, until the end of World War II, the national visions of Poland and Ukraine continued to be mutually exclusive.

Polish nationalists, be it the ethnonationalist Roman Dmowski or the more inclusivist Josef Pilsudski, continued to view the Polish-Lithuanian Commonwealth as the high point of Polish civilization. Therefore, Polish political and intellectual elites continued to view Ukraine as Poland's eastern extension and part and parcel of the Polish commonwealth. An independent, powerful Ukraine, which would have included Galicia along with Lwów with its large Polish population, was not part of the agenda of interwar Poland. Pilsudski's attempt to "liberate" Ukraine in 1920 took place only after Petliura had agreed to yield Galicia to Poland, and the Polish regime made no secret that, should an independent Ukraine emerge, it would be a junior partner in an order centered on Poland.[10]

If the aspirations of Polish nationalism were incompatible with the interests of Ukrainian nationalism, Ukraine's posture in the late nineteenth and early twentieth centuries was equally at odds with Poland. First, there was careful cultivation of the "Khmel'nit'skyi myth" by both tsarist and Soviet regimes because of its strong anti-Polish message, depicting the "resurrection" of the Ukrainian nation through a war with Poland, and as if through an inevitable progression leading to Pereiaslav. In addition, clashes between Poles and Ukrainians in Austrian Galicia over political power and later Poland's defeat of the Ukrainian-Galician state and its cultural and political repression of Ukrainians begot the birth of a powerful "integralist nationalism" in Polish Ukraine.[11] This led to political terrorism throughout the 1930s, culminating in atrocities against the Polish minority in Galicia and bloody "de-Polonization" of Volhynia (western Ukraine) during World War II. The final chapter in the Polish-Ukrainian feud was written in the first years following World War II. First, in 1945 Poland expelled thousands of Ukrainians to the USSR. Then, in order to dislodge the remaining Ukrainian nationalist resistance, the Poles carried out Operation Wisla in April 1947, in which the Polish government uprooted more than 150,000 Ukrainians, mainly of the Lemko clan, from their ancestral villages, and dispersed them across Poland.[12]

Yet, despite the initial post–World War II brutality between Poles and Ukrainians, the postwar order imposed by Stalin on Eastern Europe did much to finally put an end to Polish-Ukrainian hostilities. The redrawing of the Polish-Ukrainian line roughly along the Curzon Line, as well as the population "exchanges" between Poland and Ukraine, created for the first time a state border that was an ethnic border as well. While Poland remained sentimentally attached to Lwów (as well as to Wilno), the number of Poles in Ukraine was sufficiently small not to pose an insurmountable political problem. Similarly, while many western Ukrainians remained bitter at events in Poland from 1945 to 1947, the number of Ukrainians in Poland was also small enough not to create problems. Furthermore, as the years progressed, there was a reorientation of basic priorities in both countries. Poland's post–World War II energies were absorbed in settling the land newly acquired from Germany, and the nature of the Polish elite had changed. Unlike the interwar Polish elite, of whom large segments hailed from Lithuania or Ukraine, the new elite did not share this sentimental attachment to "Poland's East." Furthermore, in interwar Poland the question of the role of ethnic minorities had preoccupied the political elite until the very collapse of the Polish state.[13] In contrast, the main preoccupation of homogeneous postwar Poland was the scourge of communism and oppressive Soviet domination rather than the Polish-Ukrainian relationship.

In Ukraine too, the country's national frustration increasingly shifted from the cultural and political repression of Ukrainians in interwar Poland to the issue of the country's growing Russification, which, given its success, threatened the extinction of the Ukrainian language. (According to Valerii Khmelko of the Mohila Academy, only 43 percent of Ukraine's population actually feel as comfortable with Ukrainian as with the Russian language).[14]

In fact from the early 1970s, for the first time in six centuries, Ukraine and Poland started to grow together rather than apart. In Poland the political reversal of Gomulka from a national reformer to a Kremlin stalwart increasingly frustrated Polish intellectuals; these feelings were further accentuated by the political reaction after the 1967 "anti-Zionist" campaign of General Moczar and the deepening reaction throughout Eastern Europe following the suppression of the Prague Spring. In Ukraine, too, the 1972 removal of the national Communist leader of Ukraine, Petro Shelest', and his replacement with a Russifying Brezhnev protégé, Volodymyr Shcherbytsky, frustrated Ukraine's intellectuals, creating an entire new generation of dissidents. By the 1970s Poland and Ukraine actually began to view their struggles as complementary rather than contradictory.

Even before the final collapse of the Soviet Union, the brutalities inflicted by the Bolsheviks on both nations had led to a reexamination of the futility of their conflict, since they realized that this discord, to a very large degree, facilitated Moscow's domination of the two peoples. Thus, by the mid-1970s Polish scholars began to take a more benevolent attitude toward their Ukrainian neighbors, even raising painful chapters in Polish-Ukrainian relations such as the forced, brutal resettlement of the Lemko clan after World War II.[15] In fact, since the mid-1970s Polish historiography has become increasingly sympathetic to Ukrainian issues. Furthermore, while many Poles retained strong sentimental attachments to cities of pre–World War II Poland, such as L'viv (Lwów) or Vilnius (Wilno), nevertheless, even among the right fringe of Poland's body politic, territorial revisionism ceased to be respectable, thus removing a highly divisive issue between Poles and Ukrainians.

While Soviet Ukraine was governed by a succession of hardliners such as Petro Shelest' and Volodymyr Shcherbytsky, there was no apparent deviation from the extreme pro-Moscow line and little apparent change in the historic attitude toward Poland. However, the rise of Solidarity in Poland inspired many Ukrainian nationalist dissidents, and Pope John Paul II's adamant defense of the underground Uniate Church in Ukraine did much to further the relationship between Poles and Ukrainians. The defiant Solidarity movement inspired a host of Ukrainians, both nationalists and simply opponents of communism. Reacting to the turmoil in Poland, the Ukrainian nationalist poet Vasyl Stus wrote in a samizdat publication:

> Long live the volunteers in the cause of freedom! The Poles' defiance of Soviet despotism fills us with joy and their national uprisings amaze us.[16]

There is little doubt that the self-restrained yet effective tactics of the Solidarity movement served as a model, as well as an inspiration, to the Ukrainian Helsinki Group and later to Rukh.

No less important was the example of Solidarity to the reemergence of the catacomb Ukrainian Catholic (Uniate) Church. The importance of this church cannot be underestimated in light of the fact that it may well be the foremost Ukrainian national institution.[17] The steadfast defense of the Uniate Church by the Polish pontiff John Paul II, including the Vatican's 1980 declaration that the "L'viv Sobor" of 1946 (which "reunited" the Uniate Church with the Russian Orthodox Church) was invalid and null and void,[18] served to regenerate the Ukrainian Uniate Church and create a reserve of goodwill toward Poland in western Ukraine, a region where historically Polish-Ukrainian relations were tense.

By the late 1980s the Polish-Ukrainian relationship had undergone a fundamental change. Despite occasional clashes generated by property disputes between the Catholic and Uniate churches in Poland, the preoccupation with historic wrongs inflicted by either group had ceased to be the centerpiece of either nation's intellectual life.

For the Ukrainians, Poland had become a model and a symbol of a medium-size Slavic nation that had managed to preserve its culture and language as well as regain its sovereignty. For the Poles, Ukrainian aspirations for independence symbolized the disintegration of the Russian Empire, which in various guises had deprived Poland of its independence since the eighteenth century. For the first time since the onslaught of the Tatars in the thirteenth century, a symbiotic relationship between Poland and Ukraine had emerged.

Therefore, when the Communist regime in Poland, following its electoral defeat, allowed Tadeusz Mazowiecki to become the country's first noncommunist premier, many Ukrainian nationalists expected Poland to become a champion of their cause. Given the fact that Mazowiecki was a handpicked nominee of Lech Walesa and given the long-standing commitment of Solidarity and other opposition groups to reconciliation with Ukraine, this was not an unrealistic expectation. As early as 1983, Kazimierz Podalski had published his underground "Bioalorusini—Litwini—Ukraincy: Nasi wrogowie chy bracia?" (Belarusians, Lithuanians, Ukrainians: Our enemies or brothers?) calling for fundamental reconciliation with Ukraine, renouncing all territorial claims in the east, and supporting these countries' drive toward independence. A similar position was taken by the influential émigré journal *Kultura*. The 1989 declaration of the Polish parliament that Poland had no territorial demands on any of its eastern neighbors further reduced tensions between Kiev and Warsaw. Poland's powerful Catholic Church, under the leadership of its primate Cardinal Glemp, believed that the emergence of an independent Ukraine and Belarus would enhance the prospects of revival of the Uniate and Latin Catholic religions east of the River Bug. Thus, by the late 1980s there was a firm Polish consensus in favor of reconciliation and support of Ukrainian and Belarusian national aspirations and a strong belief that Poland was destined again to play the historic role as these countries' conduit to "Europe."

Yet the initial foreign policy of the Mazowiecki cabinet regarding Ukraine and Belarus was one of caution bordering on contradiction. Faced with the imminence of German reunification, along with Chancellor Kohl's reluctance to commit Germany a priori to the Oder-Neisse line as Germany's eastern border, there was serious anxiety in Warsaw. Germany's ambiguous position forced the Mazowiecki government not to join Hungary and Czechoslovakia in demanding the withdrawal of Soviet troops, but actually to request their continued presence on Polish soil. Under such circumstances Poland's ability to conduct a policy that might offend the Kremlin was limited and circumscribed. In order to reconcile Poland's precarious geopolitical position with strong public support for Ukrainian aspiration, Foreign Minister Krzysztof Skubiszewski launched the so-called two track policy. The fundamentals of this policy were that while Poland would continue to maintain its state-to-state links with the Soviet regime in Moscow, it would also expand its ties with the nations on the western fringe of the USSR to the extent that these countries attained their independence.[19] Rhetoric notwithstanding, this in effect confined Poland to a passive position. Skubiszewski's "two track" policy was not meant to last long. On the one hand, the perceived need for the presence of Soviet troops in Poland disappeared soon after the German government accepted the Oder-Neisse line and signed a friendship treaty with Poland. In fact, within a very short time the continued Soviet military presence on Polish soil was perceived by most Poles as anachronistic at best and humiliating at worst. Furthermore, Poland's measured policy toward its immediate eastern neighbors was coming under increased public scrutiny, especially following the massacre of Lithuanian civilians at the television tower in Vilnius in January 1991. However, one additional reason for Poland to temper its support for Ukrainian and Belarusian independence was the lack of clarity about how deep the aspirations toward full independence ran in these countries. Not only did the Communist governments of these two republics continue to take evasive positions on this issue, but the situation was further complicated by the fact that in both Ukraine and Belarus the populations voted in Gorbachev's referendum of March 1991 in convincing majorities (70 percent in Ukraine) to preserve a "reformed union." Because of these constraints it is not surprising that Poland's initial "two track" policy did little to inspire Ukrainian nationalists' craving for independence or to please a vast majority of Poland's electorate.

By the time Lech Walesa declared his candidacy for president and challenged his handpicked prime minister, Mazowiecki, the entire question of Poland's "eastern policy" had become a hotly contested electoral issue. Once elected and advised by Zdzislaw Naider, who advocated a far more activist policy along Poland's eastern rim, President Walesa did not wait long to signal a fundamental change. Starting with his inauguration, President Walesa startled his audience by extending his greetings to Poland's eastern neighbors, "Lithuania, Belarus, Ukraine, and Russia," ignoring the Soviet Union altogether. Walesa's seemingly open challenge to the integrity of the USSR drew an angry response from the Soviet media, with several Soviet newspapers reminding Walesa that Ukraine was a part of the Soviet Union. Yet despite Moscow's obvious displeasure, Poland's new government continued to enthusiastically pursue the cause of Ukrainian independence, witnessed by a dramatic increase in mutual exchanges and visits between the two countries. The collapse of the USSR in August 1991 provided both the Poles and the Ukrainians with an opportunity for a final reconciliation. Poland was the first country outside the Commonwealth of Independent States to recognize independent Ukraine.

Yet, despite the absence of any major issue to divide Poland from Ukraine and the presence, in fact, of a strong symbiotic relationship between the two states, the heavy baggage of ethnonationalist history has continued to cast its long shadow over Polish-Ukrainian relations. The reemergence of the catacomb Uniate Church created severe property clashes between Poland's Roman Catholic Church and the Uniate Church. The clash was especially bitter and at times violent in the dispute over the Carmelite Cathedral of St. Theresa in Przemysl. Some Polish nationalists were dismayed by the claims of the Ukrainian State Independence Organization (a self-proclaimed successor organization to the interwar OUN) that Ukraine was entitled to territories currently part of Poland, Russia, Moldova, and Belarus.[20] Ukraine's insistence on an army of 400,000, as well as the ambiguity of its position on nuclear weapons, alarmed the Polish population. In a public opinion poll conducted in Poland in June 1992, 53 percent of those responding chose Ukraine as the country posing the greatest threat to Poland.[21]

Conversely, Ukrainian popular distrust of Poland has been fueled by activities of right-wing organizations with irredentist agendas in the east. Ukraine's Orthodox Church (both the Kiev and Moscow patriarchates) was angered by what it perceived as Polish Cardinal Glemp's missionary zeal in Byzantine lands, causing an angry exchange between Moscow's Patriarch Aleksii II and Cardinal Glemp and forcing the papal nuncio to Ukraine, Archbishop Antonio Franco, to officially renounce any ambition to convert Orthodox Christians to Roman Catholicism.[22] While both the Orthodox Church and the Vatican attempted to cool tempers, and Cardinal Glemp made a reconciliation trip to Moscow during the summer of 1992, both sides agreed that, under the current circumstances, it would be inappropriate for the Polish Pope to visit the CIS.[23] The relationship between the Greek Catholic (Uniate) Church of Ukraine and the Vatican has also deteriorated as a result of policies of the Vatican, as well as those of the Polish Catholic Church in the east. The 1991 decision of the council of the Ukrainian Catholic Church (Uniate) to standardize the Ukrainian Uniate ritual along the standards of the 1720s (the high point of Latinization of that church) was received by many Ukrainians as an effort by a Polish Pope to "Latinize" and hence "Polonize" the UCC, which is Ukraine's most authentic national institution. The tensions were further aggravated by Pope John Paul II's instruction to L'viv's metropolitan, Sterniuk, forbidding his ordination of married priests, even for service in his own archeparchy, an order that, if indeed carried out, would lead to a sharp decline in the number of young Ukrainian priests and thus force greater reliance on

Polish "Latin" priests. Furthermore, some Ukrainian Greek Catholics (Uniates) responded with dismay to the Vatican's decision to create a Latin Catholic bishopric in Kiev, while abiding by the understanding with the Russian Orthodox Church that proscribed Uniate expansion outside of western Ukraine. All these actions by the Polish cardinal and Polish Pope were perceived as a part of Polish cultural irredentism.

The Ukrainian people, who have just shed their role as a "younger brother" of Russia, are in no mood to become the "younger brother" of Poland. The resentment of what is perceived as Polish highhandedness has manifested itself in the growing radicalization of L'viv's chapter of Rukh and the Ukrainian government's request to Prime Minister Suchocka to avoid L'viv during her visit to Ukraine in January 1993.

Historical baggage aside, Ukrainian-Polish relations are marked by both a need for symbiosis and inherent limitations to a mutually beneficial relationship, given both countries' broader agendas. For Ukraine, whose national agenda is integration into Europe and differentiation from Russia, Poland is the natural gateway. Upon gaining its independence, Ukraine made strenuous efforts to bolster its ties with Poland, viewing a close relationship with Poland as a means to free Ukraine from its client status vis-à-vis Moscow and as an anchor within the international system. In one of his first trips outside the CIS, President Kravchuk traveled to Warsaw and declared that "The degree of cooperation with Poland will be higher than with any other country of the CIS, including Russia."[24]

Yet Ukraine's initial enthusiasm for Poland as a means to move Ukraine out of Moscow's shadow has been met with only a partial response from Poland. The Polish government, still negotiating the terms of Russian troop withdrawal and continuing to strive to integrate Poland into the West, has shown little interest in moving Polish-Ukrainian relations beyond symbolic gestures. Two days after Kravchuk's departure, Poland's Walesa traveled to Moscow and declared that he "would like Poland and Russia to be the pillars in Eastern Europe. Poland is ready for and wants to, but it takes two to tango."[25] To the dismay of the Ukrainians, Walesa failed to include Ukraine in that configuration, evoking among some Ukrainians the specter of the treaties of Andrusovo (1667) and Riga (1921), when Poland, confronted with Russian might, twice opted to accommodate Russia at the expense of Ukraine. This notion of Poland's unreliability was certainly reinforced by Poland's offer to build a gas pipeline from Russia to Germany across Belarus and Poland, bypassing the "capricious" states of Ukraine and Lithuania.[26] In reality, however, during the first year of Ukraine's independence, Polish attitudes toward Ukraine fell into two basic categories. The Foreign Ministry tended to favor taking a remote position toward Ukraine.

Its argument was that an open alliance with Ukraine would adversely affect Poland's relationship with Russia, especially at a time when Poland had yet to see the total departure of Russian troops from its soil. Furthermore, Polish politicians have noted that, in economic terms, trade with Russia is far more important than trade with Ukraine. Relative to Poland's relationship with the West, there is concern that, given Ukraine's inability to even start reforming its economy and its growing friction with the West over the issue of nuclear weapons, an overt identification with Ukraine would compromise Poland's efforts to "join" the West, as well as complicate its delicate relationship with Russia. There is also an element of anxiety in Poland that a complete Russian disengagement from Europe may lead to a German-centered configuration, a situation that many Poles still find troubling, as manifested by Poland's adamancy about any change in the status of the Kaliningrad district.

A second school of Polish thought is put forth by Poland's former defense minister, Parys; the leader of the party Confederation for Independent Poland (KPN), Leszek Moczulski;[27] and, to a much lesser degree, President Walesa. These men believe that the only viable security—as well as economic—structure for the region is what Moczulski called *Meidzymorza* (between the sea) and basically calls for a bloc of countries between the Baltic and Black seas.[28] This proposition has received the enthusiastic support of Ukraine's President Kravchuk and Deputy Foreign Minister Tarasiuk and some qualified support from Hungary's Jozsef Antall. However, while there is anxiety in Warsaw that Ukraine may feel increasingly isolated and, thus, either turn inward or follow Belarus's lead back into the Russian fold, the dominant view in Warsaw remains that, while Poland has a practical motive as well as a moral obligation to help bring Ukraine into the international mainstream and avoid its international isolation, Poland is willing to do so only to the extent that it will not complicate its links to either the EC or Russia. For this reason, when President Kravchuk asked his Polish counterpart this May about the formation of a "Black Sea–Baltic bloc," President Walesa agreed to study the proposal "without enthusiasm."[29]

In a sense, from Poland's perspective, Ukraine—by virtue of its independence—has accomplished the most important goal of separating itself from Russia; beyond that, Poland's limited resources dictate a limited engagement with its eastern neighbor.

On the Ukrainian side as well, similar ambivalence remains. While President Kravchuk is indeed eager to see a Polish-Ukrainian bloc, other members of Ukraine's leadership, such as Prime Minister Leonid Kuchma, continue to insist that it is in the interest of Ukraine to have Poland as a "strategic ally" only so long as it does not complicate relationships with a "third party."[30]

While the tragic history of Polish-Ukrainian interactions continues to cast a long shadow over the relationship, and indeed, no meeting between the two parties passes without allusion to that lurid past, nevertheless a new phase has begun. While the two nations are pursuing different strategies in their efforts to reenter the international system, for the first time in six hundred years neither party sees the success of one as the negation of the success of the other. This sentiment was best captured by President Walesa during arrival ceremonies while he was on a state visit to Ukraine:

> We must remember that we are to build the future. The past should be corrected in textbooks, but in the future we are sentenced to one another. *Whenever we differed, a third party took advantage of us* (emphasis added).[31]

Ukraine and Russia

If the Polish-Ukrainian national clash appears to be moving toward reconciliation with a future most likely characterized by normal relations between neighbors, the Russian-Ukrainian situation is far more complex. The root of the difficulty in this relationship does not lie merely in the fact that their ties were dissolved far more recently, although that is important. Nor does it lie solely in a particularly antagonistic history. In fact, one cannot find in either Ukrainian or Russian literature the kind of antipathy toward each other that one finds in Polish and Ukrainian writings. Indeed, while Polish-Ukrainian contacts are punctuated by a history of ethnic cleansing, the history of Ukrainian-Russian neighborliness is one of common intermarriage and virtually no ethnic strife. Clearly there are dark moments in the Russian-Ukrainian relationship, ranging from Catherine II's abolition of the Hetmanate and Alexander II's *Emskii ukaz* (1876) "banning" the Ukrainian language, to the Stalinist decapitation of Ukraine's intellectual elites, followed by the horrors of the man-made hunger of 1933. However, what makes the separation between Ukraine and Russia so very complex is the fact that, unlike Ukraine and Poland where, despite centuries of cross-pollination, each group retained its distinct ethnic identity, in the case of Russia and Ukraine their respective national pathos, almost by definition, deny each other's national identity.

Even the origins of their respective states remain subject to controversy. As Professor Keenan has demonstrated,[32] until the seventeenth century Muscovy had scant interest in or understanding of what Kievan Rus' was all about. However, since the eighteenth century Russian historiography, as presented by giants such as Nikolai Karamzin, S. Solov'ev, and Vasilii Kliuchevskii, took the position that it was Vladimir-Suzdal and later Muscovy that were the heirs and successors to Kievan Rus'. Thus, the possession of Ukraine as a part of the lands of Rus' became a vital ingredient in the legitimization of the Russian Empire as a whole. In fact, one can make a case that it was the acquisition of Ukraine that transformed Russia from a nation into an empire and made Russian imperial hegemony part of Russia's national myth. This profound dependence on Ukraine as a part of the Russian national myth has become so deeply ingrained that even such highly educated and open-minded Russians as Dmitrii Likhachev, a historian who champions pre-Petrine Russian traditions, which did not include Ukraine, has the habit of using "Ukraine" and "Russia" interchangeably, referring to the Ukrainian court poet, Simeon Polotsky, as a Russian, and to Chernigov (Chernihov) as a Russian city.[33] Even Andrei Sakharov, a man with no sympathy for Russian imperialism, showed scant understanding of Ukrainian national aspirations.[34]

Conversely, Ukrainian historians of the late nineteenth century, led by Mykhailo Hrushevs'kyi, asserted that the true successor of Kievan Rus' was Galicia-Volhynia—while Muscovy was a product of a different civilization altogether.[35] Extremist interpreters of Russian historiography, such as Mikhail Pogodin, in their assertion of sole Russian "ownership" of Kievan Rus' argued that contemporary Ukrainians have absolutely no relationship to the inhabitants of Kievan Rus'. Not to be outdone, some Ukrainian national historians argued that the Russians are not a Slavic people at all, but rather a Finno-Ugric people, whose sole relationship to Kievan Rus' was dynastic. Today few in Russia would assert Muscovy's role as the sole successor of Kievan Rus' but would argue instead that Ukraine, Belarus, and Russia are one people separated due to Tatar and Polish aggression and, thus, are equal heirs to the Kievan legacy.[36] Perhaps the most correct "adjudication" of the rights to the Kievan legacy is presented by Professor Jaroslaw Pelenski, who argues that while Vladimir-Suzdal and Galicia-Volhynia did share common cultural, political, and social roots,

> The two states differed in their relationship with other powers, entered into alliances with different partners, belonged to different civilizational and commercial communities, and were in more intimate contact with their neighboring states and societies than with each other.[37]

While to the outsider this argument over the Kievan heritage may appear arcane and, indeed, esoteric, in reality the process started in Pereiaslav (1654) seriously injured the separate national identities of both the Ukrainians and the Russians.

To Ukraine, the Pereiaslav process meant the transfer of its intellectual and political elites from Ukraine to Russia and within a century undergoing a transformation from a relatively advanced society to a backwater peasant culture. As Marc Raeff noted,

> One is struck by the fact that at the moment of its subordination to Muscovite Russia, it was Ukraine that enjoyed and exercised a clear cultural predominance: much later, in the nineteenth century, at the birth of modern national consciousness, Ukraine had the status of a peasant culture adjudged inferior and harshly repressed.[38]

Ukraine's losses were further compounded by the loss of a cultural border with its Russian neighbor, as well as a nearly complete disappearance from international consciousness.

While the damage to Russian ethnic identification caused by the Pereiaslav process was less apparent and indeed, less severe, it was, nevertheless, very significant. The acquisition of Ukraine and the inflow of numerous young, talented Ukrainians had a profound impact on the Russian Orthodox Church, perhaps the only institution capable of challenging Russia's autocracy. The schism of 1666, caused in large measure by the inflow of far more educated Ukrainian clerics, finally enabled the regime to break the church and reduce it to a mere agent of the autocratic state. Richard Pipes quotes Pierre Pascal: "After Nikon Russia no longer had a church: it had a religion of state."[39] An even more serious consequence of Pereiaslav to Russia was that the national identity became subsumed into an imperial identity, before a truly national identity could develop. To some Russian "Eurasian" nationalists, such as Nikolai S. Trubetskoi, the union with Ukraine (and the inflow of Westernized Ukrainians) laid a foundation for the Petrine reforms, which in turn annihilated the traditional Russian culture and thus created a permanent gap between the elite and the masses.[40] As a result, Pereiaslav left a contradictory legacy for both Russia and Ukraine. For Ukraine, the way to develop a distinct national identity was to separate from Russia in as many spheres as possible. For the Russians, whose national identity became inseparable from an identification with the empire, an essential part of that identity was, at best, the denial of Ukraine's political aspiration or, at worst, the denial of a Ukrainian cultural identity altogether.

Thus, the ethnic identities of Ukraine and Russia continue to be at loggerheads. For Ukraine it is essential to distance itself from Russia and reassert a separate identity. For Russian nationalists, to admit that Ukraine and Belarus are indeed separate units entitled to a separate national life would mean that many parts of the contemporary Russian Federation have no less a right to secede from Russia. The Russian philosopher Aleksandr Tsipko (though his name is Ukrainian) noted that without Ukraine as a part of it "there can be no Russia in the old, real sense of the word."[41] Conversely, for Ukrainian politicians, to admit any "special relationship" with Russia is to question Ukraine's status as a separate sovereign nation.

This historic compulsion for mutual denial has been further aggravated by each group's contradictory memories of the Soviet experience. Ukrainians feel that they, along with some smaller banished nations, were the prime sufferers of the Stalinist period. Having experienced first a cultural decapitation followed by a holocaust through hunger, the prevalent feeling in Ukraine is that its people were reduced to "raw material" for a Russian empire. The Russians, in turn, feel that it was they who suffered the most cultural, economic, and physical deprivation during the Soviet era, constantly being forced to "make room" for minorities, including Ukrainians. As *Pravda* articulated:

> The Russian people . . . assumed the greatest burden in the recent wars and in the economic efforts. . . . They voluntarily *made room for others,* consciously giving their help to other nations and nationalities . . . for a long time it was not acceptable to discuss such things.[42]

Thus, Russian intellectuals, while supporting Baltic aspirations or those of other national minorities, were stunned by the demands for independence from their Slavic brethren, the Ukrainians. If one were to look at the critical period between 1988 and 1991 when the USSR showed signs of accelerated unraveling, one is stunned by the indifference to events in Ukraine. While Yeltsin continued to preach Russian sovereignty, the underlying assumption on the Russian side was that its "younger Slavic" siblings had neither the will nor the ability to assert their independence. Therefore, when the USSR disintegrated in the wake of the August 1991 coup, Russian response to Ukrainian national aspirations was a series of contradictory reactions, ranging from disbelief to anger to attempted conciliation. When Ukraine asserted its sovereignty, the initial Russian reaction was to attempt to threaten Ukraine with irredentist territorial claims. When that failed, Rutskoi traveled to Kiev trying to ease the tension, calling the situation a temporary setback. In fact, the notion that Ukraine is indeed determined to remain an independent state remains inimitable to the Russian elite. Even the act of dismemberment of the USSR agreed to during the Kravchuk-Yeltsin-Shushkevich meeting in December 1991 was initially perceived by Russia as a step toward the creation of a "more perfect union." President Kravchuk's almost immediate reneging on the Minsk agreement, which called for a single commonwealth "military-strategic space" along with a joint command structure, and Ukraine's insistence on its own armed forces were perceived in Moscow as an act of betrayal that colored the relationship from the very start.[43]

Ukraine's independence poses three main threats to Russia's ethnonational identity. First of all, the Russian Empire (at least in its Slavic context) is a part of the Russian national identity. To concede that Kiev, "Russia's mother city," "Yaroslav the Wise," and so on are all foreign entities is a loss of national symbols difficult to assimilate under the best of circumstances. Second, the loss of Ukraine and Belarus and hence the physical removal of Russia from the European mainstream is a severe blow to Russia's self-image.[44] Finally, since many, even among the elite in Russia, only vaguely differentiate between Ukraine and other parts of Russia, the secession of Ukraine is perceived as a harbinger to further disintegration of the Russian Federation, especially in regions where the population is non-Slavic and the potential for greater economic progress outside the federation is great.

It is due to the psychological impact of this baggage that Russian policy toward Ukraine is not a "realpolitik" policy toward a neighboring country of fifty-two million and an important trading partner.

Russian policy makers across the political spectrum, ranging from the pseudo-fascist Zhirinovsky to the Western-oriented Foreign Minister Kozyrev, cannot resist the temptation to treat Ukrainian independence as a temporary aberration. In fact, Russia's ambassador to Kiev went so far as to urge East Europeans not to invest in embassies in Kiev since those will soon again be consulates in a unified state.[45] The emergence of an independent Ukraine is a blow to the Russian national self-image, and, indeed, perhaps the largest single contributor to the crisis of identity that is befalling Russia. However, Russia, by virtue of its size, military power, and economic potential, continues to retain sufficient pretense of being a great power within the international system to be able to start the process of carving out a new identity in the world arena.

The impact of Ukrainian ethnonationalism on that country's foreign policy is far more severe. Relations with Russia have become a key element in Ukraine's process of nation building. One of the most difficult legacies of the Pereiaslav agreement and the success of the various Russification campaigns was Ukraine's disappearance from the international consciousness as a nation entitled to independence. Almost constantly during the twentieth century outsiders have confused Ukraine with Russia and rejected Ukraine as a legitimate player within the international system. Ukraine's delegation to Versailles was all but ignored by the Western powers, despite the latter's support for Polish, Czech, Baltic, and other drives for independence. The Allied conferences during World War II, aside from agreeing to Stalin's demands to use the Curzon line as the demarcation between Poland and the USSR and promising a seat at the UN for Ukraine, hardly raised the issue of Ukraine. Even at the height of the cold war, when Ukrainian nationalists continued to wage a bitter guerrilla war against the Stalinization of western

Ukraine, the Policy Planning Staff of the National Security Council in an internal memo insisted:

> While the Ukrainians have been an important and a specific element of the Russian Empire, they have shown no signs of being a 'nation.' ... It should be noted, as stated above, we would not encourage Ukrainian separatism; nevertheless, if an independent regime were to come into being on the territory of the Ukraine through no doing of ours, *we should not oppose it outright.* (emphasis added)[46]

While the OSS did provide the Ukrainian insurgents with some help, the West never mastered an outrage similar to the one provoked by the Stalinization of Poland, the Baltics, or Czechoslovakia. This sentiment was echoed again during the late 1980s, when the international community showed far greater sympathy to Baltic aspirations for independence than to those of Ukraine. This was manifested by President Bush's "Kiev Speech," warning Ukrainians not to push for independence or pursue "suicidal nationalism," and by Chancellor Kohl, who clearly sided with Gorbachev in his efforts to preserve the Soviet Union.

Given this historical experience, it stands to reason that any Ukrainian government would attempt, at the earliest possible moment, to establish a separate identity from Russia. President Kravchuk's efforts to establish separate embassies, or a separate navy or, on a more quixotic plane, to insist on the USSR's seat on the UN Security Council, or Ukrainian Deputy Prime Minister Iukhnovs'kyi's statement that Ukraine "cannot pass up the assets and payments of our own debt if we want to build an independent state,"[47] somehow equating indebtedness with independence, may have baffled many Western observers. However, in the context of establishing a distinct identity for Ukraine, this policy has its own logic. While a "rational" approach may dictate the perpetuation of "special relations" with Russia, Ukraine's fragile ethnonational identity at home, as well as its low profile abroad, demands a degree of assertiveness that at times appears to run counter to Ukraine's national interest. Similarly, Ukraine's defense policy —the insistence on a large army of 400,000 men, a viable blue-water fleet, and likely retention of nuclear weapons—again may appear to the West to be a shortsighted policy that antagonizes Russia and isolates Ukraine from the West. Nevertheless, these policies do have a rationale in the context of Ukraine's history. It was the absence of military power that led to the loss of Ukrainian independence during the last three centuries. Khmel'nyts'kyi's Pereiaslav agreement with Tsar Aleksei reflected Ukraine's military impotence. Mazepa's (1640?–1709) attempt to use the international system as a guarantor of Ukraine's independence through an alliance with Sweden failed after the defeat of the Swedes at Poltava in 1709, and the Rada regime's efforts (especially in the early phases in 1918) to attain an ideological understanding with Russia following the October Revolution likewise failed to secure Ukraine's independence. It would, therefore, be very hard to convince any Ukrainian government to forego a credible deterrent if Ukraine is to survive as an independent state.

This situation is further aggravated by the power base of President Kravchuk. President Kravchuk, a former ideology chief of the Ukrainian Communist Party who turned nationalist relatively late (in fact, after the collapse of the coup in Moscow), represents the complexity of Ukraine's political makeup. The referendum for independence, as well as Kravchuk's electoral campaign, was a successful attempt to please two divergent constituencies—the western part of Ukraine, along with the Kiev metropolitan area, where nationalist fervor ran high and separatist feelings were strong, and the Donbass along with the southern fringe of Ukraine, where the Russian-speaking population remained keen to preserve the existing economic order. Former president Kravchuk managed to build his power base and, perhaps, retain the unity of the country through appealing to both groups. By opposing painful economic reforms, he managed to retain the support of the industrial east, while through an assertive nationalist policy he undercut Chornovil in the western regions. Ukraine's assertive foreign policy, which would have been inimical to almost any government in Moscow, was exacerbated by the bombastic tone that Kravchuk was forced to adopt in order to retain a political hold over Ukraine's nationalist west. In fact, as Kravchuk's ability to sustain the Soviet-style economy in the industrial east faltered, his popularity in the Donbass rapidly evaporated. Meanwhile in the western part of the country, where his Communist past initially made him suspect, his ability to "stand tall" to Moscow made him the region's prodigal son.[48]

The question of Ukraine's ethnonational posture toward Russia is further complicated by the country's growing political polarization. Rukh, which started out as a broad coalition of opponents of Soviet domination under the leadership of Chornovil, has increasingly mutated to a predominantly ethnic Ukrainian party with an increasingly strident nationalist tone and growing anti-Russian rhetoric. The Rukh-led coalition of the "Anti-Imperialist Bloc" more and more favors an accelerated transfer to a market economy as well as an end to all remaining links to Russia under the auspices of the Commonwealth of Independent States (CIS). Another problematic factor is that Rukh not only has an increasingly nationalist orientation but also has a growing reliance on western Ukraine as its power base. Conversely, in the Russian-speaking eastern Ukraine there is under way a reemergence of a Communist Party that favors the resuscitation of many "Soviet" institutions, including an enhanced CIS and closer links with Russia in particular.

What we are witnessing now is a rather peculiar process. While on the elite level there is a conscious retreat from acrimonious polemics between Moscow and Kiev, on the popular level there is a growing radicalization of attitudes. As mentioned before, in Ukraine not only did Rukh shift from a broadly inclusive political entity to one of ever-growing national exclusiveness, but Valentyn Moroz, the leader of the L'viv chapter of Rukh, openly adopted the old integralist slogan of "Ukraine is for the Ukrainians." The historian Iaroslav Dashkevych defended the integralist slogan, noting, "of course Ukraine should be for Ukrainians. After all, for hundreds of years it was for everyone else but the Ukrainians."[49] The Ukrainian cultural society Prosvita organized demonstrations in Odessa protesting the fact that Ukraine's new internal passport no longer follows the Soviet practice of having an entry for ethnicity. In western Ukraine, in particular, but by no means limited to this region, a plethora of right-wing nationalist groups, such as the Social Nationalist Party, the Ukrainian Nationalist League, and other self-proclaimed successors to the OUN, more and more frequently insist on a hard-line nationalist policy toward Russia. While these organizations may well be on the political fringe, nevertheless they do represent a growing mainstream feeling that the government of Ukraine has been pandering too much to the linguistic and cultural rights of the Russian minority, without getting a Russian quid pro quo to help preserve Ukrainian culture among the four million Ukrainians in Russia, and at the same time slowing the progress of establishing the Ukrainian language as the lingua franca of the country. Ukraine's domestic political alignment is also complicated by the growing nationalist assertiveness of the Union of Ukrainian Officers, which recently escalated its demands for an accelerated "Ukrainization" of the armed forces and the retention of nuclear weapons stationed on Ukrainian soil.[50] The position of the officers' union, a powerful political lobby, can only fuel the suspicions of the Russian minority in Ukraine and heighten tensions with Russia.

A similar shift to the right has occurred in Russia. Again, while the rightist views of Zhirinovsky or Pamyat remain a fringe view, Russian nationalists effectively using their publications, such as *Literaturnaia Rossia, Nash sovremennik, Den'*, and others, have managed to create a vocal political force capable of exercising its influence far out of proportion to its actual numbers. Utilizing such emotional issues as the loss of Russian grandeur, minority rights for the twenty-five million Russians outside of Russia, and a "conspiracy" to destroy Russia, the Russian nationalist right (at times in alliance with the Communists) has managed to put the liberals on the defensive and force the Russian government to deal with issues it would rather avoid. The position of Russia's military command, citing nuclear weapons in Ukraine as the prime threat to Russia's security, and the demands of the Russian Officers' Union for a single army on CIS territory[51] has forced the Russian body politic toward a more confrontational policy toward Ukraine. The pressure from the right has not only caused an exodus of numerous Russian politicians from the liberal camp to the nationalist camp[52] but has forced relatively liberal actors, such as Kozyrev and Yeltsin, to adopt the issue of the Russian minority as their own. While both Ukraine and Russia are witnessing the emergence of vocal, radical groups that can affect policies on the governmental level, the trend at the highest levels of government is toward lowering the level of rhetoric and shifting toward more pragmatic policies.

On the Russian side, the illusion once shared by virtually the entire Russian national elite—that Ukraine's longing for independence is a fantasy limited to a handful of "Banderites"[53] in Galicia—has vanished. While few in the Russian elite have fully accepted the legitimacy of Ukraine's independence, and fewer still have reconciled themselves to the loss of Crimea, nevertheless, Ukraine's statehood is increasingly treated as a fait accompli that cannot be fully reversed. In fact, although some Russian politicians continue to complain about the "threat" to the cultural heritage of the Russians in Ukraine, the growing tendency is to attempt to come to terms with it. Increasingly, the Russian government seems to accept Fedor Shelov-Kovediaev's thesis that Russia can regain its influence with the CIS only on the basis of successful reforms at home.[54] Some of Yeltsin's closest advisors, such as Aleksandr Shokhin, have taken that notion even a step further, arguing that in order to carry out successful reform at home, Russia must reduce its bonds with the "near abroad" (even the friendly states of Belarus and Kazakhstan) to normal neighborly relations, have separate currencies, and conduct all economic intercourse on a purely commercial basis. It would appear that, since the recent referendum in Russia, there is a growing tendency toward a "Russia first" policy, and a shifting away from Russia's previous "special relationships" with other former states. It is instructive to note that, in a recent public opinion poll conducted by *Moscow News,* when Russian adults were asked which former part of the USSR they would like to see rejoin Russia, 24 percent said Ukraine; however, 20 percent said none![55]

While in Ukraine the relationship with Russia continues to loom large, there, too, the first six months of 1993 saw a growing moderation in rhetoric and substance. Unlike then president Kravchuk, who made scrappiness with Moscow a source of personal political legitimacy, Leonid Kuchma, Ukraine's then prime minister (coming from the eastern part of the country and being well aware of Ukraine's sinking economy), made the restoration of a good relationship with Russia a priority. Recognizing that Poland will not become Ukraine's gate to the West, Kuchma stated frankly that "We need an *economic union*. Ukraine probably needs it more, and Belarus and other republics need it even more. Russian needs it less. However, all need it" (emphasis added).[56] If President Kravchuk argued that Yeltsin represents the high point of Russian liberalism, and Ukraine must prepare itself for the day when it faces a reactionary irredentist Russia, Kuchma's supporters have repeatedly stressed that Russia historically expanded not into a demographic vacuum but rather into a political vacuum. Kuchma went on to insist that unless Ukraine jump-starts its economy (a virtual impossibility without Russian collaboration), Ukraine will degenerate into a political vacuum, which will tempt outside forces to inject themselves into Ukraine's internal affairs. This view that Ukraine must go beyond building the trappings of a state and concentrate on building a viable economic structure seems to be shared by the Ukrainian public. In a February 1992 public opinion poll, 40 percent of Ukrainians who responded cited domestic difficulties as the main threat to the country's security, while 22 percent cited other CIS countries, presumably Russia.

With Leonid Kuchma's popularity rating twice as high as that of Kravchuk, the president responded in two ways. Kravchuk joined Kuchma in calling for Russian-Ukrainian economic integration, albeit "on new principles,"[57] but, at the same time, relieved Kuchma of his post. Even on the vexing issue of Sevastopol there seems to be some movement. In the first few months of 1993 the two governments managed to contain the pressures from their respective fringes and move the relationship toward a more normal level. Kuchma called on Ukraine to recognize the fact that Russia is not going to withdraw from the harbor and, instead of turning the issue into a source of contention, Ukraine should lease the facilities to Russia, and turn it into a moneymaking proposition.[58] While the two countries continued to disagree on issues such as the Black Sea fleet and the ownership of nuclear weapons on Ukrainian soil, nevertheless, the level of rhetoric between the two governments remains subdued. The two countries managed to agree on how to deal with the issue of the debt of the former Soviet Union, and on 15 May 1993 both signed the draft treaty calling for a "joint economic space" within the CIS.

If one had to characterize the current state of Russian-Ukrainian relations, one can note a certain "convergence." Russian "centrists," such as Arkadii Vol'skii, feel that the prime task at hand is the internal consolidation of Russia. As far as the CIS is concerned, while these centrists see the breakup of the USSR as a tragic event, they recognize that its reconstitution is not feasible and, therefore, urge closer integration within the framework of the CIS. This attitude is not very different from the position staked out by Leonid Kuchma and later adopted by Kravchuk himself. It is because of this emerging convergence that both governments, despite their inability to reach an understanding on such important issues as the Black Sea fleet and nuclear weapons, have managed to avoid the kind of theatrical rhetoric that typified the relationship during the first year of separation. If, indeed, there is an issue that is bound to test this new "convergence" between the governments of Ukraine and Russia, it is the question of nuclear weapons, which have become the litmus test of the trust that Ukrainians and Russians have in each other. Given the historic experience of Ukraine and the fact that its military impotence ultimately led to its repeated loss of independence, General Tolubko's remark that "only idiots give up nuclear weapons"[59] reflects a deep-seated historic fear of military impotence. This fear is further reinforced by the chronic marginalization of Ukraine within the international system.

Finally, there is a constant undercurrent of belief that the Yeltsin presidency in Russia is the high point of Russian liberalism and anti-imperialism, and that it is only a question of time before Russia's imperialist urge will rear its ugly head again. Stepan Khmara of the Ukrainian Conservative Republican Party may not always reflect Ukrainian public opinion; however, his remark that "As long as the Russian empire exists, its neighbors will live under direct threat to their security and independence"[60] does reflect the feelings of many Ukrainians. It should be noted that to many Ukrainians the Russian Federation, given its size and the nature of its political psychology, continues to be an empire even after August 1991. Under such circumstances no Ukrainian government will be able to give up its nuclear arsenal soon. Even the pragmatic Kuchma urged the Ukrainian parliament to declare Ukraine a "temporary nuclear power."[61]

Should the Ukrainian government opt to renege on the Lisbon agreements and retain its nuclear weapons, the stereotype of a perfidious Ukraine (so dear to the Russian extreme right), a country that betrayed Russia during the Mazepa uprising in the eighteenth century and during World War II and then reneged on the Minsk agreement, will gain far wider currency than it has now. Russian nationalists and even large parts of the Russian center will perceive Ukraine as a country that is trying to isolate Russia from Europe and, indeed, build a "cordon sanitaire" akin to the mini-entente of the 1920s and 1930s. The Russian military establishment, which already portrays Ukraine as the greatest threat to Russia's security, will only step up its shrill anti-Ukrainian campaign. Statements such as those of Baburin, that Ukraine can be either a part of Russia or enemy territory, will be taken to heart all the more. In short, the nuclear arms issue has become a poisoned chalice to pragmatic leaders in both countries.

Even if the governments do succeed, despite the nuclear issue, in retaining this new seeming homeostasis, several severe challenges lie ahead, given the chronic internal political weakness of both Russia and Ukraine. In the case of Russia, the prospect of a "Red-Brown" coalition coming to power remains a real possibility. Should such a government emerge, the urge to present Kiev with irredentist claims would be almost irresistible. Another troubling scenario, which is all too often overlooked, is the possibility that, should the Russian Federation disintegrate, it may well cause a civil war in Russia—a war that is highly likely to spill over into ethnically Russian and Russophone areas beyond the borders of the Russian Federation.

The situation in Ukraine is hardly better. The political and economic polarization between the eastern and western parts of the country threatens internal stability and might create the kind of "political vacuum" that Moscow will find hard to resist. Ukraine's current policy of dodging economic reform has primarily benefited the Russophone Donbass, where Stalinist behemoths continue to exist thanks to massive subsidies from the Ukrainian government. This process adversely affects the western part of the country, through both the usual impact of hyperinflation and the absence of serious economic reform, and dashes Ukraine's hope of integration with its Western neighbors—a notion deeply supported in western Ukraine. However, should Ukraine undertake profound economic reform, it may well confront a situation analogous to Czechoslovakia, where the different degrees of pain associated with economic transformation rekindled seemingly dormant nationalist feelings. Given the fact that there are about 1.1 million miners in the Donbass and given the fact that according to Kuchma at least 45 percent of these mines should be immediately shut, the potential for unemployment and economic strife turning into ethnic or linguistic strife is a real threat.

Given the fact that de facto regional (and by implication linguistic) parties already have emerged, and given the fact that the economic interests of the two regions (west and east) are contradictory, it would have taken all of Kravchuk's uncanny political skills to maintain a balance that would avoid a "political vacuum" that an unreconciled Moscow would be tempted to exploit.

We should also remain mindful that in both Russia and Ukraine there are millions of "Soviet" people, ranging from apparatchiks to officers to employees of the military-industrial complex to mafiosi, who see the disintegration of the USSR as a personal tragedy and, therefore, would be delighted to see the new states fail. These people are waiting in the wings ready to capitalize on any nascent disorder.[62]

No empire dies gracefully. It took more than seventy years for a British monarch to agree to meet the Irish president "for tea." Russia and Ukraine will continue to jostle over such substantive issues as nuclear weapons and the Black Sea fleet as well as symbolic issues, such as the legacy of Kievan Rus', the historic role of Mazepa, or the power struggle between the Moscow and Kievan patriarchate within the Ukrainian Orthodox Church. However, if there is a positive legacy to the Soviet empire, it is the fact that the brutality of Stalinism created a powerful aversion to all violence and "cured" the polities of the violent and praetorian political culture that historically typified the region. It is instructive that even in the Crimea, where Russo-Ukrainian tensions are at their worst, only 3 percent of Russians and 2 percent of Ukrainians believe that the two nations will not be able to resolve their differences peacefully.[63] It is this yearning for a normal life that might ultimately be the strongest shaping force of Ukrainian-Russian relations.

Notes

1. See, for example, Kenneth Waltz, *The Theory of International Politics* (Reading, MA: Addison-Wesley, 1979). For a good discussion of the American realist school, see Michael J. Smith, "Realism in American Foreign Policy" (Ph.D. diss., Harvard University, 1982).

2. Francis Fukuyama, "The End of History," *National Interest* (summer 1989).

3. John Mearsheimer, "Back to the Future," *International Security* (summer 1990).

4. For an excellent discussion of pre-Listian Nationalism, see Roman Szporluk, *Communism and Nationalism* (New York and Oxford: Oxford University Press, 1988), chap. 6.

5. Ivan L. Rudnytsky, *Essays in Modern Ukrainian History* (Edmonton: Canadian Institute of Ukrainian Studies, University of Alberta, 1987), p. 45.

6. Neither 1339 nor 1654 implies complete domination of Ukraine, but rather a start of a process that rarely engulfed all of Ukraine, and that affected different parts of the country to differing degrees.

7. Ivan Rudnytsky, "Polish-Ukrainian Relations: The Burden of History," in Peter J. Potichnyj, ed., *Poland and Ukraine Past and Present* (Edmonton and Toronto: Canadian Institute of Ukrainian Studies, 1980).

8. For an English translation of the Haydamaks, see C.H. Andrusyshen and Watson Kirkconnell, trans., *The Poetical Works of Taras Shevchenko* (Toronto: University of Toronto Press, 1964), p. 103.

9. An ironic note in the Hollywood film of this epic—Yul Brynner and his Cossacks sing "Galinka" as they gather around the campfire.

10. For a discussion of Poland's interwar Ukrainian policy, see Bohdan Budurowycz, "Poland and the Ukrainian Problem 1921–39," *Canadian Slavonic Papers*, vol. 25, no. 4 (December 1983), pp. 473–500.

11. See John A. Armstrong's classic *Ukrainian Nationalism* (Littleton, CO: Ukrainian Academic Press, 1980).

12. For an official Polish (Communist) version of the campaign, see A.B. Szczesniak and W.Z. Szota, *Droga do nikad: Dzialalnosc OUN i jej likwidacja w Polsce* (Warsaw: Wydawn. Ministerstwa Obrony Narodowej, 1973).

13. See Joseph Rothchild, *Eastern Europe Between the Two World Wars* (Seattle: University of Washington Press, 1979).

14. Khmelko, in his presentation at the Kennan Institute during the spring of 1993, noted that in order to get a true reflection of linguistic preference in Ukraine, he distrib-

uted bilingual questionnaires. Of the questionnaires returned, 43 percent were in Ukrainian, 57 percent in Russian. There was wide regional differentiation as well.

15. See John Basarab, "Post-War Writing in Poland on Polish Ukrainian Relations, 1945–70," in Potichnyj, ed., *Poland and Ukraine*.

16. Quoted in Elizabeth Teague, *Solidarity and the Soviet Worker: The Impact of Polish Events on Soviet Internal Politics* (New York and London: Croom Helm, 1988), p. 177.

17. Ibid., p. 163.

18. See Bohdan R. Bociurkiw, "Ukrainian Catholic Church in Gorbachev's USSR," *Problems of Communism*, November–December 1990.

19. See Anna Swidlicka, "Senate Calls for Changes in Eastern Policy," *RFE/RL Report on Eastern Europe*, no. 39, 28 September 1990.

20. See Janusz Bugajski, *Nations in Turmoil: Conflict and Cooperation in Eastern Europe* (Boulder: Westview Press, 1993), p. 43.

21. PAP News Wire, 20 June 1992. A similar poll carried out by the U.S-based D–3 organization in June of 1992 noted that 34 percent of Poles felt that Ukraine is most threatening, 13 percent Russia, and 11 percent Germany (Radio Warsaw, June 1992).

22. *Interfax*, 1 November 1992.

23. *La Stampa*, 4 March 1992.

24. *Życie Warszawy*, 20 May 1992.

25. PAP Polish News Service, 22 May 1992.

26. See Jan de Weydenthal, "The Troubled Polish-Russian Economic Relations," *RFE/RL Research Report*, vol. 2, no. 7 (2 June 1993).

27. See Leszek Moczulski, *U progu niepodleglosci* (Lublin: EMBE Press, 1990).

28. It should be stressed that the concepts of President Walesa and Moczulski are by no means identical. President Walesa sees an East-Central European alliance between the Vysegrad Group or "NATO Bis" as a means to bring Poland into the West. Moczulski's KPN, with a strong similarity to the pre–World War II Endecja, is highly nationalistic, and sees a Polish-Ukrainian bloc as an anti-Western as well as anti-Russian third force.

29. Reuters, 24 May 1993.

30. PAP, Polish Press Agency, 12 January 1992.

31. PAP News Wire, 24 May 1993.

32. Edward L. Keenan, "Muscovite Perception of Other Eastern Slavs before 1654—An Agenda for Historians," in *Ukraine and Russia in their Historic Encounter*, ed. Peter J. Potichnyj, Marc Raeff, Jaroslaw Pelenski, and Gleb Zekulin (Edmonton: Canadian Institute of Ukrainian Studies Press, 1992).

33. Dmitrii S. Likhachev, "The National Nature of Russian History," Harriman Institute, Columbia University, New York, 1990.

34. See Yaroslav Bilinsky, "Political Relations Between Russians and Ukrainians in the USSR: The 1970's and Beyond," in Potichnyj et al., *Ukraine and Russia*.

35. See Mykhailo Hrushevsky, "Traditional Scheme of 'Russian' History and the Problem of Rational Organization of History of Eastern Slavs," reprinted in *From Kievan Rus' To Modern Ukraine: Formation of the Ukrainian Nation* (Cambridge, MA: Ukrainian Millennium Series, Ukrainian Studies Fund, Harvard University, 1984).

36. This position is held not only by "Soviet" historians, but also by dissident Russians as well; see Aleksandr I. Solzhenitsyn, *Kak nam obustroit' Rossiiu?* (Moscow: Pravda Press, 1990).

37. Jaroslaw Pelenski, "The Contest for the Kievan Inheritance," in Potichnyj et al., *Ukraine and Russia*, p. 13.

38. Marc Raeff, "Ukraine and Imperial Russia: Intellectual and Political Encounters

from the Seventeenth to the Nineteenth Century," in Potichnyj et al., *Ukraine and Russia*, p. 69.

39. Richard Pipes, *Russia Under the Old Regime* (New York: Collier Books, 1992), p. 239.

40. See Nikolai S. Trubetskoi, "The Ukrainian Problem," in *The Legacy of Genghis Khan* (Ann Arbor: Michigan Slavic Publications, 1991).

41. Quoted in Vera Tolz and Elizabeth Teague, "Russian Intellectuals Adjust to Loss of Empire," *RFE/RL Research Report*, vol. 1, no. 3 (21 February 1992).

42. *Pravda*, 28 March 1987. (I owe this quote to Darrell P. Hammer's article "Glasnost' and the Russian Idea" from "Russian Nationalism Today," *RFE/RL* Special Edition no. 19, December 1988.)

43. See Alexander Motyl, *Dilemmas of Independence: Ukraine After Totalitarianism* (New York: Council of Foreign Relations, 1993), p. 109.

44. The enthusiasm with which the Russian publication *Kommersant* reported on the Russian-Belarus agreement to create a joint "security space" as a means to make Russia "European again" is noteworthy.

45. See "Tough Enough," *Economist*, 3 March 1993.

46. Internal memo, S.W. Soures, Executive Secretary NSC 20/1 RG 273, 18 August 1948.

47. *Moscow News*, 20 January 1993.

48. In the December 1991 election President Kravchuk garnered around 60 percent of the votes in the east, and got less than 25 percent of the votes in L'viv Oblast (see Henry R. Huttenbach, *Analyses of Current Events*, December 1991). In a public opinion poll carried out in late 1992, Kravchuk lost his support in the east—and only in western Ukraine could he garner 53 percent of the vote. *RFE/RL Research Report*, vol. 1, no. 41 (20 October 1992).

49. Quoted in Motyl, *Dilemmas of Independence*, p. 83.

50. BBC, *Summary of World Broadcasts*, 6 January 1993.

51. See Irina Shkarinkova in *Nezavisimaia gazeta*, 14 January 1993, p. 2.

52. See Vera Tolz, "The Burden of Imperial Legacy in Russia," *RFE/RL Research Report*, vol. 2, no. 20 (14 May 1993).

53. Stepan Bandera, leader of the OUN (R) and assassinated by the KGB in 1959, remains to many Russians the symbol of western Ukrainian nationalism, which to them has little in common with the rest of Ukraine.

54. See John Lough, "Defining Russia's Relations with Neighboring States," *RFE/RL Research Report*, vol. 1, no. 20 (14 May 1992).

55. *Moscow News*, 7 April 1993.

56. Interview with Kuchma, Radio Moscow, 13 January 1993.

57. *Interfax*, 16 April 1993.

58. *Financial Times*, 2 June 1992.

59. *Washington Post*, 3 June 1993.

60. *Ekspress Khronika*, 30 December 1992.

61. *Financial Times*, 4 June 1993.

62. In a poll conducted by the Kiev International Sociological Center in January 1993, 52 percent of Ukrainians regarded the collapse of the USSR as a "great tragedy." *Reuter Library Report*, 6 January 1993. In the case of Russians when asked whether they "regret" the demise of the USSR, more than two-thirds answered yes. *Moscow News*, 7 April 1993.

63. Vladimir Ruban, *Moscow News*, 25 November 1992.

6

Development of Belarusian National Identity and Its Influence on Belarus's Foreign Policy Orientation

Jan Zaprudnik

Sovereignty as a Source of Foreign Policy

Sovereignty Institutionalized

Form breeds content. No matter how unassertive Belarusian national consciousness and how insecure Belarusian statehood, both are gaining ground as time goes on and the seminal acts of sovereignty and independence are solidified by legislation. It is true that many of the laws passed remain ineffective and do not change reality much; nevertheless they create a formal base that is being used by the more radical elements to change, if not the order of things, at least the mentality of the wider public. This is a slow, generational change, but it is clearly occurring. Events and developmental tendencies in Belarus during the past two to three years furnish much evidence to support the observation by Ronald Suny that "nationality as well as nationalism, like other social and cultural formations, is the product of real historical conjunctures, in which ethnic communities, activist intelligentsias, and political imperatives have worked together to create a new level of national coherence, consolidation, and consciousness."[1] The very concept of the Belarusian nation has been formally shifted from an earlier ethnocultural emotional plane to a more rational politico-civil one. Here is the new formula for a multiethnic Belarusian state: "Citizens of the Belarusian SSR of all nationalities constitute the Belarusian people," announces the Declaration of State Sovereignty of Belarus (Article 2). This modernization of the concept has been designed to shift the allegiance and loyalty of a multiethnic society to a more lofty ideal of a political structure with equal rights for citizens of all ethnic groups. To be sure, there are still tensions based on culture and religion, especially around the age-old equation in the popular mind of "Russianness" and Orthodoxy on the one hand, and "Polishness" and Catholicism on the other. With the rising linguistic assertiveness of the Belarusian intelligentsia and the resistance of both church hierarchies, Orthodox and Catholic, to assigning a larger role to the Belarusian language in religious life, the issue has been loudly debated in the public sphere. However, as far as legislation goes, all ethnic minorities of the republic have been treated with careful equanimity.

The national legislature, in spite of its lack of professionalism and experience, has passed an impressive number of acts elaborating and reinforcing the concept of a Belarusian sovereign state. A legal base for civil activism has been put in place, and free expression, as an instrument of political mobilization, is limited principally by the government's overwhelming economic power.

In his report to the Eleventh Supreme Council Session in March 1993, Council Chairman Stanislau Shushkevich proudly said that in less than three years the Belarusian parliament had adopted "about 500 legal acts—more than we did over the past 50 years."[2]

The Belarusian state has been evolving conceptually, politically, and physically, in terms of its borders. The latest step in the latter aspect was taken on 7 April 1993, when the Presidium of the Supreme Council approved a draft resolution conferring the status of "state borders" to boundaries with Ukraine, Lithuania, and Latvia. The parliament was reciprocating similar moves made earlier by the three neighboring states, with the purpose of "defending of the political and economic interests of the republic."[3]

All these legal developments create an atmosphere in which foreign policy concerns are still distant from a popular mind that has been depressed by economic hardships and has not yet emerged from psychological inertia. The latter becomes evident if we look at the sphere of culture.

Sovereignty's Impact on Culture and Worldview

The basic current foreign policy concern in Belarus, as mentioned above, is the government's proposal to accede to the collective security treaty with six other CIS states (Russia, Armenia, Kazakhstan, Kyrgyzstan, Tajikistan, and Uzbekistan). The move has been prompted by economic considerations, but there is undeniably also a cultural impulse involved, namely the government's pro-Russian sentiments. These are epitomized by the premier himself, Viachaslau Kebich, and are quite evident for all to see. Thus, for example, although he promised on several occasions to make his public speeches in Belarusian (which he knows), he still speaks mostly Russian. His government is very lax in implementing the 1990 law About Languages, which made Belarusian the only official language of the state. Russian still resonates in most official places throughout the republic. Insisting on use of the national language is widely perceived as a manifestation of nationalism, and Kebich does not want to be viewed as infected by it. "My personal opinion," he says, "is this: I have not shared nationalist views, do not share them, and will not share them." Quoting these words from the pro-Russian daily, *Sovetskaia Belorussiia,* his critic wrote, "When one reads his [Kebich's] answers concerning issues of Belarusianness, one gets the impression that it is not the head of government of a sovereign state who is speaking, but a high official sent from Moscow."[4]

To be fair, he does not always sound that way. At the time of his appointment as premier in June 1990, Kebich saw "only one way out—the economic sovereignty of Belarus." He also recognized the "immense damage caused to the people's spiritual strength, all that comprises the nation's foundation—language, culture, and morality" by the previous regime.[5] Two and a half years later, he elaborated on this theme in what was advertised as his major speech to the Belarusian intelligentsia. Speaking in an ancient castle, the prime minister said,

> National self-awareness cannot and should not be formed as a result of good wishes. If we are a nation, we should by all means have our own national holy places. It is not easy for us to shape our national self-awareness with the national heritage we have received, not easy to reconvince our contemporaries and successors that we do have a history of our statehood, that we are not some rootless Ivans. The fact that currently many Belarusians cannot read Belarusian and sometimes are ashamed to speak their native language and cannot overcome their shame, confirms once again how we have destroyed our national mentality. That is why any efforts, state and public initiatives, to revive our national history are so necessary and valuable.[6]

Here we have a case to illustrate the concept of "fitness," used by Walter Clemens, Jr., in his chapter "Baltic Identities in the 1990s: Renewed Fitness," as applied to Belarusians. The "fitness" of the Belarusians in relation to their environment has been severely undermined by a series of disasters: Stalinist genocide, population loss in World War II, Chernobyl radiation, and Russification. While some of the losses are irreparable, and others require huge sums of money to compensate, "fitness" is being increased through cultural rehabilitation, largely by means of reinterpreting the historical past. The nation is being redefined both in terms of its history and its place in the world. Rewriting the past begins with the drafting of the constitution, which, unlike the old one, speaks of a "centuries-old development of Belarusian statehood" that was "reflected in the Statutes of the Grand Duchy of Lithuania [written in Belarusian], the Constituent Charters of the Belarusian Democratic Republic, and the Constitutions of the Belarusian Soviet Socialist Republic."

The past, which provides a prism through which to see the present, is viewed in a new light. For the first time in decades, Belarusian historians are facing the task of developing a much-needed version of the nation's history. The rewriting of history promises to be thorough. The chairman of the republic's Main Archive, Alaksandr Mikhalchanka, speaking of a need to make a "serious review" of "many dates and events," admitted that scholars would have to "exert themselves considerably to work out their own Belarusian viewpoint about our national history."[7] It is an unusual challenge to some historians steeped in the school of "historical objectivity." The revisionists are trying to convince their hesitant colleagues that a national viewpoint does not necessarily mean distortion. "It seems to me there is no historical viewpoint which would be without a national character," said P.A. Shupliak, head of the history department of the Belarusian State University, in a roundtable discussion. "A 'Belarusian viewpoint' does not mean that we would rewrite history as if everything related to Belarus was good, and the rest was bad."[8] Nevertheless, evaluation of some major past events, whose ideological function was to mold the mentality of the "younger Belarusian brother" in a pro-Russian direction, has been reversed. Here is an example of a 180-degree turnabout. The protracted 1654–67 war between Russia and the Commonwealth of Poland (of which Belarus was a confederated partner as part of the Grand Duchy of Lithuania, Rus', and Samogitia) has been depicted as an effort to "liberate" Belarus. Now, in the opening issue of the new *Belaruski histarychny chasopis* (Belarusian historical journal), the same war is termed "predatory" and "annexationist" on the part of Russia.[9]

Historians, artists, and writers have been busy, though without much coordination, loosening their nation's past from the dead hand of the rejected Russified Marxist-Leninist dogmas. In accordance with the tenet enshrined in the draft of the constitution that Belarusian statehood has an ancient history, a new historiography is being developed to inspire and mobilize. Until the end of the 1980s, Belarusian national icons consisted exclusively of humanists: preachers, educators, philosophers, writers, and the like. Now, the pantheon is being expanded to include princes, noblemen, and war heroes who valiantly engaged not only the Teutonic Knights or Tatars, but also Muscovites. The anniversary of one victorious battle with the latter, fought on 8 September 1514, has been turned into a festive occasion and a military oath-taking ceremony by a group of officers was organized last year by the Belarusian Association of Servicemen, to the dismay of the generals.

The cultural history of old Belarus, especially of the sixteenth and seventeenth centuries—when the country was in confederation with Lithuania and Poland and enjoyed fruitful contacts with Western Europe—has become a source of debate about whether the mentality of Belarusians is different from that of Russians. Symon Padokshyn, for example, in a recent article celebrating the quatercentenary of the sixteenth-century Belarusian religious philosopher, Symon Budny, pointed to several "Western" features of the "Belarusian mentality" as "dominant"—religious pluralism and tolerance, political liberty, government by law, and freedom of travel—in juxtaposition to Muscovy (whose history was marked by despotism).[10] Intended or not, this kind of argument supports the Western-oriented foreign policy rationale as more natural and organic for the Belarusian state than staying within Moscow's orbit. Foreign Minister Piotr Krauchanka has spent considerable time cultivating a variety of ties with Western states, frequently referring to Belarus's distant cultural past. This Western orientation could enhance the nation's chances for democratic reforms if it were not for geostrategic and economic realities (discussed below) that tie Belarus to Russia. There are also considerable psychological barriers on the road to rebuilding the national mentality. The idea of a fully independent state with its own self-contained political history has yet to penetrate the popular mind. As things stand now, many Belarusians cannot think of themselves apart from Russians. A telling episode occurred during a visit of Polish journalists to Minsk: "The guests from Warsaw were quite surprised having learned from Mr. Butevich [Belarusian Minister of Information] that the Polish ethnic minority is the largest in Belarus. When the Minister was reminded that there are Russians, too, he said: 'Russians are not a minority!' At which the Poles were sincerely astonished."[11] A significant event in the process of rehabilitation of the Belarusian psyche is the appearance of the *Belaruski histarychny chasopis*, whose main goal is to guide teachers and historians themselves. Stanislau Shushkevich, in his introductory remarks, inspires them "To cleanse Belarusian history of borrowings and falsehoods, to awaken in people interest in their rich heritage and pride in it, persistence, principled positions, and deep inside a faith in renewal of the Fatherland will be needed."[12] The journal's editor, Vasil' Kushnier, elaborates:

> Historical scholarship and its researchers have never been nor will they be beyond politics. And we state openly and sincerely that our policy and the

main goal of the journal will be to enhance the process of national revival and a deepening of the national consciousness of the Belarusians.... This is state policy, anchored in legal acts of the Republic of Belarus.[13]

The chairman of the parliament, Stanislau Shushkevich, sees salubrious results of these new approaches to the national past. In his 1993 New Year's greetings he said, "I am proud of the changes in the mentality and consciousness of the Belarusian people that have taken place during 1992. Under such conditions, the legislature and the government will be able to carry out their policies."[14] Of course, what these policies should be in concrete cases is highly debatable in many instances, especially the agonizing issue of an economic-military alliance with Russia. While discussions continue, certain premises are being laid out concerning Belarus's proper place in the family of nations. Thus, Chairman Shushkevich said in a recent interview, "It seems to me that our independence, our neutrality is for the benefit of all of our neighbors and the world community. We can show an example of solving complex issues by political means and preserve our excellent image in the world."[15]

To achieve that goal, a project has been undertaken by the Academy of Sciences with the purpose of providing a "more profound and comprehensive, scientifically grounded Belarusian national idea." Explaining and popularizing the proposition, in March 1993 Academician Hienadz' Lych began a series of articles in the principal Belarusian-language daily, *Zviazda* (Star). "We Need a Vivifying Idea That Will Save Belarus," proclaimed the title of the series. On the one hand, says the author, there is "a deep crisis" threatening "the preservation even of the Belarusian ethnos itself, not to mention statehood," and on the other, "a unique chance given us by history itself to decide independently our own destiny, to overcome finally the old relationship of subordination to and dependence on another state."

Where Prime Minister Kebich sees a healthy economy as the beginning of the salutary road to sovereignty, Academician Lych points out "a great vivifying national idea that would unite the Belarusian people and bring out from its midst political leaders and statesmen who would well understand national interests and be ready to serve them selflessly." He admits, however, that so far, there is no such idea, and its formulation still lies ahead, being "a matter of the collective wisdom of the entire Belarusian people," and that he has no illusions as to the protracted nature of the process. But the agenda is there. Only, says Lych, one has to "listen very carefully to what people themselves are saying."[16]

So far, "people themselves" are not very supportive. Along with Lych's piece, *Zviazda* published in the same issue an ITAR-TASS report about the results of a poll conducted by Austrian specialists on how Belarusians and Ukrainians compare life under the old Communist regime and now. According to the poll, the present system of economic development found only 15 percent support in Belarus and merely 4 percent in Ukraine. In the sphere of politics, the old Communist rule found 61 percent approval in Belarus and 54 percent in Ukraine; as to the present political system of pluralism and democracy, it was rejected by 48 percent in Belarus and 53 percent in Ukraine; pluralism and democracy as they have been practiced up to now found approval from a minority of 35 percent of Belarusians and 27 percent of Ukrainians. One would like to see similar polling on foreign policy issues, but, as Foreign Minister Piotr Krauchanka told me in New York in April 1993, the society is utterly unprepared to discuss foreign policy for lack of specialists and scantiness of general information.

Geopolitical and Economic Background of Foreign Policy Debates

Russian Military Presence in Belarus

Belarus's geographic location, often mentioned by Western analysts as an important asset favoring the republic's integration into the European economy, is at the same time an impediment to the building of a Belarusian sovereign state because of Russia's military interests and concerns. The preoccupation of Moscow with the outward orientation of Belarus stems not only from Russia's imperialistic and messianic instincts, but also from its historical experience with the West through Belarus, in particular the "Belarusian" route to Moscow trodden by Poland's pretender, the False Dmitrii, at the beginning of the seventeenth century, Napoleon's march in 1812, and Hitler's in 1941. It was not without reason that the Belarusian SSR was described as the "Western Gate" of the Soviet Union in the pre-perestroika years. With the empire half-collapsed, the "Western Gate" has become even more important because of the weakened position of Russia vis-à-vis the Baltic states, Ukraine, and Moldova.

As a result of its geostrategic location and the fact that a third of its territory is covered by forests, Belarus had been turned into the most militarized "zone" of all the ex-Soviet republics. In a recent debate about the viability of Belarus's independence, reference was made to a report in *Argumenty i fakty* (1990, no. 6 [16 February]) that stated that 50 percent of the Soviet Union's military bases (twenty-two of forty-four) were located in Belarus.[17] General Piotr Chaus, Belarus's transitional Minister for Defense Affairs, admitted in January 1992 that 10 percent of the republic's territory was in the jurisdiction of the "military structures."[18] A part of this vast amount of land was supposed to be transferred to civilian use, but demilitarization, like privatization and other reforms, is a very slow process. For example, the ratio of troops to the civilian population in Belarus today is still dramatically higher than in any other CIS state. Prime Minister Kebich cited the following figures in February 1992. In Belarus, he said, for every forty-three inhabitants there is one military person. By comparison, in Ukraine there is one for every 98, in Kazakhstan—one for 118, and in Russia—one for 634.[19]

There is no agreement among officials as to the precise number of military personnel in Belarus. Data vary by sources vacillating between 140,000 and 400,000. Probably the real figure is around 240,000. The size of the Belarusian national army, which is being created now, has been set at about 100,000 (approximately 1 percent of the population). How many CIS "strategic" troops and arms there are on Belarusian territory remains unknown. It has been stated only that there were "many." For example, Deputy Defense Minister Piotr Chaus said, "There is currently a large number of servicemen and military equipment in the republic, since the Belarusian military command was one of the most important in the USSR. We have armored groups, missile forces, ground troops, and antiaircraft units.

All of these formations were subordinated to the Soviet defense ministry and its commanders in Moscow, and Belarus had no connection to them whatsoever. They have now been placed at the disposal of the Belarusian defense ministry."[20] However, at issue remains the division of these forces into "national," subordinated to the republic, and CIS "strategic," remaining under the centralized control of Marshal Shaposhnikov. General Chaus himself admits there are disagreements. He complained that Moscow's application of the notion "strategic" was unacceptably wide: "For instance," he said, "they tried to convince us that paratroops should be considered strategic. Such an expansion of the way 'strategic forces' is understood was dangerous to the state's sovereignty. And this is not just over our own position. The same opinion is held by other CIS countries, in particular by Ukraine and Moldova."[21]

Danger to Belarus's sovereignty is seen not only in the "strategic forces," serving Russian imperial interests, but also in the "national" army, whose officer corps does not at all reflect the ethnic makeup of the republic's population, and whose pro-Russian ideological outlook is an inhibiting factor in the development of Belarusian national consciousness. Belarus, which constituted the Belarusian Military District (abolished in May 1992), had at the beginning of 1992 "nearly 20 percent of its officers from Belarus; over 50 percent Russians; and Ukrainians, slightly more than Belarusians."[22] Newly appointed Minister for Defense Affairs General Piotr Chaus was hopeful about the prospect of building a national army, but there were strong doubts because the army leadership, "as experience has shown, is of a pro-Moscow orientation."[23] According to Defense Minister General Pavel Kazlouski (Kozlovskii), only 40 percent of the officers of the republic's armed forces were Belarusians as of February 1993.[24] While the bulk of the officer corps in the Republic of Belarus consists of ethnic Russians, the ideological outlook of the republic's army is even more Russian and pro-empire. The cultural environment in Belarus, including language on the streets and in official places, is still predominantly Russian. During the Soviet period, Belarus, "the Western Gate," had been not only flooded with the physical presence of Russian soldiers, but also saturated with symbols of Russian military history. There are still hundreds of streets, collective farms, military schools, and other institutions, let alone school programs and textbooks, propagating names of Russian generals and war heroes, like Suvorov, Kutuzov, Bagration, Chapaev, and so on.

The Russian language and historical military tradition still permeate the atmosphere of the armed forces, causing clashes between the patriotically motivated Belarusian Association of Servicemen and the Defense Ministry officials.

One such incident occurred in February 1993, when the Ministry of Defense decided to mark the fiftieth anniversary of the Suvorov Military School in Minsk. On this occasion a purportedly scholarly conference was organized where such papers were presented as "Preservation of Suvorov's Memory as a Factor of Strengthening Friendship Between Russia and Belarus." A commentator of the *Narodnaia hazeta,* an official daily of the republic's Supreme Council, called the conference an "ideological and political undertaking by the 'hawks' with white-blue-and-red [Russia's flag colors] plumage."[25] In the same issue of the newspaper (circulation over 600,000), another commentator spoke of Belarusians' "historical masochism," whereby the Belarusian nation's oppressors are presented to it as heroes. Suvorov put down an uprising in Belarus and Poland in 1794 and was richly rewarded by Empress Catherine II with enserfed Belarusian peasants.

Shushkevich took the side of the critics. As reported by Moscow Interfax, Shushkevich described as "nonsense the fact that the republican military school retains the name of Aleksandr Suvorov." Shushkevich compared Suvorov to Napoleon and Guderian (a general of the German Wehrmacht who fought on Soviet territory during World War II). "Those were skillful military leaders," said Shushkevich, "but they don't deserve respect as human beings because they caused much suffering to the Belarusian people."[26]

Hienadz' Buraukin, the republic's ambassador to the United Nations, asked a rhetorical question in an interview in New York: "Is it normal that in our country people know more about Generalissimo Suvorov than, say, about Kastus' Kalinouski?"[27] (the latter is a Belarusian national hero, the leader of the antitsarist uprising in Belarus in 1863).

The controversy around the name of Suvorov not only is indicative of a dangerous cleavage in Belarusian polity as far as national allegiance is concerned, but also symbolizes a fundamental process in reevaluating the national past. This latter phenomenon has been occurring under the impact of two basic factors: (1) the mere existence of an independent national state, and (2) increasing activism on behalf of the cause of renewal by part of the intelligentsia. The pyramid of national consciousness has begun to change mostly at the top, where political differences are often clad in ideological terms.

A recent and most dramatic example of this dilemma is the Kebich government's proposal to join Russia and five other CIS countries (Armenia, Kazakhstan, Kyrgyzstan, Tajikistan, and Uzbekistan) in a collective defense treaty (signed but not ratified yet, except for Armenia, in Tashkent on 15 May 1992), which is widely viewed as a military alliance with Russia. The plan precipitated heated debates in the Supreme Council and the media.

On the eve of the March 1993 extraordinary parliamentary session, where the dicey issue of a possible military alliance with Russia was debated, Shushkevich called for peace and national accord, admitting that "confrontation is growing between citizens who have different views of current developments."[28] Sharp divisions had to be expected in a republic that suffered heavy demographic losses from association with Russia in the 1930s, lost a quarter of its population in World War II, and is still reeling from its Afghan War losses. The most outspoken critic of the plan is Shushkevich himself. Asked if he foresaw a closer political relationship with Russia, Shushkevich answered,

> The road to a confederation, if one is possible at all, is rather long and time is needed before other republics are ready to accept the idea. For the time being, it's Kazakhstan and Russia which call for a confederation. They may have reasons for closer union but the idea of such union is unacceptable to Belarus because it runs against the Belarusian constitution, which says we are seeking a neutral status.[29]

His main objection to a military alliance with Russia is the same—the status of Belarus as "a nuclear-free and neutral state," which is embedded in the Declaration of State Sovereignty (Article 10). Arguing in favor of a referendum on the issue of the treaty, Shushkevich appealed to the sense of national identity of Belarusians, which, in his mind, implies such basic national interests as neutrality. "There is not a single Belarusian *intelihent*," said Shushkevich, "who would not agree with the principle of neutrality of the Belarusian state and even more so with the need to decide its fate by a referendum. If a person takes a stand against these two propositions, it is clear to me that he is either not an *intelihent* or not a Belarusian."[30] How many "Belarusians" there are in the republic's Supreme Council by Shushkevich's measure will be established at the May regular session of the parliament, which will resume debates on the issue of a collective defense. The results of the vote held at the March-April extraordinary session (which was barred by the rules from deciding on a referendum) did not support Shushkevich's views. By a majority of 188 votes to 34, the Supreme Council expressed endorsement for the collective defense treaty and instructed Shushkevich to sign it with some reservations. Two of these reservations exclude Belarus from sending its troops abroad and receiving foreign troops on its own territory.[31]

Some observers in Belarus are of the opinion that a majority of the voters will reject this collective defense treaty if and when it comes to a referendum. Polling, however, indicates a divided public posture, demonstrating once again the crucial importance of phrasing. The question "Do you think that Belarus should sign now a treaty on collective defense (enter into military-political union with the CIS countries)" was answered 42.5 percent in the affirmative (40.9 percent negative), whereas, asked if they would "support preservation by the Republic of Belarus of neutrality, which presupposes refusal to enter into any military-political unions," 54.9 percent said yes and only 27.2 percent said no.[32]

One of the factors influencing the Supreme Council's final decision on the defense alliance will undoubtedly be the dark horse of the military establishment, which not only is deeply ingrained in the economy of Belarus but also is where the Russian imperial spirit still reigns supreme. The concept of neutrality itself has become a subject of varying interpretations. Shushkevich and Defense Minister Kazlouski are at opposite ends of the semantic spectrum. While Shushkevich steadfastly argues against a military alliance because it contradicts neutrality, the latter, speaking on the eve of the vote in parliament, predicted that "the policy of neutrality, recognized by no one and conducted at a time of an economic crisis, is doomed to fail."[33]

Nothing illustrates this better than the hurdles faced by the patriotic Belarusian Association of Servicemen (BAS). Engendered by the August 1991 putsch and formally constituted on 13 October of that year, the association set as its main goal "to contribute by constitutional means to the creation of the armed forces of the republic and the defense of democracy and the sovereignty of Belarus."[34] This task, as it turned out, has not been easy. Since its inception, the BAS has faced harassment of its members by army commanders. Complaints about persecution of Belarusian patriots in the army and controversies around the issue of Belarusization of the army have become a standard feature in the newspapers.

In an open letter to Shushkevich, the BAS leadership, describing its goals as the "patriotic education of servicemen, studying the history and the state language of the republic, and fighting corruption in the army," explained that harassment of BAS members was "part of a wider campaign directed against the implementation of the decisions by the Supreme Council About the Establishment of the Armed Forces of the Republic of Belarus."[35] This view was based on the conviction of BAS members that without an army "in which the Belarusian language would sound and history and culture be respected, there can be no independent Republic of Belarus."[36] On the other hand, Defense Minister General Pavel Kazlouski complains, "The BAS officers make political statements in which they assess the military readiness of the Army, the Defense Ministry command, call for the derussification of the Army.... In a recent radio broadcast, they called on soldiers and sergeants of Belarusian nationality not to obey officers who are not Belarusians. BAS activities are instigating and illegal."[37] Shushkevich is of quite a different view. He thinks "political activities are conducted in the Army by other structures." "Let there be an association," he says, "which helps patriotic education, including soldiers."[38] The controversy over the activities of the BAS is now with the Justice Ministry, which should decide on the legality of the effort by Belarusian patriots to see their armed forces patriotically disposed.

The process of achieving sovereignty for Belarus is slow by nature and by design. Besides the understandable psychological inertia and endurance of cultural habits, there is a dire lack of the knowledge, cadres, and expertise needed for developing and implementing programs of the people's rehabilitation from what is popularly labeled as "national nihilism," in other words, unfamiliarity, neglect, and even scorn for one's own national values and criteria. For example, there is a lack of Belarusian-language teachers in military units where there are volunteers to learn the language. There is not a single textbook of Belarus's military history written from the viewpoint of national interests. To remedy the situation, the Belarusian-language daily *Zviazda* serialized "A Brief Outline of Belarus's Military History," written by eleven historians, in eight of its February 1992 issues. For the first time in the history of the Soviet period, a Belarusian soldier could read not only about the brutality of the Mongol and German invaders, but also about atrocities committed by Muscovite occupiers of Belarusian territories.

One can imagine the disgust that such presentation of the past would evoke in officers steeped in the old ideas of Russians being the selfless rescuers of their younger Belarusian "brothers." It has been suggested that such sentiments were one of the reasons why it took more than fifteen months after the proclamation of independence to bring the republic's army to a military oath (administered on 31 December 1992).

On the other hand, the leaders of the republic of all political persuasions, by and large, are extremely careful not to force issues, but to work through consensus, taking the ideological and cultural complexities of the society into consideration. There is a conscious effort to preserve what has become one of the two principal arguments used by the government to justify its policies: political stability. The other is the economic situation, which traditionally has been somewhat better than in the surrounding states, with the exception of Poland.

Belarusization of the armed forces of Belarus is slowly but inexorably moving ahead, spearheaded by the mere existence of the national state and prodded by an awakening national intelligentsia. Political mobilization revolves largely around the cause of renewing the ancient Belarusian nation. The preamble of the new constitution (which begins with the familiar words "We the people") opens with an assertion that the Belarusians have "a centuries-old history of development of Belarusian statehood" as reflected in "Statutes of the Grand Duchy of Lithuania, Rus', and Samogitia [the sixteenth-century legal codes written in Belarusian], the Constituent Charters of the Belarusian Democratic Republic, and the Constitutions of the Belarusian Soviet Socialist Republic."[39] Shushkevich supports the activity of the Belarusian Association of Servicemen and "wishes to see more Belarusian features in the military and greater expressions of national consciousness."[40] Some steps are being taken toward that end. Thus, teaching Belarusian was introduced to a small group of students of the Minsk Higher Military Engineering School.[41] It was also reported that the Defense Ministry has decided on "the usage of the Belarusian and Russian languages with a gradual transition of the armed forces to the state language."[42]

Gains on the road to "more Belarusian features" embolden the critics of the status quo. Political temerity grows as the public becomes more accustomed to the sensitive issues that are being debated. Anatol' Sidarevich, a member of the Central Council of the Belarusian Social-Democratic Party, did not hesitate to bring up one of the most delicate of such issues, Russian messianic expansionism. In the newspaper that has become a clarion of the nationally conscious intelligentsia, *Nasha slova* (Our Word), Sidarevich wrote,

> We know and see that our eastern neighbor has not abandoned its messianic complex and that any trouble might be expected of it. It has in Belarus its Fifth Column not only in the persons of our state bureaucrats, predominantly of the old-nomenklatura type, and not only in the persons of the officer corps (80 percent of which consists of Russian natives), but also in the persons of certain circles of the intelligentsia.[43]

The author called attention to a "bloc" of organizations, the Coordinating Committee for Sociopolitical Associations, headed by Colonel Siarhiei Haidukievich. "That is where the domestic danger lies," the critic pointed out. "All the anti-democratic, anti-Belarusian organizations of red and brown color have united in this bloc."

Having now more access to historical truth and more freedom to speak up about it, the Belarusians are increasingly doubtful that overly close ties with Russia, including military ones, are to their advantage. In opposing the signing of the CIS collective defense treaty, which, for all practical purposes, is seen as a military alliance with Russia, a group of fifty-eight Minsk city councilmen based their position on the conclusion that "the history of Belarus testifies that the siding of our people with Russia in wars during the nineteenth and twentieth centuries brought them nothing but uncounted material and human losses."[44]

However, besides history there is the economy, which is more immediate and, like history itself, quite ruthless.

Economic Ties to Russia

The idea of the national independence of Belarus is being tested by the country's ability to feed its people. In the wide public debates about the ongoing program of Belarusization—which stands for reintroduction of the Belarusian language into official usage and subjects with a Belarusian emphasis into school curricula—the expression "sausage psychology" has gained currency. "Sausage psychology" connotes indifference to national cultural values, and thus poses a crucial question about the relationship between liberty and bread in general and between the Belarusian economy and national culture in particular. This question has a pronounced foreign policy aspect because of Belarus's heavy reliance on Russia's raw material, energy supply, and export markets.

During the pre-independence period, Belarus was turned into an "assembly shop" of the Soviet Union. Industry made up 70 percent of the republic's gross national product and was heavily engaged in supplying the military-industrial complex. With only 3.6 percent of the former union's population, the republic's share was 39 percent in precise optics, 23 percent in the radio industry, 100 percent in heavy trucks, 30 percent in computers, and from 10 to 20 percent in tractors, lathes, industrial robots, bearings, motorcycles, mineral fertilizers, synthetic fibers, and watches. Nearly 90 percent of these goods was exported, mainly to other Soviet republics. The bulk of exports, between 70 and 80 percent, went to Russia. From Russia, to a similar extent, Belarus received raw materials and energy.[45]

Belarus's labor force is about five million. Of this number, more than 250,000 are employed in the defense industry. With the huge number of troops in Belarus and the shortage of civil employment, one can imagine the gravity of the situation created by the necessity to export the production of those militarized plants that until now relied on Russian markets.

At present, with former economic ties ruptured and a decline in production continuing unabated throughout the CIS states, nominally independent Belarus has to prove the viability of independence by both cultural and economic arguments. Paraphrasing the popular French advice given to a woman that the way to a man's heart is through his stomach, the love of independence in Belarus has to be brought out not only through a revival of national culture, but even more through improving the national economy, because the clamor for "sausage first" is getting louder with every step in the economic descent.

A close psychological relationship between the idea of Belarusian independence and the facts of economic performance in the popular mind can be observed in the adjacent Belarusian ethnic territories in the Smolensk region in Russia and the Bialystok region in Poland. While in the former, the idea of Belarusian statehood enjoys a putative attraction, in the latter it does not, because the economic situation in Belarus looks better vis-à-vis Russia and worse vis-à-vis Poland. A similar rationale can be seen in calls by the opposition to "return to Europe," where the material needs of its citizens are known to have been satisfied much better than in the East. There is also, of course, the powerful cultural attraction of the "West European" model. This, naturally, implies a basic reorientation of foreign policy away from Moscow to Western capitals. Western countries have the capital needed for joint ventures, which are associated with economic recovery. It is true that, to this point, this capital has been insignificant, and 60 percent has been in the service sector (40 percent of the joint ventures have Polish partners, and 10 percent German or American).[46] Belarusian economists, aware of the peripheral status of their republic in the world economy, are currently looking for a model that would provide prosperity as well as an escape from the Russian center.

A culturological argument has been brought into play to boost the economic consideration. In his article "Russian Culture, Belarusian Character, and the Economy," Pavel Bich argues that there is a correlationship between the economy and national culture, and that the Russian cultural stereotype, that is, the way Russians view themselves, is quite different from what Belarus would be if it were permitted to develop freely. But so far Belarusians have been thwarted by an inability to defend their own interests. The Russian cultural stereotype, says Bich, has been shaped in part by the abundance of the country's raw materials and is known for its "aversion to precision, scrupulousness, and judiciousness." This stereotype, "repeated in thousands of versions by Russian literature," has helped the Russian businessperson strengthen the country by establishing higher prices for raw material. It is not difficult to imagine, argues Bich, "how this stereotype influences Belarusian businesspeople with a Russian education—they will reduce the cost of goods produced with imported raw materials." Suggesting that price agreements are influenced by national culture, seeing many press reports about the ongoing plundering of the Belarusian economy, and being convinced that "Russian culture has thwarted the will to resist in Belarusians," the author of the article concludes, "In order to build a normal statehood, economy, and policy, the Belarusians should liberate themselves from spiritual submission to Russian culture."[47]

The opposition persistently calls for a "return to Europe," an invitation that is strongly supported by cultural considerations and a historical tradition that is being refurbished and "Europeanized." Prime Minister Kebich's rejection of such calls is based primarily on the hard-to-reject argument that the republic has not much to offer to Western markets, whereas there are buyers in the East. Besides this realistic economic reasoning, there is a strong cultural and ideological bias within the Kebich government propelling it toward Russia, and not necessarily for ideological convictions, which may be of secondary importance to Kebich. Supreme Council Deputy Uladzimir Hrybanau, for example, characterizes the prime minister as follows: "He is an educated man, but he cannot escape from the vise of yesterday, not simply from the ideological vise, no. For quite some time, if ever, he has not believed in the Communist idea. But besides ideas, there are life, people, relationships. He is tied to the past through specific individuals."[48] Of course, this does not mean that Kebich is free of pro-Russian tendencies, but he has not abandoned the ideal of Belarus's independence either.

In one of his major speeches, mentioning the historical experience of European states, the Belarusian prime minister said, "I have come to an unequivocal conclusion: authentic statehood and independence begins with an independent and strong economy."[49] This axiomatic proposition, however, becomes highly political as soon as one has to decide how to rescue

Belarus's crumbling economy, which has been solidly bound with Russia's through raw materials, energy, and export markets. The Kebich government sees no other way than to move closer to Russia. And the opposition charges that this is being done at the cost of the republic's sovereignty.

The prime minister insists that sovereignty will be preserved. "His" economic union, he says, (1) "must be beneficial to all members," (2) "cannot do without a reliable legal framework," and (3) should have "a fruitfully functioning [regulatory] mechanism." Speaking on this subject at the extraordinary session of the Supreme Council, Kebich laid special emphasis on the first point, drawing attention to the fact that "the mechanism of interstate relations in the civilized world" is evidence that "no economic union affects its members' sovereignty."[50] But, as the opposition deputies maintain, no economic, political, or military union with Russia will solve the republic's domestic problems. It is, they say, a dangerous shift of attention to external factors, politicizing the blame for economic disorders and omitting inner human resources and the need to restructure the national economy.

Arguing on behalf of a union with Russia before the Supreme Council session, the prime minister painted quite a compelling picture of economic disruption. "Over some two years," said Kebich, "the deliveries of oil, ferrous rolled metal, steel pipes, synthetic rubber, and industrial timber have decreased 1.5- to twofold. The supplies of natural wool have fallen threefold, cotton—1.5-fold, and grain—1.4-fold.... Numerous enterprises, especially in the machine-building industry, are by 70 to 80 percent dependent on deliveries of spare parts and units, through cooperation, from other regions."[51] Last year, Belarus's GNP decreased by 11 percent.[52]

The other side of Belarus's dependence on Russia is the republic's own army. "We are facing a dilemma," said Leanid Pryvalau, deputy chairman of the parliamentary Commission on National Security, Defense, and Crime Prevention: "in the military sphere, we are now dependent 80 to 90 percent.... Collective security is a component part of the economic union." Pryvalau explained that Belarus has now 112 industrial enterprises of the military-industrial complex employing "more than 250,000 people."[53] The Kebich government says it is trying to avert the threat of unemployment and social disruption. But the critics maintain that the old nomenklatura refuses to reform the economy and relies on old orders from Russia. And, with sound logic, they warn that a military alliance with Moscow will not bring any improvement, since "Russia's own military manufacturers' workload does not exceed 60 percent of their potential."[54] The answer to the crisis, according to the opposition, is defense conversion and utilization of new energy sources and markets.

The Foreign Policy Mechanism:
Problems of Cadres and Public Involvement

In a recent interview, Belarusian Ambassador to the United Nations Hienadz' Buraukin spoke of his republic as a "beginner" in the field of foreign relations. There is no systematic and consistent approach to foreign policy issues; no interest on the part of appropriate high officials in Minsk in what is going on in the world; no instructions about how to vote; and no adequate technical facilities to maintain steady communication with the Ministry of Foreign Affairs.[55] Some of these woes, evidently, are caused by the financial crisis that the republic is in, in other words, the scarcity of hard currency. Another cause is the republic's "adolescence" in the field of diplomacy. There are very few professional diplomats with international experience. And because schooling of diplomats had been for decades the prerogative of Moscow, Minsk has neither proper educational institutions nor qualified educators to prepare new cadres of diplomats.

The roots of the problem go even deeper. There is an almost total lack of public involvement in foreign policy issues as such. Debates, of course, are conducted on the treatment of Russians, Poles, and other minorities in the republic or visitors from the immediate neighboring states, but this is done mainly with cultural or economic considerations, not state-to-state relationships. Perhaps the clearest indicator of a retardation of the foreign policy field is the fact that out of a total of some 650 periodical publications in the republic, there is not a single one specializing in foreign relations. The same can be said about journalists. "We have no *mizhnarodniki* " (foreign affairs specialists), was Foreign Minister Krauchanka's answer in April 1993 to my query about why foreign policy articles are so rare in Belarusian newspapers. Also, according to reliable information I received, a classified forty-page document entitled "Foreign Policy Conception of the Republic of Belarus" was submitted to the Presidium of the Supreme Council for analysis and approval in September 1992. The document had been lying around for six entire months without any action taken on it. And when the time came to discuss principles of the republic's foreign policy, Chairman Shushkevich, in a major report to the parliament, devoted his attention exclusively to criticism of the Foreign Ministry's performance, which the chairman found abysmally wanting, instead of considering the principles and directions of foreign policy. A conception of the state's foreign policy still awaits a full-fledged debate by the parliament.

For a wider public debate to occur, appropriate institutions have to evolve. So far, there have not been very many. Only in 1993 was a Chair of International Relations funded in the history department of the Belarusian

State University. In April 1993, the first nongovernmental organization was set up to deal with foreign policy matters—the National Center of Strategic Studies headed by a *Narodnaia hazeta* staff columnist, Ivan Makalovich. In a brief report about the establishment of this center, it was said that "The main subject of studies will be questions of war and peace, international cooperation, and national security." Timely and important pursuits. KGB chief General Eduard Shyrkouski (Shirkovskii) was the first to announce that his agency "will become one of the Center's customers." How sporadic the efforts in the foreign policy area are can be seen from a remark by People's Deputy Miechyslau Hryb, chairman of the parliamentary Commission on National Security. Hryb expressed "amazement that the idea of establishing such an organization did not arise earlier," and this because "nobody in the republic is seriously preoccupied with the training of politicians and experts."[56]

Conclusion

The emerging Belarusian state is sundered by its history and its economy. The historical past, as it is gradually being adumbrated, reattaches the country to the West, with which Belarus had fruitful contacts for at least five hundred years. Economic conditions, on the other hand, keep the republic tightly connected to the Eurasian Russian colossus and dictate an Eastern orientation. In addition to economic ties, there is a harsh geostrategic reality that makes Belarus more important for Russia as Moscow's influence in the Baltics and Ukraine weakens. On the level of the individual, this basic equation is complemented by elements of language, religion, ethnicity, and views inherited from the Communist regime, which are clearly persistent and even resilient in view of material deterioration. All this results in considerable confusion that affects foreign policy views and actions.

However, barring a cataclysmic upheaval in Russia or some other major armed conflict engulfing Eastern Europe, the Belarusian national state will survive the test of endurance, thanks mainly to the ethnic and historical self-awareness of the Belarusian people. Statehood and national consciousness are in a dialectical relationship, mutually nurturing each other. Under the impact of the present de jure sovereign Belarusian political state, enjoying international approbation and steadily acquiring security guarantees, Belarusians will eventually recuperate from the "national nihilism" with which the Communist regime infected them. Some observers already see signs of such a recovery. For example, Leanid Lych of the History Institute of the Belarusian Academy of Sciences is convinced that "our present new generation, in terms of national consolidation, is visibly above its counterparts of the 1970s–1980s," and Lych is "firmly convinced" that young Belarusians in the new millennium's first decade will in turn surpass their counterparts of the 1990s by a comparable measure.[57]

As far as Minsk's foreign policy rationale is concerned, it seems to fit such a development, taking into account both Belarusian cultural needs and economic exigencies. Foreign Minister Krauchanka, before his departure for the World Economic Forum in the Swiss town of Davos in January 1993, said what he has been repeating at every opportunity: "We predict that there will be two main geopolitical and economic units in Europe by 2005—the European Economic Community, that will probably unite 16 states by 1996, and the East European Economic Community, which means the Commonwealth of Independent States. . . . It is only then that the idea of a common European home will acquire definite outlines."[58] A "European home" is looked on by most Belarusians as a symbol of economic prosperity, cultural diversity, and humaneness. Realistic or not, this symbol is a powerful psychological impulse.

Notes

1. Gail W. Lapidus et al., eds., *From Union to Commonwealth: Nationalism and Separatism in the Soviet Republics* (Cambridge: Cambridge University Press, 1992), p. 24.
2. Foreign Broadcast Information Service, *Daily Report: Central Eurasia* (hereafter FBIS), 9 April 1993.
3. *Narodnaia hazeta,* 9 April 1993.
4. *Nasha slova,* 1992, no. 34 (26 August).
5. *Chyrvonaia zmena,* 26 June 1990.
6. *Zviazda,* 23 December 1992.
7. *Zviazda,* 17 November 1992.
8. *Zviazda,* 13 January 1993.
9. *Belaruski histarychny chasopis,* 1993, no. 1, p. 83.
10. *Litaratura i mastatstva,* 30 April 1993.
11. *Znamia iunosti,* 16 December 1992.
12. *Belaruski histarychny chasopis,* 1993, no. 1, p. 3.
13. Ibid. FBIS, p. 5.
14. FBIS, 29 January 1993, p. 54.
15. RFE/RL Research Institute, *Belarus Today: Belarus Media News Budget,* no. 97 (20 April 1993) p. 28.
16. *Zviazda,* 18 March 1993.
17. *Zviazda,* 16 April 1992.
18. TASS (Minsk), 11 January 1992.
19. *Zviazda,* 13 February 1992.
20. FBIS, 12 February 1993, p. 48.
21. FBIS, 12 February 1993, p. 49.
22. *Zviazda,* 1 January 1992.
23. Ibid.
24. *Zviazda,* 23 February 1993.

25. *Narodnaia hazeta*, 18 February 1993.
26. FBIS, 22 February 1993, p. 35.
27. *Narodnaia hazeta*, 17 February 1993.
28. FBIS, 24 March 1993, p. 65.
29. FBIS, 28 December 1992, p. 33.
30. *Zviazda*, 9 April 1993.
31. *Zviazda*, 16 April 1993.
32. *Zviazda*, 6 April 1993.
33. FBIS, 8 April 1993, p. 54.
34. *Naviny BNF*, 1991, no. 7 (November).
35. *Sovetskaia Belorussiia*, 27 November 1991.
36. *Nasha slova*, 1992, no. 35 (2 September).
37. FBIS, 7 April 1993, p. 75.
38. RFE/RL Research Institute, *Belarus Today: Belarus Media News Budget*, no. 97 (20 April 1993), p. 19.
39. *Zviazda*, 22 August 1992.
40. *Nasha slova*, 1992, no. 30 (29 July).
41. Ibid.
42. *Nasha slova*, 1992, no. 31 (5 August).
43. *Nasha slova*, 1992, no. 41 (14 October).
44. *Narodnaia hazeta*, 9 April 1993.
45. *Delo*, 1993, nos. 1–2, pp. 9–13.
46. Ibid., p. 23.
47. *Litaratura i mastatstva*, 19 February 1993.
48. *Narodnaia hazeta*, 17 January 1992.
49. FBIS, 30 December 1992, p. 39.
50. FBIS, 29 March 1993, p. 96.
51. *Zviazda*, 30 March 1993; FBIS, 2 April 1993, p. 54.
52. FBIS, 2 April 1993, p. 50.
53. RFE/RL Research Institute, *Belarus Today: Belarus Media News Budget*, no. 88 (8 April 1993), pp. 4, 5.
54. FBIS, 2 April 1993, p. 49.
55. *Narodnaia hazeta*, 17 February 1993.
56. *Zviazda*, 21 April 1993.
57. *Litaratura i mastatstva*, 7 May 1993.
58. FBIS, 29 January 1993, p. 54.

7
The Influence of Ethnicity on the Foreign Policies of the Western Littoral States

Algimantas Prazauskas

Ethnicity, or rather ethnonationalism, may, and often does, become one of the main factors determining sociopolitical processes in multiethnic countries. The cases of the Soviet Union and Yugoslavia during the last few years of their existence and those of Cyprus, Ethiopia, and Sri Lanka illustrate this point. The influence of ethnicity on the foreign policies of particular states, except for countries beset with ethnic strife, is generally less evident.

The governments of independent states, unlike ethnic leaders who usually strive to achieve a certain single aim (cultural autonomy, revision of administrative borders, local self-government, secession), have to take into consideration a variety of political, economic, security, ecological, and other issues. As the experience of militant nationalist leaders such as Zviad Gamsakhurdia of Georgia has shown, overreliance on a policy of ethnic mythology and ethnocentrism to the exclusion of other issues may become disastrous for both the nation and the regime.

Indirectly, however, ethnonationalism, national identity, and ethnicity *always* affect the foreign policies of any state. The collective experience of a nation, and its history, as reflected in group memory, attitudes, and systems of values, largely shape the approach to major foreign policy issues, assessment of particular situations, and expected outcomes. This relatively stable and universal collection of factors sets certain limits on foreign policy options of groups in power, except puppet regimes, which do not have foreign policies of their own. Even more important, under representative systems of government, it is one of the factors determining the eligibility of political parties and leaders for a share of power. Any discussion on the impact of ethnicity and national identity on the foreign policies in a particular region has to elucidate how and to what extent certain ethnic characteristics determine the approach to, and the interpretation of, the major foreign policy issues of governments. This is a delicate task for the analyst, academically and politically: academically, because there is no consensus among social scientists concerning the approach to the problem; politically, because the examination of ethnicity as a factor in international relations lays stress on ideas, values, and loyalties, which are generally regarded as parochial, primordial, conservative, and even irrational, against the modern background of universal human rights and values, rational policy planning, and global trends toward integration. The difficulties increase if the object of analysis is not a single country but a vast region comprising six nations and a number of ethnic minorities, all of which have a number of common features, determined by their Soviet past, yet simultaneously are very different from historical, cultural, and geopolitical viewpoints.

These complexities and limitations determine the aims and structure of the present chapter, which focuses on the western littoral states of Ukraine, Belarus, Moldova, Lithuania, Latvia, and Estonia. Its purpose is to examine those common and specific features of national identity that shape foreign policy strategies and options, that is, collective historical memory, external orientation of particular nations, ethnic survival syndrome, and perceptions of security, which remain of crucial importance for the newly independent states of the western littoral, owing to the presence of large and politically mobilized minorities and the problems they pose for the formation of nation-states in the region (see Table 7.1).

Ethnic Survival and Security

As the wave of "national revivals," or ethnonationalism, swept over the Baltic republics, Moldova, and Ukraine in 1988–89, it became evident that perestroika, as interpreted in the non-Russian republics, was primarily an opportunity to reassert national identities and check the trend toward the erosion and virtual disappearance of ethnicity. Such a turn was logical and inevitable.

The Soviet nationalities policy was rather inconsistent and self-contradictory. Nominal statehood for both union and autonomous republics within the USSR was conducive to the growth of nationalism and the emergence of nations even in regions where ethnic identity and solidarity previously did not exist, or was ill-formed, as in Central Asia, Siberia, parts of the North Caucasus, and the Volga-Urals region. In the union republics, which

Table 7.1

Linguistic Situation of the Western Littoral States, 1988–89

	Ukraine	Belarus	Moldova	Lithuania	Latvia	Estonia
Russian as mother tongue for persons of titular nationality (including diaspora in other republics) (percent)						
Total	18.8	28.5	7.4	1.8	5.0	4.4
For urban residents	26.0	38.7	16.4	2.2	6.6	5.8
Kindergartens with language instruction (percent)						
Titular nationality language	58.2	19.3	53.4	85.9	43.7	67.3
Russian	40.2	72.7	31.7	9.1	38.8	27.1
Percentage of students in schools with medium of instruction (percent)						
Titular nationality language	47.5	20.8	59.1	82.2	52.4	63.5
Russian	51.8	79.2	40.9	15.8	47.6	36.5
Newspapers (number of titles)*						
Titular nationality language	1,241	131	85	192	78	75
Russian	509	89	114	38	51	36

Newspapers (number of copies per issue, in thousands)						
Titular nationality language	15,682	1,773	1,143	4,044	2,008	2,048
Russian	8,044	3,579	1,237	402	764	502
Books published (number of titles)						
Titular nationality language	1,934	439	522	2,072	990	1,316
Russian	6,225	2,437	910	518	854	523
Books published (number of copies, in thousands)						
Titular nationality language	95,231	9,404	9,520	20,355	13,110	13,345
Russian	91,683	48,133	11,063	2,038	3,518	3,596
Library collections (percent)						
Titular nationality language	38	16	30	64	46	58
Russian	61	82	69	31	47	35

Sources: Soiuz, 1990, no. 51, 1991, no. 2; *Narodnoe obrazovanie i kal'tura v SSSR: Statisticheskii sbornik* (Moscow: Finansy i statistika, 1989), pp. 41, 88, 274; *Pechat' v SSSR v 1989 godu* (Moscow: Finansy i statistika, 1990), pp. 144–47, 222–23.

*Papers published in respective republics only. Russian-speakers mainly read central press, that is, newspapers (and magazines) published in Moscow, particularly *Trud*, *Komsomol'skaia pravda*, *Izvestiia*, *Pravda*, and *Pionerskaia pravda*.

enjoyed wider cultural autonomy than the autonomous republics, regions (oblasts), and districts (okrugs), the development of mass media and modest film production in the local languages, the foundation of Academies of Sciences and museums of regional history and culture, and other developments permitted national identity to survive and even grow. However, since the times of Marx and Engels, the Communists thought in terms of supranational states. Lenin expected that nations would simply merge and disappear in the course of economic integration, but later agreed to postpone the "coalescence of nations" until the nationalist aspirations of the non-Russian periphery became neutralized in a roundabout way, through the union of nominally sovereign republics. The official idea adopted in the 1960s of the "Soviet people, a new historical community" actually meant the return to the merger theory. National identities were supposed to be relegated to the background and become irrelevant with the growth of Soviet patriotism and the formation of the new identity, the *sovetskii chelovek* (*homo sovieticus*).

Although it was never stated publicly and it may well be that the founders of the "Soviet people" theory were not aware of the parallel, it seems that the idea was inspired by the American example. The "melting pot" scenario, with Anglo-Saxon Protestants providing the language and normative culture but renouncing their British identity, and other groups contributing something to produce the American uniqueness, seemed to be an excellent model, especially as the Soviet regime during several decades was preoccupied with the idea of "catching up and overtaking America."

The "*homo sovieticus*" blueprint may have looked good on paper, but it was as utopian as the idea of communist society itself. Although millions of people, especially Russians who settled in different regions outside their own ethnic areas, adopted the Soviet identity, since it served the need to rationalize both their geographic mobility and their superior attitude toward local languages and cultures, the vast majority (more than 80 percent of Ukrainians, Moldovans, and so on, and more than 95 percent of Latvians, Lithuanians, and Georgians) stayed within their homelands and hardly felt any need to change their national identities in favor of the Soviet one. On the contrary, many intellectuals were not willing to accept the Russian culture and language as normative and obligatory features of the "Soviet people" and regarded the attempts to impose them as Russification pure and simple. There was enough evidence for anyone to see that the formation of the "Soviet people" actually meant assimilation of non-Russian nationalities. In the Central Asian republics, Belarus, Ukraine, and Moldova the local languages were increasingly ousted by Russian in all spheres of life, and among urban populations some titular nationalities became minorities due to intensive immigration of Russophone groups. The net result of these trends was that an increasingly larger share of non-Russians were linguistically assimilated (see Table 7.2).

Acculturation and assimilation of minorities is a worldwide phenomenon and need not necessarily be regarded in negative terms. In the Soviet case too, many authors wondered, what was wrong with such a perspective, and why should modernizing, increasingly urban communities set high value on their ethnic characteristics, which were anyhow becoming irrelevant, and adhere to their parochial loyalties?

One general explanation, proposed by Marxists and cosmopolitically minded liberal social scientists, is that the resistance to assimilation is consciously inspired by "ethnic entrepreneurs" and middle-class ("petty bourgeois") intellectuals, especially journalists, writers, and teachers, apprehensive of competition in the wider market of a multiethnic state. This explanation may be plausible in certain cases, but it does not explain the causes of nationalism and separatism in the regions like the Baltic republics and Ukraine, which by any criteria cannot be regarded as backward in comparison with the core area, that is, Russia. At least in the western periphery of the former Soviet Union, the problem of ethnic survival as the principal idea of ethnonationalism had little, if anything, to do with conservatism and isolationism. Large sections of the population, or even the majority in the case of Estonians, Latvians, and Lithuanians, never shared the official image of the USSR as the socialist paradise, the "hope of all mankind," and did not wish to become parts of the "Soviet people" as shaped by the regime. As the terms "Russian" and "Soviet" became almost synonymous in the Soviet Union (and abroad), the fear of assimilation, often bordering on Russophobia, reflected the unwillingness of non-Russian groups to identify with the system and society they regarded as backward and inefficient. Unlike migrants in the United States, who are determined to become "real Americans" at least in the second generation, the educated sections of the Balts and, to a lesser extent, Moldovans and Ukrainians, regarded Russian acculturation and assimilation as a move in the wrong direction, away from the modern global ("Western") civilization, into a stagnant society, deemed hopeless even by many Russian intellectuals. It became the conviction of the nationalists in the western Soviet republics that the nations had to resist assimilation and survive until "something happens" in the distant future and the survivors would be able to join the international community of nations as equal partners.

The advent of independence in 1991 did not immediately dispel the old fears. It came too unexpectedly in Belarus and eastern Ukraine, without a prolonged freedom movement and its corollaries, the institutional and psychological changes. Even more important, the former Soviet realities, re-

Table 7.2

Nationalities and Major Ethnic Groups in the Western Littoral States (1989 USSR Census)

State	Total population (thousands)	Titular nationality		Russians		Others		Disapora of titular nationality in Russia (thousands)
		thousands	%	thousands	%	ethnic group	thousands	
Ukraine	51,707	37,419	72.4	11,356	22.0	Jews	486	4,363
						Belarusians	440	
						Moldovians	324	
						Crimean Tatars	250*	
						Bulgarians	234	
						Poles	220	
						Hungarians	163	
						Romanians	135	
Belarus	10,200	7,905	77.5	1,342	13.2	Poles	417	1,206
						Ukrainians	291	
						Jews	112	
						Lithuanians	7.6	

Moldova	4,338	2,795	64.4	562	13.0	Ukrainians 600 Gagauzes 154 Bulgarians 88 Jews 66 Belarusians 20	644
Estonia	1,573	963	61.2	475	30.2	Ukrainians 48 Belarusians 28	46
Latvia	2,680	1,388	52.0	906	34.0	Belarusians 120 Ukrainians 92 Poles 60 Lithuanians 35	47
Lithuania	3,690	2,924	79.3	345	9.4	Poles 258 Belarusians 63 Ukrainians 45 Latvians 4	70

*Estimated number of Crimean Tatars in February 1993. The 1989 census figure was 46,807 persons.

garded by the nationalists as the legacy of Russian rule, still persist despite formal attributes of independent statehood. Culturally, large regions, particularly urban areas in Belarus, eastern Ukraine, some parts of Moldova, and the Baltic states, remain hardly distinguishable from the periphery of Russia. The local languages in many regions remain out of public life and schools. Especially disturbing for the nationalists is the vision of the Soviet Union being restored. These fears are not totally baseless. As the militant nationalists and the orthodox Communists converge politically, the prospect of the "Red-and-Brown" alliance coming to power is considered fairly probable by many observers in Russia. Even if the worst does not happen, these patriots have sufficient influence at the highest levels of power in Moscow to issue, through the representative bodies, militant declarations and warnings to the governments of the former Soviet republics.

In the smaller states of the western littoral the fear of reannexation is reinforced by the presence of Russian troops on their territory and the existence of a large Russian minority, generally loyal to Russia. If some would-be regime in Moscow opts for expansionist policies, it can easily inspire appeals by the "toiling masses" for "brotherly assistance" and reannex some of the former Soviet republics. With the memory of the Soviet interventions in Hungary, Czechoslovakia, and Afghanistan fresh in their minds, the nationalists in the western littoral states have no illusions that the international community in such a case will do anything except offer verbal protests and certain symbolic actions.

There is sufficient evidence to conclude that the problem of survival forms the very core of nationalism in the western littoral states and that nationalism is the dominant ideology. Since Russia is regarded as the principal, or even the only, source of threat to their independence, nationalism in the region remains basically anti-Russian or, rather, anti-Moscow, irrespective of all official protestations. Unless one bears this specific feature in mind, it is difficult to gain an understanding of the foreign policies and interstate relations in the region. The preoccupation with the problem of survival and suspicion of Russia's intentions form, although in varying degrees, the basis of the external policies of the majority of states in the region.

The perception of a Russian threat is particularly strong in Estonia and Latvia, two small countries that are of strategic importance for Russia and that have large Russian minorities. The fear of the great and unpredictable neighboring power causes the governments of Latvia and Estonia to distance themselves from Russia. As these policies are not welcomed in Moscow, the result is that among all western littoral states these two Baltic nations have the least satisfactory relations with Russia. The sense of insecurity is less evident in Lithuania, although the heavy concentration of Russian troops in the adjacent Kaliningrad region and the military traffic along and across the territory of Lithuania is causing concern in Vilnius. The perceived Russian threat is the main reason why all three Baltic states insist on early withdrawal of Russian troops from their territory and regard this problem as one of the top priority aims of their foreign policies.

Among the western littoral states Ukraine, due to its size and military potential, is the only nation able to challenge Russia and, therefore, not specifically sensitive to the hypothetical Russian threat. The major foreign policy task for the Ukrainian government seems to be preventing the transformation of the CIS into a modified version of the USSR. So far Kiev has been successful in pursuing this aim. Simultaneously Ukraine, due to geography, provides a reliable anti-imperial shield for its small neighbor, Moldova, whose position otherwise would be highly precarious.[1]

The problem of ethnic survival and security exists also for Belarusian nationalists, who have on numerous occasions made declarations about the "threat from the East." However, the majority of Belarusians obviously do not share the idea of an unfriendly Russia and would rather welcome close alliance with their eastern neighbor or even restoration of the united federal state.

Historical Memory and External Orientation

Historical memory is, generally, the central component of national identity. In its textbook version and/or in the form of popular myths, self-images, and ethnic stereotypes, historical memory affects the assessment of the international environment and foreign policy issues, and often determines particular decisions and choices. Another aspect of historical memory that is relevant for international relations is the external orientation of particular ethnic groups and nations, that is, traditional images of "foes" and "friends," desirable and unacceptable partners. In many cases traditional attitudes and images outweigh military, economic, and other rational considerations.

Although the historical memory of each nation is unique, the similar historical experiences of the western littoral nations since the early nineteenth century have shaped certain common features of the historical identity of Ukrainians, Belarusians, Balts, and Moldovans. These features, although not readily observable, in certain cases influence approaches to foreign policy issues and need to be mentioned for the purposes of this chapter.

Due to their geographical position the western littoral nations have been exposed to conflicting pulls and pressures from their eastern neighbor, Russia, and from the West, particularly Germany and Poland. During the Soviet period the Iron Curtain drastically reduced direct contacts between the western periphery nations of the USSR and their Western neighbors, while Russian influence became overwhelming and, as noted above, threatening for their existence as nations. The net result of the policy of Russification, dating back to the nineteenth century, was that nationalism in the region became anti-Russian by definition. (Pro-Russian nationalism would mean only the official "internationalism," or Soviet patriotism, and would amount to a contradiction in terms.)

Another common feature of nationalism in the region is a specific minority complex. For several generations the nations of the Soviet periphery were actually minorities in a large multiethnic state. Besides being permanently molded into uniform parts of the "Soviet people," they were remote from the decision-making process at the center and could hardly influence its policies at the regional level. This subject position intensified the minority syndrome by adding the colonial one, and made the nationalists and the emerging political elites especially sensitive to perceptions of, and opinions about, their nations by the outside world. The western littoral elites are far more nationalist and ethnocentric than those of the Scandinavian and other Western nations. In the area of foreign policy, they often tend to overreact to international events concerning their states. As the experience of other postcolonial states suggests, these syndromes disappear with the coming of a new generation of intellectuals and politicians educated during the independence period.

The third feature common to western littoral nationalisms is a somewhat unrealistic assessment of the historical and political importance of their respective nations. Having survived the Communist regime and dependence, interpreted as an imperial yoke, many nationalists, including some politicians, expected that the international community of nations would be excited about the new independent states and offer them generous assistance and support. Appeals by the parliament of Lithuania following the declaration of independence in March 1990 illustrate this kind of wishful thinking and expectations. The cool attitude of the Western powers and, particularly, the suggestion that Gorbachev was more important than some obscure nationalities of the Soviet periphery, as well as the experience of the period after the achievement of independence, compelled the nationalists to revise their expectations. However, a certain disillusionment is likely to persist for some time, in some cases causing the governments of the newly independent states to adopt a hard line or defiant attitude on specific issues of bilateral relations and international obligations.

Latvia and Estonia

Among the western littoral nations, the Latvians and Estonians are least burdened with memories, images, and symbols of the distant past. Like some other small nations of Eastern Europe, they draw inspiration from the fact of their own survival after seven centuries of foreign domination. Moreover, despite adverse conditions, they had emerged by the end of the nineteenth century as the most advanced nations in the Russian Empire. At the turn of the century, fairly large groups of intellectuals and entrepreneurs existed in Riga and Revel (Tallinn). In 1897 about 20 percent of the total one million Latvians lived in the cities, mostly in Riga (127,000), while the somewhat less urbanized Estonians had the distinction of being the only autochthonous nation in the empire with a literacy rate close to 100 percent.

In the Russian Empire the Latvians and Estonians were the most Westernized nations. For seven centuries they had been exposed to the influence of German culture and followed the Germans in converting themselves to the Lutheran branch of Protestantism. Although the emerging nationalism of the Balts had a certain anti-German slant, the German acculturation of the Latvians and Estonians made them culturally closer to the West European and Scandinavian nations than to the Slavs of the empire. Hence, their external orientation was generally rather to the West than to the East.

During two decades of independence Latvia and Estonia became developed modern nation-states, comparable by all standards with the Scandinavian countries and much ahead of the Soviet Union. The annexation in 1940, followed by mass deportations of Balts to Siberia, the large-scale influx of Slavs, the imposition of the Iron Curtain, and the rapid deterioration of living conditions were regarded by the Latvians and Estonians as a disaster and caused them to look back to the independence period as the golden age of their history. Therefore, the Estonian and Latvian nationalists did not need to revise and rewrite the history of their nations for the purposes of national awakening and political mobilization in the course of liberalization in the late 1980s.

With independence restored, many Estonian and Latvian politicians and nationalists tend to regard the Soviet period as an interlude between the prewar and the present independent states. Legally, this approach serves to rationalize claims to eliminate such negative consequences of the Soviet regime as the presence of one million Russians, now insisting on citizenship and political rights, and to restore the borders as they had been recognized in treaties with Soviet Russia in 1920. To a certain extent, this approach shapes the stand of Estonia and Latvia on the citizenship and border issues and affects negatively the relations of the two Baltic states with Russia.

Ironically, as the Russian government tends, at least in public polemics, to adopt a similar attitude, that is, to dismiss the Bolshevik regime as illegal, Russia may repudiate responsibility for the policies of the Soviet government in the region, including the treaties with the Baltic states, annexation, migration, presence of Russian troops, and so forth. It is in this legal impasse that pressure can be exerted on the Baltic states to accept the "realities" of the Soviet legacy.

Lithuania

Lithuania, in addition to these issues, has some specific problems of historical legacy. Lithuanians were a small minority in the Grand Duchy of Lithuania (which in the thirteenth to sixteenth centuries included the whole of modern Belarus and the larger part of Ukraine) and were increasingly assimilated by the Russian/Slav and, after unification with Poland in 1569, Polish majorities. The dual process of Russification and Polonization gathered momentum after Lithuania was annexed by Russia in 1796, as only the Russian language was permitted in schools and offices, and divine service in Catholic churches was conducted in Polish. By the late nineteenth century it seemed the nation would disappear completely, especially as the more dynamic and mobile individuals were emigrating to America en masse. In these circumstances, the national revival that began originally in East Prussia in the 1870s turned both anti-Russian and anti-Polish.

Twenty years of independence completed the emergence of Lithuania as a modern nation. However, the international situation of the first republic was precarious, its relations with Warsaw being hostile due to Polish annexation of eastern Lithuania, including the old capital, Vilnius, and the Germans in autonomous Memelgebiet (Klaipeda), annexed by Lithuania in 1923, plotting to reunite with their Vaterland. However, it was neither Poland nor Germany, but the Soviet Union that annexed Lithuania in 1940.

The very existence of their state threatened from all quarters, feeling betrayed by everybody—including the Vatican and the League of Nations, who had recognized the Wilno region as part of Poland—and driven to the wall, the Lithuanians became a house divided. The majority was frustrated, but a great portion became embittered in its nationalism, and after World War II ended, armed resistance to the Soviet regime continued for some eight years. Even now, consciously or not, the old fears and phobias still persist. Lithuanian nationalism is, generally, anti-Russian and anti-Polish, occasionally even apprehensive about possible German intentions toward East Prussia and the Klaipeda region. Culturally part of East-Central Europe, Lithuanian nationalists are somewhat suspicious of their immediate neighbors, except Latvia, and would prefer to avoid any close relationship with Belarus or Poland, not to mention Russia. Historical memory, burdened with negative experiences of relations with larger neighbors, makes Lithuania less responsive than Latvia or Estonia to external influences and impels the Lithuanian nationalists to seek wider contacts beyond the region in Western Europe and the United States.[2]

While feeling nostalgic about their prewar republics, Baltic analysts and the wider public are generally skeptical about their foreign policies. The reliance on neutrality and the League of Nations proved to be ineffective in safeguarding their independence after the conclusion of the Nazi-Soviet pact. The events of 1939–40, revived during the last few years by numerous reprints of memoirs, have prompted Baltic politicians to look for new ways to ensure the preservation of independence. One of them is the development of closer cooperation and coordination of foreign policy strategies among the three Baltic states. Estonia, Latvia, and Lithuania had shown a remarkable solidarity in the course of the independence movement in 1988–91, but they still fell short of close political alliance.

Another strategy common to newly independent states in any part of the world is the expansion of external relations and regional integration with neighboring states. However, neither the policy planners nor the public at large seem to believe that these strategies would prove effective if Moscow turned expansionistic in the region. Against the background of their past experience the Baltic nations cannot be expected to feel safe as long as they have not become an integral part of the emerging united Europe. Hence, the principal strategic aim of the Baltic states is full membership in the European political, military, and economic structures.

Belarus

Unlike the Baltic nations, until 1991 Belarus never existed as an independent nation. Originally part of the ethnic territory of several East Slavic groups, during some five hundred years since the thirteenth century it was under Lithuanian and Polish-Lithuanian rule. Due to long isolation from the rest of Russia, intermixture with Lithuanians, and Polish cultural influence, the population of White Russia developed certain specific traits, and its language, regarded by many as a mere Russian dialect, retained some archaic features of the Old Russian.

Polonization and, during the nineteenth century, the efforts of the tsarist regime to reclaim the region for the Russian language and culture effectively prevented the formation of a clear ethnic identity among Belarusians.

The basis of identity was rather confessional, as the religious cleavage divided them into "Russians" ("of the Russian faith") to the east of Minsk, and "Poles" ("of the Polish faith," i.e., Catholics) in the western part of the country. Belarusian identity as such was and, generally, remains regional and civic rather than cultural and historical.

Belarusian enlighteners in the past, unlike those of other East and Central European countries, were preoccupied mostly with folklore and language, which could boast of being the official language of the Grand Duchy of Lithuania and of one of the earliest translations of the Bible in Europe (published in 1517); they were not interested in writing what they regarded as a history of alien (Lithuanian) rule. Not until 1919 did a leading Belarusian historian, V.M. Ignatovskii, propose a new version of the history of Belarus.

In his *Short Outline of the History of Belarus,* which had four editions before it was banned by Soviet censorship in 1930, Ignatovskii put forward several ideas that were important for the formation of Belarusian historical identity. He insisted that the Belarusians were the purest race among the East Slavs, as the Russians and, less so, the Ukrainians had mixed with Tatar, Mongol, and Finnish tribes, while the Belarusians had only marginally intermixed with the Lithuanians, who were at least "as good Aryans as the Belarusians themselves." Further, he asserted that the Polotsk principality of the ninth–twelfth centuries was actually a Belarusian state, only nominally dependent on Kievan Rus´. And finally, Ignatovskii challenged the Russian historiography that regarded the Grand Duchy of Lithuania as a Lithuanian-Russian state, and insisted that from the very beginning it was a Lithuanian-Belarusian state, where the Belarusian language and culture dominated until the seventeenth century.[3]

Modern Belarusian interpreters of history went a step further and claimed that the disputed medieval principality was a Belarusian national state pure and simple, incidentally ruled by a dynasty of Lithuanian origin. In this manner the present independent state was provided with impressive historical legitimacy and background. This reinterpretation of history by the patriotic scholars and Popular Front ideologists was accepted even by the Communist majority of the Supreme Soviet, which stressed the ancient origins of the Belarusian state by adopting the symbols of the medieval principality as the coat of arms and the state flag of the present republic.

However surprising for the uninitiated observer, these problems of medieval history have become very relevant for Belarus's relations with neighboring countries.

The nationalist leaders in Lithuania initially welcomed the Belarusian national revival and even arranged for the founding congress of the Belarusian Popular Front (BPF) to meet in Vilnius in 1989, as the Communist regime of Belarus would not permit the holding of a "nationalist gathering" in Minsk. The efforts of the Belarusian nationalists to rewrite medieval history caused some amusement in Lithuania, but the amusement gave way to concern when the patriots of the neighboring country started claiming that "Vilna," "the ancient capital of Belarus," had been unjustly ceded to Lithuania under the Nazi-Soviet pacts of 1939. Territorial claims have become especially popular among BPF members and the militantly nationalist Belarusian Association of Servicemen. The official establishment also stresses that Belarus does not renounce its right to "restore historical justice" and settle the territorial dispute with Lithuania in a peaceful way, but regards the present moment as unsuitable for the purpose.[4] The reaction in Vilnius being predictable, Minsk expects trouble with its smaller neighbor and does not consider Lithuania a strategic ally. Significantly, in its search for transit facilities to the Baltic Sea, the Belarusian government is looking toward Poland and has expressed its readiness to construct a few hundred miles of Russian-gauge railway to the port of Gdynia in Poland instead of choosing the much shorter and cheaper way to Klaipeda in Lithuania.

Belarusian claims on Lithuania, as a means to promote national identity, are likely to persist also for the reason that the Belarusians remain a house divided on the issue of Belarusian culture and language. The nationalists' viewpoint has been formulated by V.M. Ignatovskii, who wrote in 1919:

> Belarus was one of the first among the cultured Slav peoples, much ahead of Muscovy, which was the backwoods of the Slav world at that time [up to the eighteenth century A.D.] and, much like a parasite plant, nourished itself on the spiritual juices of White Russia.[5]

However, the majority of Belarusians seem to remain so far indifferent or even hostile to the anti-Russian slant of the emerging nationalism and fail to see a significant difference between themselves and their eastern neighbors, who traditionally have been regarded as a model and reference group. Not strong enough to become anti-Russian at this stage, Belarusian nationalism is bound to concentrate at least for some time on settling historical and territorial accounts with the smaller neighbor to the west. Territorial disputes with Lithuania can hardly aim at actual revision of the frontier, but it may serve the purpose of stimulating the formation of the Belarusian national identity. At the present stage of "national revival" and nation building Belarus is likely to preserve close contacts with Russia and expand its relations with other Slavic countries, particularly Poland.

Ukraine

The ethnic history of Ukraine is broadly similar to that of Belarus, and the two nations share a number of common features. East Slavic history began with the emergence of the Kievan Rus' principality in the late ninth century, which expanded rapidly and included most of the whole territory of modern Ukraine, Belarus, and a large part of Russia to the north. As this amorphous state broke up into a dozen principalities, the larger part of Ukraine came under Lithuanian (fourteenth century) and Polish (since 1569) rule. In several stages (in 1654 and 1793) Ukraine was attached to Russia, except for a western fringe, which was annexed by the Soviet Union as late as 1939.

In the Russian Empire the Ukrainians were not recognized as a nation with its own language and culture and were subject to intensive Russification. Mykhailo Hrushevs′kiy, a leading authority on Ukrainian history and chairman of the provisional body of the independent Ukraine in 1917–19, wrote in 1906,

> The treatment of the Ukrainian nationality by the government of Russia was an uninterrupted history of repressions. Aiming at formal uniformity instead of inner unity ... it strived to smooth out and exterminate historical forms of Ukrainian life and national features, to erase everything that was different from the life of the Russian people and did not conform with the imperial attitudes.[6]

As in Belarus, there were two opposite trends in the evolution of the Ukrainian nation. Large sections of the population, particularly in the eastern part of the country, were increasingly assimilated, while growing Ukrainian nationalism, stimulated by the national renaissance in Galicia, the Ukrainian region in the Habsburg Empire, took the inevitable anti-Russian turn. After the revolutions of 1917 in Russia, the Ukrainians desperately fought for independence but finally were overwhelmed by the Red Army.

During World War II the Ukrainians fought on both sides, as many of them, led by Stepan Bandera, hoped to restore the independent state under German protection. After the war, the *banderovtsy* resistance movement continued for several years before it was crushed by Soviet troops. During the last decades the rate of Russification increased rapidly with the spread of education in Russian and under the impact of the Russian-language mass media. In large industrial cities of eastern Ukraine the Ukrainian national identity was on the verge of disappearing.

Thus, the Ukrainians had both a long list of national grievances and a vast pool of historical symbols for a successful nationalist movement. Ukrainian historians explained that Kievan Rus' of the ninth–twelfth centuries was actually the Ukrainian state, and some of them, including Hrushevs'kiy, insisted that even the term *"Rus'"* had been appropriated by Muscovy for prestige considerations. There were also sufficient facts and many names to prove that the Ukrainians never had accepted the loss of independence and strived to restore it. Finally, there was also pride in being one of the largest nations in Europe.

Statistically, the Ukrainians are on a par with the British, French, and Italians, and ranked as the second largest nation in the Soviet Union, yet as a nation they had every reason to feel themselves permanently humiliated. Since the nineteenth century they had been regarded as a countryside edition of Russians, and the bucolic image of the Ukrainian nation and lifestyle persisted despite obvious evidence to the contrary. Their language was the object of jokes, and in the cities of eastern Ukraine even speaking it amounted to a nationalist ("separatist" before 1971) challenge. Both in the Russian Empire and the USSR Ukrainian nationalism was considered a worse crime than nationalism of any other group, simply because it just had "no right" to exist.

Nationalism in latent form and as a dissident movement never disappeared in Ukraine and was especially obvious in the western regions of the country. As a major political force it emerged in 1989 with the foundation of the Taras Shevchenko Ukrainian Language Society and the Rukh movement, the Ukrainian version of the popular front. It grew rapidly and compelled the Communist government to adopt at least some of the nationalist demands. On 16 July 1990, the Supreme Soviet approved the Declaration of State Sovereignty of Ukraine, one month *after* a similar declaration was adopted by Russia. At least legally it came close to a proclamation of independence, as it stressed the right of Ukraine to form national armed forces and establish diplomatic relations with foreign countries, and did not even mention Ukraine being part of the Soviet Union.

The dissolution of the Soviet Union, precipitated by the refusal of Ukrainian leaders to enter the new union treaty, provided the newly independent state an opportunity to shape its foreign policies according to the national interests as interpreted by the groups in power. The former Communists, who enjoy a comfortable majority in the Supreme Soviet of Ukraine, are at one with anti-Communist nationalists visualizing the future Ukraine as a power to be reckoned with internationally. Unlike the small Baltic states, Ukraine is actually capable of shaping its environment within the post-Soviet area (and less so in Europe) by way of effectively challenging Russia and insisting on its own interpretation of the CIS blueprint.

The emergence of independent Ukraine drastically reduced the role of Russia in European politics, and Kiev is using the situation for its own purposes, but its foreign policy is not specifically anti-Russian. Strategically, Russia is less important for Ukraine than Ukraine is for Russia, although economically the reverse may be true. A careful examination of relations between the two states since the fall of 1991 shows that, against the historical background, there is surprisingly little evidence that the Russian policy of Ukraine is influenced by ethnic identity and priorities. If anything, in their mutual relations Moscow seems to be more influenced by ethnic stereotypes and attitudes than Kiev.

Kiev obviously attaches high importance to the formation of a regional alliance, wherein Ukraine would be at least one of the core partners, serving the double purpose of adding extra weight to Kiev in its relations with Moscow and paving the way into the European Community. With these aims in view, the CIS is rather a burden for Ukraine, and the occasionally mooted idea of the Baltic and Black Sea states alliance, despite its certain political and economic advantages, is of not much value for Ukraine. At least economically, cooperation among Black Sea littoral states, including Turkey, Bulgaria, and Romania, along with Russia, Ukraine, and some others, may have better prospects. Ukraine took part in the summit meeting of ten littoral states, held in Istanbul in June 1992, and joined the interparliamentary assembly of these states, founded in February 1993. However, politically a regional alliance of Russia, Turkey, Ukraine, and the Balkan and Transcaucasian states can hardly become a viable arrangement. Probably for these reasons Ukrainian policy planners seem to set a higher priority on integration and regional alliance with the neighboring East-Central European countries, Poland, the Czech Republic, Hungary, and Slovakia, which have wider contacts with Western Europe and are generally more advanced than the post-Soviet and Balkan states. Several multilateral and bilateral agreements concluded between these states and Ukraine may become the first steps toward a regional alliance in this part of Europe. However, the prospects of regional integration do not look very promising. The former "socialist democracies" may regard Ukraine as a desirable economic partner (primarily as a vast market for their goods), but its political value may appear ambiguous: Partnership with Ukraine ensures the security of their eastern borders, yet too close an alliance may negatively affect the process of their integration with the European heartland. Unless a genuine threat from the East (i.e., Russia) arises, there are hardly sufficient common motives for such an alliance, especially as none among these states is in a position to make regional integration economically attractive.

At the present stage it is far from clear which of several possible associations will materialize, especially as the international politics in the region not only depend on the respective states, but are also open to the influence of the European Community and the United States, provided the Western nations will opt for active policies in the region. The situation being what it is, Kiev cannot arrange its foreign policy priorities as definitely as, for example, Estonia. Having reappeared out of oblivion on the map of Europe, Ukraine is looking for ways to assert itself as a major regional power, and it is not particularly relevant for the analysis of Kiev's foreign policies to determine how far this aspiration is shaped by past experience and ethnic characteristics of the Ukrainian nation.

Moldova

Among the western littoral nations, the Moldovan nationalists probably have the most reason to be unhappy about their modern history and to look back to what they regard as the glorious past of their nation. Originally part of the Roman world, during the past two centuries they have been exposed primarily to the influence of Russian culture and drawn into its orbit. Once a fairly large kingdom, during the past fifty years Moldova has been reduced to the status of the second smallest republic of the USSR, as considerable parts of its territory, including the whole coastal area, were transferred to Ukraine following annexation by the Soviet Union in 1940. Relatively advanced in the earlier period of its history, Moldova became a backward periphery of the Russian Empire and generally preserved the same position under the Soviet regime. Finally, the Moldovan language, which was a fairly well developed written language in the late Middle Ages, during the last decades was increasingly ousted by Russian from public life and higher schools.

For all these reasons, stated here but briefly, the Moldovan nationalist movement was bound to become irredentist and anti-Russian.

Language was the basic issue during its early phase in 1989, as the Popular Front came into being in May, and on 31 August the Language Act was adopted, which renamed Moldova's language Romanian, restored its Latin/Romanian script (instead of Cyrillic/Russian) and declared it the only "state language." This decision was considered of such importance that 31 August was proclaimed a regular national holiday, Language Day.

However important, the language issue was but a component part of the national interests as interpreted by Moldovan intellectuals and nationalists. For them, Moldova is an integral part of the Latin world and culture, by force of geopolitical and historical circumstances torn away from the Mediterranean civilization. According to this view, in order to reassert themselves as a nation the Moldovans have to distance themselves from the allegedly alien Slavic culture and "return" to the Latin world. Therefore, after Moldova declared independence on 27 August 1991, the principal foreign policy issue was the dilemma of either remaining independent or reuniting with Romania. Reunification seems appealing to a significant section of intellectuals and nationalists and is the declared aim of the Christian Democratic Popular Front. The irredentist argument is that reunification will in one stroke detach Moldova from the Slavic world, speed up de-Russification, formally restore Moldova as part of Roman/Mediterranean civilization, and ensure Moldova's security in case the USSR is reanimated in some form. However, the majority of the population, if the opinion polls are a reliable guide, do not seem enthusiastic about joining Romania, which for two generations has been regarded as a foreign country. Reunification is also not desirable for the higher levels of administration and a fairly large section of politicians, who have a vested interest in preserving the institutions of the independent state. Finally, it is vigorously opposed by the Russophone groups, who constitute one-third of the total population and form the majority in the industrial Trans-Dniestrian belt.

Ethnic interests have become a crucial factor for the foreign policies of Moldova. The opposite pulls and pressures of the pro-Romanian, "independentist," and minority-separatist factions make impossible any consensus on foreign policy and present the Moldovan government with the unsolvable task of accommodating incompatible demands and approaches. For this reason, Kishinev's foreign policy is pulled in diverse directions simultaneously. To appease the pro-Romanian irredentist faction, it does not reject the idea of reunification at some future date, and promotes cultural and economic integration of the two countries. At the same time, the present regime, staffed mostly by ex-Communists, directs its efforts toward the consolidation of independence. This strategy, labeled the "Snegur Doctrine" by the Christian Democratic Popular Front, has been summarized by the president of Moldova in the following way:

> One has to proceed from the reality: in the immediate perspective I see the path of independent development of Moldova. . . . We stand for open borders with Romania, for joint ventures, but simultaneously for the preservation of our statehood.[7]

Although President Snegur was among the eleven signatories of the Almaty Declaration that announced the formation of the commonwealth on 21 January 1991, Moldova has not signed the agreement on the status of the armed forces (14 February 1992), the treaty on collective security (15 May 1992), or the inter-parliamentary assembly (15 August 1992). It did not sign the Statute of the CIS, and as of this writing (May 1993) the Moldovan parliament has not ratified the Almaty Declaration.

ETHNICITY AND FOREIGN POLICY *171*

Between the two extreme points of reunification and independence a compromise cannot be ruled out. There may be actual Romanization and de facto reunification, while formal attributes and institutions of separate statehood (constitution, parliament, government, armed forces, foreign office) will remain intact, although following the Romanian pattern. Legally, this kind of alliance would amount to the emergence of a confederation of Moldova and Romania.

The absence of consensus among the major political forces, reflecting the diverging and incompatible orientations of particular segments of the population, sets certain limitations on the foreign policy choices but does not completely rule out certain preferences. The majority of the Moldovan intellectuals and politicians regard Italy and France as the most desirable partners and role models. Within the region, Moldova, along with Romania, has shown keen interest in the development of cooperation among the Black Sea littoral states, while standing somewhat aloof from the former "socialist" countries of East-Central Europe, which are regarded as rather alien culturally.

Minority Nationalism and Foreign Policies

The population statistics (Table 7.2) suggest that all western littoral states face the problem of national integration and consolidation of nation-states. Statistics indicate, besides, that each of these states has a "Russian problem," which may affect its relations with Russia.

Absolute figures and percentages are relevant to determine whether minorities cross a certain threshold to become politically significant. However, the types of demands they make depend largely on other factors, particularly their settlement patterns. Urban and dispersedly settled minorities generally claim certain political and cultural rights, but it is compactly settled groups that form a majority or a significant part of the population within particular areas who can raise claims to territorial autonomy or insist on "self-determination," usually meaning secession.

In the western post-Soviet republics most minorities are urban diasporas and do not form compact ethnic enclaves. The largest among them, the Slavic nationalities outside their respective states, are heavily concentrated in the cities, 86 to 92 percent of Russians in the littoral states being urban, but only in certain cases do they constitute the majority of the population in certain compact areas (northeastern Estonia, two eastern districts of Latvia, the Crimean Peninsula in Ukraine). Other minorities, too, are dispersedly settled, the major exceptions being the Poles in those regions of Belarus, Lithuania, and Ukraine that were part of Poland in 1920–39, the Hungarians in the Transcarpathian region of Ukraine, and the Gagauzs in southern districts of Moldova. It is precisely in these areas, although not in all cases, that minority nationalism has emerged as a powerful force, affecting interstate relations in the western littoral of Russia.

Political mobilization of minorities on the platform of ethnonationalism is, essentially, the counterreaction to the formation of nation-states and the loss of previously held special status. The former Soviet regime provided certain privileges for the Russophone groups, who were supposed to (and actually did) spread among the titular nations the Russian language, culture, and way of life. Although their superior status was not readily accepted by the local population in some republics, over the course of decades it became a norm, and the majority of Russian migrants took their special status for granted. The process of the "national revival" in the late 1980s, which strove to reassert the status of local languages and cultures, challenged the status of the Russian-speakers and made them suspicious of the nationalist movements. Following the formation of the popular, essentially nationalist, fronts of the titular nations in 1988–89, militant "internationalist" organizations with the platform of Soviet patriotism came into being in the Baltic republics and Moldova, but not in Belarus and Ukraine, where the nationalists did not have overwhelming political influence and the Communist regimes remained loyal to Moscow. Not without inspiration and guidance from Moscow, there were strikes in several republics against the new linguistic policies, and in some ethnic enclaves separatist movements came into being. By the time the Soviet Union was dissolved in late 1991, ethnic antagonisms became intensive enough to affect relations among the newly independent states.

Among the western littoral states, Belarus is least burdened with the minorities problem. For the ethnic Russians in Belarus, hardly anything has changed since the republic declared independence. Some friction is likely to appear with the growth of the Belarusian national identity, the reinterpretation of history, and the efforts to make the Belarusian language, so far not taken seriously by Belarusians themselves, the official language. However, in the midterm perspective these developments can hardly cause ethnic polarization comparable to that in the neighboring Baltic states and capable of affecting relations between Belarus and Russia.

Potentially, the Polish minority may cause some problems for Belarus. Until recently it had virtually nothing to satisfy its ethnocultural needs, as there were no Polish lessons at schools, no local mass media in Polish, and the Poles could not even dream of launching their own political organization and challenging the policies of the Communist government. The situation improved somewhat during the past two years, as the Poles in Belarus were granted some cultural autonomy and their contacts with Poland expanded dramatically. If the process of political liberalization goes on, some factions of the local Poles may demand territorial autonomy or even reunification with Poland. However, the Polish government cannot be expected to support irredentism in Belarus, since any hint about the revision of the border between the two countries is bound to raise the issue of the Polish-German border, and without active support from Warsaw the Polish minority in Belarus can hardly start a militant nationalist movement.

In neighboring Ukraine, the Polish problem, with analogous implications, is but a minor issue. Although a huge Russian minority does not have an umbrella nationalist organization and lacks intraethnic solidarity, in some regions Russian ethnonationalism has become a force to be reckoned with. Fortunately for Ukraine, the situation in the eastern region, where the larger part of Russians is concentrated, is similar to that in Belarus, and there is no obvious ethnic antagonism along the ethnically diluted Russian-Ukrainian boundary. In another region with a large Russian minority, which includes Odessa and adjacent areas, some Russian political factions demand the formation of Novorossiia (New Russia) either as an autonomous unit or as part of the Russian Federation. However, this southern region is too remote from Russia proper for the purposes of unification, and this irredentist claim is not taken seriously either in Ukraine or in Russia.

It is the Crimean issue that is causing the greatest ethnic problem for Ukraine and accounts for much of the uneasy relations between Ukraine and Russia. The Crimean khanate, with a predominantly Turkic population, was annexed by Russia in 1783. During the following century the Turks, designated as Crimean Tatars, were increasingly ousted from the peninsula (especially after the Crimean War, when more than 200,000 of them fled to Turkey and inner regions of Russia), while many Russians settled in Crimea. In 1920 among the total population of 719,000 persons, there were 317,800 (44.1 percent) Russians, 186,600 (26 percent) Crimean Tatars, and sizable groups (20,000–50,000) of Ukrainians, Jews, and Germans. There was a new wave of Russian and Ukrainian immigration after the Crimean Tatars were deported in 1944. At present among the total population of 2.5 million, Russians constitute two-thirds, Ukrainians one-fourth, and the returning Crimean Tatars number some 250,00 persons, or one-tenth of the total.

The Crimean Autonomous Republic, formed in 1921 as part of the Russian Federation, was downgraded in 1945 to the status of an administrative region of Russia and in 1954 transferred to Ukraine in exchange for some of its northeastern areas contiguous to Russia. During recent years Crimea became a bone of contention between Russians and Ukrainians, with Tatars playing a minor part in the dispute. After the Supreme Soviet of Ukraine adopted the declaration on sovereignty on 16 July 1990, the Crimean regional soviet decided to proclaim a republic and insist on becoming a party to the union treaty, which was being negotiated at that time. The referendum, held on 20 January 1991, gave impressive support to this decision, with 81 percent of eligible voters taking part and 93 percent of the participants approving the restoration of the Crimean Autonomous Republic.

The conciliatory attitude of the Ukrainian parliament, which approved the restoration of the republic shortly (12 February) did not reduce the separatist aspirations of the Crimean politicians. On 5 May 1992 the Supreme Soviet of the Crimean Republic adopted an incomprehensible act on independence within Ukraine and decided to hold another referendum on the issue, but two weeks later was compelled to repeal the act. After several rounds of negotiations with Kiev a working arrangement was reached: The Crimean Republic remained part of Ukraine, but the local legislature was granted wide powers. However, this compromise caused dissatisfaction with both Ukrainian and Russian nationalists, as well as with the Crimea Tatars. The militant Russian Association of Crimea, closely connected with the National Salvation Front in Russia, publicly denounced the agreement between Simferopol and Kiev as collusion and treason.

Crimean separatism evoked sympathy in Russia. Nationalist organizations and many members of parliament insisted, for both ethnic and historical reasons, on reattachment of Crimea to Russia, and this claim was supported by large sections of the population. The attitude of the Russian government on the issue was ambiguous and inconsistent, causing a strain in relations between the two countries. The bilateral treaty, signed by Yeltsin and Kravchuk on 19 November 1990 and ratified shortly by the parliaments, declared that both states "recognize and respect the territorial integrity ... within the presently existing borders within the USSR."[8] This position, without the USSR being mentioned, was reiterated in a joint declaration on 6 November 1991. However, in January 1992 the Supreme Soviet of Russia denounced the 1954 transfer as illegal, and in April Vice President Aleksandr Rutskoi and presidential counselor Sergei Stankevich during their visit to Sevastopol announced that they regarded Crimea as part of Russia.[9] Finally, in December 1992 the highest legislative body, the Congress of People's Deputies, empowered the Supreme Soviet to examine the status of Sevastopol with its huge naval base and headquarters of the disputed Black Sea fleet.

The Russian claims invariably evoked strong negative reaction in Kiev. In January 1992 President Kravchuk publicly accused "certain Russian politicians" of "imperial ambitions," and the Foreign Office charged the Congress of People's Deputies with actions undermining relations between the two countries and violating the UN principles of territorial integrity. During their regular meetings the presidents of Russia and Ukraine generally manage to sort out their differences and make conciliatory statements, but this official harmony is soon destroyed by the appeals of legislators and influential politicians in Moscow.

It has to be noted that the ambiguous and inconsistent approach of Moscow to the Crimean issue is caused not only by the power struggles in Russia, but also because, from the Russian standpoint, every possible solution would have both positive and negative consequences. However valuable the peninsula may be for its health resorts and the naval base, its acquisition or, worse, its independence would create a precedent for the minorities that are insisting on "self-determination" or the redrawing of existing boundaries within the Russian Federation. For this reason, despite the pressure by militant nationalists both at home and in Crimea, it is unlikely that the government of Russia will press the issue too far.

For both internal and foreign policies the Crimean problem has another aspect, the Tatar one. The Crimean Tatars regard the peninsula as their historic homeland and do not consider themselves a national or ethnic minority. Their small number being compensated by efficient organization and a high degree of political mobilization, the community has become a significant force in Crimean and international politics. The Tatar leaders do not support the irredentist and secessionist aspirations of local Russians and pledge their allegiance to Ukraine; their show of force in October 1992 was one of the reasons the Crimean administration dropped the idea of holding a referendum on the independence issue and was forced to seek conciliation with Kiev. For the Ukrainian government, the Crimean Tatar community is an asset for containing Russian irredentism and, potentially, as a factor stimulating the participation of Turkey in the development of the peninsula.

All aspects of the Crimean problem considered, it seems hardly probable that the autonomous republic might secede from Ukraine. The issue is likely to be utilized by militant Russian and Ukrainian nationalists for their political purposes, and occasionally it may be used by Moscow to exert pressure on the Ukrainian government, thus reducing Crimean politicians to the status of pawns in a larger political game. In the long run, the existence of the Crimean republic may promote closer relations between Ukraine and Turkey and, in domestic politics, may become a precedent for the ethnoregional movements, particularly in western Ukraine, that are striving for greater autonomy and the transformation of Ukraine into a federation.

Among the western littoral states, Moldova is most threatened by the nationalist movements of ethnic minorities that are compactly settled along the left bank of the Dniester and in the Budjak region, or southern Bessarabia. These movements, particularly the former, have become major foreign policy issues for Moldova.

In Trans-Dniestria, Moldovans constitute 38 percent, Ukrainians 30 percent, and Russians 25 percent of the total population of 612,400. Historically, this narrow strip, in some places barely a few miles wide, has never been part of Moldova, or Bessarabia, and was granted nominal statehood for the first time in 1920 in the form of a Moldovan autonomous republic within Ukraine. After Moldova was annexed in 1940, a larger part of this tiny republic was attached to the Moldovan SSR, but by way of territorial exchange Ukraine obtained northern Bukovina and the coastal region of southern Bessarabia.

During seven years of the Soviet regime, the population of Trans-Dniestria developed a certain common, basically Soviet, identity. In the late 1980s the local elites looked with suspicion at the Moldovan "national revival" and were openly hostile to its double strategy of Romanization and de-Russification. The Trans-Dniestrian officials, factory managers, and army officers, inspired and supported by leaders in Moscow, who were trying to force Moldova to join the union treaty, found it an easy task to mobilize a large part of the population with the platform of Soviet patriotism and to launch a powerful separatist movement.

The local authorities in Trans-Dniestrian districts, after rejecting all the "nationalist" acts (on language, script, state symbols, and even introduction of local time) of the Moldovan parliament, declared the Trans-Dniestrian Moldovan SSR, separate from Moldova, on 2 September 1990. In November, simultaneously with elections to the Supreme Soviet of the self-proclaimed republic, a referendum was held on the independence issue, and a majority of the voters supported secession from Moldova. The failure of the August coup precipitated the crisis in Trans-Dniestria. Its Supreme Soviet once again declared independence (25 August), held one more referendum to approve the decision, and held presidential elections. The situation deteriorated as armed clashes between the Moldovan police and Trans-Dniestrian guards in December 1991 and March 1992 were followed by large-scale hostilities in June 1992.

The Trans-Dniestrian conflict became a major security issue for Moldova and affected Kishinev's foreign policy in several ways.

First, the pro-Russian and strongly anti-Romanian stance of the Trans-Dniestrian leaders posed a serious obstacle to Moldova's reunification with Romania. It became evident that Kishinev would have to make a difficult choice between reunification at the cost of losing the industrial Trans-Dniestrian stretch and independence as the principal, although far from sufficient, condition for preserving the territorial integrity of Moldova. During the past few months Kishinev seems to prefer the second alternative, and has agreed to grant Trans-Dniestria the right to "self-determination" in the event of reunification with Romania.

Second, the security situation in Moldova, like numerous other cases of armed conflicts, has prompted international involvement in the solution of the crisis in Trans-Dniestria. On several occasions the government of Moldova has appealed to the UN Security Council, the CSCE, and the CIS to stop military actions that President Snegur termed "direct aggression of the armed forces of Russia against Moldova."[10] A cease-fire on the Dniester has been achieved, and negotiations between Kishinev and Tiraspol have been initiated after several rounds of multilateral talks among Moldova, Russia, Romania, and Ukraine. The Trans-Dniestrian conflict has become a major issue for international politics in the region.

Third, the problem of Trans-Dniestria has strongly affected Moldova's relations with Russia, Romania, and Ukraine.

Efforts by the Trans-Dniestrian leaders to secede from Moldova and several rounds of hostilities involving Russian troops have made the Moldovan public mood highly anti-Russian. This compels the regime, although it is less nationalistic than the Christian Democratic Front and some other opposition parties, to keep its distance from Moscow as far as possible and abstain from becoming a full member of the CIS. Kishinev's apprehensions are by no means baseless. The Fourteenth Army of Russia, stationed in Trans-Dniestria, has been openly supporting the government of the self-proclaimed republic, and its present commander, General A. Lebed', has publicly accused President Mircea Snegur of having established a "Fascist state" and has appealed to "the former great country ... to see that Fascists find their due place on the pillar [i.e., gallows]."[11]

The Trans-Dniestrian conflict has created a very awkward situation for the government of Russia. Pressed by militant nationalists at home and taking into account its own pledge to support the 25 million-strong Russian diaspora in the former Soviet republics, Russia cannot stand aloof and regard the Trans-Dniestrian conflict as a purely domestic affair of Moldova. However, direct intervention, not to mention diplomatic recognition of the self-proclaimed republic, would produce adverse effects for both external and domestic policies of Russia. Externally, any such action is bound to increase suspicion of Russia's policies toward the newly independent states and would be interpreted as a manifestation of "imperial ambitions." In domestic policies, insistence on the right to "self-determination" would lend support to similar claims of several republics of the Russian Federation, and simultaneously could be interpreted as a significant concession to the militant nationalist and Communist opposition, which is insisting on a hard line in Russia's relations with former Soviet republics.

Conflicting approaches to the Trans-Dniestrian problem are obvious at the official level. During 1992, Foreign Affairs Minister Kozyrev spared no effort to settle the conflict through negotiations on the basis of the territorial integrity of Moldova. Vice President Rutskoi, on the contrary, supported the independence of the self-proclaimed republic during his visit to Tiraspol in April 1992, and on his return to Moscow urged the Congress of People's Deputies to grant it diplomatic recognition. Because of the Trans-Dniestrian conflict the Supreme Soviet of Russia has still not ratified the treaty of friendship and cooperation between Moldova and Russia, which had been signed in 1990.

Due to these conflicting pressures, the government of Russia was slow to state its approach to the Trans-Dniestrian issue and kept silent, while volunteers from Russia, particularly Cossacks, were joining the ranks of the Trans-Dniestrian guards. Only on 24 March 1992 did Kozyrev discuss the issue with his Moldovan, Ukrainian, and Romanian counterparts during the CSCE session in Helsinki and signed a joint declaration insisting on peaceful settlement of the conflict on the basis of the territorial integrity of Moldova, respect of minority rights, disarmament of unconstitutional militia, and the withdrawal of foreign volunteers. These principles were reiterated in the Snegur-Yeltsin agreement, signed on 21 July, which opened the way for the formation of a tripartite Russian-Moldovan-Trans-Dniestrian peacekeeping force and brought about a cease-fire along the Dniester. However, the issue is not closed for Russia, as Kishinev insists on early withdrawal of the Fourteenth Army, which is regarded as an "occupier force" in Moldova, while a large part of the officers are permanent residents in Trans-Dniestria and would rather fight than leave the place. Like Crimea, Trans-Dniestria is one of those issues that form part of the Soviet legacy affecting Russia's relations with other post-Soviet states.

The Trans-Dniestrian problem causes some concern also in neighboring Ukraine. The Ukrainian government has carefully avoided any direct involvement in the conflict and has refused even moral support to the self-proclaimed republic, despite the fact that the region was part of Ukraine until 1940, and Ukrainians form the second-largest community in Trans-Dniestria. The principal factor determining the pro-Moldovan position of Kiev is the fact that northern Bukovina and southern Bessarabia, parts of Moldova/Romania until 1939, had been attached to Ukraine in exchange for Trans-Dniestria in 1940, and the problem of these territories may arise again in the event of Trans-Dniestria's secession. Besides, any revision of frontiers on ethnic, legal, or historical grounds would inevitably undermine

Kiev's position on the Crimean issue. Therefore, Ukraine took part in all multilateral talks on the Trans-Dniestrian problem, insisting on the principle of the territorial integrity of Moldova and, having warned that the conflicting parties might not use Ukrainian territory for their purposes, tightened control over its border with Moldova/Trans-Dniestria. However, in the event of a new outbreak of hostilities in Trans-Dniestria, the Ukrainian government, pressed by nationalists at home and striving to assert Ukraine as a regional power, may become less patient.

Trans-Dniestrian separatism has compelled the government of Moldova to look toward Romania for assistance and support, and at the same time has become a major obstacle to the reunification of the two countries. The present Moldovan government regards territorial integrity as a top priority task and is rather noncommittal about reunification. In Romania, the public mood is strongly in favor of the merger, compelling the government to pledge its allegiance to the idea of Romanian-Moldovan unity. However, the top leaders of Romania, despite occasional statements by high-ranking officials, cannot insist on early reunification, particularly on the basis of an accord between the two governments. President Ion Iliescu has stressed that the problem of unification can only be solved by the people of Moldova; otherwise it could amount to annexation of Moldova by Romania.

In case of reunification Romania hardly needs the Trans-Dniestrian dowry. Unnatural and inevitably troublesome land boundaries would likely become a source of friction for relations between Romania and Ukraine. Besides, with ethnic conflict in Transylvania smoldering, Romania would rather avoid one more minority problem involving such powers as Russia and Ukraine.

Compared to the Trans-Dniestrian issue, the problem of Gagauz nationalism and separatism is less important for the foreign policies of Moldova and international relations in the region. Although Gagauzes, a small community speaking a Turkic language and professing Orthodox Christianity, had proclaimed their separate republic almost four years ago (on 19 August 1990), their conflict with Kishinev never reached the stage of hostilities. Of late, a moderate faction of Gagauz leaders, including the president of the self-proclaimed republic, is ready to settle the issue on the basis of territorial autonomy and the right to self-determination in case of Moldova's merger with Romania. Turkey, which claims to be the patron of Turkic-speaking nations and ethnic groups in the post-Soviet area, has expressed its readiness to provide assistance for the development of Gagauz districts and facilities for training Gagauz students at universities in Turkey. In a way, the Gagauz community with its Turkish connections may become a certain asset for Moldova, promoting the development of bilateral relations.

In the Baltic region, too, the problem of ethnic minorities has become a factor that affects foreign policies of the Baltic states and international relations in the region. These issues have been widely discussed in the Western press, yet some important aspects need clarification for the purposes of this chapter.

After decades of the Soviet "melting pot," all post-Soviet republics, including Russia, have opted for the nation-state model of comparatively homogeneous Western (or Eastern) countries. However, the presence of large ethnic minorities in most cases (the only exception being Armenia after the Azeri exodus) is a serious obstacle for nation-state formation. Estonia and Latvia particularly, with the Russian community being about one-third of the total population, are typical plural societies in the sense of the term used by J.S. Furnivall and M.G. Smith. The titular nations and the majority of Russian-speakers (about three-fourths among them in Latvia and up to nine-tenths in Estonia) actually form separate societies, divided by culture, religion, language, segregated schools and mass media, opposite external orientations, historical memory, and occupational differences approaching ethnosocial stratification. Aspirations of the titular nations to make their own culture and language the normative framework for the emerging civil society clash with the interests of the Russian-speakers, who insist on equality and parity principles. Natural and human rights as seen by one group are interpreted in terms of discrimination, inequality, and violation of human rights by the opposite group. The absence of consensus on the type of would-be society, namely "national," according to the prevailing idiom, or "binational," segmented (like Belgium, Switzerland, and Canada) has become an almost insurmountable obstacle for the formation of stable civil societies and liberal democratic regimes.

There are no simple solutions to the "Russian problem" in the Baltic states. The Baltic Russians, used to higher living standards and quality of life than their compatriots at home, generally are not disposed to be repatriated and would prefer to stay or, if compelled to leave for different reasons, emigrate to the West. A certain section of Russians, particularly in Riga, having lived for decades in the region regarded as "little Europe" within the USSR, are somewhat more Westernized than, and often consider themselves superior to, the inhabitants of the Russian heartland. On their part, the titular nations are apprehensive of the large Russian minority, potentially the "fifth column" of the neighboring great power and the emerging "capitalist class" of Latvia and Estonia.

Baltic politicians and nationalists are aware of the implications. Therefore the regimes in the three states have adopted a double strategy of integrating those Russians who are willing to become loyal citizens and adapt themselves as an ethnic minority in a foreign country, and stimulating the repatriation of the majority, who are politically and culturally oriented toward Russia and claim double citizenship. Lithuania, with its relatively small Russian minority, could afford to establish liberal citizenship requirements for all permanent residents, and offer property and political rights to ethnic Russians. (According to the Freedom House experts, Lithuania was in 1992 the only "free country" among the post-Soviet republics.) Estonia and Latvia, which face the prospect of nearly 50:50 power sharing in case of universal suffrage without electoral qualification and the inevitable domination of Russian entrepreneurs (nowadays labeled "Russian-Jewish business"), are opting for stringent naturalization and citizenship regulations, as well as electoral qualifications. These policies, interpreted by ethnic Russians and Russia as discrimination and violation of both human and minority rights, are among the principal factors accounting for the tense relations between Russia and the two Baltic states. In order to clinch the issue, the government of Russia exerts pressure on the Baltic states by reducing oil supplies (although this measure affects primarily large industries with Russian labor) and conditioning troop withdrawal on relaxation of naturalization requirements for ethnic Russians in Latvia and Estonia. In their turn, the Baltic states have put forward minor territorial claims, and insist on compensation for the damage caused by the annexation and the presence of Soviet troops on their territory for fifty years. The Baltic-Russian controversies have been internationalized as both sides tried to mobilize international opinion to support their respective claims.

Compared to the "Russian problem," other minorities in the Baltic states are too small to become an issue in international relations, especially as, until recently, the immigrants from Belarus, Ukraine, and other republics tended to merge with the Russian diaspora and, during the past few years, joined its "internationalist" political movements. One important exception is the Poles in Lithuania, a compactly settled minority combining ethnic Poles and Polanized Lithuanians as well as Belarusian Catholics. Supported by Moscow, during the past few years the Communist leaders of the community have been demanding autonomy for two districts with a Polish majority, and have even insisted on their right to "self-determination." Apprehensive of Polish irredentism, the Lithuanian government adopted a hard line toward the militant Polish leaders, dissolved the local councils in two districts, and introduced direct rule for one year after the failure of the August Coup in Moscow. The "Polish problem" has become an irritant in relations between Lithuania and Poland, with Belarus trying to use the Lithuanian-Polish discord for its own purposes, mentioned above.

Conclusions

At the present stage of research, the analysis of the impact of ethnicity and national identity on the foreign policies of the six post-Soviet states discussed here is bound to be tentative in nature. However, certain preliminary conclusions, relevant for both academic and policy planning purposes, may be drawn.

1. The influence of ethnicity and national identity on the foreign policies in the region is of varying magnitude, depending in each particular case on a number of factors, namely,

   a. the state of interethnic relations, which is determined generally by the size, settlement pattern, external orientation, and level of sociocultural and sociopolitical integration of ethnic minorities;

   b. the ethnonational awareness and sensitivity of the majority group to nationalist ideas and attitudes, which are determined by group memory, past relations with other groups and nations, perceived threats to ethnic survival, and so on;

   c. the traditional external orientation of the majority;

   d. the size and geopolitical location of the particular state.

   Comparative analysis of these factors clarifies to a considerable extent why the influence of ethnicity on the foreign policies in the region varies from very high to relatively low, the extremes being represented by Moldova and Belarus, with Estonia, Latvia, Lithuania, and Ukraine occupying the intermediate positions.

2. After decades, even several centuries, of forced sociocultural integration and Russification, the majority of each titular nation, with the probable exception of the Belarusians, is in favor of the formation of the nation-state. The corollary of this strategy is, at the early stage of nation-state formation, ethnonationalism as the prevailing and official ideology, which exerts influence, inter alia, on the foreign and domestic policies.

3. At least in five states (Belarus being the probable exception), the majority of nations sets high value on independence, while attitudes toward the reemergence of the Soviet Union in any form are predominantly negative. Under a representative system of government, the existing attitudes do not favor consolidation of the CIS and its transformation into a political and military alliance.

4. For foreign policy strategies and international relations in the region, the historical and cultural external orientation of the titular nations is of special relevance in the process of nation-state formation. The nationalists in the western littoral generally tend to view their nations historically as part

of Europe, in contrast to Russian patriots who stress the uniqueness of Russian civilization and its Eurasian character. In Estonia and Latvia particularly, the view that the frontier between the West and the East in a cultural and political sense coincides with their eastern border has become a semi-official axiom.

5. Cultural orientation, security and economic interests, as well as the past history of the western littoral nations cause these governments to strive, with varying degrees of intensity, for membership in the European Community. The orientation toward a united Europe ranges from a top-priority strategic aim (for the Baltic states) to one of several alternatives (Belarus).

6. Political leaders and intellectual elites obviously have no illusions about their states being immediately accepted as partners and admitted to the European Community. Therefore, their immediate aim seems to be some kind of regional integration with neighboring countries. This policy may well be feasible for Estonia, Latvia, and Moldova. Lithuania is likely to be handicapped due to its intermediate position between Northern and Central Europe, and Belarus because of its gravitation toward Russia rather than Central Europe. Ukraine, larger than the rest of the littoral states combined, can hardly be expected to renounce its strategic aim of joining the ranks of the big European powers.

7. The traditional external orientation of the newly independent nations and the existence of their diasporas in the West make the western littoral states especially sensitive to the influence of particular Western countries. Moldova is more open to French than German influence, which can be more usefully directed to the Baltic states. If the Western governments opt for political and cultural integration of the former Soviet periphery, coordination of efforts could improve the expected outcomes.

8. The formation of nation-states in the western littoral affects the status of ethnic minorities in the region, especially ethnic Russians and Russophone groups, which formerly enjoyed certain political and cultural privileges. These issues have become the principal reasons for strained relations between the western littoral states (except Belarus) and Russia.

9. Due to differences of size, history, culture, and external orientation, the western littoral does not form an entity in any sense, and a stable alliance of these states (e.g., the Baltic and Black Sea states federation) is highly improbable. This, however, does not exclude certain collective security arrangements in the event of an imminent external threat to all the states of the region simultaneously if there is no prospect of assistance from other quarters.

Notes

1. Sandwiched between Romania and Ukraine, Moldova can hardly be threatened by third parties, and for the same reason separatism of the minorities cannot reach its goal unless supported by Ukraine.
2. The reasons many Balts, particularly Lithuanians, choose a pro-American orientation are fairly obvious. The existence of a relatively numerous community of Lithuanian origin in America, the position of the U.S. government on the Baltic issue for the past fifty years, and the daily broadcasts of the Voice of America and Radio Free Europe in the languages of the region have combined to produce the image of the United States as champion of the "Baltic cause." Public opinion polls support this observation.
3. V.M. Ignatovskii, *Karotki narys historyi Belarusi* (1926; reprint, Minsk: Belarus, 1991), pp. 26, 62, 73, 80–81.
4. *Nezavisimaia gazeta,* 21 July 1992.
5. Ignatovskii, *Karotki narys historyi Belarusi.*
6. Myhailo Hrushevs'kyi, *Ukrainstvo v Rossii: Ego zaprosy i nuzhdy* (St. Petersburg: Obshchaia pol'za, 1906), p. 9.
7. *Nezasiimaia gazeta,* 21 October 1992.
8. *Rossiiskaia gazeta,* 30 November 1990.
9. *Izvestiia,* 8 December 1992.
10. *Nezavisimaia gazeta,* 21 May, 27 May, 23 June 1992; *Izvestiia,* 26 May 1992.
11. *Sovetskaia Rossiia,* 7 July 1992.

8

Baltic Identities in the 1990s
Renewed Fitness

Walter C. Clemens, Jr.

Is Baltic Identity a Lost Cause?

In their efforts to preserve and enhance their respective identities, Estonians, Latvians, and Lithuanians are confronted by three profound challenges: (1) The indigenous populations of the Baltic region are small. What fate awaits cultures whose languages are spoken by only one to three million people? (2) Baltic material and spiritual life has been held back and repressed by fifty years of Communist repression and stagnation. Looking across the sea to Sweden and Finland, Balts see how far their own lives have fallen behind "world standards." Will freedom bring a strengthening—or jettisoning—of native ways? How will traditional song festivals hold up against rock concerts and other pulls of "McWorld"? Balts are tempted to mimic rather than "do their own thing." (3) Baltic identities are threatened not only by the dynamism of the West but by multiple burdens from the East. The Baltic populations are not homogeneous. Can they work out an accommodation with ethnic Russian and other settlers that does not overwhelm indigenous cultures?

Despite these and other challenges, Baltic identity is not a lost cause. The theory of fitness helps us to understand how Baltic identity rests on stronger foundations than at any time since the 1920s.

How to Think About Identity

In reference to groups, fitness refers to a people's ability to preserve and enhance its way of life. This concept helps us understand and define "identity." On the individual level, fitness depends on an individual's internal makeup in relation to the environment. Since both factors change—the individual and the environment—what we call evolution is really "coevolution."[1]

We may think of peaks on a landscape as a measure of individual fitness. The fittest individuals stand highest relative to their landscape. If an individual is in a valley, mutation and election may push it up to a local peak. Fitness changes as coupled landscapes change. Environmental disruptions have meant the end of many life forms.[2]

Fitness theory illuminates political as well as organic evolution. But political fitness is difficult to measure. First, political fitness embodies many kinds of power and influence, both tangible and intangible. Second, political fitness must be measured relative to a coevolving landscape. Third, how the government and the many groups that make up society *feel* about their fitness may differ from objective reality. Fourth, in the case of the Baltic states, objective and subjective trends differ from one republic to another. One republic may advance more rapidly than another—or even at the expense of another. Fifth, trends differ within each republic. The situation in the capitals and other cities differs from that in smaller towns and the countryside. Residents of environmental disaster zones are worse off than others. The material as well as the physical condition of the elderly is far worse than for middle-aged and young people. The ethnic identity of many young people is less rooted than that of their elders. For all these reasons, *caveat emptor*: What we say about fitness is impressionistic—a summation of trends that could be short-lived and that in some cases are contradictory. Every observer must steer between wishful thinking and undue pessimism. The more fit a people believes itself to be, the stronger its sense of national identity. Our identity—our image of ourselves—derives from many sources. It reflects what others say about us and how they respond to us. Identity also represents our own estimate of ourselves. What is our value—potential and actual? We may believe in ourselves "no matter what." Alternatively, we may doubt ourselves despite many favorable signs.

Threats to our well-being can support or undermine our self-image. Threatened, we may muster our resources to resist. But if the threat overwhelms—if it exceeds a certain threshold—we may capitulate.

National self-consciousness can be spurred by external threats as well as by perceived strengths. Before independence—before 1918 and again before 1991—threats to Baltic survival made Balts more aware of their cultural and political identity. Even under siege, however, *confidence* in their national fitness helped propel the drive toward independence. Balts believed they deserved national self-determination. They were confident that they could survive and prosper as independent states. Absent the foreign hegemon, national identity depends on the perceived capacity of each republic to maintain and enhance its way of life in the highly competitive conditions of global interdependence and rapid environmental change.

Coevolution: How Fit Are the Balts Relative to Their Environment?

In 1991 the Baltic republics regained independence, but faced old realities. A reunited Germany was the most powerful entity in Europe, but presented no immediate threat to Baltic security. Russia was down but not out. Even if Russian troops totally withdrew from the Baltic republics, they would never be far away. Indeed, Russia can threaten the Balts from the west, the north, and the east—from Kaliningrad, from the sea, and from Russia proper. Balts feared that Russian military or security forces—directed by local commanders or from Moscow—would move against one or more Baltic republics. In the early 1990s Balts often experienced (as was said of U.S. troops in Vietnam) "weeks of boredom interspersed with moments of sheer terror."

In the early 1990s the Baltic republics were still occupied and lacked the means to defend themselves. Their small size and economic backwardness prevent them from building an equivalent to the Swedish or Swiss army. Poor morale prevents training an effective nonviolent defense force.

Threats from Russia were not sufficient to stimulate strong self-help, but mere growls were too faint to make the Balts capitulate. A stalemate ensued.[3]

Balts had cause to doubt their fitness. They had nearly forgotten how to bank, borrow, trade, innovate, and produce for a free market. They had trouble creating an integrated society. How could ex-Communists and Communist victims, colonists and the colonized, live and work together?

The European Community did not want their goods. Their food would only add to surpluses and was suspect, their goods considered inferior. Everywhere Balts faced hurdles—pollution, shortages, missing links in the chain needed to manufacture anything.

Still, the big picture since independence was positive for each Baltic republic, with Estonia the strongest. Each republic's overall fitness—its capacity to maintain and strengthen its way of life—increased. Each Baltic republic was fitter—relative to its environment—than at any time in recent centuries, with the exception of the 1920s. For the Balts (as for their Polish, Swedish, and Finnish neighbors) relative fitness in the 1990s was facilitated by a change in the environment: The major external threat—Russian expansionism—had declined.

Another external threat for all Baltic states—environmental pollution—

also showed signs of abatement. (Production was down, military activities declined, and a few halting steps were being taken toward pollution control and cleanup.) Environmental gains could easily be reversed, however, by another Chernobyl-type disaster.

Lower fitness within Russia translated into higher fitness for the Baltic. The bear can still crush the Balts like gnats, but its will to lash out has nearly evaporated. To be sure, would-be restorers of empire existed.[4] Even high authorities asserted Moscow's right to protect Russians living in the "near abroad." But Russia's pressing internal problems and its drive to join the First World tended to countervail ultranationalist wishes to retake the Baltic or, for that matter, any of the former border republics.

Russia's fitness—subjective and objective—declined in the early 1990s. Russian "identity" correspondingly weakened—both within Russia and among Russian settlers in the Baltic.

Within Russia many Russians felt their ethnic identity more strongly than ever. Many had long thought of themselves as Soviet or Soviet Russian. "Soviets" and Communist power officially disappeared, but Russia remained. Many Russians were not pleased that their imperial borderlands, acquired over centuries, had broken away almost overnight. For many, outsiders became scapegoats. These charges were misplaced, because the empire had been sick at its core, a malaise that continued even after the Communist dictatorship had disappeared. In the early 1990s the threats to Russia were largely from within—testimony to the country's inability to cope. No external power threatened the Russian Federation. Still, some Russians felt beset by mad ingrates (those in Yakutia and Tatarstan as well as on the periphery) and by cunning plotters in the West aiming to wipe out the Third Rome. Others, less mystically, responded like "neorealists" to new structures of power, trying to make the most of their potential assets. Still others, like Yeltsin and his foreign minister, sometimes took a nationalist stance to guard their flank against conservative critics at home.

Within the three Baltic states many Russians felt threatened, even persecuted. Those who had supported Estonian and Latvian independence before August 1991 felt betrayed. After each Baltic republic regained international recognition, non-Balts in the *Pribaltika* felt threatened because their own fitness had declined relative to the natives'. As Baltic identity became stronger, and as support from Moscow weakened, Russians in the Baltics lost confidence in their own political identity (earlier conceived as Soviet or Soviet Russian, and later as Russian) and began to accept the need to adjust or exit. Like French *colons* in Algeria, they would have to get along with a new way of life or retreat to the metropole. The rising numbers of Russians departing Estonia and Latvia for Russia undercut the confidence of the Russians who remained. The very work sites where non-Balts were concentrated were those most vulnerable to the new market forces—defense and other heavy industry, polluting and often unprofitable.

On the negative side, it was possible that national consciousness in the Baltic states region would never return to the level of the 1920s: Soviet-trained leaders remained influential—even popular—among native Balts. Communist training—explicit and implicit—had left a mark on the expectations, work habits, and political outlook of native Balts. Several million nonnative residents remained in the Baltic, hindering efforts to dilute foreign influences.

By 1993 the Baltic republics had endured the worst challenges they expected to see for the foreseeable future. They had begun the transition to a market economy; they had changed governments democratically; the Russian armies were leaving; native Balts and nonnative residents were groping toward a modus vivendi rather than civil war. If all Russian troops departed, Baltic governments would be less "under the gun." The new governments elected in 1992–93—the first free elections since the late 1930s—could extend the franchise to more non-Balts with less fear of falling again under alien domination.

Let us review in more detail the key factors—both their negative and positive aspects—that have shaped Baltic identity in the past and will do so in the 1990s. At the end of the chapter we consider how these factors may impact the foreign policy choices of Balts and others.

Factors Shaping Baltic Fitness and Identity

Economics

The simplest measures of fitness are GNP growth and GNP per capita, followed by positive indicators for social justice (for women as well as for all classes and minority groups), public health, and public education. In all these areas Balts in the early 1990s laid foundations for future progress. Estonia took strong steps toward economic takeoff. It introduced the kroon and pegged it at 8 : 1 deutsche marks. Exports and foreign tourism boomed, sharply increasing Estonia's reserves of hard currency. Latvia also introduced a convertible currency. Each republic made a few halting steps toward privatization. Each bit the bullet of responsibility for its own fate. Production plummeted; unemployment and inflation mounted; but few Balts wanted to shift back toward a command economy.

What of the future? For Asia's four "Little Dragons,"—Singapore, Taiwan, Hong Kong, and South Korea—economic growth has probably depended far more on intangible than on tangible assets. These intangibles —among them a strong sense of identity—were probably far stronger when the dragons took off in the 1970s than they are today on the amber coast. The soft variables may be decisive for Baltic development, but they are difficult to cultivate when they have withered.[5]

Before 1940 Estonians and Latvians seemed to embody the Protestant work ethic; Catholic Lithuanians were less devoted to thrift and investment. The impact of Soviet Communism on work habits has been quite negative. Communists preached discipline but did not reward initiative or industry.[6]

Balts have long prided themselves on their devotion to education—a source of identity as well as economic growth. But education, public health, and other public sectors have suffered due to long neglect under Soviet rule. They need large injections of enthusiasm, capital, technology, and fresh thinking. Such investments are urgent and not expensive compared to road building and electric grids.

Resources

Compared to many other countries, including Asia's "Little Dragons," the Baltic republics have rich natural resources. But autarky is not feasible. Energy requirements for life and industry in the 1990s are far higher than in the 1930s, not to mention the 1830s. Balts, like many other peoples, have become hooked on cheap fuel—supplied for decades by Soviet Russia. In 1989–91 Balts faced down Kremlin threats to turn off the spigot. But one or two winters of independence on a short fuel budget dampened enthusiasm for life in a brave new world. When Russia again curtailed fuel deliveries in 1992, Lithuanians got the message.[7] They had many reasons to turn against the Sajudis coalition led by Vytautas Landsbergis, the intransigent anti-Communist. Running a state is different from leading a liberation movement. In October the former Communists, renamed the Lithuanian Democratic Labor Party (LDLP), won the most votes in parliamentary elections (44.8 percent as against 19.8 percent for the Sajudis coalition). Lithuanians hoped that the LDLP and its technocrats would be more efficient at running the economy than their predecessors. In early 1993 Lithuanians elected the LDLP leader (and former Communist Party first secretary), Algirdas Brazauskas, as president. Many hoped that he would be more successful than Landsbergis in improving economic ties with Russia. In the months after Brazauskas' election, however, disputes continued with Russia over fuel supplies and how to pay for them.[8] And the state of Lithuania's economy went from bad to worse.[9]

No Baltic republic produces coal or natural gas. Each republic depends heavily on fuel imports—mostly crude oil (65 percent of Lithuania's fuel consumption; 59 percent of Latvia's; and 48 percent of Estonia's), natural gas, and coal. Because it possesses an oil refinery, however, Lithuania could export oil products. Lithuania also has a nuclear power plant, the only one in the Baltics. Estonia has long exported electric power. In 1991 Estonia produced 24 million tons of oil shale and 17 billion kilowatts of electricity per year.[10]

In the Baltic region, as in other parts of the ex-USSR, there is much room for improved energy efficiency. *If* their energy dependence diminished, Balts' fitness would improve and their independent identities would be less vulnerable to external pressures.

Culture

Today's three major Baltic cultures and languages have ancient roots. Faced with recurrent external pressures, Balts have displayed both tenacity and flexibility, defiance and subservience.[11] Baltic armies, greatly aided by foreign forces, checked Soviet expansion in 1920; "Forest Brethren"—guerrillas who fought to undermine Soviet rule in the Baltics—fought the Red Army after 1945; brave dissidents showed their opposition to Soviet rule in the Brezhnev and Gorbachev eras. Still, Balts have no recent history of sustained, large-scale warfare against foreign dominion such as Afghans displayed in the nineteenth and twentieth centuries.

Many Baltic writers of the nineteenth and early twentieth centuries excelled at depicting Baltic life through the eyes and feelings of Scandinavian, German, and Russian overlords. Such works showed both empathy and resentment toward the erstwhile masters. A recent Estonian novel continues this tradition.[12]

Baltic feelings toward their larger neighbors were complicated by the fact that Balts gained as well as gave. With Christianity came literacy—far higher in the Baltic region, especially among Lutherans, than in other parts of the tsarist realm. The faith of the oppressor, Lutheranism preached not just discipline but obedience. In the nineteenth century many Estonians and Latvians converted to Orthodoxy in hope of finding relief from local repression. By contrast, Lithuanians came to regard Catholicism as part of their national tradition. Balts did not want to be Germanized, Polonized, or Russified.

The revival of Baltic culture in the nineteenth century owed much to the influence of Johann Gottfried von Herder.[13] Reviving their folklore, Estonians and Latvians acquired a renewed sense of their cultural worth and nationhood.[14]

Psychology: Compliance and Defiance

When V.M. Molotov summoned Baltic ministers to Moscow and demanded new pacts and base rights for the Red Army in the Baltic, he talked like a master who had called in the serf foreman for a tongue lashing. The master stated his demands and threatened the stick. Each foreman and his subjects capitulated. Baltic political and military leaders judged that resistance would be pointlessly suicidal.

Why did Finland resist similar demands, fight, and limit Soviet expansion in 1939–40? Finland's territory was larger—both in population and territory; more defensible in terms of geographical and human-made barriers; and enjoyed greater social cohesion. The three Baltic republics experienced periods of authoritarian rule in the 1920s and 1930s and were more divided internally than Finland.[15] Against the odds, each Baltic state hoped to save its own skin. When the League Assembly in late 1939 condemned Soviet aggression against Finland and called on League members to aid Finland, nine countries abstained—the three Baltic republics, the three Scandinavian countries, Bulgaria, China, and Switzerland—each of which had its own special concerns.

The USSR annexed the three Baltic republics in June 1940. As World War II exploded, Balts were again torn. What master should they serve, if any? A few volunteered—but many more were coerced—to fight with the Red Army or with the Nazis. In some respects the Germans could be seen as liberators, but the despotism and cruelties of Browns as well as Reds were well known. Stalin's planes bombed Tallinn in 1944 after most Germans had pulled back—punishment for Estonian resistance to Sovietization? When the Red Army reimposed Soviet rule, it was 1940 all over again—deportations, puppet governments, communization. Many Balts joined the "Forest Brethren."

Stalinism returned with a vengeance. Moscow tried and partially succeeded in breaking Baltic obstinacy. After Stalin's death, strains of defiant nationalism resurfaced. But when the Soviet Central Committee suspected a "Latvian bourgeois-nationalist deviation" in 1959, virtually every native Latvian was purged from positions of higher responsibility in the republic.[16]

By the 1970s one otherwise prescient observer concluded that the Estonians, Latvians, and Lithuanians were on their way to physical and cultural extinction. Each people perceived the danger, but did nothing to prevent it. "Faced with this fate, the Baltic nationalities seem not even able to react by forming a Baltic bloc [hardly a feasible option under Soviet rule]. Each becomes weaker still by isolating itself in its particularism and the things which separate it historically from the other nations in the region." Although they are the most modern, the most Western, and the least Sovietized of all nations in the USSR, "none of this can impede the Baltic peoples from advancing toward the annihilation of their nations."[17]

The explanation was that many Balts experienced a kind of psychic numbing as a natural form of self-defense. From the 1940s through the mid-1980s fear was their constant companion. A surrealistic hypocrisy developed that could readily mislead outsiders.

As Leonid Brezhnev aged and stagnation increased throughout the Soviet empire in the late 1970s, Baltic dissent surfaced in samizdat and letters to the Conference on Security and Cooperation in Europe. After 1985 the support of M.S. Gorbachev for perestroika, glasnost, and *demokratizatsiia* opened the floodgates. How widespread was Baltic resistance in the late 1980s? The independence parties were led mainly by ex-gulag prisoners and the "popular fronts" by intellectuals, many of them Communists or ex-Communists. But "signature campaigns," "calendar" anniversaries, and other demonstrations brought huge numbers of common citizens to join the demands for sovereignty and a return to full independence. More than half the Estonian population showed up for the song festival in 1990. Fear of Soviet terror diminished each time Soviet authorities failed to prevent and punish nationalist demonstrations. When Big Brother menaced and sent in special forces to overthrow local patriots, many volunteers engaged in nonviolent resistance, risking life and limb.[18]

Russia's imperial will and unity broken, the Kremlin acknowledged the independent statehood of the three Baltic republics in September 1991.

Even after regaining independence, Balts have had cause to feel differently about Russia than their neighbors to the south. Unlike Poland and Czechoslovakia, the Baltic republics had never been "liberated" (not even in theory). Rather, they had been subdued and annexed by Soviet power. Poland and Czechoslovakia had the status of independent states under international law, even when their rulers groveled before Stalin and Khrushchev. Poland and Czechoslovakia were far less integrated in the Soviet economic system than the Baltic republics—far less dependent on Russia for fuel. Poland and Czechoslovakia had large armed forces of their own. Their struggle for emancipation from Soviet rule had been far more open and better organized than comparable Baltic efforts for decades. They could far more effectively "demand" withdrawal of Soviet forces after 1989.

Even after independence, Balts could not quickly throw off the psychological chains that long bound a subjugated people. Even if all the other loads burdening the Baltic peoples were miraculously to disappear, much time and development would be needed before mutual trust and self-confidence could return.

Russian Occupation Forces

The Baltic republics were still occupied, against their will, even after "independence." But Russian forces in the Baltic were radically reduced in 1992–93. Commenting on the reductions that had taken place by autumn 1992, Estonia's outgoing defense minister, Ülo Ulots, attributed the partial Russian pullout to Estonia's overall fitness. He boasted that "Estonia is the only Baltic country to have its own constitution and parliament; we control our borders [a goal rather than a reality in 1992–93] and we have our own currency." The Russians "have no convertible currency to pay for the upkeep and most of the barter deals with Estonia have failed." But another official, Elmo Priks, cautioned that for every ten soldiers the Russians left behind, they hoped to later bring back ten thousand. He noted that Russia had insisted on keeping its submarine training center at Paldiski until 1999.[19] Moscow told Vilnius in September 1992 that all Russian forces would withdraw from Lithuania within a year. Despite some delays and sharp conflicts, the Kremlin honored this pledge by August 1993. Russia refused to set a firm date for withdrawing all troops from Estonia and Latvia.

Russian President Boris Yeltsin stated in Vancouver on April 4, 1993 that Russia would abide by its commitment to withdraw all troops from Lithuania by August 31, 1993, because Lithuania treated its Russian-speaking population fairly. But pullouts from Estonia and Latvia would be delayed until those countries ended "persecution" of minorities. Estonian and Latvian leaders were displeased that U.S. spokesmen failed to challenge Yeltsin's assertions.

Estimates varied widely, but all pointed to substantial reductions. In early 1992 there were between 120,000 and 180,000 Russian troops in the three republics, with at least 30,000 just in Estonia. In early 1993 Radio Free Europe estimated that more than 50,000 Russian troops remained in the Baltic—27,000 in Latvia alone. By April 1993 Russians claimed 7,600 troops in Estonia, while Estonians put the figure still lower—at 5,600.[20] Many of the military facilities left by the Russians in 1992–93 had been pillaged, but some were in good order, for example, radar stations on the Estonian islands of Hiiumaa and Saaremaa.

Borders

Russia's military dominance overshadows another conflict—borders. Estonia claims those guaranteed by the 1920 Tartu peace treaty. But on 19

February 1993 the Russian parliament fixed the former border of the RSFSR as the state border of the Russian Federation. This meant, Estonian Foreign Minister Trivimi Velliste told the parliament, that Russia was refusing to return to Estonia some 5 percent of its territory seized after annexation—two areas heavily populated by Russian speakers: an area east of Narva and another south of Lake Peipsi. Velliste pledged that Estonia would seek assistance from international organizations to make good its claim.

Latvia also lost borderlands to Russia guaranteed to it in 1920, but took a less firm stand on these lands than did Estonia. Irredentist claims were also voiced in Lithuania and Belarus, while some Poles wanted the return of the Vilnius region given to Lithuania by Stalin. The future of Kaliningrad is also a question mark.[21]

Russian occupation of lands that once belonged to Balts grates on their sense of identity. Why should such small countries be deprived of borderlands taken and colonized by the world's largest state? For Balts, borders become linked with another issue: the aliens in their midst.

Nonindigenous Residents

In each Baltic country Russians and other nonindigenous settlers demanded automatic citizenship. Natives were reluctant to meet this demand, especially in Estonia and Latvia, where outsiders almost outnumbered natives. Nonetheless there was movement in 1992–93 toward accommodation between native peoples and nonindigenous residents in Estonia and Lithuania. The situation in Latvia, where the population balance was most tenuous, was less clear.

Richard Nixon, Francis Fukuyama, and some news reports in the *New York Times* lamented human rights violations in the Baltics.[22] The governments of Estonia, Latvia, and Lithuania replied that citizenship is a privilege, not a right, and that human rights were vigorously upheld in their countries—a view upheld with few reservations by observers from the European Community, the United States, and the United Nations.

Each Baltic government welcomed outside observers. In February 1993 Estonian and CSCE officials announced that the CSCE would establish watch groups to monitor human rights in Tallinn, Kohtla-Järve, and Narva. In March the chairman of the UN Commission on Human Rights, Mohammed Ennaceur, acting on a request from Estonia and Latvia, urged all concerned parties to abstain from any official declarations or actions that might undermine confidence building among people living in the Baltic states. In effect, he rebuffed Russian calls for the United Nations to criticize Estonian and Latvian treatment of nonnative residents.

Generalizations about nonindigenous settlers were impossible. To be sure, the largest number were native Russian-speakers. Some had long ties to the Baltic region, but most had settled there since World War II. Endogamy was the rule, but some outsiders had married locals and produced children of mixed nationality. Many were ex-military officers who thought it more comfortable to retire in the Baltics than Russia. Some had learned or wanted to learn the local language, but most showed little interest in Baltic cultures or tongues. Russians tended to congregate—in larger cities or industrial regions. Some complained that, even if they wanted to study the local tongue, good instruction and teaching materials were in short supply.

Many non-Balts had welcomed Baltic independence and thought that it might benefit them as well as the locals. As Baltic governments debated their proposed citizenship laws, however, settlers from outside worried that they would be excluded from the benefits of citizenship—not just voting rights, but also welfare and property rights and a share in privatization vouchers.

Estonia

Like Latvians, Estonians feared they could soon be outnumbered in their own homeland by persons who did not even speak their tongue. In a century their percentage share in Estonia's population dropped from almost 90 percent to just over 60 percent. In 1881 Estonians made up 89.8 percent of the population, followed by Germans (5.3 percent) and Russians (3.3 percent). By 1922 Estonia's boundaries had expanded, taking in some Russians, so that the proportion of Estonians declined to 87.7 percent; Russians were in second place (8.2 percent) and Germans in third (1.7 percent). Germans almost disappeared during World War II. Radical demographic shifts took place after 1945, raising Russians to 20.1 percent of the population in 1959. In 1989 Slavic nationalities made up 35.2 percent of Estonia's total population—Russians 30.3 percent, Ukrainians 3.1 percent, and Belarusians 1.8 percent. That left Estonians at 61.5 percent and "others" at 8.2 percent. Estonians made up 47.4 percent and Russians 41.2 percent of Tallinn residents. In Narva, Estonians made up only 4 percent; in Kohtla-Järve, 23 percent.[23] By 1993 some reports put the percentage of Estonians in the entire country at 63.5 percent, a sign that many non-Estonians had departed.

There was talk of a possible military confrontation between nonnatives and native Estonians, but no major incident occurred in 1992–93.[24] Fights did occur, however, between fledgling Estonian defense forces and Russian troops at their bases.

Comments in the Western press about Estonian brutality led Arno Susi to write in *Postimees* (9 October 1992) that "Russia's propaganda war against Estonia has turned out to be unexpectedly successful. A small nation is being criticized as a cruel and racist oppressor. Colonists from a gigantic nation have suddenly become the poor, suppressed victims." What to do? Susi said that Estonia could follow Finland's Kekkonen model—give in to Russia and try to be useful as a satellite. "We would have to give citizenship automatically to all foreigners, allow their relatives unlimited rights to immigrate, and declare Russian the official second language of Estonia. In foreign policy we would have to recognize Russian dominance of the Baltic Sea, allow the Russians to retain some of their military bases, and agree to coordinate our foreign policy with Moscow. For these concessions we would get slightly cheaper fuel and a market with inferior purchasing power." In short, Estonia would have to give up "the major part of what we have won."

But Estonian citizenship rules were certainly more liberal than those of the United States—not to speak of Switzerland or Malta. On 26 February 1992 the Estonian Supreme Council (elected in 1990, before independence) reinstated the citizenship law of 1938. The law stipulated that Estonian citizenship is acquired by birth or by further legal procedure such as naturalization. Estonian citizens are those persons recognized as citizens when the law entered effect, persons recognized as Estonian by international treaties, children born at a time when the father (but not the mother) held Estonian citizenship.

Conditions for naturalization include two years of residency prior to and one year after submitting an application to the Ministry of the Interior, as well as a working knowledge of the Estonian language.[25] Exceptions could be made for persons of Estonian origin and for persons who have performed particularly valuable service to Estonia.

The upshot was that most non-Estonian residents could begin applying for citizenship as of March 1992. By then they would have fulfilled the residency requirement, because the initial date was set at 30 March 1990. But members of the armed forces of other countries and persons who had worked for Soviet intelligence were not allowed to apply for citizenship. While most Russian-speaking members of the Supreme Council thought the law too stringent, the Council of Estonia (elected by mostly native Estonians in 1990) opposed the Supreme Council's enactment as too generous. The Council of Estonia declared the law null and void, because the 1938 law was not meant to apply under conditions of foreign occupation. Some critics of the law worried that excuses would be found to delay elections until more Russians had obtained citizenship. But Estonia's September 1992 elections took place before this happened. When the Estonian government moved in 1993 to ease citizenship requirements, this provoked a reaction—calls for a "velvet" re-emigration of Russians, beginning with retired KGB and intelligence workers in the Soviet armed forces. The Decolonization Fund, a nongovernmental body founded in February 1993, sought to raise the Estonian share of the population to 80 percent by encouraging and subsidizing the repatriation of non-Balts. The Estonian Foreign Ministry rejected Russian complaints that the Estonian government was behind the fund, but affirmed that the government believed in assisting the "many people who do not wish to be separated from their relatives." The ministry added that the Estonian constitution guarantees the human rights of all residents regardless of citizenship.

By April 1993, however, the Estonian government had set aside 10 million kroons to facilitate civilians' departure to Russia. Each individual could receive 1,700 kroons for removal costs and passage. A Russian nongovernmental agency, Russkoe pole, provided information about possible sites for resettlement.[26]

A number of Russian groups joined to form a "Representative Assembly" to defend the interests of noncitizens. After several false starts, the group's founding congress convened in Tallinn in April 1993. Acting assembly chairman Iurii Kotenkov called for unhindered extension of Estonian citizenship to all persons. Delegate Nikolai Iugantsov reported on a meeting with Moscow Mayor Iurii Luzhkov that led to draft joint economic cooperation accords. Other speakers said that the group had become a third force in negotiations between the Estonian and Russian governments. European diplomats took the assembly seriously. The Pro Patria government of President Lennart Meri and Prime Minister Mart Laar offered to set up a consultative council for the affairs of the nonnative population. Meri's office proposed that eight council members be appointed by the president and seven by the Representative Assembly.

Latvia

The situation in Latvia was more strained than in Estonia or Lithuania. Why? From 1959 to 1989 Latvia experienced the highest population growth in all of Europe, but this was due mainly to immigration from elsewhere in the USSR while in Latvia births declined. The 1989 census showed Latvians making up only 52 percent of the population. Russians accounted for 34 percent; Belarusians 4.5 percent, Ukrainians 3.4 percent, Poles 2.3 percent, Lithuanians 1.3 percent, Jews 0.9 percent, and others less than 2 percent.[27] Jews, Ukrainians, and Russians were much more likely than

Latvians to have finished secondary and higher education. Of engineers in Latvia, 61.4 percent were non-Latvian; manual laborers, 49.9 percent; in maritime jobs, 85 percent. For such persons to learn the Latvian language might be difficult but hardly impossible—if they wished to do so.

Latvia in 1992-93 adopted no citizenship law, leaving the status of non-indigenous residents unclear in the time leading up to the June 1993 parliamentary elections. But Latvia's Supreme Council set out the *principles* for such a law in its 15 October 1991 resolution On the Renewal of Republic of Latvia Citizens' Rights and Fundamental Principles of Naturalization. Conditions for naturalization of nonnatives were stiff: sixteen years as permanently registered residents; knowledge of the constitution; and conversational ability in the language—defined in May 1992 as 1,000 to 2,500 words depending on whether persons had to deal with the public at large. The principles endorsed in 1991 denied citizenship to persons who served in the Soviet security services or who retired from the Soviet armed forces (estimated in 1991 to number 65,000 persons).

In late 1992 some Latvian officials argued for reducing the residency requirement to ten years, but the government contended that 90 percent of Latvia's residents would be eligible for citizenship even if the sixteen-year rule were adopted. A quarter of the persons who qualified for citizenship under the laws of the 1920s were nonethnic Latvians.[28]

Latvian Foreign Minister Georgs Andrejevs traveled throughout Western Europe in February 1993 condemning Moscow for "using pressure and propaganda" to annex Latvia to Russia. He asserted that Latvian laws protected all minorities. There were thirty-four cultural societies in Latvia, he said, with schooling available in sixteen languages. He demanded protection for Latvians living in Russia (210,000, he said—probably an exaggeration). Andrejevs feared that they would be compelled to pay taxes there in hard currency and be excluded from privatization vouchers.

In the June 1993 elections only citizens of the pre-1940 republic or their descendants could vote. Of registered voters, some 28 percent were Russian or other non-Latvians.[29] The upshot was that about 300,000 Latvian citizens of non-Latvian origin could vote in June 1993. But about one-third of the voting age population, those who came to Latvia after 1940, were not eligible to vote.[30]

Some twenty-three organizations fielded candidates—from "far right" groups (such as the Anti-Communist Association) that strongly opposed citizenship for non-Latvians to "far left" groups that favored quite liberal citizenship requirements. There was even a Russian National Democratic List.[31]

In the election roughly three-fourths of the vote went to parties or coalitions that favored restrictions on citizenship for non-Latvians. The Latvian Way alliance, led by parliamentary chairman Anatolijs Gorbunovs, the former Communist Party ideology chief, won 32.4 percent of the vote to take 36 of 100 seats in the Saeima. The Latvian Way was a congeries of centrist nationalists, former Communists, and Latvian émigrés that grew out of the Latvian Popular Front and the existing government. It stood for a market economy and radical economic reforms along with a moderate stance toward non-Latvians. Gunars Meierovics, a leader of the Latvian Way, said his party would act quickly on the problem of citizenship.

Other winners were the Latvian National Independence Movement (fifteen seats); Harmony for Latvia—Rebirth of the Economy (thirteen); the Farmer's Union (twelve); Equal Rights (seven); Fatherland and Freedom (six); the Christian Democratic Union (six); and the Democratic Center Party (five). The ruling Latvian Popular Front, which had led the movement against the Communist Party and the struggle for independence, did not gain the 4 percent of the popular vote required to gain entry into parliament.

The Latvian Way needed partners to make up a ruling coalition in the Saeima, but it eschewed partnerships with groups known to be liberal toward Russians and with the ultraright Latvian National Independence Movement, which won 15 percent of the vote.

Moderate rightists had gained a plurality, but much of Latvian society was polarized. Most non-Balts had voted for the Russian National Democratic List, while the strongly nationalist Latvian groups had polled 27 percent of the vote. Still, the Latvian Way leadership hoped that the elections —the first since independence—would give the new government legitimacy and that it could proceed with unfinished business.[32]

Lithuania

Compared to Estonia and Latvia, Lithuania, with a 79.6 percent native population, had a far smaller share of minorities—Russians made up 9.4 percent, Poles 7 percent, Belarusians 1.7 percent, Ukrainians 1.2 percent, Jews 0.3 percent, Latvians 0.1 percent, Germans 0.1 percent, and others 0.6 percent.

In January 1991, Lithuania's Supreme Council passed a law Concerning National Minorities, requiring them to obey Lithuania's constitution and laws and to "protect its state sovereignty and territorial unity, . . . the state language, culture, and traditions." This requirement made illegal the efforts of various pro-Soviet, pro-Russian, and pro-Polish organizations to undermine Lithuania's independence. But the bulk of the law spelled out the many protections afforded minorities by the Lithuanian state. Articles 4 and 5, for example, provided that in areas of minority concentration its language may be used with the state language on an equal basis, including informational signs.³³

The Lithuanian citizenship law was passed on 5 December 1991. It was similar to the Latvian law except that the residence requirement was limited to ten years.³⁴ For minorities the manner in which such laws were interpreted would be as important as how they were written. A language or civics exam, for example, could be given in a way easy or difficult to pass. Lithuania tended toward laxity.

Poles, concentrated in the Vilnius area, were a more difficult problem within Lithuania than Russians, because Poland had ruled Vilnius from 1920 to 1940. After most Poles voted for the Democratic Labor Party of Brazauskas in October 1992, the Lithuanian government granted representation in the parliament to the "Union of Poles" even though they failed to win more than 2 percent of the vote. Vilnius complained that Warsaw discriminated against Lithuanians, many of whom lived isolated in the Polish countryside.

State Security

Fitness and a sense of self-worth require some kind of security force for each Baltic republic. But many impediments, tangible and intangible, stand in the way. First, tight budgets limit spending for defense. The Balts have inherited or purchased very little usable equipment from departing Russian forces. Second, skeptics question whether even the greatest conceivable outlays could purchase a force capable of fending off Russia or other neighbors —even Poland. Third, young people have shown little fervor for independence and few have answered draft calls. Poor material conditions and disorganization led some draftees to just walk out. Partly out of conviction, partly from no other choice, Balts—especially Lithuanians—are trying to organize nonviolent modes of civilian defense and sabotage. Such methods proved effective in thwarting Soviet internal security troops and paramilitary groups in 1990–91.

With the return of Brazauskas to power in Lithuania, some observers suggested that Vilnius would tilt "east" instead of "west." In April 1993 Lithuania's defense minister, appointed in 1991 by Landsbergis, granted that Lithuania's national security priorities had not yet been defined. But he stated his own view: Russia was in chaos, and Lithuania should align with NATO's security structures. He opposed neutrality and called for organizing Lithuania's defense structures so that they could swiftly and easily fuse with the European security mechanisms or become autonomous if those mechanisms proved ineffective.³⁵

Despite many problems, Balts are organizing security forces meant to police borders and maintain internal security. Estonian forces have pushed their way into Russian bases. Forces from all republics have tried to stop unauthorized Russian troop movements.

International Law and Order in the 1990s

Balts count less on armed might and more on diplomacy for their protection. Now all three Baltic republics belong to the United Nations, the Conference on Security and Cooperation in Europe, and a host of European Community working groups—for example, meetings of ministers of transportation. Balts benefit from a growing belief in the West—and perhaps in the Russian Foreign Ministry—that international institutions must be strengthened to "make peace" as well as "keep peace."

Balts hope that an invasion of their territories by a foreign state might be seen in a different light from the internecine strife destroying the South Slavs. International institutions operate on the premise that every state is equal and independent. This gives some protection to the Balts even though they have no formal alliances with friendly powers or oil riches on the scale of Kuwait's.

Baltic Fitness in the 1990s

The Baltic peoples became more confident in their identity in the first years after independence was regained.

Changes in Baltic life wrought by Soviet rule were no more extreme than those brought by the Teutonic Knights, Poles, Danes, Swedes, Germans, and tsarist-era Russians who dominated the *Pribaltika* for many centuries. Collectivization of farms was no worse than serfdom. Stalin-era deportations took a smaller toll than the Great Northern War waged between Sweden and Peter the Great. The numbers of Estonians, Latvians, and Lithuanians in the 1990s were larger than at most times in the past. Their share of the world population was declining, but the absolute number of persons speaking Baltic tongues held steady or slightly increased. Even though Baltic identities were challenged by aliens within their societies, Balts were on top—a historical anomaly. If Balts proved to be wise, skillful, and lucky, they would learn to coexist with (or assimilate) these aliens in ways that permitted Baltic cultures to evolve but endure. If they could cooperate more closely with one another as well as with their larger neighbors, the three Baltic republics could coevolve toward greater mutual fitness.

Notes

For assistance with research materials, the author thanks Mari-Ann Rikken, Ruta M. Kalvaitis, and Sonja Elder; for critical comments and suggestions, Toivo U. Raun and Rein Taagepera, and many participants in the Littoral Project workshop—especially Abraham Brumberg, Karen Dawisha, Paul Goble, David Goldfrank, Algimantas Prazauskas, and Roman Szporluk.

"Baltic" in this chapter refers only to Estonia, Latvia, and Lithuania, even though many other peoples and states occupy the rim of the Baltic Sea.

1. Stuart Kauffman, *Origins of Order* (New York: Oxford University Press, 1993).
2. See Roger Lewin, *Complexity: Life at the Edge of Chaos* (New York: Macmillan, 1992), p. 59; also Russell Ruthen, "Adapting to Complexity," *Scientific American,* vol. 268, no. 1 (January 1993), pp. 130 ff. Similar problems helped inspire James N. Rosenau, *Turbulence in World Politics: A Theory of Change and Continuity* (Princeton: Princeton University Press, 1990).
3. This was also the case in a student simulation held at Boston University in April 1993. The exercise focused on all the issues being negotiated by Balts and Russians in 1992–93. No threat or carrot the Russian team devised was sufficiently compelling to induce significant changes in the negotiating position of any Baltic team. Nothing the Balts offered was sufficiently tempting to spark major Russian concessions. Our U.S. team, not unlike the Clinton administration, was paralyzed by disagreements between intervenors and America-firsters.
4. See the chapters in this collection by Gregory Guroff and Alexander Guroff, Nikolai Rudensky.
5. Walter C. Clemens, Jr., "Are East Asian Models Relevant to the Baltic?" *Issues and Studies,* vol. 28, no. 10 (October 1992), pp. 71–89.
6. See Walter C. Clemens, Jr., "Perestroika Needs a Work Ethic to Work," *Wall Street Journal,* 5 December 1989, p. A22.
7. Lithuania's refinery at Mažeikiai stood dormant most of August 1992 as Moscow demanded world prices. Lithuania moved toward privatization of fuel purchasing but hesitated to remove state subsidies for home heating oil. Estonia had promised to purchase crude oil from Russia that would be refined at Mažeikiai, with Lithuania retaining 20 percent.
8. Lithuania's industrial production fell by 51.6 percent in 1992, pulled down by a 70 percent decline in the fuel industry. *RFE/RL News Briefs,* 11–15 January 1993, p. 18. On Russian threats to suspend gas deliveries, see *Baltic Independent,* 9–15 April 1993.
9. Saulius Girnius, "Lithuanian Democratic Labor Party in Trouble," *RFE/RL Research Report,* vol. 2, no. 24 (11 June 1993), pp. 17–20.
10. These data are from "Energy in the Newly Independent States of Eurasia," CIA map 725971 (R00535) 8–92.
11. The tiny middle class of Estonians and Latvians permitted to enter bourgeois life in nineteenth-century Tallinn and Riga cherished this privilege and did not wish to risk it. Nationalist symbols were nourished not by the incipient bourgeoisie but by pastors and teachers in the countryside. Miroslav Hroch, *Social Preconditions of National Revival in Europe: A Comparative Analysis of the Social Composition of Patriotic Groups Among the Smaller European Nations* (Cambridge: Cambridge University Press, 1985), p. 82.
12. Jaan Kross, *The Czar's Madman* (New York: Pantheon, 1992).
13. Johann Gottfried von Herder, *Sämtliche Werke,* vol. 30 (1853), excerpted in Hans Kohn, *Nationalism: Its Meaning and History,* rev. ed. (New York: D. Van Nostrand, 1965), pp. 103–12.

14. The epic *Kalevipoeg* (1857) was composed by Friedrich Reinhold Kreutzwald, working from an outline by Friedrich Faehlmann. The epic poem of Latvia, *Lacplesis* (The bear slayer), was published in 1888. For the larger picture, see Edward C. Thaden, "Baltic National Movements in the Nineteenth Century," *Journal of Baltic Studies*, vol. 16, no. 4 (winter 1985), pp. 411–21.

15. Lee Kendall Metcalf, "Critical Choices: Lithuanian and Estonian Responses to the Soviet Threat, 1939" (paper presented at the annual convention of the International Studies Association, Acapulco, 23–27 March 1993). Finland, however, had a large Swedish minority, which was not always compliant.

16. Similar purges took place at different times in Estonia and Lithuania. Purges in Lithuania were much less extensive than those in Latvia and Estonia. See Alexander Shtromas, "The Baltic States," in *The Last Empire: Nationality and the Soviet Future*, ed. Robert Conquest (Stanford: Hoover Institution, 1986), pp. 183–217 at pp. 199–200.

17. Apart from her incorrect prognosis for the Baltic, professor Hélène Carrère d'Encausse may have erred in calling the Balts the "least Sovietized." In many respects Central Asians were less Sovietized. See her *Decline of an Empire: The Soviet Socialist Republics in Revolt* (New York: Harper, 1981), p. 268.

18. For incisive studies, see Rein Taagepera, *Estonia* (Boulder: Westview, 1993); Olberts Eglitis, *Nonviolent Action in the Liberation of Latvia* (Cambridge, MA: Albert Einstein Institution, 1993); Alfred Erich Senn, *Crisis in Lithuania, January 1991* (Chicago: Viewpoint Press for *Akiraciai*, 1992).

19. *Baltic Independent*, 9–15 October 1992, p. 8.

20. For 1992, see Walter C. Clemens, Jr., "Negotiating a New Life: Burdens of Empire and Independence—The Case of the Baltics," *Nationality Papers*, vol. 20, no. 2 (fall 1992), pp. 67–78 at 72–73. For Latvia, see *RFE/RL News Briefs*, 11–15 January 1993, p. 15; for an overall estimate, see *RFL/RL News Briefs*, 8–12 March 1993, p. 15; for Russian and Estonian estimates in 1993, see BALTFAX in English, 6 April 1993, in FBIS, *Daily Report: Central Eurasia* (FBIS-SOV–93–066), p. 15, and *Baltic Independent*, 9–15 April 1993, p. 3.

21. Concerning Kaliningrad, see "Fourth Republic—Yes or No?" *Baltic Independent*, 9–15 October 1992, p. 9; "Vilnius Seeks its own Foothold in Russia," *Baltic Independent*, 26 March–1 April 1993, p. 4.

22. Francis Fukuyama, "Trapped in the Baltics," *New York Times*, 19 December 1992, p. 23.

23. Toivo U. Raun, *Estonia and the Estonians*, 2d ed. (Stanford: Hoover Institution, 1991), pp. 233–34, 247.

24. In autumn 1992 there were rumors of Russians seeking to form armed units in Narva (where over 90 percent of the population was native Russian), but an Estonian government commission found the stories to be unfounded. Still, Narva City Council Chairman Vladimir Tsuikin stated that there was still "a danger of a social explosion." He praised the commission's recommendation that the government support the city with enterprise credits and new orders.

25. The Estonian parliament passed a law in February 1993 intended to lower and render more specific the language requirements for citizenship, but precise examination procedures were left for the government to decree. Estonian leaders hoped that the law would ease Estonia's way into the Council of Europe. See *Baltic Independent*, 12–18 February 1993, p. 10.

26. Alar Jaanus headed the government's Repatriation Section and was manager of the private repatriation fund. Estonian Radio, 14 April 1993, as summarized by BBC, 17 April 1993.

27. Dzintra Bungs, "The Shifting Political Landscape in Latvia," *RFE/RL Research*

Report, vol. 2, no. 12 (19 March 1993), pp. 28–34 at 29.

28. *About the Republic of Latvia* (Riga: Supreme Council on the Republic of Latvia, 1992); "Background Information Regarding the Human Rights Situation in the Republic of Latvia," Permanent Mission of the Republic of Latvia to the United Nations, 1992.

29. In 1993 there were 2,606,176 Latvian residents, including former Soviet military personnel and their families. More than 93 percent—some 2,438,949 persons—were registered as residents by May 1993. Of the total registered residents, 1,712,864 were citizens. Of them, 1,245,530 were registered to vote—51 percent of all registered residents, but 72 percent of those of voting age. Report by Juris Dombrovskis, Deputy Chief of the Immigration and Citizenship Department, 26 May 1993, cited by Dzintra Bungs, "Twenty-Three Groups Vie for Seats in the Latvian Parliament," *RFE/RL Research Report,* vol. 2, no. 23 (4 June 1993), pp. 44–49 at 48–49.

30. Commission on Security and Cooperation in Europe, "Report on Latvia's June 5–6, 1993 Parliamentary Elections" (Washington, DC).

31. Citizenship was not the main issue for all groups. Greens and two farmers' groups represented other concerns.

32. Russians were a majority in Latvia's six major cities. Even the spouses of Latvian citizens did not automatically qualify for citizenship—even when they held responsible positions in public administration.

33. *Tautines Mazumos Lietuvos Respublikoje* (Ethnic minorities in the Republic of Lithuania) (Vilnius: State Center for Nationalities Analysis, Nationalities Department, 1992), p. 4.

34. *Lietuvos Respublikos Pilietybes Istatymas* (Law of the Republic of Lithuania on citizenship).

35. Audrius Butkevičius, interviewed in *Lietuvos Aidas,* 1993, no. 58 (27 March), p. 5, in FBIS-SOV-93-070, 14 April 1993, pp. 87–8.

III

The Southern Newly Independent States

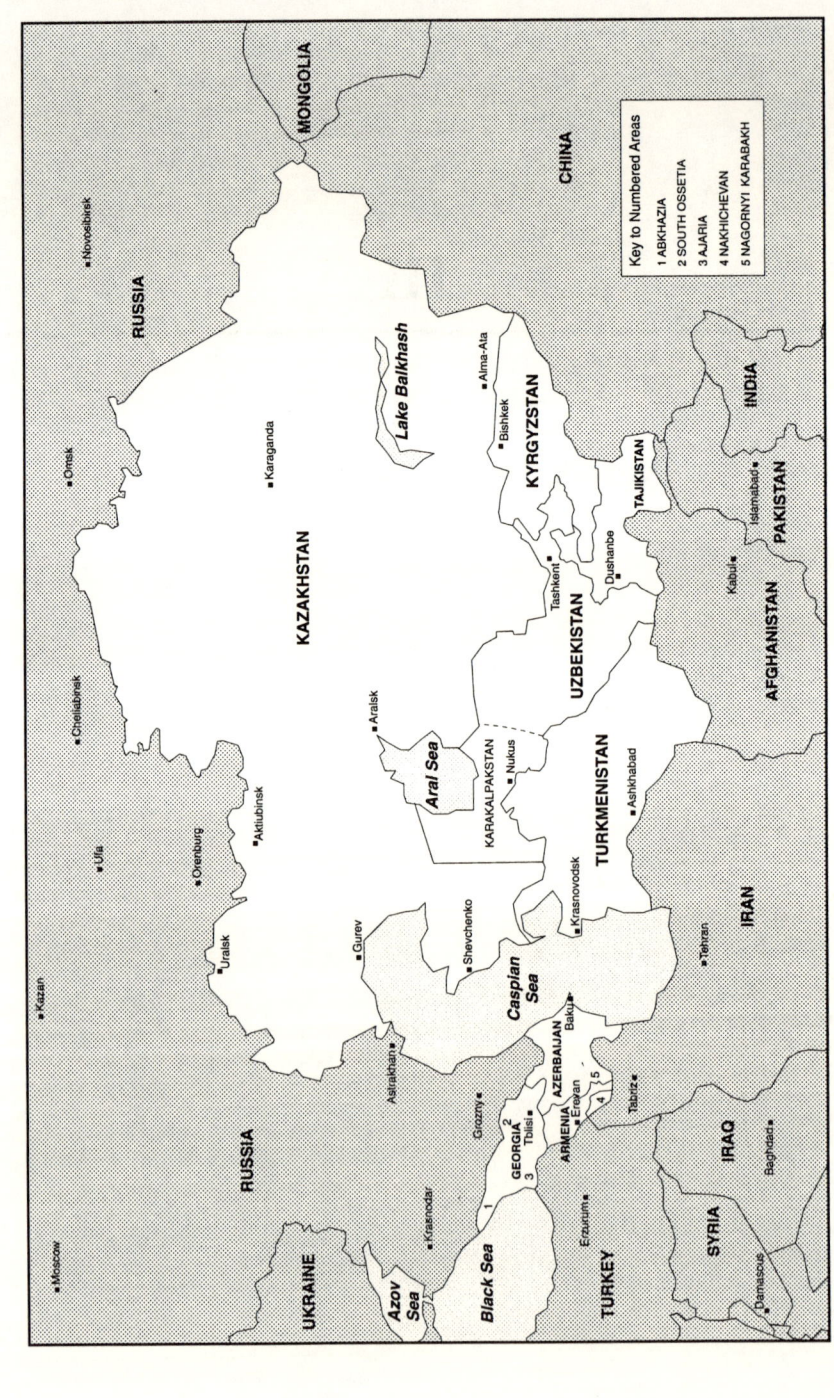

9
Nation Building and Ethnicity in the Foreign Policies of the New Central Asian States

Martha Brill Olcott

Unanticipated Independence

When independence came to the republics of Central Asia—a freedom more forced on them than acquired or won—the five new countries of Kazakhstan, Uzbekistan, Turkmenistan, Kyrgyzstan, and Tajikistan began their existence not only with no experience in the formation and conduct of foreign policy, but even more fundamentally, with almost no way of defining their national self-interests, for the simple reason that these territorial divisions were drawn to impede the exercise of statehood rather than encourage it.

Although four of Central Asia's five republics declared independence prior to the breakup of the USSR in early December 1991 (Kazakhstan's declaration was not issued until 16 December),[1] these actions were designed to put Moscow on notice that more authority had to be given to the republics, rather than to signal Central Asia's impending secession, for as late as 10 December these leaders were pressing for some form of revived union.[2]

After all, four of Central Asia's five presidents—Nazarbaev of Kazakhstan, Makhamov of Tajikistan, Karimov of Uzbekistan, and Niiazov of Turkmenistan—were career Communist Party officials who had been put in their posts by Moscow, charged among other things with the responsibility to maintain, and if possible improve, the integration of the republics within the greater union. Even Kyrgyzstan's Akaev, the one exception, was a Russian-trained physicist who had spent a good part of his adult life in Russia, working in the Academy of Sciences.

No matter how high the local level of dissatisfaction with Soviet (and read for this Russian) rule, before the breakup of the USSR there was almost no one in any of the five Central Asian republics who entertained a serious belief that these territories would ever become independent nations, with all the attendant responsibilities for economic development, provision of social services, definition of domestic and foreign policy, and other tasks of statehood.

To be sure, there was nationalism in Central Asia, as was demonstrated as early as December 1986, when riots wracked Alma-Ata (now Almaty) for three days after Kazakhstan's longtime leader, Dinmukhamed Kunaev (a Kazakh by nationality) was replaced by a Russian with no ties to the republic.[3] "Nationalism," or more precisely, ethnic violence, wracked Uzbekistan's Fergana Valley in June 1989, when Uzbeks attacked Meskhetian Turks, and Kyrgyzstan's Osh Oblast in summer 1990, when the Uzbeks and Kyrgyz turned on each other. Those responsible for these demonstrations generally were drawn from the least Europeanized of the populations, which meant that whatever separatist sentiments there may have been in Central Asian society before the collapse of the USSR were being expressed by the least worldly members of the least worldly republics in the old Soviet Union.

Certainly there were Central Asian nationalists of the European type such as those who led Uzbekistan's Birlik or Erk movements, or Kazakhstan's Azat.[4] But unlike in the Baltic republics or Georgia and Armenia, the political elites of the Central Asian republics provided virtually no support for these movements, so that prior to independence none of these groups enjoyed widespread support. Indeed, if nationalism is defined as public support for the formation of a nation-state, as opposed to the desire to advance the interests of one ethnic group, or protest the advances of another, then what was in evidence in Central Asia would more properly be called ethnocentrism.

However, when the USSR fell apart in December 1991, the Central Asian republics all became independent states, and their leaders were confronted with the responsibility of developing foreign policies that would help sustain their statehood. Each of the five men was well aware of the myriad problems that faced his republic and the region—a rapidly expanding population, a growing list of ecological problems, imminent water shortages, and failing economies; each was aware too that the 8 December 1991 meeting at which Russia, Belarus, and Ukraine had dissolved the USSR was at least in part a declaration that the Slavic part of the former USSR no longer wished to share responsibility for helping cope with problems in the Asian part.

The fact that President Nazarbaev quickly responded to the Belovezshkii meeting by convening a meeting of the Central Asian presidents in Ashkhabad demonstrates that all parties to the dissolution were aware of the ethnic dimensions of the collapse of the USSR.[5] The dire possibilities of the Slavic-Turkic confrontation that Nazarbaev's meeting implicitly threatened, however, very soon achieved the desired effect, for a second meeting of the heads of the former republics was convened, this time in Almaty. It was at this meeting that the Commonwealth of Independent States was declared.

Whatever the intentions of the presidents of the other republics may have been about the evolution of that body, there is little question that the Central Asian presidents conceived of the CIS as a perfected version of the Soviet Union that it was supposed to replace. Released from the burden of communist ideology, the CIS would become something like the European Union toward which the Common Market was evolving, with a single currency, advantageous trading conditions within the community (most prominent among them cheap energy from Russia), a common body of laws, and—very importantly—a group defense and foreign policy posture. At the same time the individual units of the commonwealth would now enjoy the greater cultural freedom for which their populations had been agitating ever louder and more openly since about 1989, and the greater economic latitude to begin to realize their economic potentials in a world arena.

To this end they had to try to take advantage of whatever "strategic" advantages they might have, especially as they recognized that now for the first time they were also objects of other states' foreign policies. Among these strategic advantages was their ethnicity. This was ironic, for during all the decades of Soviet rule, ethnicity was something the regime was on guard to restrict, while nationalism—which was little more than ethnicity in a highly politicized form—had always to be combatted. Now the leaders of Central Asia's new states hoped to use their ethnic or national composition to attract international investment and support.

Ethnicity in Central Asia

Certainly the ruling elites of Central Asia held no illusions that the five republics of the region were anything but artificial creations of the Stalinist period, drawn up in large part to dilute and divide existing populations, in order to facilitate political control by Moscow. Before the creation of the Soviet republics, although different parts of the territory had different rulers, and hence different histories, the Central Asians themselves were an undistinguished mass of various self-identifying tribes or city-states, which were differentiated from one another, first, by the nature of their economies

—whether the populations were nomadic or sedentary—and second, by the languages they spoke, whether their primary language was Turkic or Persian in origin.

To a great extent, drawing the boundaries for the five republics "created" the peoples for whom they were named, mandating new ethnic identities that earlier had been only one part of the many ways members of various Central Asian tribes had identified themselves and their kin. Closely related nomadic families who had differed from one another primarily in the manner of their migrations suddenly received passports that identified them as "Kazakhs" and "Kyrgyz," and found themselves living in neighboring republics. Similarly, sedentes who farmed in essentially the same way but spoke Turkic or Persian dialects at home now became "Uzbeks" and "Tajiks," respectively. All these peoples had small national elites for whom national identity was primary, but they were in a clear minority in 1924, when the division of Central Asia into five republics occurred.[6] Although the ethnic politics of the Soviet period directed considerable resources toward strengthening individual consciousness of the substance of those identities, the Soviet leadership worked as assiduously to prevent the transformation of ethnic identity into a sense of nation. Khrushchev believed that the "proper" social policy could manage to get national distinctions to disappear completely, but Brezhnev was more pragmatic and supported policies that were designed to neutralize the political impact of national and ethnic identities rather than eliminate them.[7] National identity was all right, but nationalism itself was a "deviation" that had to be stamped out. That distinction was clearly articulated in the "big motherland–little motherland" doctrine of the 1980s, which encouraged ethnicity-based affection for one's place of birth (the "little motherland") but transferred political allegiance, and sense of national identity, to the Soviet Union as a whole (the "big motherland").

The administrative barriers that the Soviet authorities erected to hinder the formation of ethnically exclusive Central Asian territories were even more important than their efforts to create psychological distinctions between nationality and citizenship. Boundaries were deliberately drawn to spread ethnic population concentrations among two or more administrative units whenever possible. Thus, historically Tajik cities like Samarkand and Bukhara were put under the jurisdiction of Uzbekistan, while a significant Uzbek population, by 1993 grown to be more than 550,000 people, was put inside Kyrgyzstan's borders, to form a potential irredentist community now constituting about 13 percent of that republic's total population. Large Kyrgyz and Uzbek populations also fell into Tajikistan, while two small "islands" entirely within the territory of Kyrgyzstan were left administratively under the jurisdiction of Uzbekistan; similarly, another was left part of Tajikistan.

Another effective method of slowing the rise of local nationalism was to actively encourage—sometimes even by force—the in-migration of non-Asian populations. Central Asia, and particularly Kazakhstan, became the Soviet dumping ground for unwanted peoples as early as the 1920s, when Russian and Ukrainian "kulaks" were forced to settle there, and once again in the 1940s, with the forced deportation of the Volga Germans, Crimean Tatars, Chechens, Ingush, and other North Caucasian peoples. Russian and Soviet policies in Kazakhstan during the Civil War, and then during collectivization, killed or forced into exile about two-thirds of the prerevolutionary Kazakh population;[8] in World War II the area was subjected to forced industrialization, because of its distance from the German lines; finally, beginning in the 1950s, Khrushchev's Virgin Lands campaign of aggressive agricultural cultivation brought millions of Russians and Ukrainians to the republic, where they were settled especially in the north and west, and their numbers were augmented by the "industrializers" of the 1960s and 1970s.[9] The result by the time of Kazakhstan's independence was a republic that was only about 40 percent Kazakh, and more than 50 percent Russian, Ukrainian, and other European. Similarly, Kyrgyzstan was more than one-fifth Russian and Ukrainian, and the remaining Central Asian republics about one-tenth European.

Soviet economic policies, those of Khrushchev and Brezhnev as much as those of Stalin, provided an additional barrier to the development of serious separatist movements. Although many of the republics possess natural resources that give them great potential wealth, Moscow's policy was to use Central Asia as a kind of contiguous Third World that mined and grew raw materials but did not process them. Although Uzbekistan, Kazakhstan, and, to a lesser extent, Kyrgyzstan all had industrial sectors, these tended to be extraction industries rather than manufacturing ones. They also remained overwhelmingly in Russian and European hands, particularly at the administrative level; for example, at the time of the August 1991 coup, only 8 percent of Kazakhstan's industrial sector was under republican control, with the rest administered through Moscow (as part of all-USSR ministries), or, effectively the same thing, through joint USSR and republican control. Soviet policy also established supply and delivery lines in such a way that no region could easily become economically self-sufficient. Kazakhstan again provides an example: Although the republic has prodigious reserves of oil, it has no facilities for refining its own oil, nor for shipping it anywhere other than to Russia. In the last year of the USSR's existence Kazakhstan shipped to Russia what at world prices would have been $2.7 billion worth of petroleum, but had to purchase from Russia the world price equivalent of $1.2 billion worth of processed fuel and lubricants.

These policies all inhibited the development of nationalism in Central Asia, and seriously hampered the development of ethnic politics as well. Never intended to be sovereign states, the new Central Asian states begin their lives as very fragile creatures. Though Central Asia's leaders are of course free to play their ethnic "cards," to do so brings potential gain but also potential risk, for to play to the ethnic identity of the majority is to risk a backlash from a minority.

Kazakhstan is a Turkic state, but also a Russian one; Tajikistan is a Persian state, but also a Turkic one; Uzbekistan is a Turkic state, but also a Persian one. In the end, all are in fact multinational states, formed from a multinational society that dissolved after its ideology was discredited. This would be a bad beginning under the best of circumstances, and the Central Asian states began their statehood under far from the best of circumstances.

Central Asia's First Diplomatic Steps

In general, the Central Asian republics were slow to evolve anything that could be called a true foreign policy, a system for dealing with other nations based on an understanding of the interests of their own nations. There are several causes for this: the republic presidents were all trained in a single Soviet system, which was rigidly hierarchical, rewarding conformity, not individuality, and encouraging reliance on group action rather than initiative; the republic elites were predominantly Russified, accustomed to seeing the world as intellectuals and other elites in Moscow would, which often made the desires of their putative conationals—for laws mandating use of the local language, for example, or for greater adherence to Islam—as alien and threatening to them as they would have been to a Russian, and thus heightening their uncertainty as to how best to proceed; and, not least important, the sudden creation of fifteen new nations led to an immediate shortage of qualified, trained personnel with any international, not to mention diplomatic, experience.

This shortage was especially acute in Central Asia. Throughout the Soviet period the path an ambitious individual had to follow if he or she was to rise led away from Central Asia, toward Russia. Parents who wished their children to succeed in life placed them in Russian-language schools and urged them toward university in Moscow, in spite of the strict quotas that made entrance almost impossible.[10] There were always a few handfuls of non-Russians who trained at Soviet diplomatic academies, who worked in the Foreign Ministry, and who served in the Soviet embassies and missions abroad, but they were obvious and deliberate exceptions, who tended to play very tightly defined roles, usually as examples of Soviet ethnic liberalism. Armenians and Jews were included disproportionately in this group, and certainly none of the Central Asians were included in the processes of foreign policy formation at the highest levels.

A vivid example of the insignificance of the leaders of the Central Asian republics in the formation of Soviet foreign policy that directly affected their republics was offered by General Secretary Gorbachev's attempt to increase foreign revenues to the USSR by the codevelopment, with Chevron Oil, of the Tengiz oil fields in western Kazakhstan. As recently as 1990 it was not considered necessary to involve Nursultan Nazarbaev, then first secretary of the Kazakhstan CP, and the head of the republic, in the negotiations until the final stages; the basic outline of the deal, including the terms of the profit split, were determined by Moscow.[11] Indeed, even after being elected president (by the parliament) of a "sovereign" Kazakhstan, Nazarbaev did not travel abroad except on Moscow's command until early August 1991, just days before the attempted coup.

It is probably a combination of this lack of experience and the failure to comprehend the full significance of their new independence (or, alternatively, too great a belief in the reality of a functioning CIS) that led to a certain naivete, bordering at times on euphoria, in the first foreign policy efforts of the new Central Asian republics.

Relatively secure in their faith in the continued functioning of their relations with their immediate neighbors, the ex-Soviet republics, which were quickly dubbed the "near abroad," the Central Asian republics turned their attention to the world community, those countries that had always been foreign, now dubbed "the far abroad." Sharing a similar disposition to improve the economies of their republics, and free now of the ideological constraints imposed by the alignments of the cold war, the leaders of the Central Asian nations, like those of the other ex-Soviet republics, expanded the search for world partners and donors that they had first begun in the last year of the Soviet Union's existence.

To a great degree, that search was conditioned by the desire to establish the international existence of the new nations and by the prudent calculation that the best place to look for either markets or help was among the wealthy nations. Thus all the Central Asian nations joined the United Nations and the Council on Security and Cooperation in Europe (in the process extending the geography of "Europe" right to the Afghan and Chinese border), applied for membership in the World Bank and the IMF, and began to talk of applying for membership in the Common Market and in NATO.[12] They also joined two "Eastern" groups, EKO (the Economic Cooperation Organization)[13] and the Islamic Confederation Organization.[14]

Presidents Nazarbaev and Karimov were particularly active travelers, each of them traveling extensively in Europe and Asia, as well as to the Middle East, and in Nazarbaev's case to the United States as well.[15] President Akaev has been almost as avid a traveler. Diplomatic recognition was sought and gained from the United States, Germany, Austria, Great Britain, Japan, and the other large industrial nations; by 1993, for example, Uzbekistan had been recognized by 125 nations, with ambassadorial relations with 64 of them, and plans to open 39 of its own embassies, while Kyrgyzstan has been recognized by 120 nations, and has diplomatic relations with 61.[16]

However, during the first few years of their existence there has been an amateurish quality to these efforts. "Exclusive" rights of representation were sometimes given out to multiple foreign agents, such as in the case of Kyrgyzstan's mineral wealth. Leaders like Turkmenistan's Niiazov traveled abroad under the false impression that as head of state he was a welcome guest wherever Turkmenistan was officially recognized. Though some leaders have learned more quickly than others, and Presidents Nazarbaev and Akaev have both made several successful trips to the West, their nations' diplomatic efforts have been uneven ones.

Few of Central Asia's new ambassadors speak the languages of the states they have been assigned to. Kazakhstan's first ambassador to the United States did not speak English. More telling, neither the first Kazakh nor the first Kyrgyz sent to Ankara spoke Turkish, highlighting the problems that arise when semi-assimilated former Soviet elites try to make the transition to national leaders.

Central Asia's Ethnic Cards

For all the catholicism of their search for foreign investment and aid, it is clear that the leaders of the Central Asian republics intended to take advantage of aspects of their ethnicity and religious history, in order to give them a competitive edge in the scramble for international affiliations that was set off both by the collapse of the USSR and, even more, by Russia's unilateral usurpation of the USSR's overseas presence. Broadly speaking, there were three ethnic "cards" the Central Asians could put into play in the international arena. These are their Turkic or Persian nationality, their Islamic religion, and their "Asianness."

The most immediately obvious of these was nationality. The Turkmens, Uzbeks, Kazakhs, and Kyrgyz speak Turkic languages, and share many cultural affinities with the people of Turkey, while the Tajiks have similar linguistic and cultural connections to Iran. For their part, both the Turks and the Iranians were eager to reciprocate the interest of the new nations.

For the leaders of the Turkic-heritage nations, Turkey was an obvious and, at first glance, attractive model for emulation, much like an "older brother," in President Karimov's words, that seemed to incorporate features of both East and West.[17] Turkey was the first nation to recognize Uzbekistan and Kazakhstan, and was among the first to open embassies in the Central Asian capitals, save for Tajikistan's. Both private business and the government have aggressively pursued business and cultural contacts, creating scholarships for Central Asian students—two thousand per republic—hiring Central Asians skilled in traditional crafts like leatherwork, and opening or assisting in the creation of banks, telecommunications systems, and food processing plants. In early 1992 Turkey announced plans to begin independent television programming, via satellite, with the capability to cover the entire area;[18] in mid-1992 Karimov, Niiazov, Akaev, and Nazarbaev all went to Ankara, to be present at celebrations of the sixty-ninth anniversary of the Turkish state, and numerous high-level delegations have gone from Ankara to the various Central Asian capitals.[19]

The situation with Iran was more delicate, both because of Iran's own orientation toward Islam and because of the extremely unsettled nature of politics within Tajikistan. Politically unstable even in the months before the collapse of the USSR, Tajikistan was quickly preoccupied with internal problems that rapidly degenerated into a full-fledged civil war. President Kakhar Makhamov was removed from office in September 1991 by a temporary coalition of ousted Communists, Islamic activists, and democrats, led by former Communist Party First Secretary Rakhman Nabiev, whom Gorbachev had removed from power in 1985. Nabiev, though, quickly broke with the Islamic activists and democrats, who in turn resorted to force to make him share power with them (May 1992). The power sharing then turned to outright ouster (September 1992), with the Islamic activists and democrats forced out themselves in November 1992. Iran's diplomatic presence in the republic has been substantial throughout, but Tajikistan's Islamic-Democratic coalition sought a broader range of support from Iran than did the Communist or former Communist rulers.[20]

Tajikistan's relations with its Afghan neighbors is another variant of the "Persian national" card. Since coming to power in November 1992, the government of Emomali Rakhmonov has turned with real fury on Tajikistan's Islamists, placing them under death sentence and driving them into exile. Many of them (along with tens of thousands of other Tajiks) have taken refuge in Afghanistan, and throughout the summer of 1993 they staged border raids on Tajikistan from Afghanistan, firing on Russian, as well as other Central Asian, detachments and on pro-Tajik government troops.[21]

A second ethnic "card" the Central Asian leaders hoped to play was that of Islam, an ethnic rather than religious "card" because, save for Tajikistan's brief period of Islamic-Democratic coalition rule, all of the region's leaders are committed to the development of secular societies. All five of the republics are historically and culturally Muslim, although the degree to which the religion had been established before the revolution, and the extent to which practice had survived the state atheism of the Soviet period, varied from the thorough Islamization of Turkmenistan and Uzbekistan to the generally more superficial practice of the faith in Kazakhstan and Kyrgyzstan. There is little doubt that the primary interest of all the Central Asian leaders in Islam was financial, for the oil-rich Gulf States are obviously attractive sources both for aid and for business. Here too Turkey and Iran played roles, vying as different models of the integration of Islam into economic development.

Unlike the nationality card, however, the way Islam has been "played" varies among the republics. In Turkmenistan and Uzbekistan, where the population was relatively more devout and knowledgeable, and the leaders were both associated with the Communist, antireligious policies of the past, there was good reason to aggressively pursue contacts with the Muslim states. The leaders of both republics made highly publicized pilgrimages to Mecca,[22] and both have traveled widely through the Arab states and have encouraged commercial and missionary representatives to expand activities in their respective republics.[23] Saparmurad Niiazov has been particularly keen to portray himself as a devout Muslim, replacing the large Lenin in Ashkhabad's main square with a statue of himself as a hajji, and, accompanied by Nursultan Nazarbaev, recently dedicating a large mosque in his own honor in his home village.[24] Karimov, fearful that an Islamic movement could threaten his rule, has been somewhat more cautious in his embrace of Islam. Yet even Karimov has taken great pains to reassure Uzbeks that he is an observant Muslim.[25]

The situation for Kyrgyzstan and Kazakhstan was more delicate. The former has a small but important Russian population, which forms a strong support bloc for President Akaev, while the latter is at least half Russian. Anxious to develop his republic's oil to best advantage, President Nazarbaev was eager to make use of Omani, Iranian, and Saudi technical expertise, but was reluctant to acquire any Islamic "baggage" that might come with it.

Although Akaev jested that he would be delighted to make hajj if that would help bring Saudi money into his republic, and has made two traditional Muslim feasts into Kyrgyzstani state holidays, neither Akaev nor Nazarbaev has made much use of his Muslim heritage in diplomacy. Akaev's one attempt, a clumsy reference to Palestinian autonomy during a state visit to Jerusalem, became something of an embarrassment, although it did not disrupt the development of a trade partnership between Israel and Kyrgyzstan.[26] Kazakhstan and Uzbekistan have also developed diplomatic as well as trade relations with Israel, with all three republics encouraging former Jewish residents-turned Israeli citizens to invest their capital in new Israeli–Central Asian joint ventures.[27]

Nazarbaev has gone even further to distance himself from a religious identification. Alone of all the Central Asian republics, Kazakhstan recognizes no Muslim holidays, and does not mention Islam in its constitution; religiously based political parties have been refused legal registration, and the closest Kazakhstan has come to violating international human rights standards has been in its handling of Azat, an Islamic-nationalist party that is banned in Kazakhstan.

The third basis on which the new republics of Central Asia sought to reach rapport with particular countries was a broadly defined attention to successful Asian nations. Not fully articulated, or even necessarily understood as having ethnic overtones, there was nevertheless a general recognition throughout Central Asia that the developmental models of Europe and America are more remote to the experience of these five nations than are the success stories of the Asian "tigers"—Singapore, South Korea, Malaysia, Hong Kong, Japan, and China. These models are most important in Kazakhstan and Kyrgyzstan, where some of the interest is racial, but the rapid economic gains that each of these Asian countries has made make all of interest in each of the Central Asian republics, for the miracles that those countries have performed are ones that all these new states would like to replicate. It must also be said that the tight social control and strong state sector that development has required in the "tigers" is also something the Central Asian presidents find familiar and fathomable, unlike the more confusing diffuse democracies of the West.[28] Missions and delegations have been sent to each of the Asian nations, and a number of investment and joint venture possibilities have been opened. Numerous joint projects with China have already begun in both Kyrgyzstan and Kazakhstan.[29] The technical expertise of the Asians has also been encouraged in the Central Asian republics. President Li Yuan Kew of Singapore has advised both Nazarbaev and Karimov on development strategies, and the first foreign adviser Nazarbaev put on his staff, even before independence, was a Korean-American economist who was reputed to have ties to important industrial families in Korea. One of the first foreign factories to open in Kyrgyzstan was an electronics assembly plant owned by the Korean Goldstar Corporation; Kyrgyzstan also offered significant incentives to the Japanese, in exchange for assistance in developing the electronics industry further and a $60 million line of credit, and to Hong Kong bankers, who it was hoped would assist the republic to become an "Asian Switzerland."

Disappointments

Although the ethnic "cards" on which the Central Asians had first hoped to stake their futures have had some effect, none of them has proven to be the hoped-for trump. Turkey and Iran's much-publicized competition for Central Asia has seemingly already peaked, with neither side investing the sort of sums that Central Asians hoped would be forthcoming. Iran remains extremely interested in its new neighbors. But its hopes of using these new states to improve Iran's geopolitical and economic positions are not likely to be realized anytime soon, as Iran remains a pariah for the international monetary community. Turkey too has been frustrated in its hopes to serve as a bridge from the West to Central Asia, as Turkey's leaders have found Central Asia more inaccessible and Western investors more wary than anticipated.[30]

Relations with Turkey remain good throughout Central Asia, but are considerably less sanguine than they were in the fall of 1991. The cultural and linguistic similarities between most of the Central Asians and the Turks have turned out to be much less in practice than people had assumed; save perhaps with the Turkmens, Turkish and the Central Asian languages have not proven to be mutually intelligible in any practical sense, especially since Russian was and for the time being remains the business and scientific language for the great majority of the Central Asian elites, especially when outside their own country; even those members of the elite who speak their "native" languages fluently have a "kitchen" language vocabulary, one ill-suited to the purposes of international negotiation. At the same time, the greatly increased access that Central Asians have enjoyed to the world at large has shown them how far the "Turkish model" lags behind other economies; while remaining happy if they could reach the Turkish level immediately, the Central Asians are no longer so inclined as they once were to view the Turkish standard of living as a long-term goal.

However, Turkey too has had to face the realities of national self-interest, as it became increasingly clear that any sort of diplomatic or commercial "Pan-Turkism" would come at the expense of Turkey's trade with Russia, the volume of which is about ten times that of trade with Central Asia. Nor has Turkey's internal economy proven to be as robust as Central Asia had supposed, sharply limiting the amount of money that Turkish investors were willing to direct to the region. There have also proven to be political dimensions to the question of Turkey's potential influence in Central Asia.

Although the West in general preferred Turkey to Iran as the predominant figure for the region, the possibility of Turkey emerging as a strong Asian power was at odds with Turkey's own interest in being seen as integral to Europe, and thus a fit candidate for membership in the EC. The varieties of interplay between secular and clerical Islam in Central Asia also affected the tensions between secularists and clericalists in Turkey, bringing into question the wisdom of embracing Central Asia more tightly.

Although the experience of dealing with the Central Asian nations has had some impact on Iran's domestic politics, in the struggles between pragmatists, who see Central Asia primarily as an economic opportunity, and clericalists, who continue to place priority on the increasing religious influence, it is the Central Asian leaders who have grown leery of the Iranians, because of conditions in their own republics. The civil war in Tajikistan has thoroughly traumatized the Central Asian leadership, who were inclined to accept the characterizations of the Nabiev supporters, and now of the Rakhmonov government, that the opposition was inspired and armed by "Islamic fundamentalists," variously described as being both Afghan and Iranian in origin. All the Central Asian nations remain interested in developing friendly relations with Iran, but the economic relations between Iran and Central Asia are developing far more slowly than the Iranians planned.[31]

Central Asia's Islamic card has yielded even more uneven results. Saudi Arabia has been quick to provide Korans, but it and most other Arab states have entered the Central Asian market very cautiously.[32]

The issue that has proven to be the most politically charged, however, is Islam. Uzbekistan's Karimov made early overtures to believers, taking his state oath of office on a Koran, and publicizing his own orthodoxy, including that he eats only *halal*.[33] He permitted Uzbekistan's clerics, official and unofficial, to operate freely, and allowed religious figures to enter commerce, but he refused to register Islamic political groups, including the Islamic Renaissance Party. This has left Karimov vulnerable politically, both because of his atheist, Communist past and because Karimov could never become sufficiently Muslim to satisfy the most conservative sectors of Uzbek society.

Islamic conservatism is especially strong in the Fergana Valley, a densely populated area that is emerging as a crucial foreign policy sore point for the entire region. Frightened by the examples of Afghanistan and Tajikistan and aware of how volatile and unpredictable religious support can be, Karimov has been backing away from Islam, recently replacing the official head mufti of Uzbekistan. More importantly for foreign policy, Karimov has played a very strong, behind-the-scenes role in Tajikistan, to the degree that some observers regard the Rakhmonov government as little more than an Uzbek puppet state.

The situation in Kazakhstan is similar, but even more complex. President Nazarbaev has always been wary of Islam, preferring to cast his nation as a bridge between the Islamic East and the Christian West.

The vague "fellow-Asian" ethnicity was the most easily dispelled, as the various nations demonstrated the unsentimental business orientation that had made them tigers in the first place. All the Asian nations have been happy to do business with the Central Asians, but the principle has been one of receiving top value per dollar of investment. In cases where there is little or no advantage, the Asian investors have not been reluctant to refuse funds. Japan and South Korea have come in more aggressively, but with the exception of a $60 million Japanese loan to Kyrgyzstan, they too have chosen investment strategies that offer Central Asia's states the possibility of long-term payoffs but give little by way of short-term aid.[34] The Asian nation that has profited the most from the emergence of the new republics is China, by now Kazakhstan's largest non-CIS trading partner, and, according to President Karimov, Uzbekistan's largest trading partner overall. However, China's cooperation has come with both an economic and a political price. The Chinese are especially enthusiastic about barter commerce, so that a considerable portion of the trade has involved cash-free exchanges of Central Asian raw materials (including metal scrapped from Soviet military equipment, to the annoyance of the Russians) for Chinese consumer goods, most of them of such low durability that "Chinese" has already become an adjective of disdain for Central Asian consumers. At the same time, the Chinese are a palpable potential menace, especially to bordering Kazakhstan and Kyrgyzstan. China, with potentially nationalist-minded Kazakh, Kyrgyz, and Uigur populations of its own, has refused to recognize existing borders with Kyrgyzstan, insisting on "clarification" of twelve specific locations. Concern over offending a Beijing government fearful of rising nationalism in the Uigur-Sinkiang Autonomous Region has presumably been a major motivating factor in the Kyrgyz republic's refusal to allow the registration of a Uigur nationalist political party and in Kazakhstan's reluctance to entertain the idea of forming an autonomous Uigur region.[35] Kazakhstan in particular stands to lose if Uigur demands for creation of an independent "Uigurstan" grow, not only because of Chinese displeasure, but also because such a country would cost the republic a large chunk of its own territory.[36]

In sum, throughout Central Asia, foreign investment has been neither as rapid nor as intensive as the region's leaders anticipated. Even energy-rich Turkmenistan has found the pace of foreign investment to be slower than planned, although independence could probably be called a success in Turkmenistan.[37] Blessed with a small, largely homogeneous population and vast reserves of natural gas and petroleum, Turkmenistan has under the leadership of President Niiazov opted to become a sort of post-Soviet emirate, extraordinarily tightly controlled politically, but its current energy resources allow the government to provide food, energy, and social services to the population for a pittance. Rich enough to be politely indifferent to the further fate of the CIS, Turkmenistan has been able to concentrate on establishing the necessary relationships with its immediate neighbors, especially Iran, for ethnic—there are Turkmens on both sides of the border—as well as pragmatic reasons, and otherwise go its own, essentially inoffensive, way.

For the other four Central Asian republics, however, the nearly two years since independence have brought a steady series of disillusionments and disappointments. Not only has prosperity not come, but in every place save Turkmenistan the standards of living have dropped precipitously. In Tajikistan and Kyrgyzstan, the smallest and poorest of the Central Asian nations, the economies have essentially collapsed.[38] This unraveling of the social fabric has greatly exacerbated the social tensions that the Soviet system had managed to keep relatively dormant, so that there has been an explosion of crime and corruption, and a greatly increased risk of civic disturbance, especially along ethnic lines.

The Self-Interests of Several Nations

Perhaps it is not surprising, given the worsening economic circumstances in which most Central Asian states find themselves, that the interests of the various republics are beginning to diverge one from another, and sometimes from Russia as well. In mountainous and resource-scant Tajikistan and Kyrgyzstan, with internal tribal and clan structures that have already caused an intra-ethnic civil war in Tajikistan and that have the potential to do so in Kyrgyzstan, powerful outside sponsors are required if these states are to survive. Since the Rakhmonov government is completely dependent on Uzbekistan and Russia, Tajikistan may already be considered a client state. Kyrgyzstan is attempting a different tack, seeking world support by making itself an island of democracy and free enterprise in the heart of Central Asia; however, the harsh realities of the country's remote location and feeble economy make Kyrgyzstan extremely vulnerable to outside pressure, especially from its immediate neighbors.

How fragile that goodwill can become was clear in mid-May 1993, with Uzbekistan's response to Kyrgyzstan's introduction of an independent currency. Outraged at this show of independence, and fearing a flood of Kyrgyz rubles into his own economy, President Karimov closed the border between the two countries, cut off the natural gas pipeline that brought Kyrgyzstan energy from Turkmenistan, and introduced new regulations that would make it impossible for noncitizens of Uzbekistan to spend their rubles in his country.[39]

This bellicose decision will have an immediate impact on the ethnic stability of Kyrgyzstan, because it effectively isolates the Osh region, where Uzbeks are one-third of the population, and which is a ten-hours' land trip over rugged mountains from Kyrgyzstan's capital. Tensions between Uzbeks and Kyrgyz have already erupted into lethal riots in Osh once, in June 1990, over conditions of crowding and economic competition, which have only gotten worse since. Because of the arbitrary way the Fergana Valley was divided up among Tajikistan, Uzbekistan, and Kyrgyzstan, and because of ancient competing claims for this very fertile and desirable land, the possibility of military conflict in the region seems high.

However, the Fergana Valley is not the only such possible flashpoint in Central Asia. Tajikistan and Kyrgyzstan have long-standing disputes about water rights and grazing along their common border, the course of which Tajikistan has refused to ratify by treaty. Relations have recently been strained too by an influx of refugees from Tajikistan, including defeated opposition figures who have tried to set up bases in southern Kyrgyzystan. Bishkek has also complained of Tajik treatment of the small Kyrgyz community south of Kyrgyzstan's border.[40]

Tajikistan and Uzbekistan have long-running disputes too, about ownership of the currently "Uzbek" cities of Samarkand and Bukhara and the "Tajik" region of Khodzhent, about their borders more generally, and, more basically, about whether "Tajiks" really exist, or are, as some Uzbeks assert, Uzbeks who speak Persian.

Possessed of a large and well-equipped army, which is now gathering useful experience by fighting in Tajikistan, and unhampered by ethnic opposition or parliamentary interference, Uzbekistan will undoubtedly become a force to reckon with in Central Asia. As noted, there are Uzbek populations in Kyrgyzstan and Tajikistan, as well as in southern Kazakhstan. As inheritor of the emirate of Bukhara and of the Kokand khanate, Uzbekistan can lay historic claim to the fertile portions of Kyrgyzstan and parts of southern Kazakhstan, as well as to portions of Turkmenistan. Karimov has already shown disdain for Kyrgyzstan's sovereignty, by having his KGB arrest three Uzbekistani dissidents (two of them Uzbek, one Tajik) in Bishkek, during a December 1992 conference on human rights.

Although he has not yet articulated claims to territory beyond the present borders, President Karimov has made perfectly clear that he views political stability—for which read continuation of his own regime—as the supreme defining good in the region. Moreover, he has articulated a foreign policy similar to that of Russia—the right of Uzbekistan to intervene in the name of protecting Uzbeks, independent of where they might live.[41]

The counterweight to Uzbekistan, and competitor to the claim for regional power, is Kazakhstan, which is far larger, and because of its oil reserves and other natural resources potentially far wealthier. President Nazarbaev would like to turn Kazakhstan into a link between East and West. However, Kazakhstan has significant disadvantages in this competition with Uzbekistan. The enormous ethnic diversity of Kazakhstan, and its geographic proximity to Russia, impact on state policies there in ways Uzbekistan need never consider. Much more dependent on a strong Russia than the other republics, Kazakhstan has had to remain bound to the plummeting ruble, and has had to struggle to try to make the CIS function.[42]

Even Nazarbaev has to tread a line between the two groups, projecting an image that is sufficiently Kazakh to keep the support of the republic's eponymous nationality, but sufficiently European so as not to alarm or alienate the non-Kazakhs. He has tried to do this by creating a "Kazakhstani"-oriented foreign policy, one that advocates the interests of the republic as a whole rather than that of any particular ethnic group. Thus Nazarbaev has taken particular care not to appear in garb or settings that could be considered "Islamic"; at the same time, though, he has not had the liberty to seem anti-Muslim either.

Ethnic realities make it impossible for Nazarbaev to impose too great a one-man rule, but demographics make greater democracy risky. Privatization and economic development in the republic are fraught with ethnic dimensions—privatizing large industry favors the Russians who run them, while privatizing small service establishments favors the Uzbeks, who have the capital to buy them; privatizing land favors the Slavs and Uzbeks both, because they are able to do small-plot farming, unlike the Kazakhs, while privatizing housing legalizes the fruits of Soviet-era discrimination, when the best housing went to Russians; even exploitation of Kazakhstan's oil involves disputes between local residents, who want the proceeds of the Chevron and other deals to remain locally, rather than go to Almaty.[43]

The republic has begun to create a Kazakhstani army, air force, and even navy under Minister of Defense Colonel-General Sagadat Nurmagambetov (a Kazakh), and plans to develop its own defense doctrine, though it will continue to provide basic officer and military training in coordination with Russia. But myriad issues remain unresolved; not the least of these is that the army cannot become exclusively Kazakh, and yet if it includes Russians, the army will then have at its heart the risk that one day Russian Kazakhstanis might have to defend Kazakhstan against Russia. President

Nazarbaev has concluded treaties with President Yeltsin recognizing the existing borders between the two countries, and is committed to a shared security policy.[44]

Looking Again Toward Russia

Ironically it is Russia that is likely to be the biggest winner in the competition among the various Central Asian states. The structure of the Soviet economy was such that Russia has been left with enormous leverage over each of the republics, which it has used to secure a number of unilateral benefits. Accounting for 70 percent of Kazakhstan's goods turnover, Russia was able to change Nazarbaev's first attempts at economic policy simply by closing the border, bringing Kazakhstan's industry to a halt within a few days. In Kyrgyzstan Russia has used fuel prices to control access, effectively isolating the republic because there is no jet fuel. Citing the threat of Afghan infiltration through the old USSR border, Russia has, with Uzbekistan, effectively retaken control of Tajikistan.

However, the Central Asian leadership probably does not object to Russia's strong-arm tactics as much as it does to the fact that Russia itself seems unable to follow through on its threats and feints, to impose genuine order. The continued disintegration of central control in Russia is a constant pressure on all the Central Asian states. The presidents of all the republics have complained of Russia's financial policies, especially the hyperinflation, which has worked to Russian advantage; commodities and raw materials purchases are made at old ruble dollar equivalents, while the energy and finished goods that the Central Asians import from Russia must be paid for at newer, and far higher prices. Yet at least for now, Kazakhstan, Uzbekistan, and Tajikistan have all decided to remain in the ruble zone, and have accepted that their financial policies must mirror those of Russia.[45]

Central Asians all remain afraid of Russia's military might. Thus the one issue with which Russia has managed to mesmerize Central Asia is that of the approximately ten million Russians who have remained in the five republics. Unable to cope with the people it already has, Russia is anxious to prevent a flood of further refugees, and so has spoken ominously of the violations of "human rights" represented by state language laws, possible Islamization, and other attempts to make the Central Asian nations more monoethnic.

The history of Central Asia is one of competition between and among the region's various indigenous ethnic groups. Independence, coming so suddenly and with so little advance preparation, could well prove a catalyst for a new round of ethnic conflict. Realistically, there are probably only two ways to minimize the influence of ethnicity on the course of

Central Asian politics. The first would be to have some strong central power reimposed on the region, either by an ideological, nominally nonnational entity such as the USSR, or by one nation—Russia is the obvious possibility—in a straightforward empire.

The other possibility would be for strong economic recovery throughout the region. The strong political control of Turkmenistan makes it difficult to be certain, but the experience of the republic seems to suggest that differences among the nationalities make little difference as long as everyone has plenty of money. Certainly rivalries, even hatreds, remain, but abundance both dulls appetites and gives everyone a proportionately higher stake in preserving a system that supplies plenty of services.

The real danger in Central Asia is that for the moment neither possibility seems immediately likely. The CIS is still neither multinational nor supranational, and no replacement seems at hand, while Russia will need considerable luck even to hold onto what it now has, let alone be able to reassert its former borders; this is not to suggest that the attempt may not be made, but only to suggest that it will fail.

Economic recovery, at least in Kazakhstan and Uzbekistan, seems a better possibility, but certainly not soon. Karimov's prediction of a year to recovery has already elapsed unfulfilled, and Akaev's more cautious prediction of three years would need a miracle to achieve. Nazarbaev's outline of a three-stage process, to be completed by 2015, still looks feasible, at least for his resource-blessed republic.[46] However, two lean, demanding, and possibly very dangerous decades must pass before that possibility might come.

We are thus left with a third way, that the people of Central Asia may come to understand that the nations fate has pushed upon them will have to be built by the citizens who must live within them. Bred by a Soviet system that offered food, shelter, and succor as "rights," in exchange for the renunciation of all sense of individual responsibility for what the nation does, and accustomed to explaining their own poverty, and the comparative riches of others, as a function of the ethnic group into which they happened to be born, the people of Central Asia face real hurdles in transforming the tribalism of ethnicity into a more conscious, and more considered, understanding of citizenship. However, the possible consequences of disaster are so great if they do not that we must hope the people of Central Asia will soon come to understand that while one is born with a nationality, one must work and contribute to become a citizen.

Notes

1. *Kazakhstanskaia pravda*, 18 December 1991.
2. *Vremia* (Ostankino television), 10 December 1991.

3. For details, see Martha Brill Olcott, "Perestroika in Kazakhstan," *Problems of Communism,* July–August 1990, pp. 65–77.

4. For details of Uzbekistan's national movement in particular, see James Critchlow, *Nationalism in Uzbekistan* (Boulder: Westview Press, 1991).

5. TASS, 13 December 1991, FBIS, *Daily Report: Soviet Union* (FBIS-SOV–91–240), 13 December 1991, p. 84.

6. Kh. T. Tursunov, *Obrazovanie Uzbekskoi sovetskoi sotsialisticheskoi Respubliki* (Tashkent: Izdatel'stvo Akademii nauk Uzbekskoi SSR, 1957) offers a very detailed account of the various negotiations and boundary decisions.

7. See Martha Brill Olcott, "Yuriy Andropov and the National Problem," *Soviet Studies,* vol. 37, no. 1 (1986), pp. 103–17, for details of this policy.

8. See Martha Brill Olcott, "The Collectivization Drive in Kazakhstan," *Russian Review,* vol. 40, no. 2 (1981), pp. 122–42, for details.

9. See Richard Mills, "The Virgin Lands Since Khrushchev: Choices and Decisions in Soviet Policy-Making," in *The Dynamics of Soviet Politics,* ed. Paul Cooks (Cambridge: Harvard University Press, 1976), pp. 179–92.

10. On the nonmobility of Central Asians, see William Fierman, ed., *Soviet Central Asia: The Failed Transformation* (Boulder: Westview Press, 1991), especially Fierman's own chapter 10.

11. *Kazakhstanskaia pravda,* 2 April 1992.

12. *Interfax,* 4 February 1992, FBIS, *Daily Report: Central Eurasia* (FBIS-SOV–92–025), 6 February 1993, p. 70.

13. *Izvestiia,* 6 February 1992.

14. *Slovo Kyrgyzstana,* 11 December 1992.

15. *Kazakhstanskaia pravda,* 15 May 1992.

16. *Nezavisimaia gazeta,* 12 February 1993.

17. *Izvestiia,* 20 December 1991.

18. *Interfax,* 4 March 1992, FBIS-SOV–92–045, 6 March 1992, p. 57.

19. Ankara television, 30 September 1992, FBIS-SOV–92–192, 2 October 1992, p. 32.

20. *Izvestiia,* 13 October 1992.

21. *Komsomol'skaia pravda,* 17 August 1993.

22. Radio Tashkent, 11 April 1992, FBIS-SOV–92–072, 14 April 1992, p. 60.

23. Radio Tashkent 20 February 1992, FBIS-SOV–92–037, 25 February 1993.

24. *Kazakhstanskaia pravda,* 18 May 1993.

25. *Nezavisimaia gazeta,* 7 January 1992.

26. *Vechernyi Bishkek,* 18 January 1993.

27. *Izvestiia,* 24 February 1992.

28. *Izvestiia,* 21 September 1991.

29. *Panorama* (Bishkek), 15 August 1992.

30. Tansu Ciller, address to Turkish-American Business Council, Istanbul, November 1992.

31. On Iranian credits to Turkmenistan see *Postfactum,* 5 March 1992, FBIS-SOV–92–045, 6 March 1992.

32. Riyadh SPA, 21 February 1992, FBIS-SOV–92–037, 25 February 1992.

33. *Nezavisimaia gazeta,* 7 January 1992.

34. *Komsomol'skaia pravda,* 26 August 1993.

35. *Erkin Too,* 30 June 1993.

36. See *Birlesu,* 1992, no. 46.

37. Consultations with Turkmen foreign economic officials, March 1993.

38. See *Kommersant,* 1993, no. 8, for detailed figures on the deterioration of economic conditions in the various CIS nations.

39. *Slovo Kyrgyzstana,* 15 May 1993.
40. Interviews in Bishkek, January 1993.
41. *Vechernyi Bishkek,* 15 May 1993.
42. *Komsomol'skaia pravda,* 9 September 1992.
43. Interviews in Almaty, June 1993.
44. *Kazakhstanskaia pravda,* 15 December 1992.
45. *Kommersant,* 14 August 1993.
46. *Ekonomika i zhizn'* (Almaty), 1992, no. 8.

10
Ethnic Demography and Interstate Relations in Central Asia

Robert J. Kaiser

Changes in the relative demographic "strength" of ethnonational communities in their ancestral homelands have had a profound effect on interethnic and interstate relations, not only in the former USSR but throughout the world political system. Changing rates of population growth and decline due to natural increase, migration patterns, and ethnic reidentification have all served as catalysts for rising nationalism during the post–World War II period, and have been interpreted as critical processes with respect to the future viability of the nation by nationalists and outside observers alike. This chapter examines the recent ethnodemographic trends in Central Asia,[1] and assesses how these trends have influenced interethnic and interstate relations in the region. The impact of interethnic relations on demographic processes, especially migration patterns, is also analyzed. After a general discussion of ethnodemographic trends in Central Asia during the postwar period (1959–89), the chapter examines the most recent demographic developments (1989–92), and discusses them in the context of the emerging interethnic and interstate relations in the region.[2]

This chapter assesses the relationship between ethnodemographic trends and interstate relations in three distinct geopolitical arenas. First, the ethnodemographic-interstate relationship between the Central Asian successor states and the other states of the former Soviet Union, and particularly the Russian Federation, is one of the most critical aspects of the new ethnopolitical realities in Central Asia. Second, the relationship between ethnodemographic trends and interstate relations among the Central Asian successor states themselves has become an increasingly important issue in the region. Third, since there are members of each ethnonational community across the interstate border in Iran, Afghanistan, and China, this chapter also attempts to assess the role of this cross-border population in the emerging interstate relations in the broader region of Central Asia, to the extent that this is possible.

The data used for this chapter are drawn from a variety of sources. The primary source of demographic background information is the postwar Soviet censuses (1959, 1970, 1979, and 1989). In addition, statistical yearbooks provide important information on fertility rates, mortality rates, and migration patterns, although these data sources are rarely cross-tabulated with ethnonational identity. Survey data are also used to assess recent developments in interethnic attitudes and prospective migration from the region. Estimates of the most recent ethnodemographic trends, and in particular the development of refugee migration, are taken from a variety of sources, but rely primarily on news reports. These sources are, of course, less reliable.

As used in this chapter, a nation is defined as a community of interest and belonging, whose members share both a sense of common genealogical and geographic origins (i.e., ancestry and homeland), and also a belief in a shared fate or destiny together. This makes the nation both an ascriptive group (a community of belonging) and an instrumental group (a community of interest). However, although nationalists typically paint a primordialist image of the nation (i.e., that it has existed essentially unchanged from time immemorial), nations are essentially modern collectivities. The making of nations is best seen as a historically contingent process that begins with the "ethnicization" of elites (the interest of indigenous intellectuals in the history, geography, archeology, anthropology, language, etc. of their group), and proceeds to the "nationalization" of elites (the politicization of ethnic intellectuals and their attempts to nationalize the masses and gain control over the fate of the "nation," often by attempting to gain greater political control over the region identified as the ancestral homeland). The third and final stage of this historically contingent process is the nationalization of the masses, or their vertical and horizontal integration as members of a community of belonging and interest larger than their local kinship group and of a homeland more geographically expansive than their locality. Several factors are critical to the success of this final stage, including the mass acceptance of the nationalist message (both their adoption and adaptation of it); the increasing geographic mobility of the masses, which helps to break down their localist mentality; and the increasing social mobilization of the masses, especially rising literacy in a standardized "national" language and rising educational attainment, with the political socialization that this entails.[3]

Nationalization of the masses should be seen as an ongoing process that is never really completed, since it must be reenacted with each generation. In Central Asia, the nationalization process began later than for most European groups, and was impeded by the limited geographic, social, and political mobilization of indigenes in the region. Nationalization of the indigenous masses in particular is a process without deep roots in many parts of Central Asia.[4] More localized ethnic solidarity continues to be relatively more important in Central Asia, although it does not appear that supranational identities (Pan-Turkic, Pan-Islamic) are likely to supplant either nationalism or ethnic solidarity. Overall, the trend during the postwar period has been toward the increasing nationalization of the population into Uzbek, Kyrgyz, Kazakh, Tajik, and Turkmen national communities, and the events of the last few years have tended to accelerate this nationalization process.[5]

Since nations are essentially subjective communities of belonging and interest, the essence of national consciousness is not quantifiable. However, this does not mean that the study of nations and nationalism is not amenable to empirical analysis. The use of ethnonational data from the former Soviet Union does raise a question regarding the degree to which the national categories that appear in the censuses and statistical handbooks accurately reflect the national self-consciousness of the population. The "national" communities of Central Asia—Uzbeks, Tajiks, Turkmens, Kyrgyz, Kazakhs, Karakalpaks—have been declared artificial creations of the Soviet regime, as opposed to the more "natural" subnational localized ethnic groups and supranational Turkic and/or Muslim communities.[6] It is certainly true that a national consciousness had not become mass-based in Central Asia prior to 1917, and that even indigenous elites at that time were divided as to which level of identity was most important (subnational, national, supranational). During the interwar period, a nationalization of elites occurred, with the creation of "national states" in the region and attempts to fill these political spaces with nations. *Korenizatsiia* (nativization or indigenization) policies favoring members of the titular "nations" for preferential treatment in their home republics, coupled with the dramatic social and geographic mobilization that occurred during this period, began a process of mass-based nationalization. However, this process was impeded in Central Asia by the in-migration of upwardly mobile Russians and members of other European groups to the growing urban/industrial complexes of the region. During the post-Stalin period, nationalization of the masses in Central Asia increased, though it continued to be impeded by ethnic stratification in the region. Evidence for nationalization includes the attainment of complete literacy in standardized national languages; rising education rates among the Central Asians, rivaling rates among the most developed nations in the state; and intensive intermarriage among the subnational ethnic groups that make up the nation, even while international marriage rates continued to be quite low.[7]

The Soviet censuses asked each individual for his or her ethnonational identity, and so provide a reasonably good gauge of national belonging and changes over time. However, the national communities listed in the censuses are somewhat artificial, since they include not only all individuals who declared themselves members of that nation (e.g., self-declared Uzbeks), but also all individuals who declared themselves to belong to ethnic groups considered subnational communities of that nation (e.g., Kipchaks and Kuramas in the case of Uzbeks; the so-called Pamir Tajiks of Gorno-Badakhshan in the case of the Tajiks).[8] Unfortunately, the extent of this identity problem is unknown, since data for the "subnational" ethnic groups are not provided. However, the limited data that are available indicate that the overwhelming majority of members in each national community declared themselves members of that nation, and not of some other ethnic community. According to data published along with the 1989 census, only 0.01 percent of all Tajiks, 0.003 percent of all Uzbeks, and 0.001 percent of all Turkmens declared themselves members of some other ethnic group.[9] Of course, this does not mean that a more localized ethnic identity has disappeared or become unimportant, and in certain contexts this more localized form of identity may assume primacy. Nevertheless, it does appear that the vast majority of individuals in Central Asia consider themselves members of the major nations in the region. For this reason, the national data as provided in the Soviet censuses are considered a reasonably accurate reflection of the national identity of peoples in the region, and are clearly the most extensive and reliable source of information about ethnodemographic trends in Central Asia.

Ethnodemographic trends have an impact on the nationalization process and on interethnic, international, and interstate relations. Geographic mobility and levels of interethnic interaction (particularly the in-migration of ethnic outsiders), as well as ethnosocial mobilization and changes in the pattern and intensity of interethnic competition, have been critical processes in the making of nations. This is not to say that ethnodemographic trends are the only or even the most relevant factors in the nation-making process. They are one of several important factors that influence interethnic relations and intranational consolidation, which in turn often alter the pace and/or direction of ethnodemographic trends.

General Postwar Patterns

In Central Asia, two major ethnodemographic changes have occurred during the post–World War II period. First, following the war the in-migration

Table 10.1

Demographic Indigenization, 1959–89
(indigenous and Russian percent of total population, by republic)

Republic	Titular nation				Russian			
	1959	1970	1979	1989	1959	1970	1979	1989
Uzbekistan	62.1	65.5	68.7	71.4	13.5	12.5	10.8	8.3
Kazakhstan	30.0	32.5	36.0	39.7	42.7	42.4	40.8	37.8
Kyrgyzstan	40.5	43.8	47.9	52.3	30.2	29.2	25.9	21.5
Tajikistan	53.1	56.2	58.8	62.2	13.3	11.9	10.4	7.6
Turkmenistan	60.9	65.6	68.4	72.0	17.3	14.5	12.6	9.5

Sources: 1959: Tsentral'noe statisticheskoe upravlenie (TsSU) SSSR, *Itogi Vsesoiuznoi perepisi naseleniia 1959 goda* (Moscow: Gosstatizdat, 1962), vol. 16, pp. 206–8; 1970: TsSU SSSR, *Itogi Vsesoiuznoi perepisi naseleniia 1970 goda* (Moscow: Statistika, 1973), vol. 4, pp. 321–24; 1979, Goskomstat SSSR, *Itogi Vsesoiuznoi perepisi naseleniia 1979 goda* (Moscow: Goskomstat SSSR, 1989), vol. 4, pt. 1, bks. 2–3; 1989: Statisticheskii komitet sodruzhestva nezavisimykh gosudarstv (SNG), *Itogi Vsesoiuznoi perepisi naseleniia 1989 goda* (Moscow: Statisticheskii komitet SNG, 1992), vol. 7, pt. 2.

of Russians and other nonindigenes continued a historical migration pattern that preceded 1917. This in-migration of Russians and other nonindigenes, particularly to the growing urban/industrial complexes in Central Asia but also to rural areas of Kazakhstan and Kyrgyzstan, shifted the ethnodemographic balance in these regions away from the indigenous population and toward the Russians. Second, beginning in the 1960s, rapid population growth resulting from a high natural increase among the Central Asian groups brought about an ethnodemographic shift in favor of the indigenous nations in their respective home republics (Table 10.1). This second trend, which continues at present, has been enhanced by the reversal of the first trend—since the mid-1970s, there has been a net out-migration of nonindigenes from the region, which has accelerated greatly since the late 1980s. Each of these trends has had and will continue to have a serious impact on interethnic relations in Central Asia, and also on interstate relations between the newly independent states of Central Asia and the other successor states of the former USSR. This is particularly true of relations between Central Asia and Russia. Each of these major ethnodemographic trends is examined in greater detail below.

In general, the indigenous groups of Central Asia have remained highly concentrated in their respective homeland areas (Table 10.2), even in the face of rising population pressure resulting from rapid natural increase coupled with stagnant economic growth and more recently economic decline.

Table 10.2

Indigenous Concentration in Home Republics and Central Asia, 1959–89

Nation	% in Home republic				% in Central Asia			
	1959	1970	1979	1989	1959	1970	1979	1989
Uzbeks	83.8	84.0	84.9	84.6	99.4	99.2	99.3	99.0
Kazakhs	77.2	79.9	80.7	80.3	89.3	90.8	91.9	91.9
Kyrgyz	86.4	88.5	88.5	88.0	99.3	99.2	99.0	98.1
Tajiks	75.2	76.3	77.2	75.1	99.2	99.1	99.2	98.7
Turkmens	92.2	92.9	93.3	92.9	98.4	98.5	98.7	98.3

Sources: 1959: TsSU SSSR, *Itogi Vsesoiuznoi perepisi naseleniia 1959 goda*, vol. 16, pp. 206–8; 1970: TsSU SSSR, *Itogi Vsesoiuznoi perepisi naseleniia 1970 goda*, vol. 4, pp. 321–24; 1979: Goskomstat SSSR, *Itogi Vsesoiuznoi perepisi naseleniia 1979 goda*, vol. 4, pt. 1, bks. 2–3; 1989: Statisticheskii komitet SNG, *Itogi Vsesoiuznoi perepisi naseleniia 1989 goda*, vol. 7, pt. 2.

Between 1959 and 1979, all the major indigenous nations of Central Asia became more highly concentrated in their respective home republics. This was not due to return migration of those living outside the home republic, but rather to a more rapid rate of natural increase among the members of the indigenous nations living in their homelands than among those who lived outside. This in turn was due primarily to the fact that a higher proportion of members living in the home republic lived in rural than in urban areas, while those members living outside tended to be more urbanized. Ethnonational reidentification was undoubtedly also higher among members living outside their homeland, and especially among those living in urban areas. However, this reidentification or assimilation to another national identity was minimal during the entire postwar period for the indigenes of Central Asia.[10]

Between 1979 and 1989, a dispersal from the home republic was registered for all the Central Asian nations (Table 10.2). This deconcentration was caused primarily by out-migration, and was particularly high among Tajiks, whose economic conditions and standards of living at home were according to several indices the worst in Central Asia. Nevertheless, the geographic dispersal of Central Asians from their respective home republics remained very limited throughout the 1980s. In addition, most of the deconcentration that did occur was absorbed within Central Asia. On average, the national dispersal rate from the home republic for the nations of Central Asia (e.g., Uzbeks from Uzbekistan) was 0.7 percentage points for the decade 1979–89, but only 0.4 percentage points from Central Asia as a whole.

Map 10.1. The Ethnic Composition of Central Asia

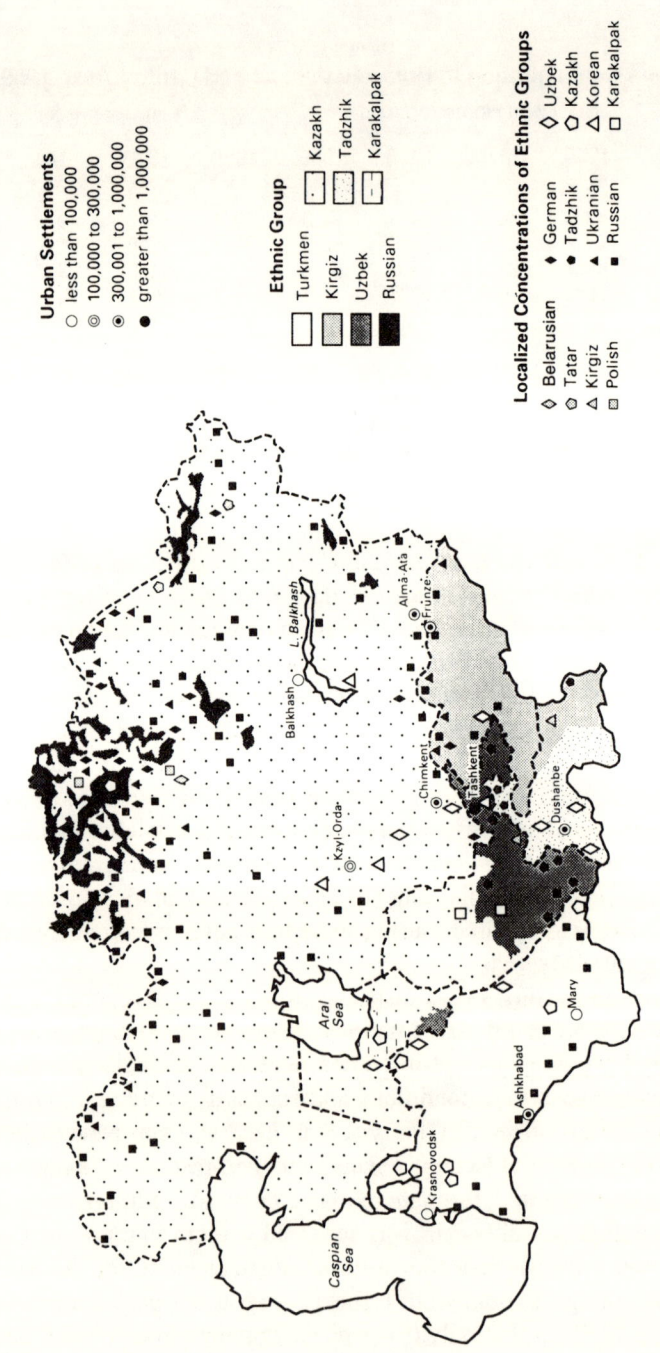

Source: Robert Kaiser, "Nations and Homelands in Soviet Central Asia," in *Geographic Perspectives on Soviet Central Asia*, ed. Robert Lewis (London: Routledge, 1992), p. 283.

Table 10.3

Percentage of National Community Currently Resident in Republic Who Were Born There, 1989

Republics	Nations				
	Uzbeks	Kazakhs	Kyrgyz	Tajiks	Turkmens
Uzbekistan	98.2	92.5	na	96.2	na
Kazakhstan	92.3	95.1	na	na	na
Kyrgyzstan	93.8	na	98.5	na	na
Tajikistan	95.2	na	90.1	98.5	na
Turkmenistan	94.3	92.3	na	na	98.9

Sources: Statisticheskii Komitet SNG, *Itogi Vsesoiuznoi perepisi naseleniia 1989 goda*, vol. 12, pp. 649–54.

Note: Data given only for largest of national communities in each republic. In cases where data were not provided, "na" is used.

The majority of those members who live outside their home republic are found in bordering oblasts of neighboring republics (Map 10.1). According to the place of birth data provided in the 1989 census, a very high percentage of members living outside their home republics but in Central Asia have lived there from birth (Table 10.3). Many of these so-called nonindigenes have lived in these areas for generations (e.g., the Tajiks of Samarkand), and consider these places part of their extended ancestral homeland. On the other hand, the borders of the former union republics have taken on real meaning, and the members of each titular nation have come to consider their homeland to encompass at least all of their eponymous home republic.[11] Not surprisingly, the border regions in which more than one national community has developed a sense of homeland have become the sites of rising ethnoterritorial tensions and conflict.

Each of the major indigenous groups in Central Asia also has members living in adjacent regions of neighboring states. An estimated 350,000 Turkmens, 1.5 million Uzbeks, and 3.5 million Tajiks live in Afghanistan; 650,000 Turkmens live in Iran; and 115,000 Kyrgyz and 930,000 Kazakhs live in China.[12] There was little movement across these essentially closed borders throughout the postwar period, although Uigurs did migrate into Central Asia from China during the 1960s. During 1992–93, an estimated 75,000–90,000 refugees from the conflict in Tajikistan fled to Afghanistan; meanwhile, an estimated 60,000 Kazakhs have immigrated to Kazakhstan from China and Mongolia.[13] Given the increasing fluidity of movement along these interstate borders and the increasing likelihood of rising claims to border regions in Iran, Afghanistan, and China as part of the extended ancestral homelands of the Central Asian nations, cross-border ethnoterritorial tensions and the potential for conflict are certain to increase. I return to this topic near the end of the chapter.

Indigenous Dilution and Demographic Russification

Central Asia is normally depicted as a crossroads region that has experienced several periods of foreign rule and several migration waves during its history. The most recent of these occurred from the mid-nineteenth century to the 1960s, during which time Russian conquest and incorporation of the region was accompanied by Russian in-migration, first of peasants in search of new farmland and later of semiskilled industrial workers who entered with regional economic development under socialism.

Analysts have often noted that the in-migration of outsiders serves as a particularly potent catalyst for rising nationalism,[14] and this is certainly the case with Central Asia. The first rural–rural migration stream primarily affected Kazakhstan, and had a number of important consequences. Russian peasant in-migration and appropriation of nomadic pastureland forced Kazakhs from their traditional lands and way of life. This rural Russian in-migration, estimated at 400,000 between 1893 and 1905, increased enormously to some 1.5 million between 1906 and 1912.[15] The rapid increase in Russian in-migration and the geographic displacement of Kazakhs was accompanied by a significant rise in anti-Russian sentiments, which provided the foundations for an emergent Kazakh national consciousness.[16] In the other regions of Central Asia (i.e., Turkestan), in-migration was more limited during this early period, due to the limited potential for the more arid region to the south to absorb a large influx of Russian peasants. While Kazakhstan and to a lesser extent Kyrgyzstan fit the general imperial model of frontier expansion, the conquest and incorporation of the remainder of Turkestan was much more closely akin to colonialist expansion.[17] This history has become important again—Russians in the region today are viewed as imperialists by many indigenes, and anti-Russian sentiments have escalated along with rising "decolonization" nationalism.[18]

The second major wave of in-migration also involved primarily Russians, and accompanied the economic development of the region under socialism. Although part of this in-migration was also rural–rural (e.g., the Virgin Lands program), the majority of this second wave involved the movement of Russians to the growing urban/industrial sectors in the region (Table 10.4). Demographically and culturally, the cities of Central Asia

Table 10.4

Demographic Russification of the Total and Urban Population, 1926–59 (%)

	Total population				Urban population			
	Indigenes		Russians		Indigenes		Russians	
Republic	1926	1959	1926	1959	1926	1959	1926	1959
Uzbekistan	74.2	62.2	5.4	13.5	57.0	37.2	19.2	33.4
Kazakhstan	57.1	30.0	19.7	42.7	14.4	16.7	52.6	57.6
Kyrgyzstan	66.6	40.5	11.7	30.2	4.6	13.2	37.2	51.8
Tajikistan	74.6	53.2	0.7	13.3	73.6	31.8	9.9	35.3
Turkmenistan	70.2	60.9	8.2	17.3	7.0	34.7	46.4	35.4

Source: Viktor Kozlov, *Natsional'nosti SSSR* (Moscow: Statistika, 1975), pp. 86–88.

increasingly became Russian enclaves in a sea of rural indigenes, and this segregated pattern was indicative of the ethnically stratified nature of society in Soviet Central Asia.[19] The demographic dominance of Russians and other nonindigenes in the urban/industrial work force denoted a system of ethnic stratification that favored Russians over indigenes, and this became increasingly intolerable as Central Asians became more educated and aspired to be more upwardly mobile.[20] Russians and other nonindigenes blocking the path to this upward mobility served as a catalyst for rising nativism during the late 1980s. However, this anti-outsider nativism has been directed not exclusively or even primarily against the formerly dominant Russians, but against a number of weaker subordinate groups whose members were perceived as receiving preferential socioeconomic treatment (e.g., Meskhetian Turks in Uzbekistan, Lezgians in Novyi Uzhen', Armenians in Dushanbe and Tashkent). This rising anti-outsider nativism has in turn sparked a rise in out-migration from the region that has all the appearances of a refugee migration stream. I return to this topic below.

Demographic Indigenization

Beginning in the 1960s, the more rapid natural increase among the indigenes of Central Asia began to outpace the demographic Russification that was occurring as a result of in-migration. This resulted in a demographic indigenization in all Central Asian republics, and in urban as well as rural areas (Table 10.5). The reason for the higher rate of natural increase among indigenes in Central Asia as compared with the Russians living there was most obviously a higher indigenous birth rate, which in turn was a conse-

Table 10.5

Demographic Indigenization of the Urban and Rural Population, 1959–89
(indigenes as a percentage of the urban and rural population, by republic)

Republic	Urban population				Rural population			
	1959	1970	1979	1989	1959	1970	1979	1989
Uzbekistan	37.2	41.1	48.1	53.7	74.8	79.5	82.8	83.5
Kazakhstan	16.7	17.1	20.8	26.7	40.4	48.2	53.5	57.0
Kyrgyzstan	13.2	16.9	22.9	29.9	54.4	59.9	63.4	66.2
Tajikistan	31.8	38.6	42.8	50.5	63.4	66.6	67.2	68.0
Turkmenistan	34.7	43.4	47.6	53.8	83.5	86.1	87.2	87.0

Sources: 1959: TsSU SSSR, *Itogi Vsesoiuznoi perepisi naseleniia 1959 goda*, volumes for Central Asian republics, table 53; 1970: TsSU SSSR, *Itogi Vsesoiuznoi perepisi naseleniia 1970 goda*, vol. 4, pp. 202–316; 1979: Goskomstat SSSR, *Itogi Vsesoiuznoi perepisi naseleniia 1979 goda*, vol. 4, pt. 1, bks. 2–3; 1989: Statisticheskii komitet SNG, *Itogi Vsesoiuznoi perepisi naseleniia 1989 goda,* vol. 7, pt. 2, pp. 192–655.

quence of a more rural, agrarian, and patriarchal society in which traditional desire for larger families continued to prevail.[21]

Demographic indigenization occurred throughout Central Asia during the entire 1959–89 period, and was not simply the result of higher natural increase among rural Central Asians. In fact, demographic indigenization was more rapid in urban areas than it was in rural areas for all republics except Kazakhstan.[22] This urban indigenization was in part the result of rural–urban migration and the upgrading of previously rural places to the status of "urban-type settlements," but primarily resulted from a higher rate of natural increase among urban indigenes than nonindigenes, coupled with nonindigenous out-migration. This demographic indigenization of the urban population in Central Asia occurred not only in the small and medium-sized cities, but also in the capital cities of each republic. By 1989, only Bishkek and Almaty had more Russians than indigenes.[23] Nevertheless, while there was rapid urban growth and urban indigenization, rural growth was nearly as rapid, and consequently little urbanization of the indigenous population occurred (Table 10.6).

For all republics, Russian out-migration from urban areas increased after 1970, and this enhanced the rate of urban indigenization. This trend toward urban indigenization has accelerated with rising emigration of nonindigenes from the region since 1989.

Some analysts interpreted the rapid population growth among Central Asians in positive terms, as a sign of ethnic vitality:

Table 10.6

Urbanization by Nation and Republic, 1959–89
(percentage of indigenous and Russian population in urban areas)

Republic	Indigenes				Russians			
	1959	1970	1979	1989	1959	1970	1979	1989
Uzbekistan	20.2	23.0	28.6	30.5	83.7	89.1	93.4	94.8
Kazakhstan	24.3	26.3	30.9	38.4	59.0	69.1	73.9	77.4
Kyrgyzstan	11.0	14.5	18.3	21.8	57.8	65.9	68.6	69.9
Tajikistan	19.6	25.5	25.2	26.4	86.9	93.8	94.1	93.9
Turkmenistan	26.3	31.7	33.0	33.8	94.5	95.7	96.5	96.9

Sources: 1959: TsSU SSSR, *Itogi Vsesoiuznoi perepisi naseleniia 1959 goda*, volumes for Central Asian republics, table 53; 1970: TsSU SSSR, *Itogi Vsesoiuznoi perepisi naseleniia 1970 goda*, vol. 4, pp. 202–316; 1979: Goskomstat SSSR, *Itogi Vsesoiuznoi perepisi naseleniia 1979 goda*, vol. 4, pt. 1, bks. 2–3; 1989: Statisticheskii komitet SNG, *Itogi Vsesoiuznoi perepisi naseleniia 1989 goda*, vol. 7, pt. 2, pp. 192–655.

A new geography is emerging for the USSR, in which the divisions seem almost biological. On the one hand, the western part of the country seems to have had its vitality sapped by its repeated and fearful trials. On the other hand, the eastern part, which is better preserved even though it has had its share of common disasters, is where living conditions tend to be more comfortable. . . . . and where the high birth rate reflects exceptional vigor and probably greater confidence in the future.[24]

This notion of a relationship between rapid population growth and a nation's biological vitality is a belief shared by nationalists the world over, and is certainly found in the writings of nationalists in the former Soviet Union. It is also clearly absurd, particularly since differential rates in population growth between "west" and "east" resulted from a conscious choice on the part of those in the European part of the state to limit family size (i.e., not the result of genetic damage, "sapped vitality," etc.).

The linkage between demographic trends and ethnic vitality was also made by Bennigsen, Carrère d'Encausse, and others to strengthen the case being offered in the late 1970s and early 1980s that Central Asia represented the greatest challenge to the Soviet Union, and would be the first to rise up against Moscow. Outlandish claims that the Muslim peoples of the USSR, treated as one monolithic "Islamic nation," would attain majority status by the year 2000,[25] and then rise up against the infidels to the north became the standard formula during the 1970s and 1980s, and continues to influence judgments about the region and its relationships with its neighbors.

A number of serious flaws are present in this formulation of ethnic demography and geopolitics in Central Asia.[26] First, all Muslim groups of Central Asia made up 12 percent of the total USSR population in 1989, and all "Turkic and/or Muslim peoples" in the USSR[27] made up roughly 19 percent of the total USSR population.[28] Although this does represent an increase over 1979, when Central Asian indigenes made up 10 percent and all "Turkic and/or Muslim peoples" were about 16 percent, the rate of increase was clearly nowhere near what it would have needed to be to attain majority status by 2000. In fact, the attainment of demographic majority status by the year 2000 was beyond the reproductive capacity of humans.

Beyond the flawed demography in the "revenge of the cradle" argument, the more fundamental error was the belief that rapid population growth was not only a sign of ethnic vitality, but that this would result in a more separatist southern tier of Islamic states, or alternatively of one super Islamic state incorporating all Muslim peoples in an extended *Dar al Islam*. Quite to the contrary of this scenario, the Central Asian republics were the least secessionist of the fifteen union republics during the late 1980s and early 1990s, and if anything rapid population growth helped undermine the strength of the independence drive by increasing the region's dependency on the center. One conclusion to be drawn from the errors of the *Homo Islamicus* school is that while ethnodemographic trends are important, they must be interpreted with much greater caution.

Several consequences of rapid population growth and demographic indigenization in Central Asia have manifested themselves, and each has implications for interstate relations today. Economically, the rapidly growing population in Central Asia has been detrimental for the region. This is not the depiction normally presented by nationalists in Central Asia, who tend to argue that it is the economic underdevelopment and dependency on Russia that is the problem, and not population growth per se. However, as Critchlow rightly points out, rapid population growth itself undermines the ability of the Central Asian economies to gain greater independence, and so has become part of the problem.[29] The high proportion of the population in the young age cohorts is making it increasingly difficult to sustain standards of living for the population, especially in rural areas of the republics. Population growth rates, coupled with the decrease in investments allocated to Central Asia by Moscow during the Gorbachev years,[30] resulted in rising underemployment and unemployment throughout the region during the late 1980s, and a dramatic decline in standards of living has continued during the early 1990s. This in turn has become a potent catalyst for rising interethnic tensions and conflict in the region.

The "population pressure" (a relative decline in living conditions due to rapid population growth and/or economic decline) building in Central Asia caused some demographers as early as the 1970s to predict substantial out-migration of Turkic Muslims from the region to the more industrialized European USSR or the resource-rich, population-poor Siberian hinterland.[31] The predicted massive out-migration never occurred, though there was some net out-migration among Central Asians between 1979 and 1989 (Table 10.1), particularly among the Tajiks, whose standards of living and population growth rates marked them as the least developed homeland and nation in the region.

Several reasons exist to explain why this wave of Central Asian out-migration did not occur. First, during the early 1980s at least, socioeconomic conditions in rural Central Asia were not declining, and in fact the rural peasants of Central Asia during that period were earning at least as much as they could expect to earn by moving to the cities of Central Asia, and more than they could expect to earn in rural regions of Russia, especially when cost of living differentials were factored in.[32] Economic incentives for migration were further undermined by the federal structure of the state itself, which accorded a privileged status to the indigenous nation in its home republic but not outside. These indigenous privileges included ethnocultural as well as socioeconomic and political advantages to being indigenous, and consequently also meant discrimination against those who chose to leave their home republics. This clearly served as an impediment to interrepublic migration for all but the Russians.[33] Finally, although less easily measured, an emotional or subjective attachment to one's ancestral homeland also exists, and impedes interhomeland migration. All of this is not to say that it is impossible for Central Asians to leave the region, but rather that there were significant impediments to out-migration for indigenes from the region, and that these impediments were not overcome during the 1980s.

Population pressure has grown enormously since the late 1980s, primarily due to the collapse of the local economy, and one could predict heightened efforts on the part of young Central Asians to emigrate from the region.[34] However, in the former USSR the obstacles to emigration are rising along with the pressure to leave. First and foremost, the new immigration laws and an unwillingness on the part of Russia and other CIS member states to accept large numbers of Central Asians will impede emigration. It is also unlikely that significant emigration to Europe will be attempted or allowed, for a variety of ethnocultural, socioeconomic, and political reasons.[35] In addition, the economies of the other successor states, or alternatively of those in Southeast Asia, are also not thriving, so that the geographic differentials in economic opportunity necessary and sufficient for emigration to occur are not in place today. Finally, each successor state has begun to restructure the system of ethnic stratification through declarations of independence, new constitutions, language laws, citizenship laws, property laws, and so on to ensure the sociocultural, economic, and political dominance of the indigenous nation over all others in its homeland. The economic downturn in Central Asia that might have precipitated greater indigenous out-migration has thus far been more than offset by the increase in territorial nationalism in the areas of potential immigration. Aside from the refugee migration of Tajiks to Afghanistan, Central Asians have not been moving from the region in significant numbers, and this is unlikely to change in the near future unless conditions in Central Asia become dramatically worse than those in the surrounding states.

The declining economic conditions in the Central Asian states have been cited increasingly as a catalyst for the rising anti-foreigner nativism in evidence throughout the region. This nativism, which Myron Weiner defined as "intense opposition to minorities because of their foreign origin,"[36] has tended to dramatically increase the rate of out-migration among nonindigenes, and thus has accelerated the process of demographic indigenization in the region. This latest ethnodemographic phase is examined below.

Rising Nationalism and Refugee Migration

Whenever indigenous nationalism increases, a reactive ethnicity is likely to develop among nonindigenes resident in the region. Two nearly universal nonindigenous reactions are possible, and each is likely to have an impact on interstate relations. First, nonindigenes are likely to vote with their feet and emigrate in increasing numbers from the more nationalistic regions, and these "refugees" are most likely to move toward their nominal homelands (i.e., Russians to Russia, Ukrainians to Ukraine, etc.). These individuals are likely to be highly nationalistic as a result of their experiences, and are likely to serve as a catalyst for rising tensions and conflict between the two states in question. Second, in regions where nonindigenes live in concentrated settlements, constitute a significant proportion of the local population, and have lived there for a long time, rising indigenous nationalism is likely to result in increasing calls for secession and the establishment of an independent state, or alternatively for irredentism and the inclusion of the region within the extended national state of that group.[37] Russians and other nonindigenes facing rising anti-outsider nativism have also supported conservative, "internationalist" (i.e., pro-centrist) Communist Party elites in these republics. Each of these reactions has accompanied rising nationalism in Central Asia.

The latest rise in anti-outsider nativism, coupled with a more assertive nationalism by the indigenous groups of Central Asia, has resulted in a third wave of migration—the emigration of Russians and other nonindigenes from Central Asia, and also the gravitation of Central Asians toward their respective "national states" within the region (i.e., Tajiks to Tajikistan, Uzbeks to Uzbekistan, etc.). The out-migration of nonindigenes began as early as the 1970s, and reflected not only the decreasing economic opportunities in Soviet Central Asia with the move away from regional equalization under Brezhnev, but also the rising competition from a rapidly growing and more highly educated indigenous population, whose elites were increasingly using their positions of authority to promote members of their own group over nonindigenes. As a result, Russian dominance was eroding throughout the 1970s and 1980s, and at the same time Russians were being made to feel increasingly unwelcome in the region. Other nonindigenes were placed in an even more precarious position. This went for Central Asians living outside their respective home republics, as well as other nonindigenes who had migrated in from other parts of the USSR.[38]

Out-migration from Central Asia began in the 1970s as a more or less voluntary decision and involved almost exclusively those nonindigenes who had recently migrated to the region. Since the late 1980s, the number of "forced migrants" and "refugees" has increased dramatically, and individuals and families who have roots in the region that go back several generations feel increasing pressure to leave.[39]

Although this forced migration is taking place in every Central Asian republic, the anti-foreigner nativism is not equally virulent in all republics. Kazakhstan in particular has been more accommodative of its non-Kazakh, and especially its Russian, population.[40] The Kyrgyz in Kyrgyzstan have also been less hostile toward Russians in the republic, particularly when compared with Uzbeks in Uzbekistan.[41] However, Russian fears are generally higher in Kyrgyzstan as a result of the ethnic violence in Osh Oblast. As I note above, Kazakhstan and Kyrgyzstan have a larger Russian population, and an older rural Russian population, which may help to explain the differential treatment here as compared with the remaining Central Asian states that experienced Russian colonial expansion. This is reflected in a recent survey of reasons for out-migration (Table 10.7). Nevertheless, there have been violent anti-foreigner confrontations in all the Central Asian states since the late 1980s.

Nationalism in Central Asia is somewhat distinct from that found in other regions of the former Soviet Union. In most of the Central Asian states, the governments have attempted to retain the skilled urban/industrial European work force that their industrial enterprises have come to depend on.[42] Language laws have made allowance for Russian as the language of

Table 10.7

Reasons for Out-Migration (%)

Reasons	Uzbekistan	Kazakhstan	Kyrgyzstan	Tajikistan	Turkmenistan
School	8	11	8	5	13
Change in place of work	10	14	13	9	14
Worsening interethnic relations	27	11	33	41	15
Worsening crime	2.5	1.3	4	6	1.3
Family circumstances	26	34	22	23	30
Unsettled living conditions	10	9	6	4	6
Other	20	20	14	12	21

Source: Statisticheskii komitet SNG, "Napravleniia i prichiny migratsii naseleniia," *Statisticheskii biulleten'*, 1992, no. 14 (October), p. 129.

international communication even while they have established the indigenous languages as the official languages of the Central Asian states. Citizenship laws were written using the "zero option" formula, to provide citizenship for everyone living in the republic at the time of independence. This is quite different from the situation in the Baltic states, where the governments are at the forefront of efforts to pressure Russians to leave. On the other hand, in Central Asia there is a tendency toward more disorganized, popular anti-foreigner uprisings, which also tend to be more violent than the anti-Russian nativism found in the Baltics. Regarding the prospects for future out-migration and ethnic homogenization of the Central Asian republics, the critical question that has yet to be answered is whether the governments will continue to position themselves between the increasingly nativistic indigenous masses and the increasingly fearful nonindigenous minorities, or whether they will side with the indigenous masses and also increase the pressure on nonindigenes to leave. A second crucial question, assuming interethnic conditions continue to worsen, particularly for Kazakhstan, is whether Russians and other so-called nonindigenes who have nonetheless lived in the same place for generations will opt for emigration to their national states, or whether they will attempt to secede and attach their home regions to their newly independent national states (e.g., northern Kazakhstan to Russia, Samarkand to Tajikistan, Osh Oblast border zones to Uzbekistan). I return to each of these questions below, following a brief description of the forced migration patterns that have developed over the past five years.

The Status of the Deported Nations

Brief mention must be made of the nations whose members were deported to Central Asia around the time of World War II and who had remained in the region since that time.[43] The experience of these groups indicates that forced migration does not facilitate assimilation, and if anything serves as a critical historical event in the formation of a national consciousness. This section deals exclusively with the four main deported nations who still had a significant proportion of their members in Central Asia in 1989: Germans, Crimean Tatars, Koreans, and Meskhetian Turks.

Volga Germans

The Germans, who were deported from the Volga German ASSR to Central Asia, Kazakhstan, and southern Siberia in 1941, have been pulled in two different directions in recent years. First, since the late 1980s increasing numbers of Germans in the region have emigrated to Germany. Since 1989, at least 300,000 Germans have emigrated, and the majority of these have come from Kazakhstan.[44] According to Shevtsova, "The 1992 exit visa applicant list includes about a million persons, which is half the ethnic Germans living in the new Commonwealth."[45] However, beginning in 1990 Germans in the former USSR have also pressed for the restoration of the Volga German ASSR as a local homeland toward which Germans can migrate and in which they can exercise a degree of self-government.[46] It appears that Germany favors this option, and the German government has placed pressure on Yeltsin to restore the autonomous republic in Saratov Oblast. The German government has also given monetary support to Ukraine for assistance in resettling Germans who were deported from that republic during the 1940s.[47] While the government of Ukraine has expressed a willingness to accept Germans returning from the east, the restoration of the Volga German Republic has been stalled by local Russian opposition.

Koreans

The Koreans were deported from the Primor'e region bordering North Korea in 1937, in a preemptive strike to secure the border. Unlike the Germans, the Koreans of Central Asia had expressed little interest in emigrating from the region prior to 1992. At a minority rights conference in Leningrad in June 1991, the Korean delegate did express an interest in the establishment of an autonomous Korean republic in Central Asia, which would provide a territorial means of protecting and preserving the local Korean community in the face of rising indigenous nationalism and anti-foreigner nativism.[48] In many ways, this is similar to the argument given for the restoration of the Volga German ASSR (or alternatively the creation of a German Republic in Kaliningrad):

> We are a people different both from the other Soviet peoples and from the other German peoples: We have our own history, our own culture, and our own language to a large extent. And our goal is continuation as a people. For this we need to revive our culture and language and our national traditions and customs, for which, in turn, the majority of us must be assembled in one place, that is, acquire sufficient territory. We must on this territory have an opportunity to resolve our problems ourselves; that is, we need our statehood.[49]

The South Korean government, like its German counterpart, expressed an interest in keeping the Koreans in Central Asia:

> We have a small country, in which more than 40 million people live. Of course, we will not close the door to our countrymen who want to return to the land of their ancestors. But we would not want a massive immigration of foreign Koreans. Soviet Koreans are citizens of the USSR, and we prefer that they remain in their country.[50]

During 1992, as conditions for nonindigenes worsened in Central Asia, and during which time Uzbekistan refused to consider the request for Korean territorial autonomy, an increasing number of Koreans began to leave the region for Primorskii Krai. The Korean returnees have been supported both by the Association of Ethnic Koreans in the former USSR and by South Korea, though they have not been warmly received by the Russians living in this Far Eastern region.[51] While not yet a major trend, this does have the potential to develop into a significant refugee migration stream (321,089 Koreans lived in Central Asia in 1989), and if it does it is likely to have a detrimental effect on Russian–Central Asian relations, Korean–Central Asian relations, and potentially even Russian-Korean relations, if anti-Korean incidents escalate in the Russian Far East.

Meskhetian Turks

The Meskhetian Turks, deported from the Georgian region of Meskhetia and mainly resettled in Uzbekistan, were the largely forgotten deportees until 1989, when the Fergana riots sparked the out-migration of 63,000 Meskhetian Turk refugees from the region, primarily to Russia and Azerbaijan.[52] Since that time, the Meskhetian Turks have attempted to return to their ancestral homeland in Meskhetia, but have been denied the right of return by the Georgian government. Georgian nationalists have argued that Meskhetian Turks are not indigenous to Meskhetia, in much the same way that they have argued that Ossetians are not indigenous to South Ossetia:

> There was a time when the Turks were strangers in Georgia. Now they claim Georgian land as their own. We cannot grant their claims, because the Turks' native land is Turkey, not Georgia. Also, the lands in Meskhetia are populated by Georgians and Armenians. What shall we do with these people?[53]

The prospects for the return of Meskhetian Turks to Meskhetia have not improved substantially since the removal of Gamsakhurdia and his replacement by Shevardnadze. In light of the situation in Georgia, two alternatives are currently being discussed by the Meskhetian Turks: emigration to Turkey or reidentification as Georgians in order to be allowed to return to their homeland.[54] The mistreatment of Meskhetian Turks by Uzbeks (though not by the government per se) has not apparently had any adverse effects on relations between Uzbekistan and Turkey. One could predict that the treatment of Meskhetian Turks by the Georgian government is much more likely to sour relations between Georgia and Turkey.

Crimean Tatars

Aside from the Germans of Central Asia, the Crimean Tatars are perhaps the most well known deported nation in the former USSR. Deported from Crimea in 1944 for alleged collaboration with Nazi Germany, the Crimean Tatars lost not only their homeland, but their separate national identity. During the entire postwar period, the Crimean Tatars disappeared from the censuses and statistics of the country, and were included with the Volga Tatars under the general label "Tatars." In the 1989 census, the Crimean Tatars reappeared for the first time. However, it is still difficult to say with any precision how many Crimean Tatars there are. The number claiming to be Crimean Tatars increased from 50,000 in 1959 to 132,000 in 1979 to 272,000 in 1989,[55] but this increase is more a reflection of changing ethnopolitical conditions that have emboldened an increasing number of Crimean Tatars to reassert their true national identity than it is a reflection of natural increase.[56] The actual number of individuals who consider themselves Crimean Tatars is likely to be substantially higher than the figure given for 1989, though the 1989 figure is obviously much closer to the actual total than is either the 1959 or 1979 figure.

As with the other deported nationalities resident in Central Asia, the Crimean Tatars have been leaving the region for their homeland since 1989. Although they had lobbied for the right of return to Crimea prior to the 1980s, their ethnoterritorial demands had consistently been denied, and they had not been allowed entry into Crimea. As of 1989, the restrictions on returnees were lifted, and since 1989, nearly 200,000 Crimean Tatars have migrated to Crimea.[57] However, it is difficult to consider this as purely a refugee migration driven by anti-foreigner nativism in Central Asia, since it is the pull of the ancestral homeland (i.e., repatriation) more than the push of anti-outsider nativism that has caused this migration pattern.

Under normal conditions, the voluntary repatriation of the members of these deported nations to their respective ancestral homelands would be viewed by most as a positive trend. However, under conditions of refugee migration from Central Asia that coincide with rising anti-foreigner nativism, this return migration from the region is not necessarily favorable, at least as perceived by the refugees themselves. In addition, none of the four deported nations discussed above has had its claim to territorial autonomy in its ancestral homeland recognized by the receiving states (Russia, Georgia, Ukraine), nor have the three that could emigrate to external "home" states been given much encouragement to do so by those states (i.e., Germany, South Korea, Turkey). The formerly deported nations are likely to remain in diaspora, or to face new interethnic confrontations on their return home.

Russians' Reaction to Their Loss of Status

As noted above, Russians have experienced a relative demographic decline in Central Asia throughout the period 1959–89, in both urban and rural areas. During the first half of this period, the absolute number of Russians continued to increase as a result of in-migration, and relative losses were due to the higher rate of natural increase among the indigenous Central Asians. However, from the mid-1970s to 1989, Russian relative decline accelerated, and was enhanced by a net out-migration from the region. Between 1979 and 1989, an estimated 319,042 Russians left Central Asia (Table 10.8).

Since 1989, Russian emigration from Central Asia has increased dramatically, and Russians are making up an increasing percentage of the emigrants from the region (Table 10.8; Map 10.2). Within each republic, they are leaving from areas where they perceive themselves to be the most

Table 10.8

Out-Migration from Central Asia, 1979–1991 (total and Russian)

Republic	1979–88				1989–91			
	Total	Russian	%	% of Russians	Total	Russian	%	% of Russians
Uzbekistan	600,332	106,290	18	6.4	374,000	100,300	27	6.1
Kazakhstan	858,353	102,159	12	1.7	273,000	87,000	32	1.4
Kyrgyzstan	183,826	46,656	25	5.1	96,000	31,900	33	3.5
Tajikistan	125,482	28,931	23	7.3	108,000	56,900	53	14.6
Turkmenistan	98,976	35,006	35	10.0	17,000	12,100	71	3.6

Sources: 1979–88: Robert Kaiser, "National Territoriality and Demographic Indigenization in the Non-Russian Periphery," paper presented at the Annual Meeting of the Association of American Geographers, 18 April 1992, San Diego. Estimating procedure described in note below. 1989–91: Statisticheskii komitet SNG, "Napravleniia i prichiny migratsii naseleniia," *Statisticheskii biulleten'*, 1992, no. 14 (October), p. 127; Russian figures compiled by Nikolai Petrov, Institute of Geography, Russian Academy of Science, Moscow, 1992.

Notes: "%" refers to the Russian percent of total out-migrants from each republic, while "% of Russians" refers to Russian out-migrants as a percentage of all Russians in the republic. For the latter columns, for the 1979–88 "% of Russians," I used the 1979 figure for total Russians as the denominator; for the 1989–91 "% of Russians," I used the 1989 figure for total Russians as the denominator.

Total migration for 1979–88 (column one) was calculated using the residual of the intercensal population for each union republic and the natural increase for the republic registered between 1979 and 1988 inclusive. Russian migration for 1979–88 was estimated using the residual of the intercensal population change (1979–89) for Russians in each of the republics and the estimated natural increase of the Russian population in each republic. The latter was estimated using the rate of population change for the total Russian population in the USSR from 1979–89 (.0565).

An alternative set of estimates is provided in A. Topilin, "Vliianie migratsii na etonatsional'nuiu strukturu," *Sotsiologicheskie issledovaniia*, 1992, no. 7, pp. 31–43. These estimates conform to those provided above for the most part, but have a much higher figure of Russian out-migration from Kazakhstan (394,000). This higher figure is clearly in error; Russian population growth in Kazakhstan could not have been as high as it was between 1979 and 1989 if net out-migration was that high. For this reason, I have opted to use the estimates provided above.

Map 10.2. Major Cross-Border Refugee Flows in the Former Soviet Union, 1989–93

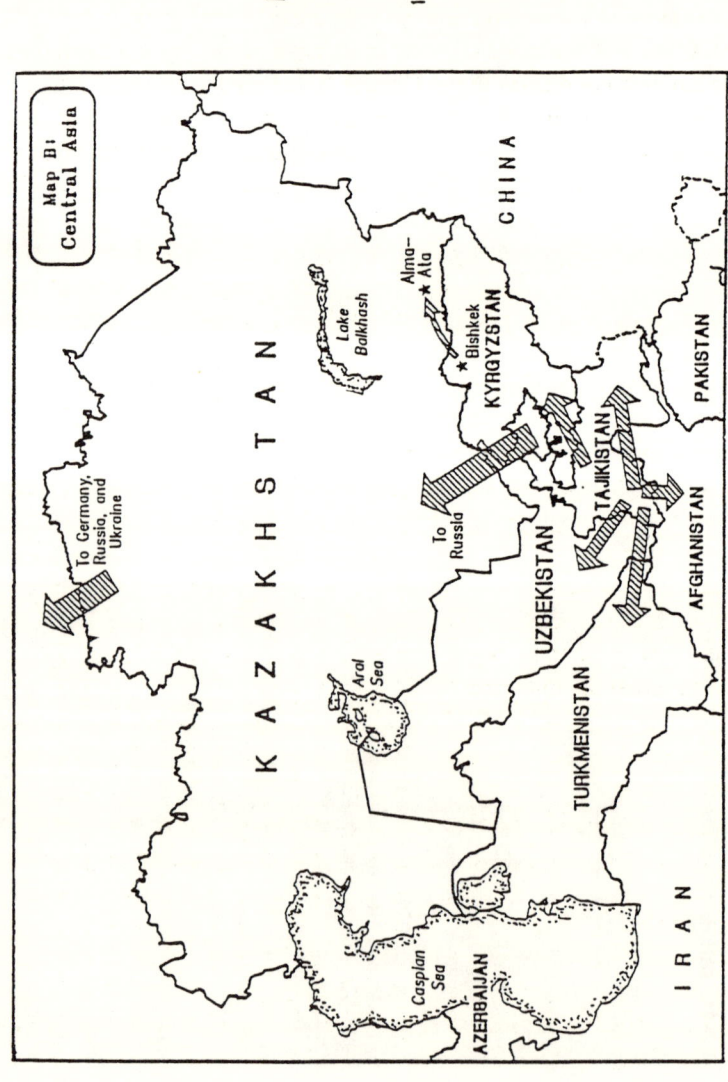

Source: Lee Schwartz, "Refugee Flows in the Former Soviet Union: Policies and Prospects" (paper presented at the annual meeting of the Association of American Geographers, Atlanta, 9 April 1993).

vulnerable to indigenous nativism (i.e., less numerous and a lower proportion of the total population).[58] In only three years (1989–91), the number of Russians leaving Central Asia was nearly equal to the number who had left in the entire preceding decade, and more Russians left Tajikistan between 1989 and 1991 than between 1979 and 1988. While the number of emigrants decreased in 1991 compared to 1990, it apparently increased dramatically in 1992 as a result of increasing unrest in the region, particularly in Tajikistan.[59] Since conditions in Central Asia in the near future with respect to economic and political stabilization as well as interethnic relations are likely to continue worsening, this out-migration stream is likely to continue as well. Ironically, the rapid increase in Russian out-migration has tended to make economic conditions in the Central Asian republics worse rather than better. Job vacancies in critical sectors of the urban/industrial complexes are being created faster than they can be filled, and numerous enterprises have had to shut down as a result of the excessive loss of skilled workers. This makes the Central Asian governments even less able to provide for the needs of their indigenous populations, which in turn fuels even greater anti-outsider and anti-Russian nativism. This vicious circle has no end in sight, though most of the political elites in the Central Asian republics have attempted to hold Russians in place.

The reasons for Russian out-migration have been noted elsewhere.[60] First, during the latter half of the 1980s the increasingly violent anti-outsider sentiments caused the most recent Russian in-migrants to leave, and also resulted in a decrease in the number of new in-migrants to the region. Second, the new language laws that established the indigenous language as the lingua franca of the republics was cited by Russians as a reason for wanting to leave the region. For example, more Russians are leaving the oblasts of southern Kazakhstan, and in part this is because the Kazakh language law is already being implemented there, while there will be a significant delay in implementation in the northern oblasts of the state.[61] Third, economic conditions became less attractive, because of both the economic downturn of the late 1980s in Central Asia and the increasing indigenous competition for higher-status positions beginning in the 1970s. However, Russians in Central Asia are not leaving due to the loss of economic position and rising unemployment per se, but rather because of the increasing indigenous challenges to their formerly dominant sociocultural position in Central Asia.

According to one survey conducted in 1991, 66 percent of Russians in Tajikistan and 72 percent of Russians in Uzbekistan felt that ethnic conflicts in these republics could lead to an eruption of violence in the future, while only 26 percent of Russians in Estonia and 34 percent of Russians in Latvia felt this way. These figures were correlated with the percentage of Russians who felt that a massive Russian exodus from the republic was very likely in the near future (44 percent for Tajikistan, 35 percent for Uzbekistan, 12 percent for Estonia, and only 3 percent for Latvia). The better interethnic relations between Russians and indigenes in Kazakhstan and Kyrgyzstan were also reflected in this survey: Only 31 percent and 48 percent of Russians in each respective republic felt that violent ethnic conflict was likely soon, and only 2 percent of Russians in Kazakhstan and 17 percent in Kyrgyzstan felt that a massive Russian exodus was very likely in the near future.[62]

Russian perceptions of interethnic threats in Central Asia were not necessarily shared by the Central Asians themselves. In a recent public opinion survey conducted by the All-Russian Center for Public Opinion Research (VTsIOM), the interethnic attitudes of indigenes and Russians did not necessarily coincide. In Latvia and Estonia, about 80 percent of indigenes felt that relations with Russians had worsened, while only about 20 percent of Tajiks and Uzbeks felt the same way. Yet Russians felt much more insecure in Tajikistan and Uzbekistan than they did in Latvia and Estonia. According to this survey, only 9 percent of Russians in Latvia and 13 percent of Russians in Estonia felt that interethnic conflict was highly likely, compared with 22 percent and 34 percent of Russians in Tajikistan and Uzbekistan respectively. This clearly had an impact on the proportion of Russians considering emigration: About 30 percent of Russians considered massive emigration from the Baltics likely, compared to 80 percent in Central Asia.[63]

The trend toward greater Russian emigration and rising anti-Russian nativism is likely to continue, but it is unlikely that all Russians will leave the region. A surprisingly high proportion of Russians living in Central Asia were born there (Table 10.9), and consider the region (or all of the former USSR) their homeland. Many have no real family ties in "Mother Russia," and these Russians may very well stand and fight rather than emigrate to a place they do not consider home. This is particularly likely in northern Kazakhstan, which Russian nationalists consider an extension of their homeland.[64] If the treatment of Russians in the region deteriorates to that point, it will clearly have a detrimental impact on relations between Russia and Central Asia. Russian nationalism is on the rise in Russia, and there appears to be increasing pressure on the Russian government to take on the role of defender of the Russian minorities in the non-Russian periphery (Table 10.9).

Thus far, however, emigration even among those with deep roots in Central Asia has been the option taken.[65] Russia has received more than one million refugees and "forced migrants" since 1989, and a significant

Table 10.9

Russians Currently Resident in Central Asia Who Were Born There, by Republic and Central Asia (1989)

	Born in republic		Born in Central Asia, living in republic		Total born in Central Asia	
	Number	%	Number	%	Number	%
Uzbekistan	909,546	55.0	110,298	6.7	1,019,844	61.7
Kazakhstan	4,145,661	66.6	110,901	1.8	4,256,562	68.4
Kyrgyzstan	541,552	59.1	90,652	9.9	632,204	69.0
Tajikistan	188,450	48.5	32,010	8.2	220,460	56.7
Turkmenistan	173,606	52.0	16,095	4.8	189,701	56.8

Source: Statisticheskii komitet SNG, *Itogi Vsesoiuznoi perepisi naseleniia 1989 goda*, vol. 12, pp. 649–654.

proportion has come from Central Asia. Although Yeltsin stated in 1992 that Russia will take all Russians who wish to live there, the cost of resettling refugees has far exceeded the amount Russia has allocated for that task.[66]

As an alternative to emigration, Russians living in concentrated settlements throughout Central Asia may seek to establish autonomous territories for themselves, much as the Koreans of Uzbekistan and the more nationalistic Uzbeks of Osh Oblast have attempted to do. Along the border with Russia in northern Kazakhstan, should interethnic conditions worsen significantly, an attempt to secede and become part of the Russian Federation is more likely than massive Russian refugee migration from this region. Thus far, surveys do not indicate a strong desire on the part of Russians in Kazakhstan for secession (Table 10.10). This is undoubtedly related to the more concerted efforts by Nazarbaev to defuse interethnic tensions in Kazakhstan.

Ethnoterritorial Conflict in Central Asia

As I note above, the majority of Central Asians living outside their home states live in adjacent regions that most have lived in all their lives (Table 10.3; Map 10.1). Up to 1989, there did not appear to be developing any significant migration pattern out of these border zones and toward the home republic. Indeed, just the opposite appeared to be occurring, with the indigenous concentration declining more sharply in the home republics of Central Asia than in Central Asia as a whole between 1979 and 1989 (Table 10.2).

Table 10.10

Attitude Toward the Revision of Interstate Borders
(Kazakhstan, % of respondents)

	Positive	Negative	Cannot say	No reply
Kazakhs	6.8	75.5	16.9	0.8
Russians	14.4	63.5	22.8	0.0
Other Slavs	12.1	70.7	17.2	0.0
Germans	7.4	79.6	13.0	0.0
Others	14.1	63.5	22.4	0.0

Source: James Critchlow, "Kazakhstan: The Outlook for Ethnic Relations." *RFE/RL Research Report*, 31 January 1992, p. 36.

Since 1989, there has been a tendency toward reconcentration in home states among the Central Asian nations. Most of this reconcentration has involved refugee migration from Tajikistan since civil war erupted there. In addition to Uzbeks, Kyrgyz, Kazakhs, and Turkmens leaving Tajikistan for their respective national states, Tajiks have also been forced to leave their home regions within the republic (Map 10.2).

As an alternative to this ethnic clearing of border regions, irredentism may also rise in a number of regions where the cross-border population has developed a strong sense of homeland. Separatism may also develop as a more serious challenge to the territorial integrity of the Central Asian states. Several cases of irredentism and separatism have already emerged (Table 10.11).[67] Some of the most noteworthy include the attempt to establish an Uzbek autonomous territory in Osh Oblast, Kyrgyzstan; the declaration of sovereignty by Karakalpakstan, and the demand by more nationalistic forces in the republic that Karakalpaks be given full independence; the rising demands for greater territorial autonomy and even secession among the so-called Pamir Tajiks of Gorno-Badakhshan; and the rising anti-Uzbek feelings among Tajiks in Samarkand, which has led to increasing calls for separating the Tajik-dominated region from Uzbekistan.

Uzbeks form a significant minority in most of the Central Asian states, and especially in Tajikistan (23.5 percent) and Kyrgyzstan (12.9 percent). Uzbeks are also by far the largest nation in Central Asia. In addition to refugee migration home (from Tajikistan) and rising demands for territorial autonomy (in Tajikistan and Kyrgyzstan), Uzbek nationalists have also been the most active advocates of the recreation of a Greater Turkestan. There are rising concerns among Central Asia's non-Uzbek population of

Table 10.11

List of Ethnoterritorial Disputes in Central Asia as of 1992

1. Transfer of the Zeravshan, Kashkadaria, and Surkhandaria oases from Uzbekistan to Tajikistan.
2. Secession of Karakalpakstan from Uzbekistan.
3. Transfer of Karakalpakstan to Kazakhstan.
4. Transfer of Karakalpakstan to Russia.
5. Transfer of the Amu Daria delta in Karakalpakstan to the Khorezm Oblast of Uzbekistan.
6. Transfer of the mountain pastures of the southern slopes of the Alay and Zaalay ranges (Tajikistan) to Kyrgyzstan.
7. Transfer of the upper reaches of the Surkhob valley (Uzbekistan) to Kyrgyzstan.
8. Transfer of the northern sections of Karateghin (Uzbekistan) to Kyrgyzstan.
9. Transfer of parts of the Tajik section of the Fergana basin to Uzbekistan.
10. Transfer of the Tajik Zeravshan to Uzbekistan.
11. Secession of Gorno-Badakhshan from Tajikistan.
12. Creation of a Kyrgyz autonomous territory in the northern Pamir of Tajikistan or the transfer of this territory to Kyrgyzstan.
13. Transfer of the Batken district of Osh Oblast (Kyrgyzstan) to Tajikistan.
14. Transfer of the high-mountain pastures of the northern (Kyrgyz) slopes of the Alay and Zaalay ranges to Tajikistan.
15. Transfer of part of the Kyrgyz section of the Fergana basin to Uzbekistan.
16. Transfer of the northern districts of Kyrgyzstan adjacent to Lake Issyk-Kul to Kazakhstan.
17. Transfer of a section of the Tashauz oasis (Turkmenistan) adjacent to the Amu Darya to Uzbekistan.
18. Transfer of the middle Amu Daria oasis (Turkmenistan) to Uzbekistan.
19. Creation of a Kurdish autonomous territory in Turkmenistan.
20. Creation of a Belujian autonomous territory in Turkmenistan.
21. Transfer of part of the Mangyshlak peninsula (Kazakhstan) to Turkmenistan.
22. Transfer of lands between the Syr Daria and Arys rivers from Kazakhstan to Uzbekistan.
23. Transfer of the northern slopes of the Transily Alatau mountains and the Kungey-Ala-Too district of Kazakhstan to Kyrgyzstan.
24. Creation of German national territorial areas in northern Kazakhstan.
25. Creation of an autonomous republic in the Russian-speaking areas of northern Kazakhstan.
26. Transfer of northern Kazakhstan to Russia.
27. Transfer of districts in the southern Urals and southwestern Siberia to Kazakhstan.
28. Creation of an Uigur autonomous territory in Kazakhstan.

Source: Ethnic and/or territorial disputes were taken verbatim from Vladimir Kolossov, *Ethno-Territorial Conflicts and Boundaries in the Former Soviet Union* (Durham, UK: University of Durham, International Boundaries Research Unit, 1992), pp. 49–50.

Uzbek attempts to assert their dominance in the region.[68] Whether or not this fear is legitimate, it is clear that as indigenous nationalism rises within each Central Asian state, the Uzbek minorities living there will increasingly be faced with the same choices faced by Russians in the region today: emigration or separation.

Ethnodemographic Interaction Beyond the Former USSR

As I note above, all the indigenous nations and homelands of Central Asia do not end at the former USSR border, but continue into the contiguous regions of Iran, Afghanistan, and China. Prior to World War II, the interstate border in this region was relatively porous, and during periods of great upheaval within Russia and the USSR, refugee migration took place to this outlying segment of the ethnonational homeland. Between 1945 and 1989, the interstate border was for the most part closed to this sort of movement, with the exception of an immigration of Uigurs from China during the 1960s and the interaction of Central Asians with their ethnic kinfolk in Afghanistan during the war.

Since independence, new opportunities for interstate contact have developed, and new migration patterns have emerged as a consequence. Two significant migration streams have developed in the past year. First, approximately 60,000 Kazakhs have migrated from the Kazakh regions of western China and Mongolia to Kazakhstan. In large part, these are former refugees from Soviet Kazakhstan and their descendants, who are taking advantage of the new "immigration law passed in August 1992, which provides free immigration for all ethnic Kazakhs, financial support for Kazakhs wanting to be repatriated from China or other former republics, and a quota system for other immigrants."[69] This, coupled with the emigration of Russians, Germans, and other non-Kazakhs from Kazakhstan, has accelerated the pace of demographic indigenization in the republic, which is undoubtedly one of the purposes behind the immigration law. Kazakhs increased from 39.7 percent of Kazakhstan's population in 1989 to 41.9 percent on 1 January 1992, adding 538,456 to their numbers.[70] As of 1 January 1993, another 224,000 Kazakhs were added to the total; Kazakhs had become 43.2 percent of the total population in the state and outnumbered Russians and Ukrainians together for the first time since the 1926 census.[71]

The other major interstate migration stream is the flow of up to 90,000 refugees from the civil conflict in Tajikistan to Afghanistan. Since interethnic conflict within Afghanistan between Pushtuns, Tajiks, and Uzbeks continues to be intense, this influx of refugees could further destabilize Afghanistan. On the other hand, fears have been expressed by the ruling elites in Dushanbe that the Tajiks in Afghanistan are forming a government in exile, and are amassing forces in preparation for a renewed assault on Tajikistan.[72] It is certainly true that the availability of contiguous ethnoterritorial safe havens has proven crucial in the success of guerrilla warfare in other regions of the world. The existence of such ethnoterritorial safe havens around the Central Asian states may facilitate similar conflicts there.

These contiguous ethnoterritorial regions may themselves become the sites of ethnic tensions and conflict, if Central Asian nationalists assert an ethnic claim to these outlying parts of their homelands. However, nationalist claims to these outlying regions are not yet very strong, since they were never part of Russia or the USSR, and since they have been separated from Central Asia for the past century. This was the period when national consolidation occurred, and the isolation of Soviet Central Asia from these ethnically related border regions during this period is certain to have weakened the sense of common national identity and sense of homeland binding together the peoples on both sides of the border. For this reason, conflict over these border zones in the name of gathering in the nation's people and homeland is not likely to become a reality, at least not in the near future.

Conclusions

Ethnic demography has emerged as a key nationalist issue in the successor states of the former Soviet Union. Indigenous nationalists in these states typically depict the ethnodemographic dilution that occurred in the past as a concerted effort on the part of Communist dictators and/or Russian imperialists to undermine the demographic standing of the indigenous nation in its homeland, with the goal of acculturating and ultimately assimilating the non-Russians to a Soviet and/or Russian identity. However, as we have seen in the cases of Latvia and Estonia, demographic dilution has not coincided with the dissipation of indigenous national consciousness, but rather with rising territorial nationalism. The in-migration of ethnic others has been a nearly universal catalyst for rising national consciousness around the creation of an "us versus them" sentiment, and has also accelerated the development of a nationalistic sense of exclusiveness among members of the indigenous nation toward their ancestral homeland.

Nationalists typically depict a nonindigenous presence in their homeland as an invasion that threatens the future viability of the nation. The nationalist depiction of utopia is drawn in equally stark terms—the future ideal from a nationalistic standpoint is an ethnically homogeneous nation-state, whose borders are congruent with those of the ancestral homeland. Given the nationalistic ethnodemographic imagery of heaven and hell (an ethnically "pure" or "polluted" homeland), the behavior that has come to be known as "ethnic cleansing" should not be seen as aberrant.[73] Indeed, in a more nationalistic setting, attempts to clear the homeland of ethnic others is just the sort of behavior that should have been predicted.

Nationalistic efforts at ethnic cleansing are clearly visible in Central Asia, as they are in Transcaucasia, the Baltics, and the Balkans. Anti-foreigner nativism has erupted into violent confrontations pitting Tajiks against Armenians in Dushanbe, Kyrgyz against Uzbeks in Osh, Uzbeks against Meskhetian Turks in Fergana, and Kazakhs against Lezgians in Novy Uzhen'. These anti-foreigner nativistic incidents, together with efforts to restructure the system of ethnic stratification to favor members of the titular nations over all others, create a general climate in which anti-foreigner sentiments are allowed to flourish, and the perceived security of nonindigenes is further undermined. These indigenous efforts to secure a dominant place in their national states are not necessarily incompatible with democracy, as we have seen in Latvia, Estonia, Georgia, and Croatia. However, it is a particular brand of "ethnic democracy" of, for, and by members of the indigenous nation that is emerging in the successor states, and not liberal democracy.[74]

Under these conditions, it is not surprising that nonindigenous emigration is increasing dramatically, and this of course fulfills the demographic indigenization goals of the territorial nationalists. In addition, in reaction to rising indigenous nationalism, minority separatism and irredentism (where relevant) are also on the rise. Almost every segment of the interstate borders among the Central Asian states, as well as segments of the border regions between Kazakhstan and Russia, have been called into question since 1989 (Table 10.11). It is relatively easy to imagine Central Asia becoming engulfed in violent ethnoterritorial conflict over the status of border regions and ethnic minorities.

Thus far the interethnic clashes between indigenes and "outsiders" have been highly localized. In Central Asia, concerted efforts to clear the region of ethnic others have been held in check (at least compared to Transcaucasia and the Balkans), due to the fact that the nationalistic message has not been carried by the governments themselves. In addition, the national front organizations that were the leading force for change in much of the rest of the USSR have not yet developed into strong political organizations capable of mobilizing mass support behind the goals of territorial nationalism. This is changing in Central Asia, and as it does, more concerted efforts to assert the indigenous nations' dominance in their homelands, clear each homeland of ethnic others, and claim ethnoterritorial space that currently lies beyond the borders of the home republic are likely to increase. This will undoubtedly create new waves of refugees migrating within the region and beyond. It will also have a detrimental impact on interstate relations in the region and beyond, and it is something that political elites in Central Asia, Russia, and the West should be actively attempting to avoid.

Notes

1. For the purposes of this chapter, Central Asia includes the following successor states: Uzbekistan, Kazakhstan, Kyrgyzstan, Tajikistan, and Turkmenistan.
2. This second part of the chapter is by necessity much more speculative, and the "data" and data analysis presented here are much less trustworthy. The reader is cautioned not to treat the information presented here as a completely accurate and fully verified depiction of actual trends.
3. For a more complete elaboration of the making of nations in Russia and the USSR, see Robert Kaiser, *The Geography of Nationalism in Russia and the USSR* (Princeton: Princeton University Press, 1994), especially chaps. 1 and 2. On the stages of the nationalization process, see Miroslav Hroch, *The Social Preconditions of National Revival in Europe* (Cambridge: Cambridge University Press, 1985). For a recent discussion of "primordialism," "instrumentalism," or "situational" identity, and also the "ethnicity as practice" approach, particularly as applied to the study of ethnicity and nationalism in Central Asia, see Jo-Ann Gross, ed., *Muslims in Central Asia: Expressions of Identity and Change* (Durham: Duke University Press, 1992). The introductory chapter by Jo-Ann Gross is especially useful in this regard.
4. Muriel Atkin, "Religious, National, and Other Identities in Central Asia," in Gross, ed., *Muslims in Central Asia,* pp. 46–72; Donald Carlisle, "Uzbekistan and the Uzbeks," *Problems of Communism,* vol. 40, no. 5 (1991), pp. 23–44; David Nissman, "Turkmenistan: Searching for a National Identity," in *Nations and Politics in the Soviet Successor States,* ed. Ian Bremmer and Ray Taras (Cambridge: Cambridge University Press, 1993), p. 384.
5. Carlisle, "Uzbekistan and the Uzbeks," p. 34.
6. Alexandre Bennigsen, "Several Nations or One People? Ethnic Consciousness Among Soviet Central Asian Muslims," *Survey,* vol. 24, no. 3 (1979), pp. 51–64.
7. Robert Kaiser, "Nations and Homelands in Soviet Central Asia," and idem, "Social Mobilization in Soviet Central Asia," in *Geographic Perspectives on Soviet Central Asia,* ed. Robert Lewis (London: Routledge, 1992), pp. 251–312.
8. For a more complete discussion of this issue, see Kaiser, "Nations and Homelands in Soviet Central Asia."
9. No "subnational" ethnic categories were provided for Kyrgyz or Kazakhs. Goskomstat SSSR, *Natsional'nyi sostav naseleniia SSSR* (Moscow: Finansy i statistika, 1990), pp. 152–53.
10. Topilin states that Uzbeks and Kazakhs lost 490,000 and 215,000 respectively as a result of assimilation between 1979 and 1988. However, much of this apparent loss was due to the ethnic reidentification of individuals to groups such as the Meskhetian Turks and the Crimean Tatars, who had claimed to be members of other nations in order to avoid persecution but who had become more ethnically assertive under perestroika and glasnost. These losses did not actually reflect a psychological assimilation from the Uzbek and Kazakh national identity to some other national identity. Anatolii Topilin, "Vliianie migratsii na etnonatsional'nuiu strukturu," *Sotsiologicheskie issledovaniia,* no. 7 (1992), p. 34.
11. Kaiser, *Geography of Nationalism.*

12. Solomon Bruk, *Naselenie mira: Etnodemograficheskii spravochnik* (Moscow: Nauka, 1986), pp. 300, 358, and 373.

13. Bess Brown, "Up to 90,000 Tajik Refugees Remain in Afghanistan," *RFE/RL News Briefs*, 5–8 April 1993, p. 8; Lee Schwartz, "Refugee Flows in the Former Soviet Union: Policies and Prospects" (paper presented at the annual meeting of the Association of American Geographers, Atlanta, 9 April 1993). In June 1993, a return migration of Tajiks to Tajikistan began, and numbered approximately 1,500. See Keith Martin, "Tajik Refugees Return Home to Uncertain Future," *RFE/RL Daily Report*, 22 June 1993.

14. For example, see Walker Connor, "The Impact of Homelands upon Diasporas," in *Modern Diasporas in International Politics*, ed. G. Sheffer (London: Croom Helm, 1986), pp. 16–46; Myron Weiner, *Sons of the Soil: Migration and Ethnic Conflict in India* (Princeton: Princeton University Press, 1978); Edward Soja, *The Political Organization of Space* (Washington, DC: Association of American Geographers, 1971); Tamotsu Shibutani and Kian Kwan, *Ethnic Stratification: A Comparative Approach* (New York: Macmillan, 1972).

15. Richard Pierce, *Russian Central Asia 1867–1917* (Berkeley: University of California Press, 1960), p. 127; and Ralph Clem, "The Frontier and Colonialism in Russian and Soviet Central Asia," in Lewis, ed., *Geographic Perspectives on Soviet Central Asia*, p. 31.

16. Martha Olcott, *The Kazakhs* (Stanford, CA: Hoover Institution Press, 1987), pp. 110–13; and Ralph Clem, "Implications of Post-Soviet Economic Development in Kazakhstan" (paper presented at the annual meeting of the American Association for the Advancement of Slavic Studies, Phoenix, 20 November 1992).

17. Frontier expansion involved a larger immigration wave of rural settlers with conquest, while colonialist expansion involved fewer rural Russian immigrants, and relied on Russian military and political elites in cities to establish and maintain control. For a detailed discussion of these two models of imperialism, see Clem, "Frontier and Colonialism."

18. For a comparative treatment of decolonization nationalism, see John Breuilly, *Nationalism and the State* (Manchester, UK: Manchester University Press, 1982).

19. Michael Sacks, *Work and Equality in Soviet Society* (New York: Praeger, 1982); Teresa Rakowska-Harmstone, *Russia and Nationalism in Central Asia: The Case of Tadzhikistan* (Baltimore: Johns Hopkins University Press, 1970); Nancy Lubin, *Labour and Nationality in Soviet Central Asia: An Uneasy Compromise* (Princeton: Princeton University Press, 1984); and Robert Lewis et al., *Nationality and Population Change in Russia and the USSR* (New York: Praeger, 1976).

20. Michael Sacks, "Roots of Republic Differences in Central Asia: A Comparison of the Labor Force and Population of Kyrgyzstan and Uzbekistan" (paper presented at the annual meeting of the American Association for the Advancement of Slavic Studies, Phoenix, 20 November 1992); and Kaiser, "Social Mobilization in Soviet Central Asia."

21. Ellen Jones and Fred Grupp, *Modernization, Value Change and Fertility in the Soviet Union* (London: Cambridge University Press, 1987).

22. The reason for this exception was that there were more rural Russians in Kazakhstan than elsewhere (Table 10.6), and that during the 1980s Russians were leaving rural Kazakhstan in significant numbers (an absolute decline in the number of rural Russians of 160,377 was registered in Kazakhstan between 1979 and 1989).

23. Mikhail Guboglo, "Demography and Language in the Capitals of the Union Republics," *Journal of Soviet Nationalities*, vol. 1, no. 4 (winter 1990–91), pp. 27–33.

24. Hélène Carrère d'Encausse, *Decline of an Empire: The Soviet Socialist Republics in Revolt* (New York: Harper & Row, 1980), p. 70.

25. Alexandre Bennigsen, "Islamic, or Local Consciousness Among Soviet Nation-

alities?" in *Soviet Nationality Problems,* ed. Edward Allworth (New York: Columbia University Press, 1971), p. 174.

26. Kaiser, "Nations and Homelands in Soviet Central Asia."

27. The formulation "Turkic and/or Muslim" was normally used by advocates of the "revenge of the cradle" scenario, because it inflated the numbers said to belong to the "Islamic nation." One nation with 45–50 million members was much more threatening in appearance than the forty plus ethnonational communities with homelands geographically spanning the USSR.

28. Statisticheskii komitet Sodruzhestva nezavisimykh gosudarstv (SNG), *Itogi Vsesoiuznoi perepisi naseleniia 1989 goda* (Moscow: Statisticheskii komitet SNG, 1992), vol. 7, pt. 1, pp. 10–12.

29. James Critchlow, *Nationalism in Uzbekistan: A Soviet Road to Sovereignty* (Boulder: Westview Press, 1991), pp. 69–72.

30. Ronald Liebowitz, "Soviet Geographical Imbalances and Soviet Central Asia," in Lewis, ed., *Geographic Perspectives on Soviet Central Asia,* pp. 101–31; and idem, "Spatial Inequality under Gorbachev," in *The Soviet Union: A New Regional Geography?* ed. Michael Bradshaw (London: Belhaven Press, 1991), pp. 15–37.

31. Lewis et al., *Nationality and Population Change,* pp. 354–81.

32. Dmitrii Ziuzin, "Prichiny nizkoi mobil'nosti korennogo naseleniia respublik Srednei Azii," *Sotsiologicheskie issledovaniia,* no. 1 (1983), pp. 109–18.

33. Kaiser, *Geography of Nationalism.*

34. In an interesting analogy, Cole and Filatotchev ask whether migration patterns in the former USSR will conform to the experience of other European empires following decolonization, which experienced first a wave of European settlers returning to their home countries, and then a wave of non-Europeans from the former colonies attempting to migrate to the former colonial core. John Cole and Igor Filatotchev, "Some Observations on Migration Within and From the Former USSR in the 1990s," *Post-Soviet Geography,* vol. 33, no. 7 (1992), pp. 432–53.

35. A. Vishnevskii and Zh. Zaionchkovskaia, *Migratsiia iz SSSR: Chetvertaia volna,* (Moscow: Tsentr demografii i ekologii cheloveka, 1991), vol. 3, p. 18.

36. Weiner, ed., *Sons of the Soil,* p. 268.

37. Shah Tarzi, "The Nation-State, Victim Groups, and Refugees," *Ethnic and Racial Studies,* vol. 14, no. 4 (1991), pp. 441–52.

38. R. Rakhimov, "K voprosu o sovremennykh Tadzhiksko-Uzbekskikh mezhnatsional'nykh otnosheniiakh," *Sovetskaia etnografiia,* no. 1 (1991), pp. 13–24.

39. The distinction between the designation "refugee" and "forced migrant" is that while both are persons migrating due to a fear of persecution, refugees are persons without Russian citizenship, while forced migrants are Russian citizens. There are 470,000 officially registered refugees in Russia, and 800,000 registered forced migrants. The number of actual refugees and forced migrants is thought by most to be much higher. Schwartz, "Refugee Flows in the Former Soviet Union," and idem, "The Realignment of Territory and the Mixing of Nationalities Along the Russian Periphery" (paper presented at the annual meeting of the American Association for the Advancement of Slavic Studies, Phoenix, 20 November 1992).

40. Clem, "Implications of Post-Soviet Economic Development."

41. Sacks, "Roots of Republic Differences in Central Asia."

42. Robert Kaiser, "National Territoriality and Demographic Indigenization in the Non-Russian Periphery" (paper presented at the annual meeting of the Association of American Geographers, San Diego, 18 April 1992); and W. Rogers Brubaker, "Citizenship Struggles in Soviet Successor States," *International Migration Review,* vol. 26, no. 2 (1992), p. 275.

43. For the most recent and comprehensive compilation of documents, data, and

maps related to the deported groups, see Mikhail Guboglo, *Deportatsii narodov SSSR* (Moscow: Rossiiskaia Akademiia nauk, Institut etnologii i antropologii, 1992).

44. Vishnevskii and Zaionchkovskaia, *Migratsiia iz SSSR*, p. 7.

45. L. Shevtsova, "Post-Soviet Emigration Today and Tomorrow," *International Migration Review*, vol. 26, no. 2 (1992), p. 247.

46. Kaliningrad Oblast has also been proposed as an alternative German homeland.

47. Schwartz, "Refugee Flows in the Former Soviet Union."

48. This issue was discussed with Mr. Kim, the Korean delegate from Uzbekistan to the Leningrad Minority Rights Conference, 2–4 June 1991.

49. "Statehood for Soviet Germans Viewed," FBIS, *Daily Report: Soviet Union* (FBIS-SOV-90-162), 21 August 1990, p. 30.

50. Vishnevskii and Zaionchkovskaia, *Migratsiia iz SSSR*, p. 8.

51. E. Matveeva, "Locals Say No to Korean Autonomy in the Maritime Territory," *Moscow News*, no. 38 (1992), p. 5.

52. "Bezhentsy v ozhidanii," *Argumenty i fakty*, no. 28 (1990).

53. Zviad Gamsakhurdia, "We Have Tolerated Separatists Too Long," *Moscow News*, no. 48 (1990), p. 7.

54. Vishnevskii and Zaionchkovskaia, *Migratsiia iz SSSR*, p. 18; and E. Panesh and L. Ermolov, "Turki-Meskhetintsy," *Sovetskaia etnografiia*, no. 1 (1990), p. 19.

55. Goskomstat SSSR, *Natsional'nyi sostav naseleniia SSSR* (Moscow: Finansy i statistika, 1991), p. 6.

56. Figures for 1959 and 1979 were not published as part of the original censuses for those years, but were provided in a comparative table with the 1989 census.

57. Schwartz, "Refugee Flows in the Former Soviet Union."

58. Schwartz, "Realignment of Territory."

59. Net out-migration from the five Central Asian republics totaled 235,000 in 1989, 419,000 in 1990, and 214,000 in 1991. See Statisticheskii komitet SNG, "Napravleniia i prichiny migratsii naseleniia," *Statisticheskii biulleten'*, no. 14 (October 1992), p. 127. Preliminary data indicate that a dramatic increase in net out-migration occurred during 1992. In Kazakhstan, the number of Russians decreased absolutely by approximately 109,000 in 1992, the first time an absolute decrease was registered. See Keith Martin, "Kazakhstan: More Kazakhs, Fewer Russians," *RFE/RL Daily Report*, 25 June 1993. As a result of the civil war in Tajikistan, an estimated 60,000 refugees left for Afghanistan, another 125,000 left for the other Central Asian republics, and up to 163,000 Russians left for Russia. See Schwartz, "Refugee Flows in the Former Soviet Union"; and Von Andrzej Rybak, "Grausamer als die Mongolen," *Die Woche*, 13 May 1993, p. 24.

60. Kaiser, "Nations and Homelands in Soviet Central Asia," and idem, "National Territoriality and Demographic Indigenization."

61. Oblasts with a majority Kazakh population are to implement the new language law mandating the increasing usage of Kazakh immediately, while oblasts with a majority Russian population (i.e., in northern Kazakhstan) are allowed to delay full implementation of the language law until 1 January 2000. See Martha Olcott, "Kazakhstan: A Republic of Minorities," in Bremmer and Taras, eds., *Nations and Politics in the Soviet Successor States*, p. 320.

62. Carlisle, "Uzbekistan and the Uzbeks," p. 40.

63. Vishnevskii and Zaionchkovskaia, *Migratsiia iz SSSR*, p. 12.

64. Olcott, "Kazakhstan: A Republic of Minorities," pp. 322–24; and Aleksandr Solzhenitsyn, "Kak nam obustroit' Rossiiu," *Komsomol'skaia pravda*, 18 September 1990 (special issue), p. 2.

65. Critchlow, *Nationalism in Uzbekistan*, p. 205.

66. "Okhota k peremene mest," *Argumenty i fakty*, no. 5 (1992), p. 4; and Schwartz, "Refugee Flows in the Former Soviet Union."

67. See also Gregory Gleason, "Uzbekistan: From Statehood to Nationhood," in Bremmer and Taras, eds., *Nations and Politics in the Soviet Successor States*, p. 350.

68. V. Yemelianenko, "Uktam Bekmukhamedov" (interview with leader of the Samarkand Society of Tajiks), *Moscow News*, no. 30 (1992), p. 9; and Gleason, "Uzbekistan: From Statehood to Nationhood," p. 351.

69. Schwartz, "Refugee Flows in the Former Soviet Union," p. 8.

70. Gosudarstvennyi komitet Respubliki Kazakhstan po statistike i analizu, "Naselenie," *Statisticheskii press-biulleten'*, no. 4 (1992), p. 87.

71. Martin, "Kazakhstan: More Kazakhs, Fewer Russians."

72. See the chapter by James Critchlow, "The Ethnic Factor in Central Asian Foreign Policy," in this volume.

73. Ethnic cleansing is defined broadly here as the attempt by indigenous nationalists to clear the homeland of ethnic others, which may include genocide, physical expulsion, or attempts to forcibly assimilate these foreign elements.

74. Smooha and Hanf define "ethnic democracy" as "a democracy in which the dominance of one ethnic group is institutionalized." For a further elaboration of this concept and the comparison of ethnic democracy with other democratic models, see Sammy Smooha and Theodor Hanf, "Modes of Conflict-Regulation in Divided Societies," in *Ethnicity and Nationalism*, ed. Anthony Smith (Leiden: E.J. Brill, 1992), pp. 26–47.

11

The Ethnic Factor in Central Asian Foreign Policy

James Critchlow

Five sovereign nations emerged in Central Asia from the collapse of the Soviet Union. Despite their varying degrees of adherence to the Commonwealth of Independent States, all five have demonstrated a strong sense of independence and a determination to pursue their own interests free of outside direction.

In particular, independence has confronted the new Central Asian nations with sudden responsibility for conduct of their own foreign relations. For each of them, the sphere of foreign policy is not some remote interest; it is intimately related to their future viability as states. With the collapse of the Soviet system, the central authority in Moscow that orchestrated foreign relations for the constituent republics (both with one another and with countries outside the USSR) has disappeared from the scene. Any expectation that its functions would be taken over in substantial form by the Commonwealth of Independent States has not withstood the test of time and political reality; at the insistence of Ukraine, CIS coordination was limited to economic issues,[1] and even there cooperation was rudimentary, and one of the Central Asian states, Turkmenistan, was an abstainer. This created a vacuum in critical areas that could be filled only through painstaking creation of a new fabric of regional and bilateral relations. From the standpoint of the international community, the new situation posed a potential threat to the stability of Asia, particularly if one of the major powers of the continent, Russia, China, or Iran, were to bring Central Asia under its control.

General Context

Before examining the ethnic and other domestic factors that are the central topic of this chapter, it may be useful to sketch the general context of Central Asian foreign relations.

At the outset, the Central Asian republics were ill-equipped for the task facing them. Prior to independence, each had its own "Ministry of Foreign Affairs" under the federal system, but these largely fictitious bodies had only small staffs and facilities and were used largely as a means for enabling Moscow to impart a measure of credibility to the supposed "autonomy" of the republics. The "ministries" had no real authority; all foreign relations were handled through Moscow. Even in foreign relations at the federal level, the Central Asian republics were severely underrepresented: With the exception of a few token Central Asian ambassadors assigned mainly to Muslim countries as an adjunct of Soviet efforts to woo them, the Soviet foreign service was essentially Slavic.

This meant that on achieving independence the Central Asian republics lacked trained and experienced staffs capable of administering their foreign relations at a professional level. Nonetheless, they rushed to exploit their new sovereign status by emerging as independent actors in the global arena. Their haste is explainable in terms of three priorities:

1. internal political considerations (establishment of independent foreign relations was popular because it symbolized the new freedom from central control and helped legitimize the republican governments in power, most of them holdovers from the Soviet period);
2. the urgent need to develop new trading ties to replace those that had vanished with the Soviet system;
3. the desire to deal directly with foreign governments to solicit economic assistance and political support (in the case of some foreign partners, such as Iran, by discouraging them from giving support to dissident or opposition elements within the new countries).

The Central Asian republics' initial experiments in foreign relations were successful in that they resulted in quick recognition by other countries and, in the case of major powers, establishment of diplomatic relations and the exchange of diplomatic missions. The republics were also accepted with little hesitation into the United Nations and other international bodies.

At the same time, many problems remained. Lack of staff, facilities, and funds forced the republics to continue to depend on Russian missions abroad (as successors of the former Soviet ones) for much of their representation. This led to anomalous situations in which Russian officials continued to make decisions for their nominally sovereign clients on such matters as issuance of entry visas. Since Moscow continued in the early period to be the main point of access to Central Asia from abroad, Russian immigration and customs officials also controlled traffic and goods to and from the republics.

Lack of trained and experienced personnel has also been an embarrassment in the development of foreign trade. While businesspeople from abroad have been actively courted by the presidents of the new countries and welcomed in style, the former complain about the frustration of legal ambiguities, overlapping jurisdictions, and grasping and incompetent bureaucracies, a problem that has prevented many agreements from coming to fruition.

Still, despite these problems, it is clear that the Central Asian states are determined to control their own foreign relations without delegating decision-making authority to the CIS or any other extranational body. In attempting to advance the security and economic interests of their countries, they face a set of discrete (if overlapping) areas that are definable in geographic terms:

1. other Central Asian states;
2. other CIS states outside Central Asia;
3. neighboring states of Asia and the Middle East (i.e., Iran) outside the former Soviet Union;
4. the Muslim world;
5. the global community at large.

Foreign Minister Sadik Safaev of Uzbekistan has shown that his government conceptualizes its foreign policy in such geographical categories: He has enunciated its top three priorities as Central Asian cooperation, integration into the Asian world, and cooperation with CIS countries, primarily Russia.[2] (He seems pointedly to have ignored the United States and Western Europe in this formulation.)

Central Asian Regional Relations

For reasons discussed in the next section, the Central Asian states, with the possible exception of Uzbekistan, are not disposed toward any form of regional organization that would mitigate their individual sovereignty. Still, they share economic and environmental problems whose solutions can be achieved only through some form of regional cooperation. This fact has been given recognition through various regional "summits" that have been held both before and since independence. Progress in this area has been slowed, however, by preoccupation with other options. There was an initial inclination on the part of some of the states to look to the CIS as a coordinating mechanism; this expectation has now been largely dashed. Similarly, attention to regional solutions has been somewhat distracted by a tendency to look outside the region for assistance in dealing with such critical multinational problems as reclamation of the Aral Sea basin. (The problem of nuclear contamination in Kazakhstan is a special case, related to the sensitive issue of dismantlement of Kazakhstan's nuclear arsenal on the basis of multilateral cooperation with Russia and the United States.)

Relations with Other CIS States

The CIS concept has been hamstrung by the zeal of members to protect their newly won sovereignty and by differences in approach. Within Central Asia, Kazakhstan has been the most enthusiastic about CIS cooperation, and Turkmenistan—with its mineral resources and long Middle Eastern border—the least. Relations among states of the CIS community have depended on a network of ad hoc bilateral and multilateral arrangements. Thus, in March 1993 the three Central Asian states bordering China (Kazakhstan, Kyrgyzstan, and Tajikistan) participated together with Russia in negotiations with China on border issues.[3] Uzbekistan has worked out a barter arrangement with Russia (cotton for petroleum) to replace the old dictates of the *goszakaz.*

The problem of ties with Russia, given its special interest in the region due to issues of proximity and security, its dependence on Central Asian raw materials, and the situation of the Russian minorities, is most sensitive.

Asian Cooperation

In foreign policy declarations, the Central Asian states have generally emphasized awareness of their situation as Asian powers. President Nursultan Nazarbaev of Kazakhstan, mindful of his country's long borders with Asian Russia and China, called in October 1992 at the Forty-seventh UN General Assembly for an Asian cooperative security treaty along NATO and CSCE lines. For Kazakhstan and Uzbekistan, a special relationship with South Korea is facilitated by their large Korean minorities (see below). Another non-Muslim Asian country with developing economic interests in the region is India; for example, Indian firms are building new hotels in the major cities of Uzbekistan. (There is a tradition of Indian economic presence: in prerevolutionary times Hindu moneylenders played a special role in Muslim Central Asia.) President Islam Karimov of Uzbekistan, alarmed by unrest in neighboring Tajikistan and Afghanistan, has sought to improve relations with Iran and Pakistan, a task complicated by his close association with Russia in helping to defeat Islamic and democratic forces in Tajikistan.[4] Considering its economic strength, Japan has been relatively inactive in the area, its reluctance a reflection of its dispute with Russia over the Kuril Islands and its unwillingness to become involved in the ruble zone; at least in the case of Kyrgyzstan, it has extended modest credits.

The Muslim World

The situation of the Central Asian republics is deeply affected by the history of their region as a traditionally Muslim land. This age-old tie is a standard point of reference in speeches by government leaders, both to domestic audiences and when meeting representatives of foreign Muslim countries. At the same time, the threat of encroachment by "Islamic fundamentalism" is a source of alarm, even panic, for the secular elites now in power in the republics (see below). Kazakhstan, with its relatively liberal Muslim population and the incendiary potential of upsetting its large Russian minority, and Uzbekistan, with its proximity to trouble spots in Tajikistan and Afghanistan, have been especially leery of close involvement with Islam, although the latter has felt constrained for domestic reasons to adopt an ostensibly pro-Islamic stance (while banning Islamic political parties). The conservative government of Tajikistan has also banned Islamic (and other) political parties. President Saparmurad Niiazov of Turkmenistan has exploited the question of fundamentalism for his own conservative political purposes, cautioning that it is a reaction to democratization along European lines: "By insisting that European principles are so universal, Western politicians, one way or the other, are provoking growth of anti-Western sentiments in some of the Muslim countries."[5]

Since independence, Tajikistan has been the most unstable of the five republics, the scene of civil war among different political factions, with both religious and regional overtones. While description of these hostilities as a conflict between "Communist" loyalists and "Muslim" rebels is an oversimplification, there is little doubt that mujahideen remnants in Afghanistan have attempted to support the rebels of Tajikistan with infiltration of personnel and arms, rumored to be financed by Saudi Arabia or Iran.[6] One result has been to strengthen the residual Russian presence in the region, with Russian border and security forces deployed on the territory of Tajikistan by request of the Central Asian governments.

The Central Asian republics have joined the Economic Cooperation Organization founded by Pakistan, Iran, and Turkey, and have expressed openness to economic ties with those and other Muslim countries. At the same time, relations with the relatively poorer Islamic coreligionists have tended to stress educational and cultural exchanges as much as actual economic assistance.

Other Nations of the Global Community

While the affluent nations of North America and Western Europe are geographically and culturally the most remote from Central Asia, in the all-important sphere of financial and technical assistance they more than any other may hold the key to the region's future. The Central Asian republics have recognized this in their early and enthusiastic acceptance of diplomatic relations with the United States and other Western countries, and their espousal in principle of Western market principles. At the same time, they have shown apprehension about being labeled too "pro-Western" by radical Islamic elements.

Among the ruling elites, the pull of Western culture (and Western economic achievement) is strong. On becoming independent, all the Central Asian nations rushed to join the Conference on Security and Cooperation in Europe; an official of one of them noted proudly, "This makes us Europeans!" The five have welcomed establishment of American and other Western embassies in their capitals (along with diplomatic missions from Turkey, Iran, and other countries). Speaking of his Turkic republic's orientation to Turkey, a Kyrgyz intellectual expressed approval of that country as a secular Islamic model, but noted that his own values were conditioned by the works of writers like Tolstoy and Turgenev, and by the world literature that he knows through Russian translation; he expressed doubts about Turkey's contribution in such areas as human rights. The thirty-nine-year-old foreign minister of Uzbekistan studied at Harvard, one of six Uzbeks who studied there in 1990–91. Another of the six is back in Tashkent, lecturing to his economics classes in English ("so that they will be at home in the global terminology"). Still another has returned to the United States as an Uzbek diplomat.

In practice, the Central Asian posture toward the West has varied by country:

• Kyrgyzstan under its liberal President Askar Akaev quickly embraced Western values; if anything, he damaged his country's economy by rushing too quickly to adopt Western ideas.

• President Nazarbaev of Kazakhstan, after initially hiring an economic advisor and loudly proclaiming devotion to market principles, has lately backtracked, concluding that in this area the government must proceed more gradually so as not to lose control.

• Presidents Karimov of Uzbekistan and Niiazov of Turkmenistan have paid lip service to market ideas but look askance at Western political models. Karimov (whose daughter is married to an Uzbek-American and has lived in the United States) is visibly piqued by U.S. criticism of his human rights record, which has reportedly made Washington cool to the idea of his paying a state visit. Niiazov, as noted above, has problems with Western democratic principles.

• Given the turmoil in Tajikistan, it is difficult to write here of a coherent foreign policy, although it has managed to maintain ties with the United States and other Western countries even when the diplomatic staffs had to be evacuated.

If one considers the attitude of the Central Asian states toward the West (especially the United States) in the light of recent negotiations over dismantlement of Kazakhstan's (and Ukraine's and Belarus's) nuclear weapons, one is led to find emerging affirmation of the principle applied decades ago to the newly independent colonial states of Asia and Africa that "states are likely to get what they want if they raise a sufficient fuss and unlikely to get it if they fail to do so."[7]

National Differences

Their brief post-Soviet history of independence has demonstrated that the Central Asian republics are not the homogeneous "Muslim bloc" that some observers had assumed them to be. Under Soviet rule, the difference between "Muslims" on the one hand and Russians or other European nationalities on the other was the salient fact of Central Asian identity. The republics of the region were united by a common status vis-à-vis Moscow and a set of common grievances against the center, especially in economic and cultural areas. Since independence, they have joined in rather halfhearted mutual attempts to establish regional coordination in such areas as water resources and environmental recovery, but their political union into some such entity as "Turkestan"—once the object of intense speculation—now seems remote and improbable.[8] As independent states, the five republics have demonstrated that the differences among them are as important as the common features. Ironically, those differences were exacerbated as the result of an officially sanctioned drive during the early Soviet period to create, through "nation building," a separate and distinct national identity and tradition, reinforced by its own historiography. Although slowed by Stalin's reversal of policy and liquidation of "bourgeois nationalists," the nation-building drive regained its momentum after his death, especially in the latter Brezhnev period, which has been described as one of "decolonialization."[9] The differences among the Central Asian republics are capable of influencing their separate foreign policies. What will be the prime domestic ingredients of those policies? In particular, what will be the role of ethnicity, both that of the majority ethnic group and of minorities resident in the republics? What other internal factors will influence foreign policy?

In all five republics, patterns of identity are complex and overlapping.

Writing in the Soviet period, Alexandre Bennigsen elicited three broad classifications of identity: *supranational* (such as "Asian," "Eastern," "Muslim"), *national* (identification with the individual republic), and *subnational* (tribal, local, etc.)[10] Trends since independence have tended to bring the first and last categories, supranational and subnational, to the fore, presenting in some cases a threat to stability by detracting from the cohesiveness of the nation.

While even in the post-Soviet period empirical study of identity in the region has been limited by both political and practical considerations, it is clear from existing evidence that identity is very much a function of social stratification. We are far from being able to construct a comprehensive matrix of identity and social variables, but such diverse sources as the vernacular literature or casual contacts of foreigners with the indigenous population have demonstrated, for example, that national identity (versus supranational or subnational) is most deeply entrenched in those classes (e.g., administrative and professional) who are most socialized to the political system.[11] On the other hand, the less educated rural inhabitants are more inclined to both the supra- (e.g., Muslim) and subnational (e.g., local, tribal) sets of identity. This is not a rigorous distinction: Feelings of Muslim identity may be strong among intellectuals (although apt to manifest themselves in more secular or cerebral forms) and clannic divisions are said to operate at the upper levels of some republics, while ideas of national identity may have been nurtured in the lower social groups, especially those (such as military recruits) who have been exposed to multinational situations. Yet certain truths of operational importance seem to be evident, such as the greater vulnerability of rural populations to the appeals of "fundamentalist" Islam, which tends to be viewed with distrust or alarm at higher socioeconomic levels.

Ethnic Factors

The Core Populations

All the Central Asian republics are heirs to the Soviet political culture. Whatever the changes wrought by independence, it is likely that in the near term that culture will continue to influence their outlook and actions. In particular, the Soviet system, despite its official "internationalism," accorded pride of place, in foreign relations as in other spheres, to the dominant Russian nationality. As Adam Ulam wrote in the context of Soviet foreign policy, " 'Soviet patriotism' today is an ideological veneer over good old-fashioned Russian nationalism."[12] We see a parallel to this in the controlling position exercised in the Central Asian republics by their core nationalities. This position is made even more commanding in Central Asia by the heritage of the "cult of first secretaries," which reached its apogee in the Brezhnev era, the practice of highlighting the figurehead role in each republic of the party first secretary, always a member of the eponymous nationality. Over time, the first secretary role grew into one of real power and was replicated by appointment of first secretaries of the same nationality at regional and district levels.[13] As a result of this heritage, the core nationality is paramount in each republic, with little tradition of power sharing with other nationalities.

At the same time, it must be recognized that the concept of "nationality" is a relatively recent one that did not exist before the Soviet period. The nationalities are in fact amalgams of different local, tribal, and clannic groups. These subgroups retain influence within the nationality to the present day. For example, the national government of Uzbekistan is constrained to balance the interests of geographic subgroups from Tashkent, Samarkand, and the Fergana region. (It is rumored in Uzbekistan that the first Uzbek ambassador to the United States owes his appointment to the fact that the president needed his former post of minister of justice to satisfy the demands of one such subgroup.) In Kazakhstan, affiliation with the three main tribal groupings, the Larger, Middle, and Smaller Zhus, is reportedly still a factor in such areas as job preference. In Kyrgyzstan, there is rivalry between northern and southern groups. The civil war in Tajikistan reportedly has local and clannic as well as national (Tajik versus Uzbek) elements.

Four of the republics (Uzbekistan, Kazakhstan, Kyrgyzstan, Turkmenistan) have titular nationalities of Turkic origin. The fifth, Tajikistan, belongs to the Iranian ethnic family. Even within the Turkic group, there are significant differences that inhibit the development of Pan-Turkism.

The Uzbeks, together with the urban Tajiks, are heirs of the ancient sedentary civilization of the mixed Turkic-Iranian population known before the revolution as "Sarts." Oasis cities of present-day Uzbekistan like Samarkand and Bukhara owed their growth to the flourishing caravan routes that from ancient times constituted the major East-West trade artery and made the region in many ways more advanced than Europe well into the Middle Ages. With the arrival of Arab armies in the seventh century, the oases became an integral part of the burgeoning Islamic civilization that extended from India in the east to North Africa and Spain to the west. "Holy" Bukhara was a major center of Islamic learning, visited by pilgrims and seminarians from throughout the Muslim world. In the Soviet period, the Uzbeks were at the cutting edge of resistance to Moscow, yet their first president after Uzbekistan became an independent country is the former Communist Party chief (as is the case in all the Central Asian republics except Kyrgyzstan). (An Uzbek minority in Tajikistan has charged discrimination by the authorities there, with similar complaints by the large Tajik minority in Uzbekistan.)

The Turkmens, whose ancestors were nomads into the twentieth century, are affected geopolitically by their long border with Persia to the south and their proximity to Azerbaijan across the Caspian Sea. Turkmen bandits who plundered the caravan routes through their area were famous in the traveling lore of earlier days. Today, Turkmenistan is arguably the Central Asian republic that has least changed politically since the Soviet period.

Kazakhstan and Kyrgyzstan along the northern periphery of the region differ from the others by their relative remoteness from the former centers of Muslim influence, in consequence of which Islam came to them later and penetrated their societies much less deeply. It is common to hear members of both nationalities boast, "We are the least Islamic and most European of all the Central Asian peoples." The nomadic Kazakhs and Kyrgyz stood out among the Muslims of the Russian Empire for their refusal to sequester or veil women. Before the advent of the Russians in the eighteenth century, both of these peoples ranged freely over vast stretches of grassy steppe, a situation in which their chieftains had to practice a kind of tribal democracy to encourage cohesion and keep members from simply wandering off. Kyrgyzstan is today regarded as the most liberal of the five republics, having deposed its Moscow-appointed Communist Party ruler even before the breakup of the Soviet Union. Kazakhstan, although still ruled by a president who is the former Communist first secretary, has displayed more democratic tendencies than its southern neighbors.

Within the Turkic group, Kazakhstan—with a territory a third the size of the continental United States—is a special case because of its large Russian minority, which constitutes some two-fifths of the population and is barely exceeded by the eponymous Kazakhs themselves. Moreover, the Russians are concentrated in northern oblasts of the republic where they outnumber other nationalities, including the native Kazakhs, and pose a potential secessionist threat. The postindependence government has demonstrated sensitivity to this issue, avoiding any commitment that might make Kazakhstan appear to be a Muslim-bloc or Pan-Turkic nation in which the Russians would feel disadvantaged. Yet, thanks to the legacy of the pro-Kazakh cadre policy of Dinmukhamed A. Kunaev, who led the Kazakh Communist Party from 1960 to 1986 (with a two-year hiatus from 1962 to 1964), members of the Kazakh nationality have much higher visibility in the central government organs in the capital of Almaty than do Russians and other nationalities.[14]

Tajikistan is set off from its Turkic neighbors in the region by its majority population of Iranian Tajiks. In the emirate of Bukhara, urban Tajiks coexisted closely for centuries with Uzbeks in the oasis cities they shared, where bilingualism was the norm. Today, Tajikistan laments the fact that the two largest "Tajik" cities were assigned to Uzbekistan in the Soviet national delineation of 1925, which divided the emirate and the rest of the Asian region into separate "nations" in the European sense.

The Tajiks are tied linguistically to the Iranian populations of Iran and Afghanistan. In the case of Iran, those ties have been mitigated in history by the religious split between Sunni Central Asia and Shi'i Persia (although recent visitors to the republic report hearing crowds chanting, "Ya, Ali!" a Shi'i slogan). With largely Sunni Afghanistan, however, there is no such pronounced religious divide.

Transborder Cognates

Another potential ethnic factor in the foreign relations of the Central Asian states is the presence in countries adjacent to the region of significant numbers of cognate groups: Kazakhs in Russia and China, Kyrgyz in China, Uzbeks in China and Afghanistan, Turkmens in Afghanistan and Iran, Tajiks in Afghanistan. Conversely, the republics have in their own populations minority representatives of outside ethnic groups: among them, Russians, Ukrainians, Germans, Volga Tatars, Koreans, Crimean Tatars, Jews. In some cases, the political importance of these groups in the affairs of the Central Asian countries is being reduced by out-migration: Slavs (especially from Tajikistan and Uzbekistan) to Russia, Ukraine, and other republics, Germans to Germany and Russia, Crimean Tatars to Crimea, Jews to Israel. The Kazakhstan Russians are a special case: While their conationals in the other Central Asian nations have been fleeing in the face of real or perceived threats to their security, Russian settlement in Kazakhstan has remained largely stable.[15] The Koreans are another exception: Large numbers of them live in Uzbekistan and Kazakhstan, where they have established a strong economic position in the decades since their deportation from the Soviet Far East prior to World War II, and have shown little inclination to emigrate to the unfamiliar environment of Korea.

Whether these minorities can play a role of any importance as interest groups in the formation of foreign policy is questionable. If one considers the analogy of the parent Soviet political culture, it is unlikely: Analysts could never find convincing evidence that ethnic groups materially influenced Soviet foreign policy, and could only "posit" such a phenomenon as possible.[16]

What is more certain is the potential of minorities as mediators with those foreign countries with which they have ethnic ties. Republic of Korea businesspeople have expressed confidence in their coethnics in Central Asia as a reliable bridge to the local economies. Especially in Kazakhstan, South Korean economic activity is now quite visible. (A Kazakh made this bittersweet comment to a visitor: "The Koreans are taking over our economy, but at least they won't butcher it the way the Russians did!") Reversing the pattern, Uzbek émigrés from Saudi Arabia have been active in trying to promote trade between that country and Uzbekistan.

Nonethnic Factors in Foreign Relations

Religious and Cultural

Apprehensions about a tide of religious fundamentalism that could threaten to transform their young nations into "Islamic republics" on the Iranian model are endemic among secular and moderate elements in Central Asia. Such fears are fed by the presence of local Islamic movements; even in relatively secular Kazakhstan, the banned nationalist Alash Party has a strong Islamic tinge. (A drive to recruit volunteers in Kazakhstan to fight for the Islamic side in Nagorno-Karabakh was discouraged by the government; its motivation seems to have been more religious than ethnic.) Civil conflict in Tajikistan has had a pronounced religious component, although the alleged threat of "Islamic fundamentalism" has also been used as a scare tactic to rally support from secular elements. The response of the national governments has been to co-opt "loyal" believers by lifting Soviet-era restrictions on religious practice and providing state support for the construction or repair of religious buildings; at the same time, the governments are trying to channel religious activity by encouraging tame "official" religious establishments like the Muslim religious board in Tashkent. (Leaders of the official clergy have specifically repudiated Islamic political activity; while this may have enhanced their position with the governments, it doubtless detracts from their influence with the broad Muslim *umma*.) At the same time they have sought to maintain good relations with the governments of Muslim nations like Iran, Saudi Arabia, and Pakistan, presumably to provide leverage to discourage them from supporting religious subversion of the political structure.

A cultural issue closely related to religion and ties with foreign countries is the issue of alphabet reform. Prior to Sovietization, all of Central Asia used the Arabic script. In the 1920s and 1930s, partly under the influence of reform elements in Turkey, the new Soviet republics went over to the Latin alphabet, which was subsequently replaced by Cyrillic. Now that the republics are independent, there has been agitation to replace Cyrillic with either Arabic or Latin. Generally, religious elements propose adopting the Arabic, with Turkey-oriented secular ones favoring the Latin. (All parties concede the utility of teaching the Arabic script to enable students to read prerevolutionary literature.) Change has been slowed by practical considerations, especially the cost involved. In March 1993, representatives of Turkic-language countries, including the four Central Asian Turkic states, agreed at a meeting in Ankara on a common Turkic alphabet; however, the agreement was subject to government ratification.

Economic

In all the republics, the economic crisis is the central fact of political life and the main threat to stability. In consequence, the political and security goals of Central Asian foreign policy are balanced by often contradictory considerations of economic interest.

The breakup of the Soviet Union has disrupted the old patterns of trade. This has been not without its advantages: the Central Asian republics are no longer compelled to supply goods at confiscatory prices to fulfill Moscow's *goszakaz*. This has tended to improve local food supplies. Moreover, the republics, all of which are rich in raw materials, are now free to sell at world prices for hard currency, provided that they can find buyers. Turkmenistan, with its long border with Iran, was one of the first to take advantage of its new status, selling its natural gas abroad (and causing turmoil in Ukraine, which was once heavily dependent on supplies of Turkmen gas at low Soviet state prices). On the other hand, Russian textile factories initially balked at paying new, higher prices for Central Asian cotton; the impasse was eventually resolved through a barter arrangement: cotton for badly needed Russian petroleum. (In dealing with such issues, the role of the CIS has been secondary to negotiation of direct bilateral agreements.)

The Central Asian republics complain that under Soviet rule their economies were not allowed to develop in balanced fashion, that they were exploited by the center as "raw materials bases" while their industry was stunted by Moscow's refusal to provide capital investment. The result is that they are now short of manufactured goods traditionally exported from other parts of the Soviet Union. In the entire region, not a single automobile, television set, or refrigerator is produced.

The governments have set about an urgent quest abroad for hard currency to meet current needs and finance development of local industry. This is to be obtained partly through sale of raw materials, partly—it is hoped—through aid and credits. Presidents and other officials have been energetically traveling abroad in pursuit of economic ties. Although foreign businesspeople have been welcomed with open arms in the region, potential partners are put off by the difficulty of negotiating agreements and doubts about the security of investment there. For example, an $11 billion deal concluded between Kazakhstan and Chevron Oil is reportedly still being held up by obstacles. Newmont Mining, an international firm, has had difficulty getting operations under way on a proposal, agreed to long ago in principle by the government of Uzbekistan, to refine low-grade gold ore under terms that would apparently be advantageous to both parties.

The economic objectives of Central Asian foreign policy sometimes transcend ethnic or cultural ties. With economic and technical benefits no doubt in mind, President Akaev of Kyrgyzstan was the first Central Asian leader to visit Israel, where he created a storm in the Islamic world by offering to set up his country's embassy not in Tel Aviv but in Jerusalem (a position he later modified in the face of the Iranian foreign minister's cancellation of an impending visit). The United States (which has granted most-favored-nation status to all the republics but Tajikistan and Uzbekistan), Western Europe, China, and South Korea have all been courted assiduously.

Conclusion

In the foreign policy of the Central Asian nations, the potential role of ethnicity is complex, depending on many variables. Ethnic factors may help facilitate agreements with other countries where they coincide with other goals, if only by providing a congenial topic of political rhetoric. Yet at present, with each republic being ruled by a nationalistic and Muslim (in the broad sense) but secular elite exposed, ironically, through Soviet education to Western influences, it is economic power interests, with related security considerations, that are the main determinants of policy. Political and social upheavals could eventually change the situation, bringing to power governments more concerned with ethnic, cultural, and religious questions, but for the foreseeable future that does not appear to be in the cards. Facile ascription of Central Asian actions in the international sphere to "Muslim" or "Pan-Turkic" motives are apt to be misleading.

Notes

1. By mid-1993 there were signs that Ukrainian policy had evolved in the direction of accepting new forms of cooperation with Russia and Belarus, as suggested by the 10 July adoption of a joint declaration on "common economic space" by the prime ministers. The practical effect of this declaration and its consequences for the Central Asian republics were not immediately apparent.

2. Uzbekistan APN Service in Russian, 15 February 1993; cited in FBIS-SOV-93-030, 17 February 1993, pp. 70–71.

3. *RFE/RL News Briefs,* 15–19 March 1993, p. 8.

4. See Christopher J. Panico, "Uzbekistan's Southern Diplomacy," *RFE/RL Research Report,* 26 March 1993, p. 39.

5. Interview carried by *Interfax* (Moscow) in English, 24 March 1993; cited in FBIS-SOV-93-056, 25 March 1993, p. 62.

6. For a discussion of the conflict in Tajikistan, see Eden Naby, "Tajik Political Legitimacy and Political Parties," *Central Asia Monitor,* 1992, no. 5, p. 10, and other materials on the subject in that and more recent issues of the same publication.

7. Inis L. Claude, *Swords Into Ploughshares* (New York: Random House, 1956), as quoted in Rupert Emerson, *From Empire to Nation: The Rise to Self-Assertion of Asian and African Peoples* (Boston: Beacon Press, 1960), p. 399.

8. For a discussion of this question, see James Critchlow, "Will There Be A Turkestan?" *RFE/RL Research Report,* 10 July 1992, p. 47.

9. For an illuminating discussion of nation building and decolonialization in the USSR, see Gerhard Simon, *Nationalism and Policy Toward the Nationalities in the Soviet Union: From Totalitarian Dictatorship to Post-Stalinist Society* (Boulder: Westview Press, 1991).

10. Alexandre Bennigsen, "Several Nations or One People?", *Survey,* no. 108 (1979), pp. 51 ff.

11. See Donald S. Carlisle, "Power and Politics in Soviet Uzbekistan: From Stalin to Gorbachev," in *Soviet Central Asia: The Failed Transformation,* ed. William Fierman (Boulder: Westview Press, 1991), pp. 118–20.

12. Adam Ulam, "Russian Nationalism," in *The Domestic Context of Soviet Foreign Policy,* ed. Seweryn Bialer (Boulder: Westview Press, 1981), p. 14.

13. For a discussion of the patrimonial system of first secretaries at different levels and Moscow's attempt to deal with it, see James Critchlow, *Nationalism in Uzbekistan: A Soviet Republic's Road to Sovereignty* (Boulder: Westview Press, 1991), pp. 17–54.

14. I am indebted to Martha Brill Olcott for pointing out to me Kunaev's special role in this during a seminar at Harvard University.

15. According to Kazakhstan's State Committee for Statistics, the percentage of Russians in the republic's population declined from 37 to 36.4 percent, but this appears to be attributable largely to the higher birthrates of the Kazakhs together with in-migration of Kazakhs from Russia and Mongolia. ITAR-TASS, 23 June 1993, cited in *RFE/RL Daily Report.*

16. Jeremy Azrael, "The 'Nationality Problem' in the USSR: Domestic Pressures and Foreign Policy Constraints," in Bialer, ed., *Domestic Context of Soviet Foreign Policy,* p. 149.

12

War in Abkhazia

The Regional Significance of the Georgian-Abkhazian Conflict

Gueorgui Otyrba

The problems of ethnicity, national minorities, and national self-determination are critical issues in the Caucasus today. Their activation in recent years can be linked to several factors, among them the compact settlement of minorities in the territories of the present republics of the Caucasus (in Georgia there are three autonomies) and the radicalization of national thinking and mentality. In full measure these issues are promoting the rise of centrifugal tendencies in some republics.

The drive for separatism from the Union of Soviet Socialist Republics was particularly strong in Georgia and Checheno-Ingushetia. Following the disintegration of the USSR, Georgia became a nation in its own right, and through a rather peaceable partition, Chechnia and Ingushetia became republics of Russia. But if the Chechens and the Ingush have never been in conflict, Georgia threatens to change that. Indeed Georgian nationalism, in part in reaction to Abkhazia's drive for autonomy, has revived other regional ethnic minorities' fears of state domination and repression.

In Georgia one can find examples of all the major causes of ethnic strife in the Caucasus: the legacy of the national-territorial division of the USSR, the problem of the right of nations to self-determination, the tension between federalism and unitarianism, and the frustrations of peoples subjected to repression. The ethnic conflicts in Georgia and Abkhazia exert a direct influence on the situation in the Caucasus and in Russia.

The Georgian-Abkhazian conflict is not well known in the West. Abkhazia's position, for that matter, has been subsumed by Georgia's greater eminence as a new nation and through its more familiar history. One need only read about the Georgian point of view on the ethnic problems in Georgia and Abkhazia in current reports compiled by the staff of the Conference on Security and Cooperation in Europe.[1]

For a better understanding of the Georgian-Abkhazian confrontation, one needs to look at the history leading up to the crisis. The November 1992 "Report of the Unrepresented Nations and Peoples Organization Mission to Abkhazia, Georgia and the Northern Caucasus," upon which this chapter is based, is an excellent source. The Unrepresented Nations and Peoples Organization is held in respect in Abkhazia, and its position may be regarded as the most objective.[2]

Abkhazian History Under Tsarist Russia and the Soviet Union

Abkhazia is a country with a long and distinctive history. At different times in its past, Abkhazia was independent, dependent on tsarist Russia, part of an independent North Caucasus Confederation, a republic of the Soviet Union, and an autonomous republic of Georgia. Today's conflict in Abkhazia and in other areas of the Caucasus cannot be understood without some sense of the history of the region.

There are many problems in studying the ancient history of Abkhazia, as attested to in the most objective official historical documents written before the 1980s.[3] One could write about the history of Abkhazia only in its close connection with that of Georgia. In fact, any attempt to connect the histories of the Abkhazians and related peoples of the North Caucasus was suppressed by Georgian officials. For years Georgian and Abkhazian historians have been arguing over the ethnic identity of Abkhazia's first settlers. In the 1950s, and again in the 1980s, some Georgian historians actually publicly challenged the view that Abkhazians were indigenous to Abkhazia, suggesting that the Abkhazians had settled in later centuries, displacing the original Georgians.[4]

The first textbook history of Abkhazia that was free from political ideological tenets was published in Abkhazia in 1989.[5] It was suppressed by Tbilisi as well. The Georgians said that it was impossible to study the history of Abkhazia in the educational institutions because there was no history of Abkhazia itself, only the history of Georgia.[6]

The Abkhazian people were among the earliest settlers of the Caucasus and the first to be Christianized in the fourth century. The area came under the domination of the Greeks, Romans, Byzantines, and Turks, and each left aspects of its culture for Abkhazians to absorb. Under Ottoman rule part of Abkhazia was converted to Islam.

When the Russian tsars conquered Ottoman Transcaucasia in the first half of the nineteenth century, Abkhazian and other northwest Caucasian peoples fought for their independence. Their resistance was finally put down in 1864, when the North Caucasus came under imperial Russian domination.

At the time of the Russian conquest, Abkhazia was the southernmost part of the self-contained homeland of three northwest Caucasian peoples: the Abkhaz-Abazians, the Ubykhs around Sochi, and the Circassians in the uplands. The Russian conquest led to great population movements. The Ubykhs who were not killed fled to the Ottoman Empire, as did the Abkhazians. Armenians who survived the genocide of the Turks and Greeks settled in Abkhazia.

Tsarist Russia resettled Abkhazia with Russians and Ukrainians. The rich lands left behind by those who had been killed or had fled Abkhazia were also colonized by Kartvelians (Georgians, Mingrelians, Svans, and Laz). By the end of the nineteenth century, Abkhazians made up only slightly more than 53 percent of the population of Abkhazia. (The population of Abkhazia was reduced from 75,698 to 43,734.)[7]

As a result of these population movements and Russian conquest, Abkhazia lost its related people and ally, the Ubykhs, and was separated from other related peoples in the North Caucasus: Kabardians, Adyges, and Circassians. The geopolitical situation in the northwest Caucasian region radically changed. The only Caucasian people with which the Abkhazians stayed in close contact were the Kartvelians, a Russian ally; the Abkhazians were separated from others by Russian military settlements in the rich lands left behind by the Ubykhs (the modern territory of Krasnodar Krai) and in the North Caucasus. Although the Kartvelians and the Abkhazians were not related by nationality—they speak different languages, and have different traditions—some of their people formed other connections through intermarriage.

After the Russian conquest the Abkhazians and the North Caucasian peoples had no means of continuing active anticolonial resistance, and so they resorted to passive resistance. Their historical connections may have weakened, but the Abkhazians, Adyges, Circassians, and Kabardians never forgot that they were members of one ethnic group who were artificially separated by tsarist Russia and then by Soviet nationality policy. Whenever an opportunity presented itself to take their destiny into their own hands, such as at the time of the Bolshevik Revolution, they revolted. In between, passive resistance persisted.

During the Russian Revolution, Abkhazia formed an independent state within the North Caucasus Confederation—a politically independent confederation of North Caucasian states that in 1918 was being considered for membership by the League of Nations.

In 1918 the Mensheviks took control of Georgia and claimed Abkhazia as part of Georgia. They ruled the region with an iron fist until the Bolsheviks established control in 1921. That period was the first attempt at the "Georgianization" of Abkhazia.

As one historian has noted,

> [The conflicts] between Abkhazians and Georgians in 1918–1921 have become historical lessons on the ethnic incompatibility of both sides, and underlined the weakness of Georgian democracy. Although the Georgian government could legitimately claim it was fighting for the integrity of the new state, its methods—occupation, military governors, and military tribunals—reflected an inability to incorporate ethnic minorities into the political system. Arguably, if economic conditions and the threat of invasion had not been so pressing, and if the government had had a less corrupt and more effective civil administration, these ethnic disputes might have been resolved in a more democratic manner. As it was, the experience of Georgian rule reinforced the minorities' alienation from the new Georgian state and led Georgians to view the universities as a potential "fifth column." This situation has been repeated today.[8]

The establishment of Soviet power led to the creation of the Soviet Socialist Republic of Abkhazia on 31 March 1921. Despite its reduction in status to a "treaty republic" on 16 December 1921, for some ten years the country maintained an independent status within the Soviet system and in practice governed itself autonomously from Tbilisi.

With the rise of Joseph Stalin the situation changed. In February 1931 Abkhazia's status was changed to that of an autonomous republic within Georgia. The oppression of Abkhazians and other North Caucasian peoples during the Stalin era is not forgotten today, and is an important factor in understanding the peoples' determination to defend their self-government or statehood.

The Abkhazians, as is true of other peoples of the North Caucasus, have repeatedly suffered cultural persecution and political oppression at the hands of Russian tsars and Soviet leaders. Under Stalin and Lavrenti Beria this oppression reached new heights.

Deportations were conducted on a large scale. The entire Chechen and Ingush population was deported to Central Asia during the war years. Large numbers of Georgians (primarily Mingrelians) were transferred to Abkhazia. Georgian minorities were pressured to assimilate into the majority Georgian population.

The Georgianization of Abkhazia, from 1933 to 1953, involved the systematic destruction of cultural institutions. When other non-Russians had their alphabets "Cyrillicized," the Abkhazians had theirs "Georgianized," and all native-language schools in Abkhazia and South Ossetia were closed. The teaching of and in Abkhaz was prohibited.

Through deportation and population transfer during the Stalin era, the native population of Abkhazia was reduced drastically. Today, native Abkhazians constitute a mere 18 percent of the population. Georgians, Mingrelians, and other Kartvelians (loosely referred to in Soviet statistics and elsewhere as Georgians) make up 45 percent of the population, and Russians, Armenians, Greeks, and Estonians account for the remainder.

Following Stalin's death, Georgian policy toward the Abkhazians improved gradually, but discrimination continued. Abkhazian schools reopened, Abkhazians reentered local politics—from which they had been excluded—and broadcasting and publishing in Abkhaz were once again allowed.

Under Leonid Brezhnev tensions again increased, and came to a head in 1977–78 in connection with the new Soviet constitutions. Troops were sent in to quell public disturbances. A commission was sent from Moscow, and Georgian authorities were forced to implement some of the Abkhazians' demands. No fundamental change resulted, however, with respect to Abkhazia's autonomy, which remained largely theoretical.

The Struggle for Independence

The situation in the Soviet Union in the late 1980s encouraged both the Georgians and the Abkhazians to revindicate their respective claims to independence, as it did other republics of the former Soviet Union. From 1988 to 1990, the Supreme Soviet of the Georgian Soviet Socialist Republic adopted a number of measures that paved the way for Georgia's exit from the Soviet Union. All state structures established after February 1921, when Georgia officially became a part of the USSR, were declared invalid. Legislation passed after that date was also declared null and void.

Mikhail Gorbachev's perestroika also brought new hope to the Abkhazians and other minorities. Sixty leading Abkhazians transmitted a letter to President Gorbachev in June 1988 detailing grievances and proposing the re-creation of the original Abkhazian Soviet Socialist Republic with special treaty ties to Georgia, so that the region would have true self-government for the benefit of all its inhabitants. The proposal received support from Abkhazians and non-Abkhazians (including Georgians) alike.

In March of the following year thirty thousand people signed a petition at a mass meeting at Lykhnyi demanding the restoration of the sovereign status Abkhazia enjoyed before 1931. Georgia's official reaction to these events was very negative, and a number of measures, including the establishment of a branch of Tbilisi University at Sukhumi, were taken to consolidate Georgian power and influence in Abkhazia. This action led to clashes in Sukhumi and Ochamchira in July 1989.

Nationalist feeling in Georgia rose with the country's own hope for independence from Russian domination, and a state program for the Georgian language, drafted in late 1988, became law in August 1989. The law, which made the teaching of Georgian mandatory in all schools and required Georgian language and literature tests as prerequisites for entry into higher education, raised fears of a renewed attempt at Georgianization, and of a revival of the images of 1918–32 and 1935–53.

In August 1990 the Supreme Soviet of Abkhazia, in the absence of Georgian deputies, declared its sovereignty, but emphasized its willingness to enter into negotiations with the Georgian government for the formation of a federative relationship that would preserve Georgia's territorial integrity. Similar sovereignty declarations were adopted by all autonomous republics of the Soviet Union before the supposed signing of the new union treaty.

In December 1990 the Abkhazian Supreme Soviet elected the historian Vladislav Ardzinba as its chair. Ardzinba enjoyed great respect in the Abkhazian community for his active role in the defense of rights of minorities in the USSR, especially during his tenure as deputy in the union parliament.

A major catalyst of tensions between Abkhazia and Georgia was the 17 March 1991 all-union referendum on Gorbachev's new union treaty. Georgia's parliament prohibited the population in Georgia from taking part in it, but Abkhazia's electorate did take part and voted overwhelmingly to enter the new proposed union of sovereign republics as an autonomous republic. The Georgian government immediately annulled the results of the referendum as a violation of its own earlier decision.

In negotiations with the elected Georgian government of Zviad Gamsakhurdia, Abkhazian leaders proposed a two-chamber parliament for Abkhazia. One chamber would represent the entire electorate on the basis of proportional representation; the other would represent the various national groups constituting Abkhazia. After protracted negotiations, the Abkhazian leaders agreed to a new election law in Abkhazia that allocated a certain number of seats to each ethnic group. Of the sixty-five parliamentary seats, twenty-eight were to be allocated to Abkhazians, twenty-six to Georgians, and eleven to other minorities.

As an additional measure of protection for each of the minority groups, certain decisions were to be made only with a qualified majority of 75 percent. In December 1991 a new parliament (Supreme Soviet) was elected on this basis. Within months the parliament was paralyzed owing to the formation of two blocs: that of the Georgian deputies on one side, and that of Abkhazian, Armenian, Greek, Russian, and other minority deputies on the other. Decisions taken by a majority of votes were repeatedly rejected by the Georgian deputies (who formed the minority bloc in the parliament). This disagreement led to a walkout by Georgian deputies, who continued to meet in separate quarters.

During this turmoil, intra-Georgian tensions increased between the once popular Gamsakhurdia and a growing opposition movement. A bloody military coup (December 1991 to January 1992), led by the head of the Georgian National Guard, Tengiz Kitovani, resulted in the flight of Gamsakhurdia (who eventually received political asylum in Chechnia) and the installment of a State Council of Georgia headed by Eduard Shevardnadze. Kitovani was then appointed minister of defense of the State Council.[9]

One of Shevardnadze's first tasks and successes was obtaining international recognition of Georgia, which took place in March 1992. International recognition of Georgia also implied recognition of the borders claimed by that country's government and, therefore, the inclusion of Abkhazia in its territory.

In June 1992 Abkhazia's president sent a draft treaty to the Georgian State Council that would have provided for federative or confederative relations between Abkhazia and Georgia and the maintenance of Georgia's territorial integrity. The draft contained provisions for the guarantee of the rights of all minorities in the territories under Abkhazian and Georgian jurisdiction, and for rejection of the use of military force to resolve differences. The State Council of Georgia did not reply.

In response to Georgia's February 1992 decision to reinstate the 1921 Georgian constitution, in which there was no specific mention of Abkhazia, the Abkhazian rump parliament reinstated, on 23 July, the Abkhazian constitution of 1925, in which the status of the republic from 1921 to 1931 was set down.

Under Article 4 of that constitution, Abkhazia was "united with the Soviet Socialist Republic of Georgia on the basis of a special union treaty" and through that treaty entered into the Transcaucasian Socialist Federative Union Republic "and through the latter into the Union of Soviet Socialist Republics." Article 5 includes the provision that "the Abkhazian SSR reserves the right of free secession both from the Transcaucasian Federation and from the USSR." The Georgian parliament immediately annulled the Abkhazian decision.

On 12 August 1992 the Abkhazian Supreme Soviet again sent an appeal to Shevardnadze for negotiations on future federative relations between Abkhazia and Georgia. In the appeal the Abkhazian leadership proposed that discussions should address both the extent of powers and responsibilities of separate Abkhazian and Georgian governments and those of their future joint (that is, federal) bodies. It also proposed discussions about the representative structure of union or federal bodies and the procedures for their formation, including the holding of elections. Consultations between senior leaders of Abkhazia and Georgia took place until the military action started on 14 August.

On that day the Abkhazian parliament also was scheduled to discuss the draft treaty proposed to the Georgian State Council. The immediate cause of armed conflict in Abkhazia was the decision of the Georgian State Council to send units of the National Guard to the Abkhazian capital, Sukhumi. The official reason for sending troops was to put an end to ongoing sabotage and looting, particularly on the railway line, and to search for, and free, Georgian officials kidnapped by supporters of ousted Georgian president Zviad Gamsakhurdia.

Abkhazian officials maintained that both reasons were pretexts to impose military control over Abkhazia, for neither could be substantiated. They stated that, with few exceptions, sabotage and looting occurred elsewhere in Georgia, outside Abkhazia, and that to their knowledge the hostages were not being kept in Abkhazia.

Moreover, the Abkhazian authorities had offered their support, if necessary, to find and free the hostages. Several days later Defense Minister General Tengiz Kitovani of Georgia explained that the goal of the military operation was to put a stop to the "secessionist" moves of the Abkhazian parliament.

The Abkhazian parliament protested the incursion of Georgian troops, calling it an "invasion" and "occupation." The parliament also termed it a violation of agreements made in April 1992 with Kitovani and other Georgian officials, by which Georgian troops would be allowed to enter Abkhazia only with the prior permission of the Abkhazian authorities. The Georgian State Council chair, Eduard Shevardnadze, maintained later that it was Georgia's sovereign right to "relocate" troops within its territory. The Abkhazians pointed out that even under the repressive Soviet constitution of 1978, military units could not be brought into the territory of an autonomous republic without the consent of the Supreme Soviet of that republic.

The Abkhazians were ill prepared for the entrance of Georgian troops—a surprising fact, given that tensions had been high for a long time and talk of war was in the streets of Sukhumi. The Abkhazian Civil Guard (also called the Abkhazian National Guard) briefly attempted to oppose the advancing Georgian troops, but with little success. The Georgian troops, with the support of tanks and helicopters, took control of Sukhumi, and declared the Abkhazian Supreme Soviet dissolved.

Four days later fresh Georgian troops arrived, and serious fighting broke out between them and Abkhazian volunteers. Georgian troops, under the command of Jaba Ioseliani (Mkhedrioni military groups) and Gia Karkarashvili (special forces), also took the strategically important city of Gagra on the northwestern coast of Abkhazia, close to the Russian border.

By this time volunteers from the North Caucasus had started arriving in Abkhazia to help Abkhazian units. Their support came as a result of the 1989 formation of the Confederation of North Caucasus Peoples, largely at the initiative of the Abkhazians.

This Confederation of North Caucasus Peoples, uniting community organizations of all the peoples of the North Caucasus, has as its main decision-making body an elected parliament modeled after the European Parliament. Its object is to promote cultural and economic exchanges and cooperation, to mediate territorial and other disputes among its members, and to help any of its member peoples defend themselves against outside attack. It was born out of a realization that, as history has taught the peoples of the North Caucasus, unity among them is the only hope they have to withstand the inevitable attempts to suppress their desire for national and cultural self-realization.

The Abkhazian leadership left Sukhumi for the coastal city of Gudauta, about forty-five kilometers northwest of the capital. There the leaders established the temporary seat of their government. Thousands of Abkhazians, Armenians, Russians, and other non-Georgians also fled Sukhumi. In less than three months of heavy fighting, tens of thousands of civilians of all ethnic groups, including large numbers of Georgians, had fled Abkhazia. Some estimate that half the population of Abkhazia was displaced. Loss of life on both sides of the conflict was considerable, particularly among civilians.

On 21 August Shevardnadze denied all responsibility for the military action in Abkhazia. Then an unsuccessful attack was staged by Georgian troops on Gudauta. Three days later, on 24 August, Shevardnadze threatened the Abkhazians with full-scale war if they continued their struggle. On the same day, the new commander of Georgian troops in Sukhumi, Gia Karkarashvili, warned the Abkhazians in a televised address that they literally faced the possibility of extinction if they persisted.

On 3 September, a cease-fire agreement was negotiated between Russian

President Boris Yeltsin and Shevardnadze in Moscow. The agreement was also signed by President Ardzinba and by the leaders of the North Caucasian republics. (Ardzinba has consistently stated that he was pressured into signing the agreement, and Shevardnadze has confirmed this fact.)

The principal aspects of the agreement were the reaffirmation of the territorial integrity of Georgia, the implementation of a cease-fire on 5 September, the disarming and withdrawal of all illegal armed forces active in Abkhazia, and the reduction of Georgian armed forces to a number sufficient to prevent sabotage of railways and other important installations. The agreement also provided for the resumption in Sukhumi of government functions by legitimate authorities of Abkhazia by 15 September 1992, and called on the United Nations and the Conference on Security and Cooperation in Europe (CSCE) to support the principles of the agreement.

The cease-fire agreement was never fully implemented. According to the Georgian authorities, including Shevardnadze, the Abkhazians never demonstrated their willingness to implement it, and attacked positions vacated by Georgian troops. Abkhazian leaders, including Ardzinba, on the other hand, say the Georgians did not withdraw troops as agreed and consistently violated the cease-fire. They believe a precondition for any agreement is the withdrawal of all Georgian troops from Abkhazia.

On 3 October, Abkhazian units took Gagra after three days of heavy fighting. They also liberated other areas in northwest Abkhazia near the border with Russia. The Georgians say they did so in violation of the 3 September cease-fire agreement.

On 29 October, Minister Kitovani clarified the Georgian State Council's position that Georgia must be a unitary state in which there was no place for any type of autonomous area.

In a departure from his earlier position, Shevardnadze was reported by Russian television, on 3 December, as stating before parliament that a peaceful solution to the conflict in Abkhazia was no longer possible. He was reported to have said that only military means could solve the issue and that this would have to happen soon.

Georgia as an Initiator of the National Movements in the Caucasus

The Georgians and the Abkhazians give different explanations for the rising tide of national conflicts in Georgia and Abkhazia since 1988. The arguments from the Georgian side follow this line: The center is guilty of arousing passions in ethnic conflicts. Many years ago the center established the autonomous republics, rewarding Abkhazian and Ossetian revolutionaries because of their help in the annexation of Georgia. With the assistance of Georgian Communists, the center was instrumental in installing Armenians and Azerbaijanis in Georgia as a means of realization of a "divide and rule" policy. Now it is necessary to abolish the autonomies and put into practice a policy of increasing the percentage of Georgians among the nationalities inhabiting Georgia.

The representatives of the Abkhazians, Ossetians, and other non-Georgian national minorities have an opinion of their own, that is, that the principal cause of ethnic conflicts is connected with the policy of official and "nonformal" structures in Georgia since 1988. Abkhazian, Ossetian, and other non-Georgian national movements emerged in response to the slogans of various Georgian parties about expelling of Armenians and Azerbaijanis from Georgia, and abolishing all the autonomous republics. Soon each side could find reasons for ethnic conflicts in Georgia. The national Georgian bodies began to evict Lezgian families from Kahetia in 1989 after the events in Marneuli, Bolnisi, and Dmanisi. In 1989 many Armenians moved from Georgia to Armenia, and in 1990 a limited group of Meskhetian Turks were forced to leave their homes. With the conflict that broke out in South Ossetia in 1990 (through Zviad Gamsakhurdia's fault, as the present Georgian government claims), and the beginning of the war in Abkhazia in August 1992, it became clear that ethnic conflicts were indispensable elements of Georgian official policy. The ethnic conflict in Abkhazia would give Tbilisi an opportunity to consolidate the Georgian nation while sparing Shevardnadze the risk of confrontation with Georgian subethnoses and armed groups. The Georgians were aiming to "forget all offenses and to defend their native land together" against a common enemy, the Abkhazians.[10]

But this policy has led to unfortunate results for Georgia. A process of consolidation began among the national minorities of the Caucasus. Whereas the problems with the Armenians and the Azerbaijanis were settled in negotiations with Armenia and Azerbaijan, the problems with other peoples had yet to be resolved. The republics of Transcaucasia were at war with one another and had no time to discuss the problems of their peoples in Georgia. As for the Abkhazians, they have had no opportunity to be involved in negotiations with Tbilisi. The Georgians apparently did not want to negotiate with the Abkhazian government and reach a peaceful settlement of the "Abkhazian problem." Abkhazia was forced to look for an ally.

The conflict between Georgia and Abkhazia in July 1989 led to the convening of the Assembly of Mountain Peoples of the Caucasus (AMPC). The AMPC had as its object a peaceful settlement of interethnic conflicts in the Caucasus at that time, when the USSR with its republics was still intact.

Significantly, at the first stage the leaders of all national movements who were members of the AMPC took an active part in supporting Russia's leadership. But the hesitation of the Russian government as to its own future in the disintegration of the USSR impelled the AMPC on a course of self-determination. That course led to the foundation of the Confederation of Mountain Peoples of the Caucasus (CMPC) and gradual expansion of its sphere of influence to the nonmountain peoples, which led in October 1992 to the declaration of the Confederation of Peoples of the Caucasus.[11]

Another, and not least important, factor promoting the formation of the CMPC in November 1991 was the so-called Chechen revolution, when Moscow missed an opportunity to take control of the Chechen government after the overthrow of D. Zavgaev. But even after the foundation of the pseudo-state structure of the CMPC, most national leaders of the North Caucasus continued to orient themselves toward Russia.

Eventually, some provocative statements of the Russian leadership about the situation in South Ossetia in June 1992 led to dissidence in the CMPC, dividing it into two camps: a moderate one, standing for cooperation with Russia, and a radical one, supporting Chechnia's anti-imperial position.

The Confederation of Mountain Peoples of the Caucasus

The history and destiny of Abkhazia are closely connected with those of all the peoples of the North Caucasus. Today they share a common history of suffering and oppression, of deportations and cultural destruction, and of fighting powerful enemies. They also share a determination to protect themselves against a repetition of history. They have seized the opportunity created by the disintegration of the Soviet Union and by Russia's and Georgia's relative weakness, to assert their rights and bring about a situation that can provide better guarantees for their survival in the future.

The North Caucasus is of strategic importance to Russia. It is the gateway to the entire Caucasus, a region in which Russia wants to maintain its sphere of influence. Russia's military presence in the Caucasus (as evidenced, for example, by the visit of Pavel Grachev, Russia's minister of defense, to Abkhazia and Adzharia in March 1992) is still considerable, and the country has an interest in preserving a dominant position on the Black Sea.

Russia has traditionally followed a divide-and-rule policy in the North Caucasus, playing one people against the other. Today it appears that the policy is being revived in a significant way to prevent the various peoples of the region from forming a united front against Russia. Russia may have lost its best chance when it failed to recognize the CMPC in 1989. The

CMPC is not a confederation of states or governments, but a confederation of peoples represented by local community rather than government leaders. Its objective is to unite the North Caucasian peoples, promote cultural cooperation, and provide an avenue for the peoples to help one another in case any one of them is under attack.

The president of the CMPC, Musa Shanibov, says the peoples of the North Caucasus are all too well aware of the fact that they are too small to defend themselves individually. Their only chance for survival in the long run, therefore, is to help and defend one another. Abkhazia is an important case in testing this principle. If the Abkhazians, with the help of volunteers from the North Caucasus, can show that an attack on such a people cannot take place without serious consequences for the aggressor, future attacks against any of the CMPC's members will be discouraged.

The governments of various North Caucasian republics so far have not taken part in the Abkhazian conflict. Even the government of Chechnia has remained neutral, despite the fact that a large number of volunteers fighting alongside the Abkhazians and other peoples of Abkhazia are Chechens. After the disintegration of the Soviet Union, Russian-Georgian relations became a solid factor of President Dzhokar Dudaev's stability.

His government wishes to maintain good relations with both sides. Chechnia certainly has an interest in maintaining good relations with its neighbor, Georgia; however, the people and government of Chechnia morally support the right of all North Caucasian peoples to self-determination and will not abandon the Abkhazian people at this time. If volunteers from Chechnia want to fight alongside their brethren in Abkhazia, the government will respect their choice.

President Dudaev's principal preoccupation is to strengthen his republic's independent position in regard to Russia. The republic has vast mineral and other natural resources (oil, gold, uranium, etc.), and hopes to establish economic links with the outside world, thereby discouraging Russian military intervention. Chechnia, in fact, is the only region of the former Soviet Union where there are no Russian troops or military installations. They were forced to withdraw. Subsequent Russian troop movements on two occasions nearly provoked conflict, only to be withdrawn again after a threat of war from Chechnia. Even the power crisis in Chechnia in April 1993 did not lead to the republic's withdrawal from the CMPC.

Throughout the North Caucasus and in Georgia, the prevailing feeling is that Russia is promoting or taking advantage of divisions and conflicts among the peoples of the region. In the Ossetian-Ingush conflict, for example, Russian involvement on Ossetia's side was barely distinguishable, though the official Russian government's position was that Russian troops were involved to separate the two fighting sides. It is a widespread belief in the region that Russia promoted or used the dispute between North Ossetia (traditionally an ally of Russia) and Ingushetia (a small republic that until recently was part of the Chechen-Ingush Republic) to reintroduce its army into Ingushetia. The object would be to prepare a future advance into Chechnia—a symbol of a new resistance to Russian hegemony.

In keeping with this view of Russian policy, each side in most disputes in the region, including the Abkhazians and the Georgians, sees Russia as a taciturn ally of the other side. The Abkhazians, for example, point out the Russian-provided military equipment that Georgia is using against them and the use of Russian technicians for operating almost all the sophisticated military equipment, including tanks, helicopters, and artillery; the Georgians, in their turn, point out the Russian political bias in favor of Abkhazia and the alleged use of Russian air support in battle.

In fact, there are quite a few potential conflicts among the peoples of the North Caucasus. Many of them are the result of arbitrary or intentionally divisive border demarcations between various republics and administrative units dictated by Moscow under Stalin and other Soviet leaders who followed his lead. The leaders of the CMPC say they are trying to serve as a go-between to settle such disputes peacefully through mediation and other methods. They believe that their efforts are being hampered by Russia. Russia says it is trying to play a peacekeeping role in a volatile region where ethnic rivalries are bound to erupt into violence. Whatever Russia's intentions may be, its involvement in the region is seen as most unhelpful by virtually all the people concerned. In any case, with regard to the bloody conflict between North Ossetia and Ingushetia, the North Caucasian peoples were under the strong impression that Russian involvement was an important factor in the escalation of the conflict and in the disproportionately high number of casualties suffered, particularly among civilians.

Violations of Human Rights

Allegations of human rights violations by all sides in the Caucasian conflict, especially atrocities committed by the armed forces, have been numerous. Allegations of cultural genocide in Abkhazia are particularly poignant. When the Georgian troops under the general command of Defense Minister Tengiz Kitovani first entered Sukhumi on 14 August 1992, Georgian soldiers attacked non-Georgian civilians, robbing and beating them, killing many, and looting houses and flats. Such was the case in all parts of the Abkhazian territory occupied by Georgian troops. Reports of assaults on Abkhazian, Armenian, Russian, and other non-Georgian minority group civilians, including killing, torture, looting, and the destruction of property, still persist.

It is important to remember that the traditions of North Caucasian peoples, Abkhazians included, are sometimes cruel, and that conflicts are fed by vendettas and the need to exact revenge.

Medical authorities in Gudauta (the Abkhazian center of resistance) report that virtually all men who come through the Gudauta hospital after having been held prisoner by Georgian authorities appear to have been severely tortured. In substantiation of what appeared to be more than mere isolated instances of extreme atrocities, medical authorities reported the case of an Abkhazian woman brought in for autopsy who had been shot both down her throat and up her vagina. They also reported the case of a man brought in for autopsy (after a large sum of money was demanded by Georgians for his body) whose genitals had been cut off and stuffed into his mouth. Atrocities against members of other non-Georgian ethnic groups have also been reported.

Examples of extreme brutalities are important for understanding who is fighting Abkhazians. Such cruel acts are typical of Caucasian criminal customs. And it is no wonder, as most individuals making up the Georgian troops, such as the Mkhedrioni detachments headed by Jaba Ioseliani, are criminals like their chief. Nor should it come as a surprise that when one of the Abkhazian towns, Gagra, was occupied by Georgian troops, all local criminals and drug addicts were set free to go anywhere they wanted. In one way, the activities of Georgian soldiers may be partly attributed to what Georgian authorities admitted, even maintained, was a lack of control and discipline in the armed forces. A Georgian commanding officer taken prisoner by Abkhazian forces in Gagra confirmed reports that Georgian troops had indeed committed atrocities there.

President Shevardnadze himself agreed that there was no regular army in Georgia, and Deputy Prime Minister Aleksandr Kavsadze, chair of the Georgian State Committee for Human Rights and National Relations, admitted that soldiers had behaved like vandals and had been in the habit of looting, saying they were "out of control."

The "out of control" explanation is not satisfactory, however, because evidence points to authorization or encouragement by Georgian officials for attacks on Abkhazian and other non-Georgian civilians. Georgian soldiers who are reported to have entered Abkhazian homes and to have beaten, raped, or otherwise terrorized the inhabitants, and to have looted or destroyed their property, are repeatedly said to have had lists of names and addresses of Abkhazians to treat in this manner.

The assaults, therefore, do not appear to be made at random. Georgian service personnel and police are reported to have asked people in the streets, particularly in bread lines, to show their identity papers. When an Abkhazian is discovered, he or she is subject to serious abuse. One of the results of this practice is that fewer Abkhazian residents in Sukhumi, for example, ever dare to leave their homes.

Regarding the characteristics given by Georgian military authorities to the behavior of their troops during and after battle, Kitovani is reported to have told his troops that according to the law of war, soldiers have the right to loot for three days. But their right is already, at the time of this writing, in its ninth month.

The Geneva Convention forbids the use of cluster bombs, yet Abkhazian medical personnel in Gudauta report having treated a number of cluster bomb victims brought in from battle areas. Cluster bombs, extensively used during the month of August 1992 by Georgian forces, continue to be employed.

Another extensively used weapon is the "Grad" (Hail) artillery system, which delivers a large number of shells in a chessboardlike pattern, causing a heavy loss of service personnel—and civilians when used on civilian targets. Moreover, the commander in chief of Georgian troops in Abkhazia, General Gia Karkarashvili, warned in his televised formal address to the Abkhazian and Georgian people in Sukhumi on 24 August that "no prisoners of war will be taken" by the Georgian troops, that he was prepared to sacrifice a hundred thousand Georgian lives to destroy ninety-seven thousand Abkhazians (the official figure for the total Abkhazian population in Abkhazia) and that "the Abkhazian nation will be left without descendants."[12]

In contrast to such evidence, it appears that two months after Georgian troops had been brought into Gagra and while that area was still under Georgian control (for about two weeks), Georgian troops stationed in South Ossetia as a peaceful military unit were flown in to Gagra. The commander of those troops, who was taken prisoner by the Abkhazians, claimed that they were sent by Georgian authorities in Tbilisi to restore order and protect the local civilian population from ongoing rampages by the troops already stationed there.

It is also worth noting that in contrast to many reports of Georgian civilians cooperating with Georgian military authorities in some of the acts against Abkhazian civilians and members of other minority groups, there are numerous accounts of local Georgians helping Abkhazians and other persons in danger to escape, sometimes at great risk to themselves.

Nevertheless, the destruction of Abkhazian cultural centers in Sukhumi continues. Victims thus far have been the Abkhazia State University, the offices of several Abkhazian cultural journals, an Abkhazian language and printing house, an Abkhazian secondary school, the Abkhazian Institute of Language, Literature, and History, the Abkhazian National Museum, and the Abkhazian National Archives.

The Abkhazians in Gudauta and elsewhere believe that the Georgian government is engaged in a systematic attempt to destroy Abkhazia as a nation and the Abkhazians as a people. They point to the methodical attacks on and killing of Abkhazian civilians, and the destruction and looting of Abkhazian homes. They also point out General Karkarashvili's television statement and the destruction by Georgians of the principal Abkhazian institutions of cultural and historical significance in Sukhumi. They see all this as a continuation of an ongoing Georgian government policy that follows in the steps of the now-exiled Georgian president Zviad Gamsakhurdia, who apparently advocated in his speeches a need to eliminate the Abkhazian intelligentsia along with other extreme and oppressive policies.

Regarding human rights violations by Abkhazians and allied forces, it can be acknowledged that some human rights violations have occurred against Georgian civilians. Those acts, however, do not appear to be systematic, and they have never reached anything like the scale or gross nature of those committed by the Georgian military.

Abkhazian authorities have been taking steps to prosecute and punish Abkhazian perpetrators of human rights violations. Georgian prisoners of war have been treated well by Abkhazian authorities. They reported they were relaxed, shared the same rations with Abkhazian service personnel, and appeared to be on relatively good terms with their captors.

Not a single delegation from neutral powers was able to find any evidence of two major allegations put forward against the Abkhazian side: a story of hundreds of Georgians being driven into a stadium and killed there, and another to the effect that Abkhazian soldiers had gone to a hospital and killed doctors and patients. What had really taken place was the burning of many houses of the Georgians who fled the area before the Abkhazian advance.[13]

Political Positions

Though there has been no declaration of war by either side, the current conflict in the Caucasus is a war nevertheless, among the citizens of Russia, Chechnia, Abkhazia, and Georgia. Specialists continue talking about "the positions" of each side in the conflict, between Abkhazia and its allies and Georgia, in which the position of Russia and other states is an important factor.

The position of Georgian leaders, including President Eduard Shevardnadze, has been stated to the world's opinion in clear terms: Georgia is a unitary state. Its independence and its borders have been recognized by the international community, including the United Nations. Its territorial integrity must be protected. Abkhazian political leaders, President Vladislav Ardzinba in particular, have created the present crisis. Georgia cannot let Abkhazia secede and is therefore acting entirely within its rights under international law in putting down the Abkhazian separatist movement. Georgian leaders had done much to meet the demands of Abkhazians, but the Abkhazian leadership was being unreasonable and could not be trusted. They explained the need for sending troops to protect the railway and other installations from looting.

Shevardnadze is not pleased with the role played by Russia, which he sees as encouraging Abkhazians in the conflict and assisting them. He said he regretted having involved Russia in the cease-fire negotiations of 3 September. It was clear for Shevardnadze that the only basis for a cease-fire, as a preliminary step toward a political solution, was the September cease-fire agreement, which Ardzinba had also signed. He said this also meant a return to the military situation that existed on 3 September: the return of Gagra and other areas taken by Abkhazian forces after that date to Georgian forces.

With respect to a third-party involvement, Shevardnadze expressed support for "an active and effective mediation," but not for other forms of third-party interests or involvement. The UN could have a role to play in affirming and promoting the implementation of the 3 September agreement.

Such is the position of Georgia.

The Abkhazian point of view is contained in a number of statements issued by the Supreme Soviet of Abkhazia. The basic issue for which the Abkhazians, together with other minority communities in Abkhazia, are struggling is a sufficient degree of self-government to safeguard the preservation and development of Abkhazian culture and national identity with those of the other minority nationalities (in particular Armenian, Greek, Russian, and Estonian), and to implement social and economic policies suited to the specific conditions of Abkhazia.

These demands must be seen in the context of the region's history and the repeated attempts by outside powers (primarily Russia and Georgia) to destroy the distinctive cultural, ethnic, and political identity of the peoples of the North Caucasus. Emphasis is put by the political leaders on the need for guarantees of a settlement to be reached so that the people can live without fear of persecution.

Abkhazian leaders believe that a political solution must be sought in a confederative or federative structure, wherein Abkhazia's self-governing statehood is recognized and relations between it and Georgia are laid down in a treaty to be signed between the two states. That, in their view, would safeguard the territorial integrity of Georgia and meet the basic needs of the peoples of Abkhazia, including the Georgian (and Mingrelian) populations.

President Ardzinba has emphasized the multinational character of Abkhazia and the need to protect the rights of all minorities in the territory of Abkhazia. Abkhazians throughout the world, and particularly those in Turkey who were forced to leave their country, should be allowed to return if they wish to do so.[14]

Ardzinba and other leaders believe that the longer the conflict lasts, the more suffering and destruction it will cause, and that the more offensive the Georgian anti-Abkhazian propaganda is, the more difficult it will be to find a mutually acceptable solution. It will become ever more difficult to negotiate in good faith with a counterpart that has declared and shown the intent to destroy the Abkhazians as a nation. Nevertheless, at the present time Abkhazian leaders remain prepared to enter into negotiations with Georgian leaders on the issue.

A condition for meaningful negotiations to take place, according to the Abkhazian side, is the withdrawal of Georgian forces from Abkhazian soil. A withdrawal of troops is now necessary if only to demonstrate Georgia's goodwill before negotiations can start.

The attempts made by a number of missions representing the UN, CSCE, and others to organize peaceful talks between Abkhazia and Georgia have proved unsuccessful. Neither the Abkhazians nor the Georgians were satisfied with the work done by these missions.

The Abkhazians expressed regret that those missions spent very little time in Abkhazia listening to Abkhazian and other minority witnesses and political leaders, as compared with the time they spent listening to the Georgian point of view in Georgia or in occupied parts of Abkhazia. The Abkhazian leaders also felt offended that neither the CSCE nor the UN had taken the trouble to send the Abkhazian government copies of its reports, whereas such reports were duly dispatched to the Georgian authorities.

Georgian officials felt that the missions were poorly accomplished and the reports did not lead to any action.

In fact, the nature of the UN report, attached as an annex to UN Document S/24633 of 8 October 1992, has added fuel to the widespread feeling in Abkhazia and the North Caucasus that the United Nations and other intergovernmental organizations serve the interests of the governments seated in those organizations and cannot be counted on to protect the rights of peoples oppressed by them.

Resolution of the Abkhazian-Georgian conflict, it seems, will have to be worked out by the players themselves, including Russia. Georgia, however, holds the key.

In assessing the direction of the conflict, it is necessary to take into account Georgia's intent. Georgia's military intervention in Abkhazia afforded Shevardnadze time to stabilize his position in Tbilisi and Mingrelia, as a means to put an end to confrontation among Georgian subethnoses and armed groups. But the failure of the "victorious advancement" of the Georgian troops in Abkhazian territory, the steady military assistance rendered by the peoples of the North Caucasus to Abkhazia, and the tenacity of the Abkhazians themselves, after a period of nine months of war, have made Shevardnadze's position tenuous. Meanwhile Georgia's economy has grown weaker. Russia is losing its prestige in the North Caucasus and is gaining nothing in Transcaucasia. Shevardnadze can now lose his Russian trump card: the Russian army in Transcaucasia is no longer a guarantor of stability. Shevardnadze will have to rethink Georgian policy if he hopes to survive likely political repercussions.

There is also a need for a clear and open policy on the part of the Russian Federation in this region. Though a third party, Russia has historical influence in the Caucasus, and its opinions are sure to carry great weight. It remains for Russia, however, to prove its value in helping to resolve regional differences through trust and reassurance, particularly with the Abkhazians and the peoples of the North Caucasus.

As for the applications for membership in the Council of Europe and other international organizations by the governments of the region, they should be assessed in the light of each government's respect for the rights of its people and those of minority nations.

Other Participants

"If there was no war in Abkhazia, it would break out elsewhere in the Caucasus." Russia's inability to act as a viable third party in the Abkhazian-Georgian conflict has been forcing some Russian leaders to come to similar conclusions. With Russia trying to hold ground in the Caucasus, the most active participants in the Caucasian events currently, besides Georgia, the Confederation of Peoples of the Caucasus (CPC), Abkhazia, and Chechnia, are the Ukrainian Cossacks and the leaders of other North Caucasian republics, North Ossetia in particular.

The Russia-Georgia tandem, as was the case at the end of the nineteenth century, is threatening to lead once again to a new, protracted, and bloody war. Russia's refusal to allocate financial resources to Tbilisi, and Moscow's anxiety over the unceasing attacks of the Georgian guard on Russian military units have resulted in the appearance of a new Georgian ally, Ukraine. Shevardnadze has attempted to bring into play the contradictions between Moscow and Kiev: indeed, his meeting and negotiations with Leonid Kravchuk, Ukraine's head of state, were completed by the signing of a number of agreements. As many as eight hundred mercenaries are already participating in the war on Georgia's side in Sukhumi,[15] funds have been promised, fuel for military aircraft is being supplied, and so on. Moscow's growing dissatisfaction with this development is underscored by the firmer tone of statements and appeals to the Georgian leadership on the part of the military and the Ministry of Foreign Affairs.

The CPC has taken a number of steps toward cooperation at the negotiations with the Cossacks' representatives. In early 1993 a meeting of the CPC and the Cossacks' Union of the South of Russia (CUSR) took place in Abkhazia. It was decided that after the meeting there was to be a roundtable of the CPC and the Cossacks' union, with an agreement on different issues ensuing. On 28 April in Stavropol, the CPC and the CUSR agreed to cooperate in defending rights and freedoms in the region, eliminating the use of force in solving territorial problems, and respecting the right of peoples to self-determination, without raising any territorial claims on each other. In contrast to agreements on an intergovernmental level, such as those between Georgia and Ukraine, an alliance of this type is not binding, hence unenforceable should conflict arise. Both parties were bold enough to dissociate themselves from the federal power, however, though the Cossacks have since gained Yeltsin's official support. The CPC has not been acknowledged so far. But a loss of trust in Moscow as a neutral arbiter of Caucasian affairs has forced the CPC, whose zone of influence extends beyond Russia's state borders, to come to the fore and stand up for the rights of minorities, without waiting for state structures to emerge. The CPC president, Shanibov, has declared that for the confederation Abkhazia is not an external but an internal problem.

The chair of the CPC parliament, Chechnia's representative Y. Soslambekov, who may soon take up a high-ranking post in the Chechen state structure, has said that the CPC does not need to depend on Moscow for an acknowledgment of Chechnia's independence. In Chechnia itself there has been a political split between the opposition and President Dudaev. Should Dudaev's position or that of his opponents weaken, however, there is not much threat to the existence of the CPC, as it is not a union of states but a union of nations. To avoid bloodshed, the "Afghantsy" and "Abkhaz" detachments of the CPC have taken upon themselves the task of separating opposing parties.

A crisis has sprung up in North Ossetia as well. The Ossetian-Ingush conflict is the first armed collision in Russian territory since the breakup of the USSR. Whereas North Ossetia has always been and remains Russia's ally in the North Caucasus, Ingushetia, having ruled out a joint path with Chechnia toward independence, has found itself in an uncompromising situation. Neither the CPC nor Chechnia nor Russia succeeded in averting bloodshed. Russian troops brought into the frontier districts of North Ossetia and Ingushetia once again became a "thin line" for the defense of civilians, but not a force large enough to guarantee a settlement. The CPC has offered its services for pacifying Ingushetia and North Ossetia in their conflict; it appears, however, that the CPC does not itself have enough military strength to maintain order, and is capable only of carrying on negotiations and organizing meetings with the representatives of the two parties.

In early April a session of the Supreme Soviet of North Ossetia acknowledged the Republic of South Ossetia. Some officials in North Ossetia, in response to a statement by the Russian Ministry of Foreign Affairs to the effect that the abovementioned acknowledgment is invalid, noted that acknowledging the Republic of South Ossetia did not mean an acknowledgment of its independence, but rather an acknowledgment of the constitutional system in its territory. Nevertheless, there is no doubt that North Ossetia will render military assistance to South Ossetia in case military action with Georgia resumes. If the question of a federal state system in Georgia is not positively solved, there is a possibility of a fresh military action in South Ossetia at the beginning of summer, an action in which the CPC detachments will take part in fighting the Georgian army.

For the first time during the nine months of the war, on 22 April 1993, there was a call by the Supreme Soviet of Georgia to enter into peaceful talks with the "Abkhazian separatists." Shevardnadze assured that this call was not "one of the regular tricks or an attempt at gaining time but a serious intention to sit down at the negotiating table and to peacefully settle all the conflicting issues." The Abkhazian side stated in response that it was ready to get such a negotiations process started, but as a first step it was necessary to discuss the mechanism of Georgian troop withdrawal from Abkhazia. In response to this demand, which has been voiced since the first days of the war, the Georgian leadership declared part of Abkhazia "an occupied territory" —occupied by no one else but Russia—and formed the Defense Council of Abkhazia (defending it from Abkhazians?). The fighting resumed.

It appears that both Georgia and Abkhazia do not foresee a real possibility of a peaceful settlement to the war. A number of important political considerations, ambitions, wounded feelings of national pride, and of course international law guarantee a long life to the Abkhazian conflict.

While Russia is busy trying to solve the issues of federalism and the Chechen problem, intergovernmental relations in the North Caucasus will be solved by means of Russia's troops. As for the war in Abkhazia, as has already been stated, it is an internal issue within the CPC. Its outcome will tell on the strengthening of positions of the leaders of national movements in the North Caucasus during the republics' reelection campaigns of directing bodies. Russia is striving for support of the existing state structures in the North Caucasus in order to counter the growing influence of the CPC, but will only succeed in aggravating an already complicated situation.

Escalation of the Georgian-Abkhazian Conflict

The war in Abkhazia has been painful for both parties. Georgia counted on its being a blitzkrieg. Now that it is clear that the Abkhazians will not surrender, Georgia has found itself in a very awkward predicament. Even if it manages to carry out a sort of military operation, and gets as far as Adler, the population might flee, but the Abkhazian troops would take to the mountains. And through the mountains they could communicate with their brethren, and then the whole of the North Caucasus would become a battleground, and intensify as shipments of arms and tanks made their way over macadamized roads. Georgia would have to enter a protracted war without any prospect of victory. It would be blocked from all sides, and forced to undergo guerrilla warfare with acts of terrorism and sabotage and a complete paralysis of economic life.

The Abkhazians have the prospect of getting to the Inguri River bordering Georgia, but this war of liberation waged until victory is achieved will probably cause a great loss of life, which the Abkhazians can ill afford, given their small numbers. Following Georgia's assault of 16 March on Sukhumi, the Abkhazians have undertaken a serious attempt to put their armed forces in order, even organizing combat subunits out of detachments of people's volunteer corps. The Georgians have amassed a large but motley army. In Sukhumi, for example, the various military contingents consist of a people's volunteer corps, Kitovani's guard, Ioseliani's Mkhedrioni, Karkarashvili's special combat unit, Akhalaia's military police, a battalion of Afghani soldiers of an obscure subordination, a regiment of internal forces of the Georgian Ministry of the Interior, and, finally, mercenaries. All of them are being forced to submit to a unified command, but self-interests and divided loyalties (according to the various sources of support in Tbilisi) threaten to undermine authority, which could spell defeat.

It is too early to speak of mercenaries in support of Abkhazia. One fights here not for money but for the idea of independence. As the Slavic idea drove partisans to help the Serbs and the Muslim idea drove Turks to help the Bosnians in the Balkan conflict, so too will mercenaries come to Abkhazia's assistance as the war progresses.

But what idea will drive a Russian or Ukrainian to shed blood for the sake of the "territorial integrity of Georgia"? That is why the Georgians need to attract mercenaries: airmen, artillerymen, specialists in communication, antiaircraft defense specialists. Recruitment is under way in Russia, Ukraine, and the Baltic states. The Georgians are also in need of cannon fodder. Of the two thousand men dispatched from Georgia to Abkhazia in April, 60 percent have deserted.

The Georgians needed an easy victory as badly as a mouthful of Georgian wine. Enough toasts had been proposed in both Moscow and Tbilisi, in both the UN and the CSCE. The phrases bandied about in the central press during the first days of the war, to the effect that talking with the Abkhazians and the North Caucasian peoples for Shevardnadze was not the same as talking with the Americans, the French, and the Germans, were not as offensive as they were nonsensical. Georgia, blinded by nationalism, seems incapable of believing that its army, with all its tanks, artillery, and aircraft, has not been able to suppress an armed resistance of the Abkhazian home guard. And now accusations of the Chechens fighting on the Abkhazian side have given way to threats of a mythical, all-out mobilization of the Georgians in response to "Russia's aggression."

Georgia is now in a precarious position. Desertions have thinned the ranks of its national army. In April many mercenaries had their contracts terminated, and Georgia has been unable to retain them because it has not yet paid for the previous terms of service. The prospect of getting 60 billion rubles in cash from Russia to pay for the war effort has not materialized. So Georgia has had to introduce coupons, while pressuring the populace to yield up its hoarded rubles. No doubt problems will arise as more mercenaries, for example, leave their posts for lack of compensation, with the possible exception of Ukrainians, who have probably been paid beforehand by their government. Hence the Georgian military leadership is hurriedly arming the local home guard, to train them and then substitute them for the mercenaries, with weapons withdrawn from the mercenaries.

Of late, word has been spreading of the possibility of a coup in Georgia. Ioseliani's Mkhedrioni detachments, which are faithful to Shevardnadze, are being drawn up to Tbilisi. It appears that Kitovani has come to terms with the Mingrelians and Gamsakhurdia's supporters. The Russian intelligence service has livened up to the extent that Kitovani is suspected—not without grounds—of being in touch with it. There is also gossip to the effect that detachments of Gamsakhurdia's supporters might serve as a kind of peacekeeping force to separate Abkhazian and Georgian troops wherever they oppose each other, the argument being that they did not take part in the original Georgian military expedition to Abkhazia. But it looks as if time has been lost.

Something like the Vance-Owen plan for resolving the Balkan conflict was suggested for Abkhazia at the beginning of 1993. It was even intended to reorganize the Galskii district, populated for the most part by the Mingrelians, into a sort of territory under joint control. But nothing official has been brought forward.

It stands to reason that Georgia will gradually weaken both as a result of internal political problems and the strengthening of the CPC's position. In any case, both Georgia and the republics of the Caucasus are expected to be active internationally. Georgia, in fact, is pinning hopes on U.S. and West European humanitarian aid. Whatever their respective positions might be, they will be equally dependent on Russia's influence.

Untying the Caucasian Knot

Russia's mistakes in its Caucasian policy, if there ever was a policy on a serious level, have led to nothing but warfare. And current attempts by the state bodies of Russia to create a counterpart to the CPC—in the form of diverse North Caucasian roundtables, economic unions, and the like—will only result in postponing resolution of the differences between the leaders of the various national movements of the North Caucasus. After settling its own internal problems, Russia will either have to enter into a dialogue with the CPC or resign itself to the loss of the Caucasus.

There are serious structural changes in store for the CPC. For the time being, only two state formations acting as sovereign republics are participants in this organization of peoples: Abkhazia and Chechnia. A strengthening of the influence of national movements in the republics of the North Caucasus will probably result in a change of leadership, and posts in state bodies will be filled by representatives of the CPC. In that case a confederation of peoples will either grow into a union of states or remain in its present CPC form, but will have a decisive role to play as to the choice of leadership positions of those republics.

Russia underestimated the strength of the CPC. Its position of non-acknowledgment was as gross a miscalculation as its expectancy that democracy would settle in Georgia once Shevardnadze came to power. Georgia did have a chance of joining the CPC once, but it likewise underappreciated that organization. As a result, the Caucasian knot is an intricate web of the positions held by the CPC, Georgia, the republics of the North Caucasus, and Russia—not a single one of which puts forward optimal solutions to the problems. In the event of a peaceful solution of the war in Abkhazia, however, the CPC will have at its disposal not just reservists, but ready mobile detachments, in which case they will be able to make their appearance in the areas of interethnic unrest in the Caucasus earlier than their Russian counterparts.

Even today the CPC is keeping under control all imminent conflicts in a number of North Caucasian republics. Not everything goes smoothly in Kabardino-Balkaria, for example. This somewhat strange amalgamation of two different peoples accomplished by Stalin within one republic, as well as the cases of Karachaevo-Cherkessia and Georgia-Abkhazia, causes the CPC much anxiety over the state of affairs in that republic. As recently as 1991, a congress of the Balkar people formed a national council that took upon itself the task of preparing documents for the declaration of the Balkar Republic. According to that project, Balkaria was to separate itself from Kabardia. Initially, Kabardino-Balkaria's Supreme Soviet agreed with the decision of the First Congress of the Balkar People. Likewise, the First Congress of the Kabardian People agreed with the Balkarians' decision and, in its turn, decided on Kabardia's forming a sovereign republic of its own. The First Congress of the Kabardian People also elected its organs, the National Congress and the Executive Committee, but the separation did not take place. The authorities of the Kabardino-Balkarian Republic managed to organize general elections and got a unified Supreme Soviet and president elected.

At the Second Congress of the Kabardian People, which took place on 24 March in Nal'chik, decisions were to be taken as to the passage of constitutional power on the Kabardian territory into the hands of the National Congress. Questions concerning the frontiers arose, and passions egged on by the leadership of the Kabardino-Balkarian Republic ran high. But no divorce decision was taken. It was then that the Abkhazians and the CPC took an active part in peaceful negotiations between the Kabardians and the Balkarians.

At present the situation in Kabardino-Balkaria remains quiet, though all problems and questions concerning the self-determination of the Kabardians and the Balkarians have not been completely settled. The Kabardians take an active part as volunteers in the fighting in Abkhazia on the CPC's side: The Balkarians, who are members of the CPC, are not actively involved in the Abkhazian conflict, although they claim to be on the side of the "war of liberation of the Abkhazian people." In case the situation deteriorates drastically, and Russia withdraws its support for the present leadership of the republic, it would be reasonable to admit to power the leaders of national movements of the Kabardian and Balkarian peoples, who would then be able to carry on negotiations not only on an interrepublic level, but as full-fledged members of the CPC enjoying equal rights with others.

A similar situation is regretfully hardly possible in Karachaevo-Cherkessia. A strong feeling of mistrust toward Russia is being felt in the republic, and centrifugal forces inside the republic itself are at work. In September 1991 the peoples of Karachaevo-Cherkessia stood up for a unified republic, then later on came a series of declarations constitutionalizing the independence of five republics: Karachai, Cherkessia, Abkhazia (representing peoples of the North Caucasus), Zelenchuksko-Urupskii, and Batal-Pashinskii (the latter two Cossack republics). The complexity of the situation is due to a large number of districts with compact populations representing different ethnoses dispersed all over the republic. The most suitable choice here would be the creation of a unified elected body with each of the peoples in possession of an equal number of mandates so that any decision to be made on even the most complicated matter would have to be taken on the basis of mutual agreement. Time will show whether it will be possible for the peoples of Karachaevo-Cherkessia to realize such a project. What is beyond doubt is the obligatory participation of the CPC in the negotiation process in the republic.

It is to be regretted that nowadays the frame of mind of the mountain peoples of the Caucasus is based on the assumption that in the Caucasus the interests of two imperial powers have come together, namely, those of Russia and Georgia. Whereas Russia has not completely lost its position in the Caucasus, Georgia is under a real threat of inheriting, as a result of the Abkhazian war, a formidable rival—the Caucasus. For Georgia, instead of entertaining the idea of the Abkhazians' military defeat, which is sure to be transformed into a horrible guerrilla warfare, it would be more reasonable to turn to the CPC in search of mediators for settling its disputes with Abkhazia, with an obligatory decision by the Georgians on the introduction of a federal state system in Georgia. Such a way out is not completely unrealistic; on the contrary, it is the only chance for the nation to preserve its interests in the Caucasus, Georgia having changed its attitude toward the CPC from that of an enemy to that of an acknowledged partner. This process of transformation, however, is very painful for Georgia, considering Georgian nationalists, who are not willing to give up the idea of creating a "great unified Georgia" and are indulged in the belief in the international support for the "military power of the Georgian people." But the time of such statements as "We will be taking decisions that will correspond to our national interests" by Shevardnadze regarding Georgia's autonomies is gone forever. Russia as the guarantor of Shevardnadze's stability seems to be changing its position.

Today, without defending Abkhazia or South Ossetia, without securing the stabilization of the situation in the whole of the Caucasus (with due pressure to be exercised on the aggressive forces in Georgia), without starting contacts with the CPC, Russia is actually losing its allies in the region, which in cooperation with Russia is bound to become an important strategic point, with a prospect of exerting its influence and representing Russia's interests. It was for a fairly long time that Russia had been ignoring the aspirations of the peoples of Abkhazia and South Ossetia to be taken under its protection. In the last century Russia used to advance into the Caucasus as a colonial power; now the situation is quite the contrary: in the geopolitical situation that has taken shape of late, the mountain peoples and Abkhazia are seeking Russia's protection of their own free will. That is why, taking into consideration the importance of choice for all external and internal policies, Russia must make its final decision: either completely withdrawing from the Caucasus, with Turkey and Iran taking its place, or moving to meet the mountain peoples, who are now all too willing to stay under its protection and defense. A temporizing position will not win peace in the region.

Very popular now in the North Caucasus is the idea of federalism—irrespective of all possible critical situations. This assertion is proved not only by the unification of national movements (as in the case of the CPC), but also by the support now being rendered, as it was rendered before, by the Caucasian national leaders, including those from Chechnia, to the idea of renovation of the union and Russia. Conceivably, the idea of renovation of the union and Russia can be replaced with the idea of creation of the North Caucasus Confederation with Abkhazia and—as hard as it is to imagine—the south of Russia (the Krasnodar, Stavropol, and Rostov regions) as a confederation of states.

Notes

1. *Implementation of the Helsinki Accords; Human Rights and Democratization in the Newly Independent States of the Former Soviet Union* (Washington, DC: Commission on Security and Cooperation in Europe, 1993), pp. 138–60.

2. Certainly there are many articles about the modern history of Georgia. See, for example, Stephen Jones, "Georgia's Failed Democratic Transition," in *Nations and Politics in the Soviet Successor States,* ed. Ian Bremmer and Ray Taras (Cambridge: Cambridge University Press, 1993), pp. 288–312.

3. See, for example, D. Guliia, *Istoriia Abkhazii* (Tiflis, 1925); A.V. Fadeev, *Kratkie ocherki istorii Abkhazii* (Sukhumi, 1934); S.T. Zvanaba, *Etnograficheskie etiudy* (Sukhumi, 1955); G.A. Dzidzaria, *Vosstanie 1866 goda v Abkhazii* (Sukhumi, 1955); *Ocherki istorii Abkhazskoi ASSR* (Sukhumi, 1960).

4. Extracts from these disputes in the 1950s and 1960s are included in *Mat'iane*

(Tbilisi, 1989), the journal of the Georgian Helsinki Group led by Zviad Gamsakhurdia. See also *Ingorogva P. Georgi Merchule* (Tbilisi, 1954).

5. *Istoriia Abkhazii* (Sukhumi, 1989).
6. *Avangard*, 1 March 1989 (Gagra's town daily).
7. *Ocherki istorii Abkhazskoi ASSR,* p. 219.
8. Jones, "Georgia," p. 291.
9. In February 1992 the Abkhazian government allowed the Georgian National Guard, led by Gia Karkarashvili, to come into Abkhazia with the mission of disarming Gamsakhurdia supporters. Its stay in Abkhazia was accompanied by numerous serious delinquencies. In Gagra, for example, Georgian soldiers and Mkhedrioni murdered two men: an innocent Greek fisherman and a Russian supporter of Gamsakhurdia who was shot in his home. After numerous meetings of the non-Georgian population of Abkhazia and demands of the Abkhazian government, Georgian soldiers left the Abkhazian territory on 17 February 1992, but gave to the Cokal Mkhedrioni detachment a considerable portion of their armaments. This temporary residence of Karkarashvili's soldiers demonstrated that there was a possibility of negotiation between the Georgian government and the Supreme Soviet of Abkhazia.
10. FBIS, *Daily Report: Central Eurasia* (FBIS-SOV–92–212), 2 November 1992. In an interview on Tbilisi Radio Network on 5 April 1993, Shevardnadze said that the Mingrelians "are fighting as Georgians should fight in *the interests of Georgians* and Georgia" (emphasis added) (FBIS-SOV–93–064, 6 April 1992, p. 80).
11. It was the conflicts in Georgia that initiated the formation of the prototype of national military guards by the CMPC.
12. There is a video recording of this ominous speech available. Karkarashvili became the defense minister of Georgia in March 1993.
13. "Report of Unrepresented Nations and Peoples Organization Mission to Abkhazia, Georgia and the Northern Caucasus," November 1992, p. 19.
14. The Abkhaz-Abazians, Cherkess, and Adyges living abroad call themselves Circassians. They have preserved their traditions and language. In Turkey, Jordan, Israel, Saudi Arabia, and other countries that formed part of the Ottoman Empire, substantial compact communities of Circassians have retained their identity. In Jordan they exercise important functions as military officers and businesspersons.
15. After the 14 May 1992 talks between Shevardnadze and Yeltsin, an additional contingent (five hundred soldiers) was dispatched from Ukraine to Sukhumi. Press Center of Abkhazia, Gudauta, 28 May 1992.

Appendix: Project Participants

List of Workshop Attendees, May 28, 1993
Ethnicity and Russian Foreign Policy

  Stephen Blank, U.S. Army War College
  Steve Coffey, Department of State
  Dieter Dettke, Friedrich Ebert Stiftung
  Rosemarie Forsythe, National Security Council
  Paul Goble, Carnegie Endowment for International Peace
  David Goldfrank, Georgetown University
  Steven Grant, U.S. Information Agency
  Edy Kaufman, University of Maryland
  Jutta Klapisch, Friedrich Ebert Stiftung
  Patricia Kolb, M.E. Sharpe, Inc.
  George Liska, School of Advanced International Studies
  Natalia Melnyczuk, U.S. Institute of Peace
  Sergo Mikoyan, Institute of Peace, Moscow
  Susan Nelson, Department of State
  Gueorgui Otyrba, Abkhazia State University
  Vasilii Pospelov, Embassy of Russia
  Algimantas Prazauskas, Institute of Oriental Studies, Moscow
  Kevin Quigley, Pew Charitable Trusts
  Marion Recktenwald, University of Maryland
  Al Richman, U.S. Information Agency
  Eric Rothberg, Central Intelligence Agency
  Blair Ruble, Kennan Institute
  Lee Schwartz, Department of State
  Roman Szporluk, Harvard University
  Darius Szwarcewicz, School of Advanced International Studies
  Vladimir Tismaneanu, University of Maryland
  Astrid Tuminez, Carnegie Corporation
  Michael Turner, University of Maryland
  Adam Wasserman, Department of State
  Mary Yntema, School of Advanced International Studies

June 14, 1993
Ethnicity and Foreign Policies of Western NIS States

Ibrahim Arafat, Cairo University
Stephen Blank, U.S. Army War College
Will Blunt, Boston University
Abraham Brumberg, Chevy Chase, Maryland
Martha Chomiak, National Endowment for the Humanities
Marcus Franda, University of Maryland
Phillip Gillette, Old Dominion University
Paul Goble, Carnegie Endowment for International Peace
David Goldfrank, Georgetown University
Robert Hutchings, Woodrow Wilson Center
Israel Kleiner, Voice of America
Valeri Kuchinsky, Embassy of Ukraine
Laura Libanati, U.S. Institute of Peace
George Liska, School of Advanced International Studies
Sergei Martynov, Embassy of Belarus
Mary McIntosh, U.S. Information Agency
Melissa Meeker, Center for Strategic and International Studies
Natalia Melnyczuk, U.S. Institute of Peace
Gueorgui Otyrba, Abkhazian State University
Vasilii Pospelov, Embassy of Russia
Nikolai Rudensky, Institute for Economy in Transition, Moscow
Sonya Sluzar, Department of State
Amy Smith, Kennan Institute
Angela Stent, Georgetown University
Michael Turner, University of Maryland
Vladimir Volkov, Institute of Slavic and Balkan Studies, Moscow

June 7, 1993
Ethnicity and Foreign Policies of Central Asia and the Caucasus

Ibrahim Arafat, Cairo University
Stephen Blank, U.S. Army War College
Patricia Carley, Helsinki Commission
Kenneth Currie, National Intelligence Council
Toby Davis, Department of State
Adeed Dawisha, George Mason University
Richard Dobson, U.S. Information Agency
Rosemarie Forsythe, National Security Council
Phillip Gillette, Old Dominion University

Steve Grant, U.S. Information Agency
Hrach Gregorian, U.S. Institute of Peace
Alexander Guroff, Center for Strategic and International Studies
Shireen Hunter, Center for Strategic and International Studies
Erjan Kurbanov, Moscow State University
Laura Libanati, U.S. Institute of Peace
George Liska, School of Advanced International Studies
Petr Lunak, School of Advanced International Studies
Dan Matuszewski, IREX
Melissa Meeker, Center for Strategic and International Studies
Sergo Mikoyan, Institute of Peace, Moscow
Jayhun Molla-zade, Embassy of Azerbaijan
Nurbek Omuraliev, Institute of Philosophy, Bishkek
Vasilii Pospelov, Embassy of Russia
Algimantas Prazauskas, Institute of Oriental Studies, Moscow
George Quester, University of Maryland
Al Richman, U.S. Information Agency
Nikolai Rudensky, Institute for Economy in Transition, Moscow
Barri Sanders, University of Maryland
Lee Schwartz, Department of State
Cevdet Seyhan, Voice of America
Nasir Shanseb
Jim Steiner, Department of State
Joan Urban, Catholic University
Oleg Yaroshin, Catholic University
Karmit Zysman, International Azerbaijan Research
    and Development Institute

Index

Abdulatipov, Ramazan, 48
Abkhaz-Abazians (people), 283
Abkhazia
  ethnic identity of, 282
  history of, 282–85
  independence struggle, 285–90
  Russian conquest of, 283
  See also Georgian-Abkhazian conflict
Abkhazian Civil Guard, 288–89
Acculturation, 155
Afghanistan, 217, 231, 237, 258, 276
Akaev, Askar, 218, 227, 271, 279
Aleksandr Nevskii (film), 87
All-Union Law (Soviet Union), 29
Almaaty Declaration, 170
Alphabet reform, 277–78
Ambartsumov, Evgenii, 93
AMPC. *See* Assembly of Mountain Peoples of the Caucasus
Anarchy, 15
Andrejevs, Georgs, 199
Andrusova, Treaty of, 112
Anti-Semitism, 90
Ardzinba, Vladislav, 286, 290, 298, 299
Armenia, 96, 97
Armenians (people), 291

Assembly of Mountain Peoples of the Caucasus (AMPC), 291–92
Assimilation, 152, 155, 247
Association of Ethnic Koreans, 248
Autarky, 40
Avvakum, Father, 83
Azerbaijan, 92, 96
Azerbaijanis (people), 291
Baburin, Sergei, 99n.1
"Back to the Future" (Mearsheimer), 103
Bakatin, Vadim, 99n.13
Baku, 92
Baltic states, 29, 64–65, 93, 97, 246
  military forces in, 74–75
  and national identity, 185–203
  borders, 195
  culture, 191–92
  economics, 189–90
  factors shaping, 189–202
  minorities, 195–201
  natural resources, 190–91
  psychology of, 192–94
  Russian occupation forces, 194
  state security, 201–2
  resistance movements, 193
  Russian minorities in, 67–68, 188–89
  See also Estonia; Latvia; Lithuania

315

Bandera, Stepan, 128*n*.53, 166
Bashkortostan, 35, 42
BAS. *See* Belarusian Association of Servicemen
Belarus, 9, 11, 118, 155, 182, 183
   army of, 136–37, 145
   border disputes, 195
   cultural history of, 133
   environmentalism, 81–82
   ethnic identity, 163–64
   ethnic survival and security in, 159
   foreign policy, 129–48
      and economic ties to Russia, 142–45
      geopolitical and economic background of, 135–45
      mechanisms of, 146–47
      sovereignty as source of, 129–35
      Western orientation of, 13, 133
   historical memory and external orientation, 163–65
   historiography of, 132–34
   labor force of, 143
   minority nationalism in, 172–73
   national icons of, 132
   nationalities and ethnic groups in, 157
   and Poland, 109, 110, 181
   political mobilization in, 141
   Russian military in, 135–42
   Russification of, 152
Belarusian Association of Servicemen (BAS), 137, 139–40, 141, 165
Belarusian Popular Front (BPF), 165
Bennigsen, Alexandre, 273
Beria, Lavrenti, 284
Bich, Pavel, 144
Billington, James, 89

Black Sea fleet, 174
Bolsheviks, 284
Bosnia, 96
BPF. *See* Belarusian Popular Front
Brazauskas, Algirdas, 190–91, 201
Brezhnev, Leonid, 193, 212
Budny, Symon, 133
Bukhara (Uzbekistan), 274, 276
Buraukin, Hienadz', 137–38, 146
Burbulis, Gennadii, 93
Bush, George, 119

Catholicism, 191
   See also Eastern Orthodox Church; Roman Catholic Church; Uniate Church
Central Asia, 209–27
   alphabet reform in, 277–78
   and Asian nations, 219–20, 222, 269
   demographics, 230–61
      birthplace data, 237
      general postwar patterns of, 233–44
      indigenization, 234, 239–44
      and Russification, 238–39
   deported nation status in, 247–50
   disappointments for, 220–23
   ethnic cleansing in, 260, 265*n*.73
   ethnicity in, 211–14, 216–20, 226–27, 236
   ethnoterritorial conflict in, 255–58, 257
   foreign investment in, 222–23
   foreign policy, 214–16, 266–79
      and Asian cooperation, 269
      economic factors, 278–79
      ethnic factors, 273–77
      general context of, 266–72
      with Muslim world, 270

Central Asia *(continued)*
   regional, 268–69
   religious and cultural factors, 277–78
   identity in, 273
   in-migration to, 213, 232, 233–34, 238
   interethnic attitudes, 254
   living standards, 242
   national differences in, 272–73
   nationalism and refugees, 244–47
   nationalization process, 232–33
   out-migration, 235, 243–44, 245–46, 251, 264*n.59*
   population pressure on, 242–43
   and Russia, 226–27
   Russian emigration from, 250–55
   and self-interest, 223–26
   trade, 268, 278
   transborder cognates in, 276–77
   urbanization of, 241
   See also specific countries
Central planning, 40
Chaus, Piotr, 135, 136
Checheno-Ingushetia, 281
Chechen Republic, 25
Chechnia, 35, 38, 54*n.54*, 55*n.57*
   and Georgian-Abkhazian conflict, 293, 300, 302
   revolution, 292
   and Russia, 50
   taxes, 41–42
Chevron Oil, 215, 279
China, 219, 222, 231, 237, 258
Christian Science Monitor (newspaper), 23
Circassians (people), 283, 309*n.14*
CIS. *See* Commonwealth of Independent States

Clinton, William, 75
Cluster bombs, 296
CMPC. *See* Confederation of Mountain People of the Caucasus
Collective security agreement, 130, 138–39, 142, 145
Collectivization, 213
Commonwealth of Independent States (CIS), 95, 123–24, 148, 182, 227
   and Central Asia, 266, 268, 269
   collective security agreement, 130, 138–39, 142, 145
   formation of, 211
   and minority rights, 73–74
   and Moldova, 170
   Russia's role in, 12–13
   and Ukraine, 159, 168
Communist Party, 5–6, 24, 120–21, 152, 190
Confederation for Independent Poland (KPN), 113
Confederation of Mountain People of the Caucasus (CMPC), 292–94
Confederation of North Caucasus People, 289
Confederation of Peoples of the Caucasus (CPC), 300, 301, 303, 305–6, 307
Conference on Security and Cooperation in Europe (CSCE), 70, 74, 193, 195, 215, 271, 290, 299
Coordinating Committee for Sociopolitical Association (Belarus), 142
Cossacks (people), 105, 300
Cossacks' Union of the South of Russia (CUSR), 301
Council of Europe, 70
Council of Heads of Republics, 43

Council of the Subjects of the Federation, 47
CPC. *See* Confederation of Peoples of the Caucasus
Creativity, 82
Crimea, 65, 94, 122, 126, 173–75
Crimean Autonomous Republic, 173
Crimean Tatars, 173–75, 249–50
Crimean War, 173
CSCE. *See* Conference on Security and Cooperation in Europe
"Cult of first secretaries," 274
CUSR. *See* Cossacks' Union of the South of Russia
Czechoslovakia, 193
Czech Republic, 13, 168

Dashkevych, Iaroslav, 121
Decolonization Fund (Estonia), 198
Democracy, 135, 260, 265*n*.74
Discrimination, 67–69, 181
Dmowski, Roman, 106
Dniester Moldovan Republic, 65
Don Cossacks, 90
Dostoevsky, Fyodor, 81
Dudaev, Dzhokar, 293, 301

Eastern Europe, 10
Eastern Orthodox Church, 82
Economic Cooperation Organization, 270
Education, 62, 189, 190, 232
Emergency powers, 37–38, 43
Employment, 62–63
  See also Unemployment
"The End of History" (Fukuyama), 103
Energy, 190–91
Ennaceur, Mohammed, 195–96

Entrepreneurs, 49
Environmentalism, 81–82, 187–88
Estonia, 9–10, 29, 92, 93, 155, 187, 191, 253
  border disputes, 195
  citizenship laws in, 69, 181, 197–198, 204–5*n*.25
  and economics, 189
  foreign policy, 163
  historical memory and external orientation, 161–62, 183
  minorities in, 196–198
  nationalities and ethnic groups in, 158
  perception of Russian threat, 156, 159
  Russian military in, 74–75, 194
  Russian minority in, 58, 180–81
  state security, 202
Ethnic cleansing, 260, 265*n*.73
Ethnic democracy, 260, 265*n*.74
Ethnic homelands, 5
Ethnicity, 3, 4–5, 31, 86
  Abkhazia, 282
  Belarus, 163–64
  Central Asia, 28–29, 211–14, 216–20, 236
  and employment, 62–63
  Estonia, 158
  and foreign policy, 150–84
  Latvia, 158
  Moldova, 157
  reactive, 244
  Russian Federation, 27, 188
  survival and security, 151–59
  tensions, 64, 94
  Ukraine, 157
Ethnonationalism, 103–5, 150, 151
  See also Nationalism

Eurasianism, 11
Europe, 163
European Community, 183, 187

Federalization, 21–24
Federal Treaty, 33–38, 42, 44, 50, 51–52
Federation Council, 45–46
Fergana Valley (Uzbekistan), 210, 221, 224
Finland, 192
Fitness theory, 185–86
Food stocks, 39
Forced migrants, 263*n.39*
Foreign policy, 7
  Belarus, 129–45
  Central Asia, 214–16, 266–79
  Estonia, 163
  and ethnicity, 150–84
  historical memory and external orientation, 159–71
  Kazakhstan, 270
  Latvia, 163
  Lithuania, 163
  and minority nationalism, 171–81
  and Russian Federation, 71–76, 90, 95–99
  Ukrainian, 104, 105, 159, 168
  Uzbekistan, 270
"Forest Brethren," 191, 192
Frankland, Mark, 24
Fukuyama, Francis, 103, 195
Fundamentalism, 270, 277

Gaidar, Yegor, 34, 38–39, 41
Galicia (Ukraine), 106, 166
Gamsakhurdia, Zviad, 286, 287, 297, 304

Ganiushin, Vitalii, 47–48
Gaugauz (people), 179
Gefter, Mikhail, 32
Geneva Convention, 296
Genocide, 294
Georgia, 249
  military coup in, 287
  nationalism in, 281, 286
  See also Georgian-Abkhazian conflict
Georgian-Abkhazian conflict, 281–308
  escalation of, 303–5
  Georgia as initiator of, 290–92
  history of, 282–85
  human rights violations, 294–97, 309*n.9*
  other participants in, 300–303
  political positions, 297–300
Georgian National Guard, 309*n.9*
Germany, 109–10, 160, 187, 247
GKChP. *See* State Committee for the State of Emergency
Glasnost, 89
Glemp, Cardinal, 111
Glezer, Oleg, 32
Goble, Paul, 27, 50
Gogol, Nikolai, 105
Goldstar Corporation, 219
Gorbachev, Mikhail, 6, 29, 87, 95, 193, 215, 285
Gorno-Badakhshan, 256
Govorukhin, Stanislav, 79
Grachev, Pavel, 292
Grand Duchy of Lithuania, 162, 164
Great Church Council (1666), 83
Grushin, Boris, 76

Haidamaki (Shevchenko), 105
Haidukievich, Siarhiei, 142
Hauner, Milan, 11
Health, 189, 190
Herder, Johann Gottfried von, 192
Hitler, Adolph, 72
Horowitz, Donald, 50
"How Are We to Structure Russia?—A Modest Contribution" (Solzhenitsyn), 79
Hrushevs'kyi, Mykhailo, 115, 166
Hryb, Miechyslau, 147
Hrybanau, Uladzimir, 144
Human rights, 73, 75
 in Baltic States, 67–71, 180, 181, 195
 and Georgian-Abkhazian conflict, 267–97
 in Kazakhstan, 219
 See also Minority rights
Hungary, 168

Iaroslavl' Oblast, 40
Ignatovskii, V.M., 164, 165
Iliescu, Ion, 179
Illarionov, Afanasii, 51
India, 269
Individuality, 82
Inflation, 40, 41
Ingushetia, 55n.57, 301–3
Intermarriage, 233
International fronts, 64
Internationalization. *See* Russification
International Monetary Fund, 215
International relations. *See* Foreign policy
Iosleiani, Jaba, 289, 295
Iran, 216–21, 231, 237, 258, 269, 276

Irkutsk Oblast, 40
Iron Curtain, 160
Islam
 in Kazakhstan, 218–19, 222, 270, 275, 277
 in Kyrgyzstan, 218–19, 275
 in Tajikistan, 270, 277
 in Turkmenistan, 218–19, 270
 in Uzbekistan, 218–19, 221
 See also Fundamentalism
Israel, 219, 279
Iugantsov, Nikolai, 198
Ivan III (Tsar of Russia), 82
Izvestiia (newspaper), 12

Japan, 96, 97, 219, 222, 269
Jewish Autonomous Oblast, 27
John Paul II (pope), 108, 111
Jowitt, Ken, 10

Kabardino-Balkaria, 306
Kalmykia, 35
Kapuscinski, Richard, 13
Karachaevo-Cherkessia, 207
Karakalpakstan, 256
Karimov, Islam, 218, 221, 223–25, 227, 269, 271
Karkarashvili, Gia, 289, 296, 309n.9
Kartvelians (people), 283
Kavsadze, Aleksandr, 295
Kazakhs (people), 212, 216, 237, 258
Kazakhstan, 15, 209, 274
 and Commonwealth of Independent States, 269
 economy, 215, 227, 271, 279
 environmentalism in, 82
 foreign relations, 225–26, 270
 identity of, 214

Kazakhstan *(continued)*
  indigenization of, 258
  in-migration to, 213
  Islam in, 218–19, 222, 270, 275, 277
  military in, 136
  nativism in, 245
  and Russia, 226
  Russian emigration from, 253, 254–55, 264*n.59*
  Russian minority in, 275, 276
  Russification of, 238
Kazlouski, Pavel, 137, 139, 140
Kebich, Viachaslau, 131, 134, 136, 144–45
Khanty-Mansi Autonomous Okrug, 27
Khasbulatov, Ruslan, 42–43, 46
Khmara, Stepan, 124
Khmelko, Valerii, 107
Khrushchev, Nikita, 212
Kievan Rus', 114–15, 166–69
Kitovani, Tengiz, 287, 288, 290, 294, 296, 304
Kohl, Helmut, 119
Korea, South, 219, 222, 269, 277
Koreans (people), 247–48, 269, 276
Kotenkov, Iurii, 198
Kozyrev, Andrei, 14, 71–72, 73, 96, 178
KPN. *See* Confederation for Independent Poland
Krasnodar Krai, 39, 49
Krauchanka, Piotr, 133, 148
Kravchuk, Leonid, 112, 113, 117, 119, 120, 128, 174, 301
Kuchma, Leonid, 113, 122–23, 124
Kultura (journal), 109
Kunaev, Dinmukhamed, 210, 275
Kuril Islands, 96, 97, 269

Kushnier, Vasil', 133–34
Kyrgyz (people), 212, 216, 237
Kyrgyzstan, 209, 212, 219–20, 222, 274
  adoption of Western values, 271
  border dispute with Tajikistan, 224
  diplomatic recognition of, 216
  economy, 223
  Islam in, 218–19, 275
  nativism in, 245
  natural resources, 213
  and Russia, 226
  Russians in, 254
  Russification of, 238
  and Uzbekistan, 223–24
  Uzbeks in, 256

Laar, Mart, 198
Lake Baikal, 81
Landsbergis, Vytautas, 190
Language, 5, 7, 64, 69
  in Baltic States, 191–92
  Belarus, 131, 140, 164
  Central Asian, 152, 220, 253
  Georgian, 286
  Moldovan, 169
  Russian, 59
  Ukrainian, 107, 121, 167
  in Western littoral states, 153–54, 156
Language Act (Moldova), 169
Latvia, 9–10, 92, 93, 155, 253
  border disputes, 195
  citizenship laws in, 68–69, 70–71, 100*n.19*, 181, 199
  economy, 189
  foreign policy, 163

Latvia *(continued)*
  historical memory and external orientation, 161–62, 183
  human rights standards in, 69–71
  minorities in, 198–200
  nationalities and ethnic groups in, 158
  perception of Russian threat, 156, 159
  purges in, 192
  Russian military in, 74–75, 194
  Russian minority in, 68, 180–81
Latvian Way alliance, 200
LDLP. *See* Lithuanian Democratic Labor Party
Lebed', A., 177
Lenin, V.I., 152
Lezgian (people), 291
Likhachev, Dmitrii, 115
Literacy, 191, 232
Lithuania, 9–10, 13, 93, 155, 160, 183, 190, 191
  and Belarus, 164–65
  border disputes, 195
  citizenship laws, 181, 201
  economy, 190
  foreign policy, 163
  historical memory and external orientation, 162–63, 184*n*.2
  minorities in, 200–201
  nationalities and ethnic groups in, 158
  perception of Russian threat, 159
  Poles in, 181, 201
  Russian military in, 194
  Russian minority in, 68, 180–81
  state security, 200–202
Lithuanian Democratic Labor Party (LDLP), 190

Liubarskii, Kronid, 44, 45
Li Yuan Kew, 219
Lutheranism, 191
Luzhkov, Iurii, 198
Lych, Hienadz', 134
Lych, Leanid, 147–48

Makalovich, Ivan, 147
Makashov, Al'bert, 99*n*.13
Makhkamov, Kakhar, 217
Mazowiecki, Tadeusz, 109, 110
Mearsheimer, John, 103
Meierovics, Gunars, 200
Mensheviks, 284
Meri, Lennart, 198
Meskhetian Turks (people), 248–49, 291
Mikhalchanka, Alaksandr, 132
Military-industrial complex, 63
Minority nationalism, 171–81
Minority rights, 73, 75, 181
Minsk agreement, 117
Moczulski, Leszek, 113
Moldova, 65, 152, 159, 183
  foreign policy, 170
  historical memory and external orientation, 169–71
  minority nationalism in, 175–79
  nationalities and ethnic groups in, 157
  reunification with Romania, 170, 176, 179
  security situation in, 177
Molotov, M.V., 192
Mongolia, 258
Moroz, Valentyn, 121
Moscow (Russia), 46, 81
Movement, freedom of, 69
Mujahideen, 270

Nabiev, Rakhman, 217
Nagorno-Karabakh, 5
Naider, Zdzislaw, 110
Nasha Slova (Belarusian newspaper), 141
National Center of Strategic Study (Belarus), 147
National identity, 13, 150-51, 152, 182-83, 212
  and Baltic States, 185-203
  of Central Asia, 273
  civic versus ethnic definition of, 7
  and historical memory, 159-71
  post-Soviet, 6-7
  See also Ethnicity; Nationalism
Nationalism, 3, 48, 103-4, 155, 160
  Belarusian, 165, 172-73
  in Central Asia, 210, 212-13, 214, 238, 244-47, 248
  and ethnic survival, 156
  Georgian, 281, 286
  Lithuanian, 162-63
  minority, 171-81
  minority complex of, 160
  in Moldova, 175-79
  Polish, 106
  Russian, 79, 81, 89-90, 90-91, 93, 121-22, 254
  and Soviet nationalities policy, 151-52
  territorial, 5, 259-60
  Ukrainian, 104-5, 121, 166-67, 173-75
  See also Ethnonationalism
National Salvation Front, 90, 174
Nation formation, 3
Nativism, 244-45, 246, 248, 250, 253, 260
NATO, 13, 202

Natural resources, 37, 47, 191-92, 213
Nazarbaev, Nursultan, 8, 211, 215, 219, 222, 225-27, 269, 271
Neff, Charles, 22
Nekrich, Aleksandr, 99*n*.9
Nemtsov, Boris, 47
Neoimperialism, 16
Nestor's Chronicle, 93
Neumann, Iver B., 13
Newmont Mining, 279
A New Russia? (Salisbury), 86
Niiazov, Saparmurad, 223, 270, 271
Nikon, Patriarch, 83
Nixon, Richard, 195
Nizhnii Novgorod Oblast, 40
North Caucasus, 294
North Caucasus Federation, 283-84
Nuclear weapons, 124
Nurgamambetov, Sagadat, 225

Old Believers, 82, 83
"Operation Wisla," 106
Osborn, Robert, 39
Osh Oblast, 245, 256
Ossetian-Inguish conflict, 293-94, 301-3

Padokshyn, Symon, 133
Pakistan, 269
Pamir Tajiks (people), 256
Pamyat, 90, 121
Pascal, Pierre, 116
Pelenski, Jaroslaw, 115
Pereiaslav Agreement, 115-16, 118, 119-20
Perestroika, 151, 285
Peter I (tsar of Russia), 9
Petrine reforms, 116

Pilsudski, Josef, 106
Pluralism, 135
Podalski, Kazimierz, 109
Pogodin, Mikhail, 115
Poland, 13–14, 160, 162, 193
  and Belarus, 165
  and Lithuania, 181, 201
  two-track policy, 110
  and Ukraine, 105–14, 168
Polish-Lithuanian Commonwealth, 106
"Polish-Ukrainian Relations: The Burden of History" (Rudnytsky), 105
Popular fronts, 64
Posen, Barry R., 15
Pravda (newspaper), 117
Priks, Elmo, 194
Privatization, 39, 41, 69
Property rights, 37
Prosvita (cultural society), 121
Pryvalau, Leanid, 145
Pushkov, Aleksei, 12–13

Radishchev, Aleksandr, 81
Raeff, Marc, 115–16
Rakmanov, Emomali, 217
Rasputin, Valentin, 81, 99*n.1*
Reddaway, Peter, 50
Refugees, 237, 244–47, 252, 256, 258, 259, 263*n.39*
Regionalism, 48
Regionalization, 21, 41
Riga, Treaty of, 112
Roman Catholic Church, 111–12
Romania, 170, 176, 179
Rudnytsky, Ivan L., 105
Rukh (Ukrainian political movement), 112, 120, 121, 167

Rumiantsev, Oleg, 30–31, 33, 37, 38, 42
Russian Association of Crimea, 174
"Russian Culture, Belarusian Character, and the Economy" (Bich), 143–144
Russian Empire, 23, 53*n.7*, 115, 161, 166, 283
Russian Federation, 8–16, 188
  and Abkhazia-Georgian conflict, 292, 298, 300–301, 305–6, 307
  Asianization of, 13
  Belarusian economic ties to, 142–45
  boundaries, 11–13
  center-periphery relations in, 21–51
  constitution of, 24–25, 30–31, 33, 42–47
  Eastern versus Western orientation, 9–11, 80
  economic autonomy in, 34, 38–42
  federalization of, 21–22
  Federal Treaty, 33–38, 42, 44, 50, 51–52
  foreign policy, 90, 95–99
    toward Bosnia and Serbia, 96
    fuel deliveries to Baltics, 190–91
    future of, 90–97
    and "near abroad," 91–95
  identity, 5–6, 9, 15, 58, 78–99, 116, 118
    ethnic, 188
    and geography, 80–82
    and history, 82–88
    and national pride, 88–90
    and World War II, 87–88
  imperial legacy of, 23–25, 52–53*n.7*
  interethnic tension in, 27
  Japanese relations, 96

Russian Federation *(continued)*
  jurisdiction disputes, 36
  marginalization of, 13
  military
    in Baltic states, 74–75, 194
    in Belarus, 135–42
  minorities abroad, 58–76, 91–92, 175, 180–81
    attitudes toward, 76
    in Baltic states, 67–68, 188–89
    in Central Asia, 250–55
    demography and status of, 59–63
    impact on foreign and domestic policy, 71–76
    rights violations against, 67–69
    sociopolitical attitudes of, 65–67
    in Ukraine, 173
  nation building in, 6
  people-state relations, 11
  and Poland, 112–13
  political weakness of, 125
  population, 28, 53n.11
  presidency of, 43
  prospect of disintegration of, 23
  refugees in, 263n.39
  republic-region rivalry, 30–33
  territorial-administrative structure, 25–28
  and Trans-Dniestrian conflict, 177–79
  and Ukraine, 105, 114–26
Russian National Council, 72
Russian Officers' Union, 122
Russian Orthodox Church, 82–85, 87, 116
The Russia We Lost (film), 79
Russification, 5–6, 63, 64, 182
  in Central Asia, 152, 160, 162, 238–39

Russification *(continued)*
  in Ukraine, 107, 118, 166
Rutskoi, Aleksandr, 26, 93, 117, 174
Ryzhkov, Nikolai, 99n.13

Safaev, Sadik, 268
St. Petersburg (Russia), 46
Sakharov, Andrei, 115
Salisbury, Harrison, 86
Samarkand, 256
Sanin, Iosif, 82
Sarts (people), 274
Saudi Arabia, 277
Schwartz, Lee, 48
Separation of powers, 24–25
Separatism, 155, 256, 260
Serbia, 90, 96
Sevastopol, 123
Shakhrai, Sergei, 43, 47
Shanibov, Musa, 293
Shapshug (people), 49, 56n.103
Shcherbytsky, Volodymyr, 107
Sheehy, Ann, 30
Shelest', Petro, 107
Shelov-Kovediaev, Fedor, 122
Shevardnadze, Eduard, 287–91, 295, 297–98, 300–302, 307
Shevchenko, Taras, 105
Shevtsova, L., 247
Shokhin, Aleksandr, 122
Short Outline of the History of Belarus (Ignatovskii), 164
Shupliak, P.A., 132
Shushkevich, Stanislau, 130, 133, 134, 137–41, 146
Shyrkouski, Eduard, 147
Siberia, 33–34, 47, 81
"Siberian Agreement," 50

Sidarevich, Anatol', 141–42
Sienkiewicz, Henryk, 105–6
Singapore, 219
Skubiszewski, Krysztof, 109–10
Slovakia, 168
Snegur, Mircea, 177
"Snegur Doctrine," 170
Social justice, 189
Societism, 6
Solidarity (Polish union), 108, 109
Solzhenitsyn, Aleksandr, 79, 81, 87
Sorskii, Nil, 82
Soslambekov, Y., 301
South Korea. *See* Korea, South
"Soviet people" theory, 152
Soviet Union, 3, 12, 24, 29, 86–88, 110, 150, 182
  and Abkhazia, 284–85
  economic policies of, 213
  importance of Eastern Europe to, 10
  nationalities policy, 151–52
  nationality question, 4–5
  and Orthodox Church, 85
  restoration of, 156
  See also Russian Federation
Space program, 88–89
Stalin, Joseph, 87, 88, 192, 284
Stankevich, Sergei, 72, 91, 93, 174
State Committee for the State of Emergency (GKChP), 78
Step-by-Step Constitutional Reform, 25
Sterligov, Aleksandr, 72
Strikes, 40
Stus, Vasyl, 108
Suny, Ronald, 129
Susi, Arno, 197

Suvorov Military Academy (Minsk), 137
Sverdlovsk Oblast, 40, 54*n.23*
Sweden, 119–20
Switzerland, 24

Tajikistan, 92, 96–97, 209, 212, 214, 217, 272, 274, 275–76
  border dispute with Kyrgyzstan, 224
  civil war in, 221
  economy, 223
  Islam in, 270, 277
  out-migration of, 235, 243
  refugees from, 237, 256, 258, 259, 264*n.59*
  and Russia, 226, 254
  Russian emigration from, 253
Tajiks (people), 212, 216, 233, 237, 256, 276
Taras Bulba (Gogol), 105
Taras Shevchanko Ukrainian Language Society, 167
Tartu peace treaty, 195
Tatarstan, 29, 30, 33, 35, 38, 42, 50, 54*n.23*
Taxes, 41–42, 45, 47, 54*n.23*
Tengiz oil fields (Kazakhstan), 215
Terrorism, 106
Torture, 295
Trade, 40
Trans-Dniestra (Moldova), 176–79
Trubetskoi, Nikolai S., 116
Tsipko, Aleksandr, 116
Tsygankov, Andrei, 14–15
Tuleev, Aman-Geldy, 99*n.13*
Turkey, 151, 175, 179, 216–17, 218, 220–21
Turkmenistan, 209, 216, 227, 266, 269

Turkmenistan *(continued)*
  foreign investment in, 222–23
  Islam in, 218–19, 270
  trade, 278
Turkmens (people), 233, 237, 275

Ubykhs (people), 283
Uigur-Siankiang Autonomous Region, 222
Uigurs (people), 222, 237
Ukraine, 9, 11, 23, 65, 93–94, 97, 152, 155, 183, 266
  defense policy, 119
  economy, 123, 125
  environmentalism, 82
  ethnonationalism in, 104–5
  foreign policy, 13–14, 103–26, 159, 168
  and Georgian-Abkhazian conflict, 301
  historical memory and external orientation, 166–69
  identity, 13–14, 15
  military in, 136
  minority nationalism in, 173–75
  national agenda of, 112
  nationalities and ethnic groups in, 157
  and Poland, 105–14
  political polarization in, 120–21
  political weakness of, 125
  right-wing nationalism, 121
  and Russia, 114–26
  and Trans-Dniestrian conflict, 178–79
  Western rejection of, 118–19
Ukrainian Catholic Church. *See* Uniate Church
Ukrainian State Independence Organization, 111

Ulam, Adam, 86, 273
Ulots, Ülo, 194
Unemployment, 40, 242
Uniate Church, 108, 111–12
Union of Ukrainian Officers, 121
Unions, decentralization of, 40–41
United Nations, 70, 74, 95, 96–97, 195–96, 215, 267, 290, 299
United States, 24, 75, 93, 184*n*.2, 279
Unrepresented Nations and Peoples Organization, 282
Urbanization, 241
Uzbekistan, 209, 210, 212, 214, 217, 222, 225, 248, 269, 274
  Asian relations, 269
  diplomatic recognition of, 216
  economy, 227, 279
  foreign relations, 270
  Islam in, 218–19, 221
  and Kyrgyzstan, 223–24
  nativism in, 245
  natural resources, 213
  and Russia, 226, 253, 254
Uzbeks (people), 212, 216, 233, 237, 256–58, 274–75, 276

Velliste, Trivimi, 195
Virgin Lands campaign, 213
Volga Germans, 247
Volhynia (Ukraine), 106
Vol'skii, Arkadii, 123

Walesa, Lech, 109, 110, 112, 113, 114
Wars, 4
What Is Asia to Us? (Hauner), 11
Work habits, 190

World Bank, 215
World War II, 87–88, 106, 166, 213

Yeltsin, Boris, 6, 22, 29–30, 37, 39, 49, 78, 81, 90, 93
  and Chechnia, 50
  and Commonwealth of Independent States, 73–74
  and constitutional reform, 24–25, 42–47
  election results, 99*n.13*
  and Federal Treaty, 37
  foreign policy, 95–97

Yeltsin, Boris *(continued)*
  and Georgian-Abkhazian conflict, 290
  and Lithuania, 194
  and minority rights, 75
Yevtushenko, Yevgeny, 81
Yugoslavia, 15, 96, 150

Zavgaev, D., 292
Zhdanok, Tatiana, 75
Zhirinovsky, Vladimir, 12, 90, 95, 99*n.13*, 121
Zorkin, Valerii, 38
Zviazda (Belarusian newspaper), 140